11

ICT & COMPUTER STUDIES

PNG UPPER SECONDARY

Greg Baker
Tom Bowen

Editorial reviewers:
John Gesa Junior
Martha Lulu Aaron

OXFORD

Oxford University Press is a department of the University of Oxford. It furthers the University's objective of excellence in research, scholarship, and education by publishing worldwide. Oxford is a registered trademark of Oxford University Press in the UK and in certain other countries.

Published in Australia by
Oxford University Press
Level 8, 737 Bourke Street, Docklands, Victoria 3008, Australia.

First published 2013

Reprinted 2013, 2014, 2020, 2023, 2024

ISBN 978 0 19 557815 7

Illustrated by diacriTech, Chennai, India
Typeset by diacriTech, Chennai, India
Printed in China by Golden Cup Printing Co. Ltd

Oxford University Press Australia & New Zealand is committed to sourcing paper responsibly.

Contents

Unit 11.5 Databases

Unit 11.6 Internet

Unit 11.7 Desktop Publishing

Introduction

This book has been published to provide the information required by students in order to successfully complete both the Upper Secondary syllabus in Information Communication Technologies (ICT) and the Computer Studies syllabus at Grade 11 in Papua New Guinea. A detailed syllabus coverage chart showing how this book covers both courses is set out on pp. viii–ix. Please refer to that chart for guidance.

For students of Information Communication Technologies, Units 11.1 to 11.5 in this book follow the same order as Units 11.1 to 11.4 in the Grade 11 Information Communication Technologies Syllabus:

Unit 11.1 Computer Fundamentals

Unit 11.2 Word Processing

Unit 11.3 Computers and Society

Unit 11.4 Spreadsheets

Unit 11.5 Database 1

Within each Unit the Topics follow the main subheadings and bullet points in the Syllabus. Advanced students may choose to skip some of the Topics at the beginning of some Units, such as 11.2 Word Processing, which offers an introduction to word processing before moving on to advanced word processing. Similarly, students may skip the introductory Topics in Unit 11.4 Spreadsheets.

This book also includes:

Unit 11.6 Internet

Unit 11.7 Desktop Publishing

These two Units are important for all students of computers and information technology and they correlate with the requirements of the last two Units in the Grade 11 Computer Studies syllabus.

For students of Computing Studies, this book covers all that is needed for Grade 11 plus some of the Units in the Computer Studies Grade 12 syllabus:

Unit 11.1 Computer Fundamentals

Unit 11.2 File and Information Management (covered in Unit 11.2 in this book)

Unit 11.3 Word Processing

Unit 11.4 Computers and Society

Unit 11.5 Desktop Publishing

Unit 11.6 The Internet

Unit 12.3 Spreadsheets

Unit 12.4 Databases

Please use the syllabus coverage chart on pp. viii–ix as a guide.

The influence of information technology has gained tremendous momentum in Papua New Guinea in the last decade. It will be of increasing importance in driving the economy and the social and political environment of our country. The two syllabus documents are designed to support our growing needs and this book is designed to provide the necessary structure and content in a concise and compact format.

If you have any suggestions about how this book might be improved in future editions, please make contact with Oxford University Press:

Fax: 00 61 3 9934 9100

Customer Service Email: exportsales.au@oup.com

We wish you every success in your studies.

The authors

Acknowledgments

There are many people to be thanked for their help and assistance in enabling the publication of this series to happen. First, we acknowledge the cooperation and generosity of Mark Sayes at ESA Publications in New Zealand who responded with interest and support when the proposal to adapt his Study Guide series was put to him.

We would also like to acknowledge many other individuals who have been happy to advise and assist in different ways: Joy Sahumlal, Greg Kapanombo, Anne Sangi, Safak Deliismail, and especially two people who reviewed the manuscript and made valuable comments – John Gesa Junior and Martha Lulu Aaron.

Copyright acknowledgments

The author and the publisher wish to thank and acknowledge the following copyright holders for reproduction of their material.

AAP content is owned by or licensed to Australian Associated Press Pty Limited and is copyright protected. AAP content is published on an "as is" basis for personal use only and must not be copied, republished, rewritten, resold or redistributed, whether by caching, framing or similar means, without AAP's prior written permission. AAP and its licensors are not liable for any loss, through negligence or otherwise, resulting from errors or omissions in or reliance on AAP content. The globe symbol and "AAP" are registered trade marks, pp.189, 195; Alamy/David Pearson, p.167 /Friedrich Stark, p.155 /Henry Westheim Photography, p.164; Corbis/Morton Beebe, p.50 (top left) /Ocean, p.50 (bottom) /Sagel & Kranefeld, p.21 (bottom) /Sygma/Alain Nogues, p.163; Courtesy Cisco Systems, p.360; courtesy EA Games, p.158; Fairfax/Eddie Jim, p.165; Getty Images/Jonathan Kitchen, p.181; Getty Images/AFP/Robyn Beck, p.154; Getty Images/Bridgeman Art Library, p.12; Getty Images/SSPL via Getty Images, p.8 (top); iStockphoto/franckreporter, p.16 /pepi, p.7 (bottom) /Rubén Hidalgo, p.17 /Stephen Krow, p.39 /Victoria Short, p.7 (top); Used with permission from Microsoft, pp.30 (bottom),159; Science Photo Library/Publiphoto Diffusion/R. Maisonneuve, p.53 (bottom); shutterstock.com, pp.13, 14 (top),14 (bottom), 15 (top), 15 (bottom), 20, 21 (top), 22 (top), 22 (bottom), 23, 24, 25, 26 (top), 26 (bottom), 29, 30 (top), 31, 32, 35 (top), 35 (bottom), 37, 38, 41, 46 (top), 46 (bottom), 47 (top), 47 (centre), 47 (bottom), 48, 50 (top right), 53 (top), 58, 59, 131, 161, 162, 185, 345 (top), 345 (centre), 345 (bottom), 346 (top), 347, Copyright 2003–2005 Wearable Consult, p.27

Every effort has been made to trace the original source of copyright material contained in this book. The publisher will be pleased to hear from copyright holders to rectify any errors or omissions.

Syllabus coverage chart

The chart below shows how each Unit and Topic relates to the ICT syllabus and the Computer Studies syllabus.

Unit 11.1 Computer Fundamentals	ICT Syllabus Grade 11	Computer Studies Syllabus Grade 11
Topic 1: Information processing cycle	**11.1** *p.9*	**11.1** *p.9*
Topic 2: A brief history of computers	**11.1** *p.9*	**11.1** *p.9*
Topic 3: Generations of computers	**11.1** *p.10*	**11.1** *p.10*
Topic 4: Classification of computers	**11.1** *p.10*	**11.1** *p.10*
Topic 5: Input devices	**11.1** *p.10*	**11.1** *p.10*
Topic 6: Output devices	**11.1** *p.11*	**11.1** *p.10*
Topic 7: Storage devices	**11.1** *p.11*	**11.1** *p.12*
Topic 8: System box	**11.1** *p.12*	**11.1** *p.12*
Unit 11.2 Word Processing (Basic and Advanced)	**ICT Syllabus Grade 11**	**Computer Studies Syllabus Grade 11**
Topic 1: Introduction to word processing		
Topic 2: Creating and saving a new document		**11.3** *p.15*
Topic 3: Formatting documents		**11.3** *p.16*
Topic 4: Editing text		**11.3** *p.17*
Topic 5: Finalising and printing a document		**11.3** *p.18*
Topic 6: Working with tables and lists		**11.3** *p.18*
Topic 7: Working with graphics		**11.3** *p.18*
Topic 8: Working with styles and templates	**11.2** *p.13*	
Topic 9: Creating mail merge and labels	**11.2** *p.13*	
Topic 10: Working with columns	**11.2** *p.14*	
Topic 11: Working with outline and long documents	**11.2** *p.14*	
Topic 12: Sharing information with other programs	**11.2** *p.14*	
Topic 13: Sharing information with other people	**11.2** *p.15*	
Topic 14: Working with online forms	**11.2** *p.15*	
Unit 11.3 Computers and Society	**ICT Syllabus Grade 11**	**Computer Studies Syllabus Grade 11**
Topic 1: Impacts on society	**11.3** *p.16*	**11.4** *p.20*
Topic 2: Measures to protect computers and data	**11.3** *p.17*	**11.4** *p.21*
Topic 3: Environmental, social and ethical issues	**11.3** *p.17*	**11.4** *p.21*
Topic 4: Government controls and laws on ICT	**11.3** *p.18*	**11.4** *p.21*
Topic 5: Ergonomics in ICT	**11.3** *p.18*	**11.4** *p.22*

Unit 11.4 Spreadsheets	**ICT Syllabus Grade 11**	**Computer Studies Syllabus Grade 12**
Topic 1: What is a spreadsheet?		**12.3** *p.35*
Topic 2: Formulae		**12.3** *p.36*
Topic 3: Printing a worksheet		**12.3** *p.38*
Topic 4: Charts		**12.3** *p.37*
Topic 5: Using advanced functions	**11.4** *p.19*	
Topic 6: Integrating with other applications	**11.4** *p.21*	
Topic 7: Protecting and auditing forms and templates	**11.4** *p.21*	
Unit 11.5 Database 1	**ICT Syllabus Grade 11**	**Computer Studies Syllabus Grade 12**
Topic 1: Getting started	**11.5** *p.23*	**12.4** *p.39*
Topic 2: Working with data	**11.5** *p.24*	**12.4** *p.40*
Topic 3: Working with tables and relationships	**11.5** *p.24*	**12.4** *p.40*
Topic 4: Creating and customising queries	**11.5** *p.24*	**12.4** *p.40*
Topic 5: Creating and customising forms	**11.5** *p.25*	**12.4** *p.41*
Topic 6: Creating useful reports	**11.5** *p.25*	**12.4** *p.41*
Unit 11.6 Internet 1	**ICT Syllabus Grade 11**	**Computer Studies Syllabus Grade 11**
Topic 1: Web fundamentals	**11.6** *p.26*	**11.6** *p.25*
Topic 2: Web security	**11.6** *p.27*	**11.6** *p.26*
Topic 3: Search techniques	**11.6** *p.27*	**11.6** *p.26*
Topic 4: Website evaluation	**11.6** *p.27*	**11.6** *p.26*
Topic 5: Evaluating internet-based resources	**11.6** *p.27*	**11.6** *p.27*
Topic 6: Electronic mail (email)	**11.6** *p.29*	**11.6** *p.28*
Unit 11:7 Desktop Publishing	**ICT Syllabus Grade 11**	**Computer Studies Syllabus Grade 11**
Topic1: Working with publications	**11.7** *p.30*	**11.5** *p.23*
Topic 2: Planning and designing a page	**11.7** *p.30*	**11.5** *p.23*
Topic 3: Working with text	**11.7** *p.31*	**11.5** *p.23*
Topic 4: Drawing and working with graphic objects	**11.7** *p.31*	**11.5** *p.24*
Topic 5: Working with tables	**11.7** *p.31*	**11.5** *p.24*
Topic 6: Sending and printing the publication	**11.7** *p.31*	**11.5** *p.24*

Unit 11.1 Computer Fundamentals

Topic 1: Information processing cycle

Unit 11.1 explores computing fundamentals. Topic 1 in this Unit focuses on the information-processing cycle (see ICT Syllabus p. 9 and Computer Studies Syllabus p. 9). It covers:

- What is a system?
- What is a computer?
- What is a computer system?

What is a system?

In daily life there are many different systems that impact on our lives – for example, the water cycle, digestive systems, knowledge databases, transaction systems, accounting systems, expert systems.

A system has structure and a number of components that are related.

If we are preparing work without a computer then we might use a pen and paper. The pen is an **input device**; we store data on a piece of paper (storage device); we process that data, ie make changes; and then we output that data.

If we are going to the local store, we might do the following:

- Write a list of the items that we wish to purchase (input).
- Take the list to the store on a piece of paper (storage).
- Select and purchase the items (process the data).
- Take the items home (output).

What is a computer?

A **computer** is an electronic device that accepts, processes, stores and outputs data at high speeds according to programmed instructions. A computer is typically made up of a central processing unit (microprocessor) based on digital technology, memory (random-access and read-only), storage devices and input-output devices.

A personal computer has a base for the central processing unit (CPU), a keyboard and a mouse or other pointing device for input and a visual display unit for output.

Hardware

Hardware consists of the parts you can actually touch, hold and move (with care). This includes the central processing unit (CPU), monitor, keyboard and a mouse or pointing device. Other pieces of hardware that can be attached to a computer are called **peripheral devices**. These include printers, scanners, digital cameras and external storage devices.

Software

Software is a series of instructions that tells the computer what to do. The sequence of instructions is called a computer program. You cannot see or touch software. It is installed as electronic impulses on disc.

Each computer has an operating system. This software makes the computer usable: it provides a link between the hardware and the person using the computer. When the computer is turned on, the operating system starts up the computer.

What is a computer system?

A computer system involves the input of data that is stored and processed and then output in some manner. The figure below shows the steps in using a computer to compete a task. A computer system consists of input devices, a storage device and **output devices**. The computer system is made up of both hardware and software.

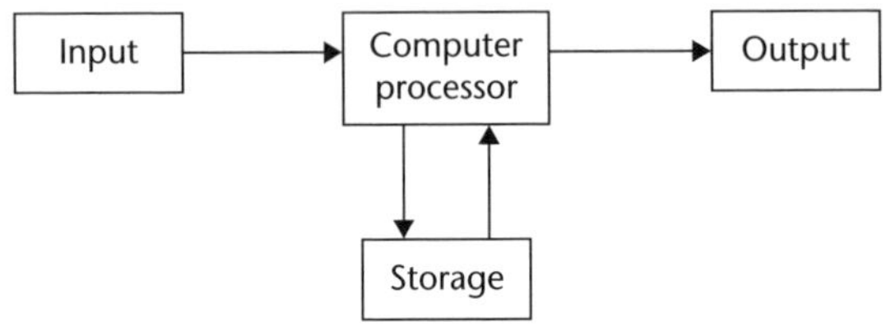

A computer system

Information systems

An **information system** involves people and information technology. People use information technology to solve problems and to communicate. Thus, the way people interact with the technology is part of the information system.

An information system involves:

- People.
- Hardware.
- Software.
- Data.
- Processes.

Most information systems now use computer systems to process, store and modify data and to provide solutions to problems.

Data

Data is facts concerning people, objects, events or other entities. There are many sources of data and many types of data. Some data is an exact measurement; other data might involve subjective judgement.

For example, the number 121 is a piece of data. It can have many meanings depending on its use and context. On its own or out of context it tells us nothing. The number 121 could be:

- A postal code in a table of postal codes, in this case Port Moresby.
- A student identification number in a school.
- An employee identification number in a business.
- The price of an item in a catalogue.
- The number of people in a village.

Data needs to be defined and organised to have meaning and to become information.

Data becomes information

When data becomes organised and has meaning it is **information**. It may enable decision-making if it meets the needs of the recipient of that information.

Telephone directory

A directory stores the names, addresses and telephone numbers of most of its subscribers.

A typical entry is:

Name & Location	Contact
Itagau Roger PO Box 313 Lae Tent City, LAE	Ph: 475 7753

An item of data

A printed directory lists subscribers in alphabetical order according to their family or business name. The items of data in the directory are:

- Family name.
- Initials or given name.
- Postal or street address.
- Town.
- Telephone number.

A directory is a report from an information system to enable people to find a subscriber's telephone number. It has functionality because it is sorted from A to Z by family name.

Unit 11.1 Activity 1A: The water cycle

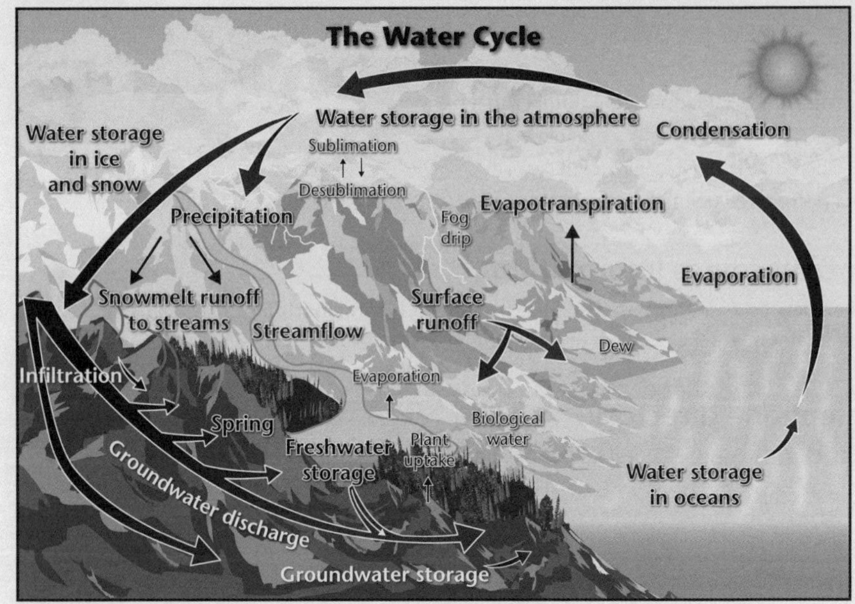

(Source: http://ga.water.usgs.gov/edu/watercyclehi.html)

Identify on the diagram the following parts of the water cycle as input, processing and output.

Input	Processing	Output
Heat (sun) Water Plants and vegetation	Evaporation Transpiration Condensation Rainfall (Precipitation)	Circulation of water between earth, storage and atmosphere

Unit 11.1 Activity 1B: Making a cup of hot chocolate

Making a cup of hot chocolate with milk is an example of a system, in that a sequence of steps must be carried out in order, using a variety of inputs and equipment.

1. List the items required for the process of making a cup of hot chocolate.
2. List the steps in making a cup of hot chocolate.

Unit 11.1 Activity 1C: Investigation into an airline information system

Passenger airlines move people from one place to another. Airlines provide online information about flight schedules, flight arrivals and departure times. Increasingly the airlines are using real-time information processing for reservations. Internet reservation systems allow customers to directly reserve seats.

1. Having registered to have access to the system, how would a customer make a reservation? What information would need to be conveyed to the airline for the reservation to be made?

2. The following are examples of information that an airline may gather about a passenger. Some information will be the same each time a passenger flies, while otherinformation will be particular to the day and time the passenger is flying.

List the information the airline may decide to access from its records and what information the airline may require input from the passenger.

	Data	Airline records	Passenger input
1	Passenger's name and address details		
2	Customer credit card details		
3	Destination of flight		
4	Frequent flyer or award scheme number		
5	Status of points from award scheme		
6	If passenger is a vegetarian		
7	Number of items of baggage		
8	Payment details for a particular flight		
9	If the passenger is male or female		
10	Number of flights in the last 12 months		
11	If a passenger has checked in for a flight		
12	Seat number on a particular flight		

3. Investigate the procedure for booking a flight on two domestic airlines. What are the differences and similarities?

4. What documentation do airlines provide for passengers? In your answer, discuss whether or not the following are used:

	Documentation	Used?
1	Airline ticket	
2	Boarding pass	
3	Baggage check	
4	Receipt for payment	
5	Confirmation when flight confirmed	

Unit 11.1 Computer Fundamentals
Topic 2: A brief history of computers

Topic 2 in this Unit explores the history of computers (see ICT Syllabus p. 9 and Computer Studies Syllabus pp. 9–10). It covers:

- Early times.
- The abacus.
- The pioneers.
- The modern computer.

Early times

Computers developed out of the need for help with calculations.

Analog devices were widely used in ancient times. Analog means 'measuring or representing data by means of one or more physical properties that can express any value along a continuous scale'. (Source www.thefreedictionary.com)

A circular clock is an analog device: time is represented by the distance that the hour hand and the minute hand have moved around a circle. A simple ruler is an analog device that measures distance on the scale on the ruler.

The mathematician John Napier invented a way in which logarithms could be used to simplify calculations: multiplications could be carried out by adding logarithms. This occurred in the early 1600s and led to the development of the slide rule, which was an analog device that allowed multiplication to be carried out by using a sliding bar adding measured lengths of timber for multiplication. Slide rules were widely used by engineers until the 1960s and the invention of the handheld calculator.

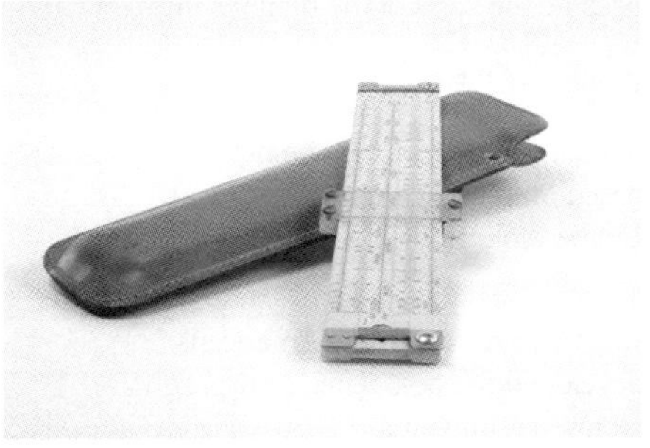

A slide rule

The abacus

Another early calculating device was the **abacus**.

An abacus is a counting tool, usually made from bamboo and widely used in Asia. It consists of a frame with beads sliding on wires. The abacus is an ancient device and dates back to ancient Greece.

The abacus is still in use in parts of Asia today.

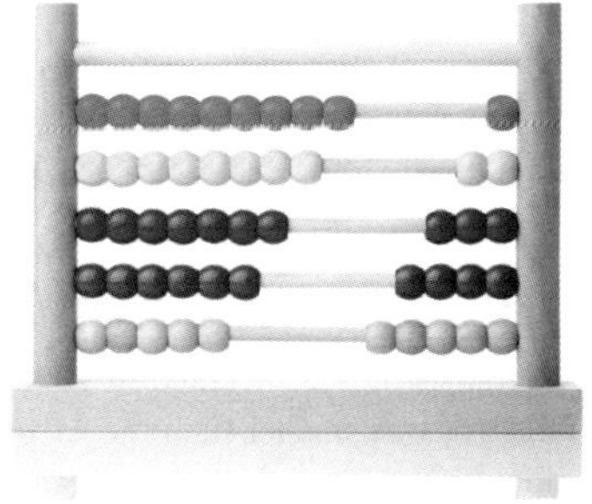

An abacus

The pioneers

Charles Babbage's difference engine

Blaise Pascal was a French mathematician who developed a mechanical calculator in the 1640s. Another mathematician, Gottfried von Leibniz, improved on this design so that multiplication and division could be carried out. Mechanical calculators gradually evolved over time and were still in use in the 1970s.

In the 1830s, the English mathematician Charles Babbage developed the difference machine that is now seen as the forerunner of the modern digital computer. He used punched cards to control the machine that is now on display in the Science Museum in London.

During the 1920s and 1930s a lot of work was done developing analog computers. Electric voltages and currents were used as the measuring devices and they were widely used in weapons during World War II.

Another English mathematician, Alan Turing, developed the Turing machine in 1932, which became the basis of the digital computer.

An early computer

A key development was the use of the binary number system in the development of computing devices. The binary system is based on only two numbers: 0 and 1. These can be replicated by a switch being on or off.

After World War II, the Americans developed the first general purpose computer, known as ENIAC (Electronic Numerical Integrator and Computer). This huge computer weighed 27 tonnes and had over 18,000 valves to enable it to work.

In 1947 John von Neumann designed a new computer architecture that replaced the design used in ENIAC and became the basis of the modern computer.

The modern computer

The transistor was invented in 1947 and this replaced the vacuum tubes in computers. The transistor was smaller than the vacuum tube, needed less energy and developed less heat. The printed circuit board was also developed and used in these second-generation computers. Magnetic tape was used for storage.

The third-generation computers used the integrated circuit or microchip that was developed at Intel in the USA. The use of silicon led to the term 'Silicon Valley', which referred to the growth of companies using the integrated circuits. Many of these companies were based in the same area about 80 km south of San Francisco in California.

The silicon chip led to the development of the microcomputer. The first of these microcomputers were the forerunners of the current personal computers in use today. These are known as the fourth-generation computers. The development of the Apple computer and other computers such as the IBM PC led to the computer becoming ubiquitous.

These developments came despite the assertion of Ken Olsen, the founder of DEC, which was at one time the second-largest computer manufacturer in the world, that 'there is no reason for any individual to have a computer in his home'.

Fifth-generation computers were a Japanese initiative to develop supercomputers that would provide the facilities for the development of artificial intelligence applications.

Unit 11.1 Computer Fundamentals
Topic 3: Generations of computers

Topic 3 in this Unit explores the various generations of computers (see ICT Syllabus p. 10 and Computer Studies Syllabus p. 10).

Generations of computers

Computer development has seen more powerful, smaller and cheaper computing relative to the previous generation.

Generation	Years (approx.)	Key technology	Key feature	Input	Output
First	1940–1956	Vacuum tube	Machine language	Punch cards, paper tape	Paper printout
Second	1956–1963	Transistors	Programming languages developed	Punch cards, paper tape	Paper printout
Third	1964–1971	Integrated circuits	Operating system	Keyboard	Screen output
Fourth	1971–present	Microprocessors Personal computer (micro-computer with its own CPU, storage, input and output devices – 1981 IBM PC)	CPU on single chip	Graphical user interface, keyboard and mouse WIMP: windows, icons, mouse, pointer	Screen output mobile devices
Fifth	From now on	Artificial Intelligence	Parallel processing	Natural language input, voice recognition	Screen output mobile devices Speech Other fifth-generation computers

Generations of computers

Moore's Law

Moore's Law is a prediction made by Gordon Moore, the co-founder of Intel, the manufacturer of computer chips. He predicted in 1965 that 'the number of transistors and resistors on a chip doubles every 18 months'.

This prediction has proved to be surprisingly accurate and the capacity of computer chips continues to increase at a remarkable rate.

Typewriters

The typewriter is a mechanical device that prints characters on a piece of paper. It was invented in 1870 and became an indispensable writing tool until late in the 20th century. In effect, it was the first word processor.

The QWERTY keyboard was invented with the typewriter and this same layout is used on most computer keyboards.

Some of the largest computer companies started as companies making office machines and developed the electric typewriter. IBM was a very large supplier of electric typewriters.

An early typewriter

Unit 11.1 Computer Fundamentals
Topic 4: Classification of computers

Unit 11.1 explores computing fundamentals. Topic 4 in this Unit focuses on the classification of computers (see ICT Syllabus p. 10 and Computer Studies Syllabus p. 10). It covers:

- Supercomputers.
- Mainframe computers.
- Servers.
- Workstations.
- Microcomputers.
- Desktop computers.
- Portable computers.
- Artificial intelligence (AI).

Computers can be classified according to their size and power, and the number and speed of the processes they can undertake. The distinction is changing as improving technology produces faster computers at a much cheaper price than their predecessors.

Supercomputers

Supercomputers are the largest computers that are always at the front line of processing power. They are used in scientific and research organisations where complex calculations and analysis are required. Weather forecasting and space exploration need to process hundreds of millions of instructions per second.

Supercomputers are typically produced for a specific purpose and are one of a kind. They are produced by large companies such as IBM, Hewlett Packard and Cray Research.

Mainframe computers

A **mainframe computer** is one that supports many users at the one time. They are made by large computer companies including IBM, Unisys, NEC and Fujitsu. Large organisations such as government departments and banks use mainframe computers for critical applications and those that require a large amount of data processing. A mainframe may do many tasks at once and usually operates 24 hours a day.

A mainframe computer

Servers

A computer **server** provides applications and databases for other computers connected to a network. Some of their functions include:

- **File servers**: store and manage files of users connected to the network.
- Print servers: manage printers and printing queues.
- Web servers: manage the internal intranet and access to the Internet.
- Database servers: manage access to databases used in the organisation.
- Email servers: manage the sending, receiving and storing of email.

A typical computer server

Workstations

A **workstation** is a computer that is part of a network. It is usually a personal computer. A workstation is more powerful than a standard desktop computer and may be used for specific purposes such as graphics, publishing, animation and engineering.

Microcomputers

A **microcomputer** is a single computer, usually used by one person at a time. The power and configuration of these computers vary significantly.

Most microcomputers are based on either an Intel chip running a Windows Operating System or an Apple chip running an Apple Operating System.

Desktop computers

Most **desktop** computers have a computer base that contains the processing unit, memory, peripheral devices and communication ports. These typically have an external monitor or screen, an external keyboard and a mouse.

Some desktop computers are built as all-in-one computers; for example, the Apple iMac. Manufacturers such as Lenovo, Acer and Hewlett Packard are also building all-in-one desktop computers.

A typical desktop computer

Portable computers

Portable and laptop computers enable use while travelling and working away from home or work.

A mobile smartphone is essentially a portable computer.

Laptop and notebook computers

A notebook computer provides a similar computing experience to a desktop computer. It can be powered by battery or electricity supply.

Notebook computers often have different chips that use less energy than desktop computers and generate less heat. They have built-in keyboards and a trackpad in place of a mouse. The size of the screen is limited by the physical size of the computer.

External monitors, keyboards and other peripheral devices can be attached to notebook computers. A notebook computer usually has an internal wireless network card.

A notebook computer

Some notebook computers are known as tablet computers. In these cases, the screen can fold down flat and the user can write on the screen with a special pen. Some of them include handwriting recognition software.

Netbook computers

A netbook computer is usually around the size of a book and has a small keyboard. It may have a cut-down version of a desktop operating system and have a more basic suite of software applications.

The small size and low weight make these ideal computers for use when travelling. However, they do not have the processing power or speed of a notebook computer and the small screen size and cut-down keyboard can make them more difficult to use.

A netbook computer

Unit 11.1 Activity 4A: Notebook computer or netbook computer?

1. Compare the features of a notebook computer and a netbook computer. You could consider the following:
   a. Cost.
   b. Size, including weight.
   c. Screen size.
   d. Hard disk size.
   e. Operating system.
   f. Connection points, eg USB ports.
   g. Network connections.
   h. Warranty conditions and length.
2. Which would you prefer to own? Why?

Handheld computers

The Apple iPad computer is the first of the handheld computers to make a significant impact in the market. The computer does not have a physical keyboard and all the interaction takes place using a touch screen. The computer is thin and light and can have an inbuilt wireless capability to allow it access to the Internet. The screen is easy to read and the applications developed for the iPad are easy to use and are proving to be very popular. There is an e-book application on the iPad allowing electronic books to be stored and accessed.

The other handheld devices that are essentially computers are smartphones such as Apple's iPhone and the Blackberry. These allow a significant number of applications to be carried out, including email, web browsing, photography, video creation and access to a GPS. These are excellent devices for receiving and displaying data but are perhaps limited in their use as content creators.

An Apple iPad

Unit 11.1 Activity 4B: Apple iPad

The Apple iPad has proved to be very popular.

1. List the features of the iPad that you believe helps make it popular.
2. List any disadvantages of the iPad.
3. Find out how to print a document from an iPad.

E-book reader

An electronic book or e-book is a digital version of a printed book, although in some cases the e-book may have only been published in a digital form. The book is read using an e-reader, which can access, store and display the book on screen for reading.

There is a variety of **e-book readers** on the market, including the Kindle, the Nook and the Sony Reader. All of these require the electronic book to be purchased and **downloaded**.

An e-book reader

Unit 11.1 Activity 4C: Advantages and disadvantages of e-books

Complete the table below regarding the use of e-books.

	Feature	Is the feature an advantage or disadvantage? Give a reason for your answer.
1	An e-book is generally cheaper than a printed copy.	
2	E-books are good for the environment.	
3	Hyperlinking and bookmarking are possible.	
4	It is easy to update to a new edition.	
5	The text remains in its original form.	
6	E-books and e-book readers are portable.	

	Feature	Is the feature an advantage or disadvantage? Give a reason for your answer.
7	E-book readers provide their own light for illumination of text.	
8	There is a lack of standardised format for e-books.	
9	E-book readers require batteries.	
10	The screen display size of e-book readers can be small.	
11	The font and formatting of some text in some e-books may not suit some readers.	
12	Consumers still like the 'browseability' of books.	

Artificial intelligence (AI)

Artificial intelligence (AI) is where computers carry out tasks in a manner similar to human beings. Robots on production lines, for example, carry out tasks that are repetitive and physically demanding at high speed.

Voice recognition software on telephone answering systems allows people to be directed to appropriate sections of the organisation based on their response to questions made by selecting numbers on the telephone keypad. There is usually an option to be put through to a person as a fall-back during the process.

It is very complex for AI to simulate the human thought and decision-making processes.

Unit 11.1 Computer Fundamentals

Topic 5: Input devices

Topic 5 explores the various input devices (see ICT Syllabus pp. 10–11 and Computer Studies Syllabus pp. 10–11). It covers:

- Keyboards.
- Pointing devices.
- Source data-entry devices.
- Scanner devices.
- Biometric scanning.
- Image-capturing devices.
- Digitising devices.
- Audio input devices.
- Sensors.
- Radio-frequency identification tag.

Input is where main memory accepts data, instructions, commands and user responses.

Software (programs), when launched, are loaded into memory. Commands from the program are entered by the keyboard or by choosing an item from a menu (such as **File** > **New** to create a new document). Data is the text, numbers, characters, images and sounds that are processed by the computer. User response occurs when software dictates a response from the user, often with a dialogue box with an 'OK' or 'Cancel' response required.

Keyboards

The keyboard is the most common device for entering data. When a key is pressed, it is translated into an instruction the computer can understand.

The standard 'QWERTY' keyboard has its origins in the typewriter. 'QWERTY' refers to the six letter characters on the top left-hand side of the keyboard.

What keys are on a keyboard?

Keyboards usually have between 81 and 105 keys. Many keyboards have a keypad with numbers on the right-hand side. This is called a numeric keypad.

Keys can be separated into the following categories:

- Letter keys – **a** to **z**, **A** to **Z**.
- Number keys – **0** to **9**.
- Punctuation keys – for example, full stop.
- Cursor keys – up, down, left, right.
- Symbol keys – for example, **%**, **&**.
- Special keys – for example, **ENTER** (sometimes called **RETURN**), **Ctrl**, **Esc**, **Alt**, **COMMAND** (Macintosh), **Page Up**, **Page Down**.
- Function keys – **F1** to **F12**, which carry out specific tasks.

Special keys

There are also keys for special tasks. These special keys include **Alt**, **Ctrl** and **Esc**. Often these keys will have a special shape to make them easier to see and touch – for example, CAPS LOCK and ENTER are larger than the letter and number keys.

Sometimes the names for these special keys will be different depending on the computer. For example, the **Backspace** key operates similarly to the **Delete** key on another computer.

The use of a special key can vary according to the software – for example, **Tab** for a word processor could set text to a position on a line, while on a database it could move the cursor to the next field. **Esc** can be used to cancel the last command before the **Enter** key is pressed.

Ergonomics of the keyboard

Ergonomics of the keyboard refers to:

- The size and position of a key.
- The shape of a key.
- The curve on the face of a key.
- The noise a key makes when it is pressed.
- The angle of the keyboard.
- The tactile response of a keyboard – that is, the finger pressure required to register the key being depressed and the distance the key moves when it is pressed.

Most keyboards are connected to a desktop computer via a cable. A wireless keyboard connects without the use of a cable. It needs a battery to provide power.

Some keyboards are designed to minimise the strain on the user. These can include contoured and split keyboards.

A computer keyboard

Unit 11.1 Activity 5A: Use and care of keyboards

1. Describe the characteristics of keyboards that are used on personal computers.
2. Why is it useful to have 'touch-typing' skills to use a computer keyboard effectively?
3. How do operating systems and software offer enhanced features where special keys and alphanumeric functions allow users to carry out sophisticated functions?
4. What guidelines should apply in places of work with keyboards so that the keyboards are used effectively and efficiently?
5. How can keyboards be abused and ill-treated?
6. Why is the 'QWERTY' keyboard so called?
7. What keyboard shortcuts are used commonly in software?

Pointing devices

The mouse

The mouse is the most commonly used pointing device. The mouse is used to select items and to access menus. A mouse typically has two buttons and a scroll bar in the middle.

A single click of the left mouse button is used to select an icon – for example, the name of a document can be changed after it has been highlighted with a single click. It is also used to select a menu command, and to move the flashing cursor in a Word document.

A double-click is used to open an item – for example, an application will be opened after its icon has been double-clicked.

A computer mouse

The left button is used to select an icon. Then, holding the button down, the icon can be dragged to another location. This can be used for copying files.

The right-click provides extra functions. Right-clicking on an icon provides another menu. Right-clicking within an application also provides an extra menu and it can be used for spellchecking in Microsoft Word.

Development of the mouse

The mouse was invented by one of the pioneers of the personal computer industry, Doug Engelbart, who worked at the Stanford Research Institute in California in the 1960s.

The first commercially successful mouse had a trackball installed inside it to track two-dimensional movements. The ball ran against two rollers inside the mouse.

As the mouse ball ran over the surface, it picked up dirt and this accumulated on the rollers. After a period of time, the mouse became unusable and it needed to be taken apart and cleaned.

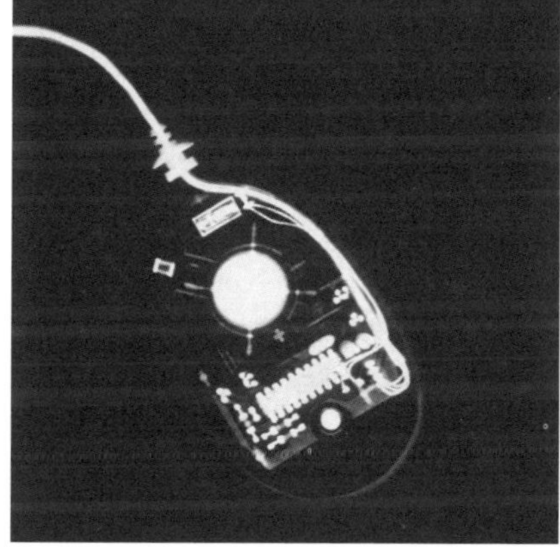

Mouse showing mouse ball

The mouse was a significant development in personal computers and quickly became a standard part of a computer system.

PS2 mouse

The PS2 connector is a six-pin connector used to connect some keyboards and mice to personal computers.

The name, PS2, came from IBM who produced the Personal System 2 series of computers in the late 1980s. The computers were produced with two such connectors: one for a mouse and one for a keyboard. The connectors were colour-coded: purple for the keyboard and green for the mouse.

The keyboard and mouse connectors were electronically similar but could not be interchanged because of the different commands needed by the keyboard and mouse.

The computer needed to be started with the keyboard and mouse connected for the devices to be able to be used.

The PS2 mouse was the standard pointing device until superseded by USB devices.

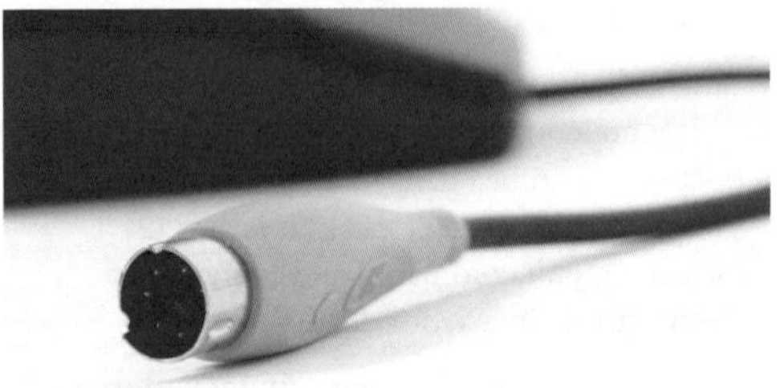

PS2 Mouse

USB wireless mouse

A USB wireless mouse has no physical connection to the computer. The mouse sends a wireless signal to a wireless USB device that is connected to the computer using one of the USB ports. Initially, the mouse and the connector need to be synchronised.

A USB mouse is powered by batteries. When the batteries run flat, the connection is lost and the batteries must be replaced.

Care needs to be taken to ensure that other wireless signals do not interfere with the transmission.

USB wireless mouse and receiver

USB optical mouse

The optical mouse was invented by Taligent in 1999. It has a tiny camera inside that takes up to 1500 photos per second to track movement. It has a small, red light-emitting diode (LED) that bounces off the surface and is used to record its position.

The computer moves the cursor on the screen based on the coordinates sent to it by the mouse.

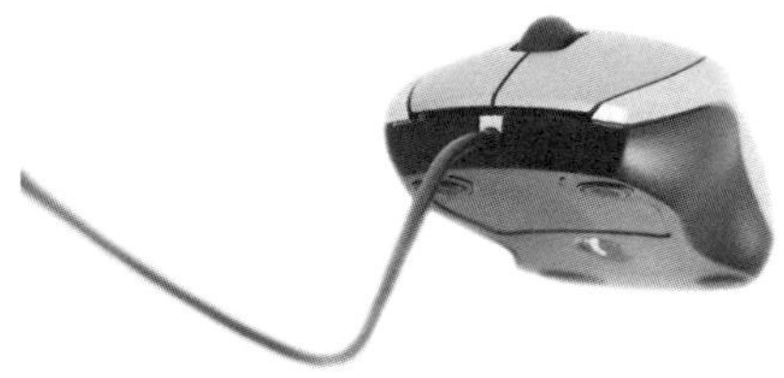

Optical mouse

The optical mouse has no moving parts, thus reducing wear and tear and the possibility of failure. It works effectively on many different surfaces and does not require a mouse pad.

Touch pad

A touch pad (or track pad) is an alternative pointing device that is a flat surface with a tactile sensor sensitive to pressure and touch. A touch pad is responsive to finger movements and tapping. Some touch pads have buttons around the edge of the pad.

A touch screen is a monitor with a sensitive layer over the top. This layer allows the user to select items with a finger or a special pointing device. Touch screens are used on tablet computers, handheld computers and in consumer kiosks such as interactive guides.

Trackball

A trackball is still used as the pointing device in some specialist areas such as computer gaming. A trackball has a ball as the central controlling device. Rolling the trackball allows navigation and selection.

Light pen

A light pen is a light-sensitive device that can be used with a CRT or TV monitor. It operates in a similar manner to a touch screen but with greater precision.

Joystick

A joystick is a stick that pivots on a base and usually has a number of buttons on the central stick to provide commands. Joysticks are widely used in games and also for navigation in aircraft.

Source data-entry devices

A source data-entry device is anything that inputs data into the computer directly from its source. These include scanners and barcode readers.

Scanner devices

Scanners can capture images in a wide range of sizes and formats. Scanners are purchased with their own versions of software to operate the scanner and to capture and edit the images.

Scanners can be flat-bed, ie a document is placed on a flat panel and is then scanned, or portable, in which case the scanner is moved over the document.

Optical character recognition (OCR)

As well as capturing images, a scanner can use optical character recognition (**OCR**) to convert a scan of text to characters that can be used by a word processor. Apart from the capability of the OCR software, the success of the OCR can be affected by the quality of the document being scanned.

A flat-bed scanner

Unit 11.1 Activity 5B: Using a scanner

1. Outline the advantages and disadvantages of using a scanner.

2. Renumber these steps for using a scanner so that they are in the correct order.

- **a.** Open the scanning software on the computer.
- **b.** Crop the scanned image using image-editing software.
- **c.** Check that the scanner is turned on.
- **d.** Check that the glass on the scanner is clean.
- **e.** Turn on the computer.
- **f.** Adjust the scanner settings.
- **g.** Preview the image to be scanned using the scanning software.
- **h.** Save the scanned image to the hard disk (as a TIFF image).
- **i.** Orientate the image on the scanner.
- **j.** Name the file of the scan.
- **k.** Resize the scanned image if required.
- **l.** Print the scanned image if required.
- **m.** Save the image in a final format, eg screen or print.

Barcodes

A **barcode** is made up of a number of vertical lines printed on products with a numeric description of the lines below it. These vertical lines can be read by a machine and translated into numbers.

At a store checkout a barcode scanner reads the barcode, identifies the item by the unique item number, inputs the price assigned to the item number and lists the item on the receipt for printing at completion of the transaction. If a code is unreadable, or the item does not have a barcode, the operator keys in the numbers.

Supermarkets are examples of businesses using information systems to measure stock movements by automatically capturing data. Barcodes printed on individual products, single cartons, a pallet of cartons and a container or load of pallets provide information about product purchases and product sales. International conventions determine how numbers are assigned to manufacturers.

A barcode

Some retailers are investigating technology where products can be inserted with a sensor. This could enable a complete trolley of goods to be registered with a single pass at the checkout.

Stock control

Supermarkets use barcode readers to record stock on shelves and stock in storerooms ready for sale. These stock levels can be compared with information from checkout sales and purchases to determine:

- Wastage.
- Shoplifting.
- Incorrectly located items.
- Fast- and slow-moving lines.
- Product ordering as it is needed, thus reducing stock levels.

Product ordering

Manufacturers and suppliers can be given orders based on the daily sales of a supermarket. Customisation of products for different supermarkets in different areas can be based on up-to-date information.

More specific information about prices allows the manufacturer's production and marketing schedules to be aligned to schedules that respond to consumer demand. Supermarkets and manufacturers will have information showing consumer responses to special price promotions.

They will be able to observe those times of the year when demand is affected by seasonal weather or special occasions.

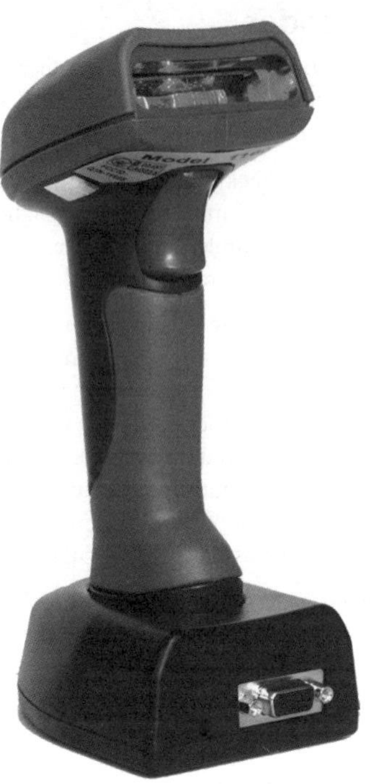

A handheld barcode reader

Product pricing

Prices of products appear on the supermarket shelf next to the item and on the printed receipt when the item is purchased. In the future, digital prices and product information could replace printed information on the shelves. This could be wireless-based technology and enable supermarket managers to change prices and promote special lines instantly.

Character and mark recognition devices

Magnetic Ink Character Recognition is a special font called MICR. It is often used on the bottom of cheques that banks use and allows a large number of cheques to be scanned by a machine.

Optical Mark Recognition (OMR) is often used on surveys or tests. The answer is marked on a form by a pen or pencil and the document is entered through a scanner to enter the responses.

An example of Magnetic Ink Character Recognition

Unit 11.1 Activity 5C: Capturing information

What tasks are being performed when you do the following?

1. Using a mouse with a computer.
2. Scanning a photograph using a flat-bed scanner.
3. Scanning a page of text with a flat-bed scanner.
4. Taking an image with a digital camera.
5. Linking a digital camera to a computer.
6. Using a computer keyboard.
7. Using a modem.
8. Speaking into a microphone attached to a computer.
9. Playing a CD or DVD and saving information to the hard disk.
10. Transferring music to a portable music player from a computer.

Biometrics

Human beings are unique and as people we are expert in distinguishing between different people based on their personal characteristics and idiosyncrasies. It is something we do without giving it much thought at all. To build this capability into an information system and use computer technology is, however, very demanding.

Biometrics uses identity to confirm access to buildings and information systems. It is also used for identification where security is important, such as in airport terminals.

Fingerprints, face recognition, iris recognition, palm prints and DNA can all be used to identify a person.

Research and development are creating possibilities for the computer to be able to relate and interact more with people. The Media Laboratory of the Massachusetts Institute of Technology has been a leader in the research and development of computer interfaces and software that will make computers act on ordinary movements and recognition of people. Use of sensors and cameras with appropriate software will make it possible for associations to be made with a person's environment. Some areas of research include:

- Wearable computers.
- Associating facial expressions, such as smiling or frowning, with a person's mood.
- Doors that open only to the person with the appropriate information embedded into a card or a badge.

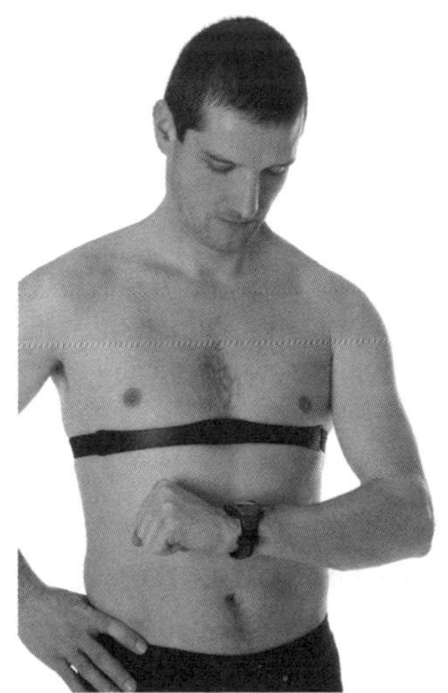

A wearable computer

Face recognition system

A human face has many nodal points that can be measured and used for comparison with a database of images. An image of a person's face is captured, points of reference determined, such as:

- Distance between the eyes.
- Shape of the cheekbones.
- Width of the nose.
- Length of the jawline.
- Depth of the eye sockets.

To date there has been limited success with these systems, particularly in law enforcement and airline security systems. Some countries use such systems as part of their entry process.

Factors that could limit the success include:

- Quality of the image captured (it could be affected by poor lighting).
- Distance and angle at which the image is captured.
- Currency of the image in the database for comparison.
- Hairstyles covering the face.

Australia has a 'smartgate' system at some airports for immigration for international passengers. A face photograph is compared with the digital photograph stored in a microchip in the e-passport. The scan is performed at a self-check-in booth.

Speech recognition

Recognition of speech as input for computers has been a goal of software developers. It is used in a number of situations, but obstacles have prevented its widespread implementation. These obstacles include:

- Background noises interfering when a user gives commands.
- Substantial memory and hard disk storage requirements.
- The spoken word being joined rather than in separate parts, making it difficult for normal speaking patterns to be recognised.
- Different accents in different countries.

Finger and palm prints recognition system

Fingerprints are a unique identifier and can be used for access to computers. Some notebook computers now include fingerprint recognition devices that can be used to log onto the computer.

Image-capturing devices

Digital still camera

A wide range of digital cameras are available with many different features. The cameras vary in size from compact to large, high-performance cameras that are used by professional photographers.

Digital cameras offer a range of image setting modes. The settings affect the style and quality of the images created, particularly file size and resolution.

Downloading images from a digital camera

Most digital cameras include image-management software that allows the downloading and printing of photographs. The camera is connected to a computer using either a USB cable or a firewire cable.

Some cameras include storage devices that can connect directly to a computer.

These include:

- Compact flash memory cards.
- Floppy disks.
- Removable hard disks.
- USB storage devices.

Some cameras can also connect directly to printers to print the photographs.

A digital camera

Digital cameras give images a default name, usually with some form of sequence. The default name does not have any relationship to the content of the image.

When the images are loaded onto a computer, they should be stored, edited and renamed.

Unit 11.1 Activity 5D: Using a digital camera

1. Outline the advantages and disadvantages of using a digital camera.
2. Describe the step by step process for using a digital camera.

Digital video camera

Digital video cameras can record directly to memory in the camera rather than a storage medium such as tape. A digital video camera does not require a video capture card. As video requires large amounts of storage space, a DV camera may be connected to a suitable storage device, such as a hard disk, and the video saved to disk at the same time as recording. Many commercial movies are recorded digitally.

Video can be compressed to decrease the size of files created at time of recording. The greater the compression, the smaller the file size and reduction in quality of the finished video.

Webcam

A webcam is a camera attached to a computer. A webcam can capture an image, image sequence or streaming video as input to a computer and then **upload** it to a web server for display on a web page. An image sequence may be updated at regular intervals.

Webcams are used in a wide variety of locations and for a wide variety of purposes. They can be used to show traffic conditions, public places, weather, classrooms and famous places.

Many personal computers have built-in cameras.

A webcam

Videoconferencing camera

A videoconference allows two or more parties to interact using video and audio in real time.

Videoconferencing systems vary greatly in scope and cost. At the entry level, webcams can be used for videoconferencing. Microsoft has developed a videoconferencing system using a specially designed camera called the Roundtable that is voice-activated and can automatically move from one participant to another.

A Microsoft Roundtable camera used for videoconferencing

Other vendors have developed systems that require the use of higher-powered video cameras. For example, Cisco has developed a system that uses large screens and they call the interactions 'telepresence' to indicate that it is close to real face-to-face **communication**.

Digitising devices

Graphics tablet

A graphics tablet is a flat, rectangular, electronic board. It is used to create drawings and sketches, particularly by artists, architects, draftsmen and designers. The tablet is sensitive to touch and it digitises the movements made on the tablet to a digital document.

Digital notepads

A digital notepad is like a clipboard that uses a special pen or stylus to record the movements of the pen and writing on the pad. The pad can record many pages of writing and transfer the data to a computer.

Some transport companies use a digital notepad to collect signatures when delivering a parcel.

Audio input devices

Music (musical instrument digital interface (MIDI))

This is a standard protocol that allows computer and electronic musical instruments to communicate with each other. It allows music to be stored as a series of instructions rather than as audio files.

Thus a MIDI file stored on a computer can be used to play a musical creation through an electronic keyboard connected to the computer.

Sensors

A **sensor** is a device, often a microprocessor, that measures a physical quantity. The measurement is read by an observer or another piece of equipment such as a computer. For example, a sensor can be used to monitor the temperature of a liquid and that temperature can be recorded on a computer. The sensor may be simple with two states (on and off) or it may be able to detect a range of states.

Microprocessors are found in a variety of commonplace goods ranging from wristwatches and motor vehicles to domestic appliances such as microwave ovens and televisions.

These microprocessors have embedded instructions and operate within parameters of pre-set instructions. They are used in manufacturing processes and control systems. Examples of the types of sensors include:

A sensor

- Light sensors are able to monitor intensities of light and when light is blocked. They are used for security lighting, to detect and count objects on a conveyor belt.
- Pressure- or touch-sensitive pads are used to operate automatic doors by detecting a person approaching the door.
- Temperature sensors allow a heating or cooling system to operate, turning it on or off according to pre-set temperature levels.
- Weight sensors are used to control food packaging on a production line so that products have a minimum correct weight.

Sensor control is used by:

- Valves: flow control for liquids and gases.
- Motors and pumps.
- Robots.
- Actuators, such as those used in hydraulic pistons.

Microprocessors in motor vehicles

Motor vehicle manufacturers are major consumers of computers. Microprocessors in a motor vehicle can be responsible for the following systems:

- Engine and power control.
- Radio, CD and audio.
- Air bag and restraint.
- Vehicle electronics control and security.
- Steering wheel remote control.
- Cruise control.
- Electronic climate control.
- Anti-skid braking.
- Vehicle self-diagnosis.

A navigation map can be displayed onscreen in a car. Evolution of the microprocessor towards miniaturisation and increased function means the signals travel faster with more operations carried out in a given time. Digital-quality sound input and output, full-frame video and speech recognition are increasingly possible because of the microprocessor's increasing power.

Miniaturisation is an important factor in developing voice recognition so that instructions to the computer can be given verbally.

Radio-frequency identification tag (RFID)

RFID transmits the details about an object wirelessly. An RFID tag is scanned by a reader and the details are transmitted to a computer. An RFID tag consists of a microchip that is attached to a radio antenna. An RFID reader has one or more antennas attached that send out radio signals and receive replies from RFID tags. The reader passes on the information it receives to a computer in a digital format.

RFID tags are used by companies to track assets.

Pager

A pager is a one-way communication device suitable for short messages. Many pagers use a radio communication protocol. A computer is attached to a radio transmitter and the message is sent to the pager by the computer via the transmitter. Pagers are alphanumeric and there are some two-way pagers available.

Pagers have been superseded by mobile phones in many areas.

An alphanumeric pager

Radar identification (IFF)

Radar is an identification system that uses radio waves to determine the location, movement, speed and direction of both moving and fixed objects. A radar dish or antenna emits radio waves that bounce off objects and part of the radio wave is returned to the dish.

Radar applications are widely used in the military and also for aircraft flight navigation.

Unit 11.1 Activity 5E: Connecting devices

The following devices can be connected to a computer.

1. How are the devices physically connected to the computer and what software is required for their use? Complete the following table.

	Device	Physical connection	Software	Example of product
1	Scanner			
2	Graphics tablet			
3	Keyboard			
4	Light pen			
5	Printer			
6	Monitor			
7	Sound input			
8	Modem			
9	Webcam			
10	Digital video camera			

2. For each of the items above find an example of a product. Identify the brand name, model number, supplier and price.

Unit 11.1 Computer Fundamentals

Topic 6: Output devices

Topic 6 explores the various output devices (see ICT Syllabus p. 11 and Computer Studies Syllabus p. 11). It covers:

- Monitors.
- Printers.
- Audio and video output devices.
- Combination input and output devices.

Monitors

A **monitor** is used to display computer output. Most computers have a monitor either attached or built-in.

Cathode ray tube (CRT)

A **CRT** monitor has a picture tube with a cathode or charged filament enclosed in it. The filament heats up and sends light particles to a phosphor-coated screen. The phosphor emits red, green and blue light that can be combined to display on a colour screen.

The picture is produced out of rows of coloured dots or pixels. The higher number of dots per inch, the sharper the resolution.

CRT monitors are relatively large because of the size of the tube. This is the same technology as has been used in television sets for over 50 years.

CRT monitors are being superseded by flat screen monitors.

A CRT monitor

Flat panel monitor or liquid crystal display (LCD)

An **LCD monitor** is a flat panel monitor. LCD monitors were first used in laptop computers.

An LCD monitor is made up of five layers including a sheet of polarised glass and a layer of liquid crystal solution that is responsive to electric charges. The crystals are manipulated by the electric charge to produce different degrees of light and colour to produce a picture.

A flat panel monitor

An LCD monitor is brighter than a CRT monitor and uses significantly less electricity. Being a flat panel, it takes up far less space than a CRT monitor.

LCD technology continues to evolve and larger screens are being developed.

E-book readers

An e-book reader is a portable electronic device with a built-in flat panel screen that is optimised for reading books. They are very similar to tablet computers but typically have specialised software optimised for displaying the contents of books.

The software is usually proprietary and e-books are mostly purchased online.

Data projectors

A data projector takes a signal from a computer, a television source or a video source and displays that signal on a large screen.

Typically, a computer is connected to the data projector by a cable and the projector acts in the same manner as an external monitor. The cost of data projectors varies significantly and depends on a number of factors including:

- Size of the display required.
- Brightness of the globe.
- Portability of the projector.

High-definition television (HDTV)

High-definition television has a much higher definition rate than standard-definition television: approximately five times higher at about two million pixels per frame.

High-definition televisions receive a digital signal rather than the analog signal that the older CRT televisions used. To receive a signal, the HDTV must have a high-definition tuner, either built-in or external.

In Australia, all television broadcasts are being changed to high-definition.

Printers

Impact printers (dot matrix)

A dot matrix printer uses a printhead that moves back and forth across the paper. It makes an impact by striking a ribbon that has been soaked in ink. The characters are made by a matrix of dots that create pressure on the paper. A dot matrix printer can print a range of font sizes and styles. It can also print carbon copies of documents.

Impact printers can be quite noisy as the printhead strikes the paper.

Non-impact printers (laser, thermal printer, inkjet)

A non-impact printer does not operate by having a printhead make an impact.

A laser printer produces high-quality print documents quickly and quietly. A laser beam projects the image onto a rotating drum. Dry toner particles are picked up by the drum and printed by direct contact onto the paper. Heat is used to ensure the print is dry.

The laser printer was invented at Hewlett Packard in Silicon Valley in 1969. The laser speed can vary greatly and many organisations use high-speed laser printers to generate large, personalised mailings.

A thermal printer operates by heating parts of special thermal paper that respond to heat. When the printhead passes over the paper, the colour turns to black in the selected area. An additional colour can be added by passing over the paper at a different temperature.

Thermal printers are generally quieter and quicker than dot matrix printers. One common application of a thermal printer is invoice printers at petrol service stations.

A laser printer

Inkjet printers create images by putting droplets of ink directly onto paper. Many of these printers are inexpensive consumer items. However, it can be expensive to replenish the ink.

The ink cartridges are black together with red, blue and yellow to produce colours. There is a wide range in the size and quality of inkjet printers. Some large poster printers use this technology.

Photo printers

Photo printers are optimised to produce high-quality photographic images. These will use special photographic paper. Both inkjet and laser printers can be used for photographs.

Plotters

A plotter uses a pen to move across the surface of a piece of paper. Plotters have been widely used in computer-aided design applications but are being replaced by large inkjet or laser printers.

Braille printer

A Braille printer prints text as tactile Braille text. This is an impact printer. A Braille printer needs its own software to translate normal text into Braille. It prints about 40 characters per line and 25 lines per page. Braille is usually printed onto special paper that is significantly heavier than normal paper.

Audio and video output devices

Sound output (audio speakers, headphones)

Most computers have an audio port, ie a port to which external speakers or headphones can be connected. Computers have inbuilt speakers that can be used for music or videos.

Generally, external speakers have a higher quality sound output than inbuilt speakers.

Video output (videoconferencing)

Most computers can play video. There is a range of different digital video formats, such as Blu-ray, QuickTime and MPEG-4.

The computer needs the appropriate software to be installed to play the various formats. Some players come as standard with the operating system, while others will need to be downloaded and installed.

Videoconferencing uses two-way video transmissions across a communication channel. Some of the videoconferencing technology uses the **Internet protocol (IP)**, the same as on the World Wide Web.

Voice output (text-to-speech system)

Text-to-speech applications take written text and output it as speech. The quality of the results is dependent on the specialised software used for this application.

There are many text-to-speech applications that can be used on the Internet in a range of languages.

Combination input and output devices

Facsimile machines

A facsimile (fax) is a document that is transmitted across a telephone line. The facsimile machine scans a document and sends the scanned image to the recipient. The recipient's fax (telephone) number is dialled and the image is received on a printer of some type.

Multifunction devices (MFD)

A **multifunction device** combines a number of these functions – printing, scanning, copying and facsimile – into the one device. Such a device can be a single-user device in a small office or home or a large, networked device.

Companies such as Fuji Xerox have specialised in large multifunction devices for organisations.

A Fuji Xerox multifunction device

Internet telephone (telephony)

Internet telephony uses the Internet protocol to carry out many of the functions of the wired telephone service.

Skype is a software application that uses the Internet for telephone and video calls. It is useful and cheap for one-to-one conversations.

Many corporations have moved to Internet telephony that also uses the Internet but provides most of the applications that were expected in an office environment. Large corporations including Microsoft and Cisco have developed suites of applications to meet business needs using the Internet.

An Internet-compatible telephone

Terminals

A computer **terminal** is a device used for entering and/or viewing information on a computer system. Terminals were used on mainframe computer systems and displayed information. They were mainly CRT devices.

If a terminal had some capacity for processing data rather than displaying it, it was known as a smart or intelligent terminal.

A thin client or network computer relies on a computer **network**. The network computer has processing power but the applications are stored on the network server. For example, for document production the word processing application is loaded from the network. It then runs on the thin client and the user chooses where to store the document.

In a similar manner, an Internet or Web computer has the application stored on the Internet and it is loaded as required by the computer.

Computer networks

A computer network is a number of computers connected to each other. A computer network allows users to:

- Work on a file that is on another computer on the same network.
- Print a document on a printer connected to the network.
- Send a message to another user on the network.

A computer network can span the whole world or be confined to a single room.

A network is made up of:

- Nodes.
- Connections or links between the nodes.
- Computer software to allow connections.

Nodes

A node on a network is any device that is connected to the network. It can be:

- A computer.
- A printer.
- Hard disk storage.
- One of many other devices.

The links between computers are made up of any combination of:

- Cable, such as coaxial cable, CAT 5 or telephone wiring.
- Satellite transmission.
- Radio waves, called wireless networking.

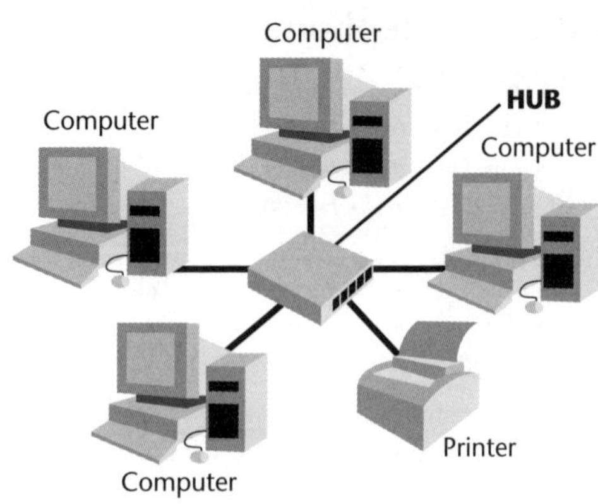

A computer network

Graphical user interface (GUI)

Most of the application packages use a **graphical user interface** (GUI) whose features include the use of a mouse or pointing device and the ability to:

- Access pull-down menus.
- Point and click on objects to cause actions.
- Copy and paste between applications.
- Drag and drop text or objects both within and between applications.

Many software applications have an interface that is consistent with other applications. This makes it easy to work with a range of applications and reduces the time it takes to learn commands. Similarly, many of the keyboard shortcuts and commands are consistent between applications.

The Microsoft Office suite of programs includes a word processor, Word; a spreadsheet, Excel; a presentation package, PowerPoint; and a database package, Access. The standard menus in Word and Excel are almost identical.

Unit 11.1 Computer Fundamentals

Topic 7: Storage devices

Topic 7 explores the various storage devices (see ICT Syllabus pp. 11–12 and Computer Studies Syllabus p. 12). It covers:

- Units of measurement.
- Primary (internal) storage.
- Secondary (external) storage.

Units of measurement

Information stored using a computer is stored in a digital format, that is, using binary digits (bits) 0 and 1. Any input is converted to a series of 0s and 1s in accordance with standards used among computer manufacturers.

American Standard Code for Information Interchange (ASCII) is a code that is used to represent characters using eight binary digits. For example:

Character	ASCII code (binary)
space	00100000
$	00100100
1	00100001
0	00110000
.	00101110

ASCII code examples

A bit stream is a sequence of bits with no formatting or spacing that is stored on an appropriate medium. The bit stream needs to be read, interpreted and reconstituted in a meaningful format.

Depending on the context, an eight-bit sequence could be interpreted in a number of ways. It could be:

- A character.
- A note of music.
- A real number.
- An integer.
- A pixel.

A bit does not know what it represents, nor does anyone without the complete bit stream.

The common standards for ASCII code are binary digits in eight-bit bytes. There are proposals to include non-English alphabets and use a 16-bit code.

Binary and decimal numbers

A **binary** number is made up of only 1s and 0s. An example of a binary number is 1010.

Any number can be represented as a binary number, ie as a series of 1s and 0s.

In binary numbers, each digit '0' represents zero and each digit '1' represents two to a power. It starts on the right side, with the first digit being 2^0 ie 1. The next digit is 2^1 ie 2, then 2^2 ie 4, and so on.

The four-digit binary number 1010 is:

$1 \times 2^3 + 0 \times 2^2 + 1 \times 2^1 + 0 \times 2^0$

$= 1 \times 8 + 0 \times 4 + 1 \times 2 + 0 \times 1$

$= 10$

An eight-digit binary number is made up of powers of 2 up to 2^7:

2^7	2^6	2^5	2^4	2^3	2^2	2^1	2^0
128	64	32	16	8	4	2	1

Thus the number 10111011 is:

$1 \times 2^7 + 0 \times 2^6 + 1 \times 2^5 + 1 \times 2^4 + 1 \times 2^3 + 0 \times 2^2 + 1 \times 2^1 + 1 \times 2^0$

$= 128 + 32 + 16 + 8 + 2 + 1$

$= 187$

The maximum eight-digit binary number is 11111111 which is equal to 255.

Binary to decimal conversion

Use the above method to convert from binary to decimal.

Example

Binary number 10010011

10010011

$= 1 \times 128 + 0 \times 64 + 0 \times 32 + 1 \times 16 + 0 \times 8 + 0 \times 4 + 1 \times 2 + 1 \times 1$

$= 128 + 16 + 2 + 1$

$= 147$

Decimal numbers

A decimal number is made up of the digits 0, 1, 2, 3 … 9. Each digit represents the number times 10 to a power.

The right-hand digit represents 10^0 ie 1, the next to the left 10^1 ie 10, then 10^2 ie 100, and so on.

The number 3421 is made up of:

$3 \times 10^3 + 4 \times 10^2 + 2 \times 10^1 + 1 \times 10^0$

$= 3 \times 1000 + 4 \times 100 + 2 \times 10 + 1 \times 1$

$= 3421$

Decimal to binary conversion

A decimal number can be converted to binary by repeated division by 2. The decimal number is divided by 2 and the remainder is written next to the number until the answer (quotient) is zero. The digits that make up the remainder give the binary number.

Example 1

Decimal number 14

2 divides into 14 with the result 7 and remainder 0.

2 divides into 7 with the result 3 and remainder 1.

2 divides into 3 with the result 1 and remainder 1.

2 divides into 1 with the result 0 and remainder 1.

Divisor	Number	Remainder
2	14	0
2	7	1
2	3	1
2	1	1
	0	

The binary equivalent is the remainder from bottom to top ie 1110.

Example 2

Decimal number 45

2 divides into 45 with the result 22 and remainder 1.

2 divides into 22 with the result 11 and remainder 0.

2 divides into 11 with the result 5 and remainder 1.

2 divides into 5 with the result 2 and remainder 1.

2 divides into 2 with the result 1 and remainder 0.

2 divides into 1 with the result 0 and remainder 1.

Divisor	Number	Remainder
2	45	1
2	22	0
2	11	1
2	5	1
2	2	0
2	1	1
	0	

The binary equivalent is the remainder from bottom to top ie 101101.

Example 3

Decimal number 122

2 divides into 122 with the result 61 and remainder 0.

2 divides into 61 with the result 30 and remainder 1.

2 divides into 30 with the result 15 and remainder 0.

2 divides into 15 with the result 7 and remainder 1.

2 divides into 5 with the result 2 and remainder 1.

2 divides into 7 with the result 3 and remainder 0.

2 divides into 3 with the result 1 and remainder 1.

2 divides into 1 with the result 0 and remainder 1.

2	122	0
2	61	1
2	30	0
2	15	1
2	7	1
2	3	1
2	1	1
	0	

The binary equivalent is the remainder from bottom to top ie 11011010.

Checking this result it is 64 + 32 + 16 + 8 + 2 = 122.

Unit 11.1 Activity 7A: Binary–decimal conversion

1. Convert the following numbers to binary:

- **a.** 45
- **b.** 67
- **c.** 109
- **d.** 221
- **e.** 567

2. Convert the following binary numbers to decimal:

- **a.** 1101
- **b.** 1011
- **c.** 10110010
- **d.** 10111011
- **e.** 1101110111

Units of storage

Computer data is measured in **bits**, **bytes** (B), kilobytes (KB), megabytes (MB), gigabytes (GB) or terabytes (TB). A single character in a text document is equivalent to a byte.

A bit is the basic unit of storage in information systems. A bit is also known as a binary digit. A bit has two states, like an electricity switch that can be either on or off. In computing, a bit is usually represented as having the value of either 0 or 1.

A byte is a series of 8 bits. A byte can have 2 to the power of 8 different values, ie 256 different values. Each byte is used to represent a separate character.

A kilobyte is 1000 bytes and a megabyte is 1000 kilobytes. A gigabyte is 1000 megabytes.

Storage unit	Abbreviation		Value (approximate)	Exact	
Byte	B		1	(2^0)	1
Kilobyte	KB	One thousand bytes	1 000	(2^{10})	1 024
Megabyte	MB	One million bytes	1 000 000	(2^{20})	1 048 576
Gigabyte	GB	One billion bytes	1 000 000 000	(2^{30})	1 073 741 824
Terabyte	TB	One trillion bytes	1 000 000 000 000	(2^{40})	1 099 511 627 776

Units of storage

Primary (internal) storage

Read-only memory (ROM)

Read-only memory (ROM) is the part of the computer where essential instructions and data for the operating system are stored. These instructions cannot be changed.

When a computer is turned on it carries out some instructions that are permanently stored in its ROM. The process of starting up a computer is known as the '**boot process**'.

The boot process involves the following tasks:

- It detects the processor type.
- It detects all the available devices including disks, keyboard, mouse and monitor.
- It looks for an operating system located on the hard disk.
- If an operating system is located, the system starts up.

The operating system is usually located on the computer's hard disk. However, the boot process looks for an operating system on other **storage devices** first. This allows the user to start the computer from another system for diagnostic purposes.

If the required files are not located, an error message is displayed.

Random-access memory (RAM)

Random-access memory (RAM) is the part of the computer where data and instructions are stored by the user and application programs. Each application requires some of the RAM to work effectively. It is temporary storage and when a computer is turned off the information it stores is lost. This means a document currently being worked upon needs to be saved to the hard drive, and if there were a power failure any unsaved portion of the document would be lost.

RAM is usually installed onto the motherboard by using a SIMM (single in-line memory module). The amount of RAM may be altered by changing the configuration of the SIMMs or adding more SIMMs. If a computer is being used for intensive tasks such as movie editing then greater RAM is often necessary.

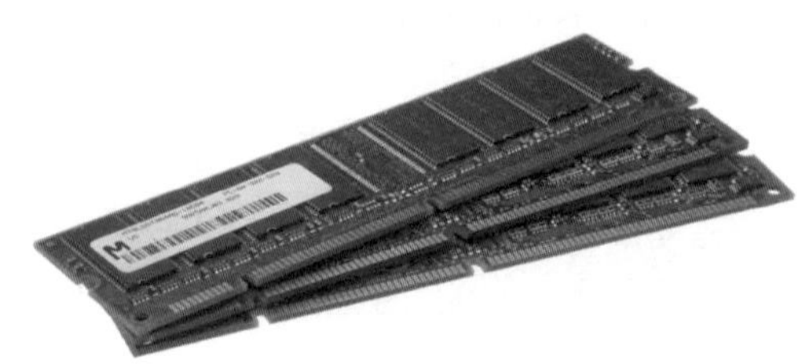

RAM for a computer

Secondary (external) storage

Floppy disks

A floppy disk is a small storage device made of flexible magnetic storage material. The disk is sealed inside a rectangular case.

The floppy disk was invented by IBM and a floppy disk drive was installed in almost all desktop and notebook computers from the mid-1970s to the mid-2000s. Floppy disks were manufactured in three sizes: initially 8-inch, then 5.25-inch and finally 3.5-inch. A 3.5-inch floppy disk had a storage capacity from 500 KB up to 2 MB.

A 3.5-inch floppy disk

When the disk is inserted into the floppy disk drive in a computer, the disk rotates and magnetic heads read the data on the disk.

These were the only storage devices on early personal computers. The operating system was stored on a floppy disk and was used to boot the computer.

When personal computers started to incorporate hard disks as primary storage, they still included an internal floppy disk drive for backup purposes. In time, the floppy disk drive was removed from personal computers and external storage was provided by flash memory, external hard drives or, in some cases, external floppy drives.

Floppy disks are now rarely installed in computers and are found mostly in legacy devices.

Memory stick (flash drive)

USB memory sticks have flash memory with a USB interface. Flash memory is a rewritable memory chip. There are no mechanical parts in the drive. Flash memory can be erased electronically and reprogrammed and therefore can contain both data and programs.

External flash drive with a USB interface

Many digital devices such as digital cameras, modems, pagers and cellular telephones use flash memory devices. Some notebook computers now use flash memory for storage rather than a hard disk.

In some cases the flash memory is a removable card that can be moved from device to device. Memory sticks are small and portable, which is a security risk if the data is valuable. Memory sticks have replaced floppy disks for external storage.

Smart cards (SD, smart media)

A smart card is a pocket-sized card that has an integrated circuit embedded into the card. Smart cards are often used for identification and authentication. Banks use smart cards to identify users and to authorise transactions. Many organisations use smart cards for controlled access to buildings and offices.

Smart cards have been developed for transport ticketing where they have a stored value and can calculate the appropriate fare.

A smart card includes an embedded integrated circuit

Hard disk drive

A **hard disk** is a storage device that is made up of one or more rigid platters coated with a material that allows data to be magnetically recorded. The disks rotate at very high speeds, eg 3600 revolutions per second. The drive has read/write heads that move across the disk surface.

Hard disks range in size from 100 GB upward.

Most personal computers are now sold with an internal hard disk drive of at least 500 GB of disk storage.

A hard disk drive

External hard disk drive

An external hard disk drive uses the same technology as the internal hard disk drive but is contained in its own case and is connected to the computer by a communications port.

For many years, the most widely used interface was the Small Computer System Interface (SCSI) and personal computers included a SCSI port to allow connection. Some high performance computers still use SCSI ports for connecting hard disks.

An external hard disk using a USB connection

Most external hard drives are now connected via the USB port on the computer. Most personal computers have a number of USB ports and hard disks can be easily connected and disconnected.

Removable hard disk

A removable hard disk is a magnetic disk that is not permanently attached to a computer system. The disk is enclosed in a cartridge and is accessed via disk drive.

Such a hard disk can be taken out and replaced by another one at the user's discretion.

Removable hard disks have become less popular as the price of large, fixed hard disks has fallen, and with the increased use of flash memory sticks.

Removable hard disks are now used mostly for backup and archival purposes.

Optical disks

An optical disk is a flat, circular disk that uses laser technology to encode binary digits onto it. **Compact disks**, DVDs and Blu-ray disks are made of polycarbonate produced by injection moulding; one side of the cavity has a mirrored surface.

An optical disk requires an optical disk drive to read and write to it. Optical disk drives are now standard items in personal computers. The optical disk drive has replaced the floppy disk drive. As with hard disk drives, optical disk drives can be both internal and external.

CD-ROM disks

A CD-ROM is an optical disk that uses laser storage technology and can store about 780 MB of files.

Many networks and libraries include banks of CD-ROM drives that can be accessed by a number of users.

A CD-ROM is a read-only device. Files cannot be written to a CD-ROM.

A computer with a CD-RW or DVD-RW drive can read and write CD-ROM disks.

CD-RW disks

A CD-ReWriteable disk is a type of CD disk that allows the user to write data to that disk a number of times. A CD-RW disk can be treated in much the same manner as a floppy disk.

In some cases, specialised software is needed to write to the disk.

DVD disks

DVD stands for digital versatile disk or **digital video disk**. A DVD looks like a CD but it has a much higher storage capacity. A DVD can consist of a number of layers and can be single- or double-sided. The storage capacity of a single-layer, single-side disk is 4.7 GB. The maximum capacity of a DVD is 17 GB.

When DVDs first came onto the market they were only used for showing videos or movies. They were played in a DVD machine connected to a television or monitor.

As the product developed, different standards emerged. There are now three competing standards that produce similar products.

DVDs are used for:

- Applications requiring a large amount of storage such as enhanced **multimedia** and games.
- High quality music.
- Video.

DVD-ROM disks

The DVD-ROM was the first DVD standard. It is a read-only format and is used for video or games. The data is burned onto the DVD and then the DVD is played on a DVD drive that is connected to a television set or monitor.

Many personal computers contain a DVD-ROM drive. Being read-only format, the data cannot be modified, nor can data be added to the disk.

DVD+R disks

DVD+R is a recordable DVD but it can record data only once. When the data has been recorded onto the disk, it is stored permanently and no further data can be recorded to the disk.

DVD+RW disks

DVD+RW is a re-recordable DVD. That is, data can be recorded and erased a number of times.

DVD+R and DVD+R disk formats are supported by companies including Philips, Sony, Hewlett-Packard and Dell.

DVD-RAM disks

DVD-RAM is another DVD format but it is only supported by the companies that manufacture the devices. These disks can be recorded, erased and modified many times. The format is not compatible with many DVD players.

Laser disks

A laser disk compared to a CD

A laser disk is an optical disk storage medium. It was largely used for movies and videos. Laser disks came onto the market in the late 1970s and were very popular in the USA and Japan.

Laser disks had higher-quality video and audio than VHS tapes. Many movies were made available on laser disks. However, laser disks were limited in that they held only about 30 minutes of video per side.

Laser disks have been replaced by DVDs. However, there are some sites that specialise in selling laser disk titles that are collector's items and difficult to find.

Blu-ray disks

Blu-ray disks are the same physical size as CDs and DVDs but they are multi-layered. A layer can contain 50 GB of storage and a Blu-ray disk can contain four layers.

Blu-ray disks use a different laser technology from standard DVDs. A blue laser light reads the data, unlike the red laser for standard DVDs and CDs.

A Blu-ray disk player

A Blu-ray disk can store about nine hours of high-definition video or television or about 23 hours of standard definition video. Blu-ray disks are becoming widely used consumer items for use with high-definition television sets and they allow users to record video and television transmission.

Online storage

Internet hard drive

An Internet hard drive is a means of storing files on the Internet. These files can then be accessed by any authorised computer connected to the Internet.

A number of different vendors offer the use of an Internet hard drive. Uploading regular backups of files to an Internet hard drive can be a useful method of backing up files.

However, the loading of files onto an Internet hard drive takes up bandwidth and is slower than directly accessing them on a disk.

Different vendors offer a range of disk space and services.

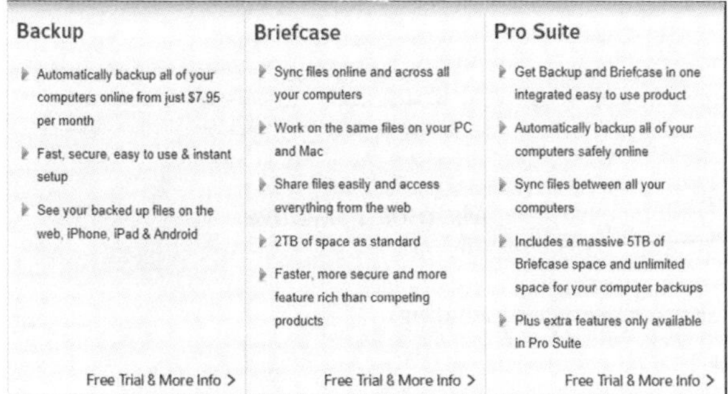

Some of the services offered by Livedrive.com

i-Drive

i-Drive was one of the first companies to provide Internet hard disks. It was founded in 1999 and subsequently taken over by a large corporation. However, it continues to offer these services.

Some of the services offered by iDrive.com

SkyDrive

SkyDrive is Microsoft's offering of storage on the Internet. It is part of the Windows Live suite of services that includes email and calendaring.

Some of the services available are:

- Document storage.
- Photograph storage.
- Public folders.
- Shared folders.

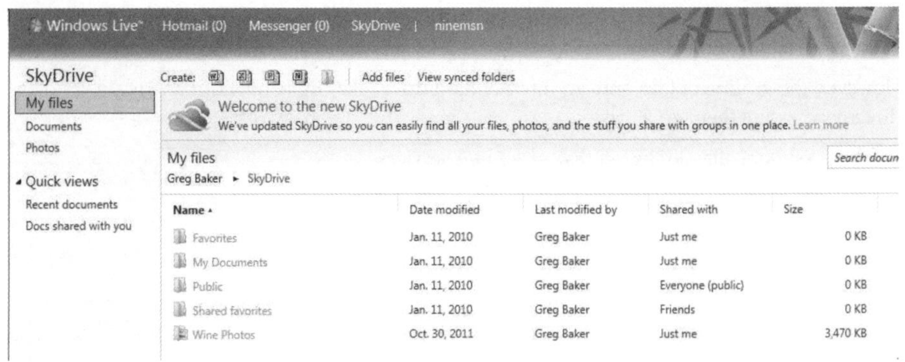

Microsoft's SkyDrive

Other vendors offer similar services including:

- Google: Gmail.
- Apple: iCloud.

Disk caching

Disk caching is a method of speeding up the storage of data onto a hard disk. This works by using part of the RAM on a computer to store data; in effect, it becomes part of the hard disk.

The most recently accessed data can be stored in the RAM. When a request for data is made, the operating system first checks the RAM to see if the data is stored there, and, if so, it is retrieved.

There are, however, risks with disk caching. If the system crashes, the data may not have been written back to the hard disk. If that is the case, the data that was cached in the RAM will be lost.

File compression

File compression is a method of reducing the amount of storage space taken up by files on a hard disk. Compression software uses the fact that there are patterns in data and it encodes the information so that the number of bits required to store data is reduced. This reduces the amount of storage needed or the amount of bandwidth required if a file is to be transmitted across a network.

However, compressed data needs to be decompressed. If a video has been compressed, it may require expensive hardware to decompress it at an acceptable rate before viewing. Because compressing removes some of the data, the decompression process may lose some of the original data, resulting in distortion of the original.

RAID systems

A redundant array of independent disks (RAID) is an array of a number of disks that is used to improve performance in a computer system. A RAID system works by dividing the data into 'chunks' and each chunk is saved for a different disk drive. For example, a 400 KB file could be split into two 200 KB chunks and saved on each of two disks.

There is a range of RAID levels from RAID 0, RAID 1 through to RAID 6.

Another commonly used feature of RAID is mirroring, where data is replicated across one or more disks. This is useful for disaster recovery purposes where a disk fails and it can be replaced without any detrimental effects to the user.

A hardware RAID system such as this can be used at home or in a small business.

Network attached storage

Network attached storage (NAS) is a storage system that is accessible to a range of users on a network. The storage is not dedicated to one computer or server but is accessible to a range of authorised users.

These hard disk systems have multiple disks and RAID configurations. NAS systems have their own unique address on the network.

NAS systems are easy to expand and extra RAID functions can be added to increase the reliability of the storage.

Storage area network

A storage area network (SAN) is a special-purpose network that connects a range of different storage devices.

A storage area network is usually part of a large organisation's information technology resources. It would typically include one or more network attached storage systems.

Magnetic tape systems

Magnetic tape is a storage medium for the sequential storing of data. The tape is made of flexible plastic and one side is coated with magnetic material, making it suitable for storing electronic data.

Magnetic tapes are usually used for archival purposes. They were originally open reels but these have been largely superseded by cartridges and cassettes. Cartridges can be easily stored offsite for archival and disaster recovery purposes.

As magnetic tape is a sequential storage device, data can be relatively slow to locate, as the particular location of the data on the tape must be found.

Some large organisations still use reel-to-reel tape in cabinets for backup purposes.

A reel-to-reel tape system

Unit 11.1 Activity 7B: Storage

1. Music, its access and storage have undergone significant change in the last twenty years. In this section of the course we are examining the technical aspects of formats. For each device identify and compare the method of storage used in each device and an advantage and disadvantage of each device for music.

Storage device	How is music stored? Describe the files and format.	Technologies required to acquire, store and access	Advantages	Disadvantages
Compact disk				
iBook				
Portable music player				
Smartphone				

Storage device	How is music stored? Describe the files and format.	Technologies required to acquire, store and access	Advantages	Disadvantages
Cloud				

2. The following devices and storage mediums are used for data storage. Fill in the parts of the tables to describe their features.

	Device or storage medium	Key features	Capacity	Where used
1	ROM			
2	RAM			
3	Floppy disk			
4	USB flash memory stick			
5	Smart cards			
6	Compact disk			
7	DVD disk			
8	Blu-ray disk			
9	Laser disk			
10	Internal hard drive			
11	External hard drive			
12	RAID system			
13	Network attached storage			
14	Magnetic tape			
15	The cloud – online storage			

Unit 11.1 Computer Fundamentals

Topic 8: System box

Topic 8 examines the system box (see ICT Syllabus p. 12 and Computer Studies Syllabus p. 12). It covers:

- Mainboard.
- Power supply unit.
- Cooling fan.
- Ports.
- Software.
- File management and organisation.

A computer is made up of:

- Central processing unit.
- Memory.
- Input and output.
- Communications and control devices.

Mainboard

Also called the **motherboard**, this is a printed circuit board that holds the main components of the microcomputer's CPU (central processing unit). The CPU is a microprocessor. A personal computer usually has a single processor, although it is becoming more common to have more than one.

Microprocessors

A microchip is a silicon wafer with electronic switches etched on the surface to make an integrated circuit. A **microprocessor** is a type of microchip that has memory and logic circuits built in. Other microchips store information that can be accessed easily and quickly by the microprocessor. Since the invention of the integrated circuit in the late 1950s, development has been such that the number of transistors per chip has increased as the cost has decreased. A megabyte of memory that cost approximately $US550 000 in 1970 today costs about $US30. Some circuits produced today have more than six million transistors.

Microprocessors are made by specialist companies who supply computer and other manufacturers. Technological development and improved capabilities of computer chips have been accompanied by demand for these new chips.

Central processing unit (CPU)

The **CPU** usually consists of:

- The main memory.
- Controller boards to manage and control other parts of the hardware such as the monitor.
- Any special processors, such as a maths processor to enable a computer to make quicker calculations.

- Input and output ports (or sockets), to enable peripheral devices such as a keyboard, mouse, printer and scanner to be physically linked to the computer.

The CPU performs the data processing of a computer and contains:

- Registers: areas for storing data or control information.
- Arithmetic logic unit: under the control of the control unit, it is where calculations and comparisons on data are performed.
- Control unit: this executes instructions and sends signals to other parts of the computer while retrieving, decoding and implementing instructions.

Image of a board with a CPU for a computer

Control unit

The control unit has four main operations:

- Fetching: returning the next program instruction from memory.
- Decoding: translating program instructions into commands the computer can understand.
- Executing: carrying out the commands.
- Storing: writing the results of the instructions to the main memory.

Computer bus

A computer bus is a set of physical connections that allows various components of a computer system to connect with each other. The width of a bus refers to how much data can transmit at once. Hence, the transfer speed of bus is an important factor in the speed at which a computer system operates.

Peripheral Component Interconnect

The Peripheral Component Interconnect (PCI) is a bus in the computer system that allows devices such as hard disks and sound cards to interact with the CPU. There are agreed standards about the physical characteristics of the system, the speed of the system, and other protocols.

Power supply unit

A computer has a power supply unit that converts electricity network voltage (240 volts alternating current) to the lower voltage (such as 3 to 15 volts direct current) required.

The power supplies vary between countries – in the USA the network voltage is approximately 110 volts AC.

Power supply for a desktop computer

Cooling fan

Computer components generate heat as the computer operates. If the system gets too hot the performance degrades and the integrated circuits can fail.

A cooling fan is a device that enables airflow and helps cool the components in the computer. All personal computers have at least one cooling fan installed.

Computer cooling fan

Ports

A port is a socket to connect a computer with a peripheral device using a cable with connectors.

Serial and parallel

The connectors at each end of a cable are a male and a female. The male is made up of one or more pins. The female has sockets to match the male pins.

Universal serial bus (USB)

Universal serial bus is an industry standard protocol for connecting peripheral devices to computers. The USB connection has effectively replaced the earlier serial and parallel connections. Most computers have a number of USB ports and USB **hubs** can be connected for extra devices if required.

Software

Computer **programs** are the sets of instructions and rules for decisions that enable the computer to work. These programs are called software.

Software is made up of a series of instructions that tell the hardware what to do. You cannot see or touch computer software. It is stored as electronic impulses on disk.

Starting a computer

When a computer is turned on the instructions stored in the ROM (read-only memory) are carried out. This is called the 'boot' process. The process:

- Detects the processor type.
- Detects the available devices attached, including disks, keyboard, mouse and monitor.
- Detects the operating system instructions (located usually on the hard drive). If this is found and is valid, the computer starts up.

Operating system

Each computer has an **operating system**. This software makes the computer usable – it provides a link between the hardware and the person using the computer. When the computer is turned on, the operating system starts up the computer.

Operating programs are generally purchased with the computer.

Some computers are able to use more than one operating system, although only one operating system can run at any one time. The operating system consists of a large range of smaller programs, each of which will have a specific job to carry out.

Operating systems are being continually modified and upgraded. For example, Microsoft offers service packs that include update and security improvements.

A computer needs operating **system software** to work. The functions of the operating system include:

- Control of the user interface, ie the way the user interacts with the computer, such as menus, **toolbars**, task bar and icons.
- Communications, including networking and Internet access.
- Font management and use.
- Controlling the display on the monitor, including the resolution and size.
- Starting, restarting and shutting down a computer.

Control panels

The Control Panels folder contains most of the software that controls the hardware in the computer and many of the settings. In Windows, the Control Panels folder can be accessed in a number of ways:

- From the **Start** button, choose **Settings** and then **Control Panel**.
- Double-click the **My Computer** icon, which will display the Control Panel icon.

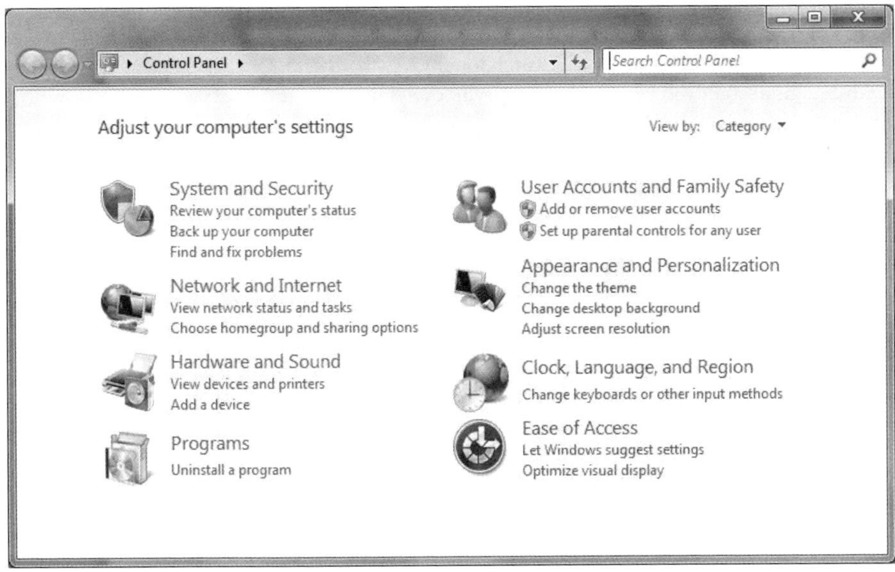

Control Panel items in Windows 7

Managing a computer

Effective operation of a computer requires a variety of tasks to be performed, including:

- Creating, naming and renaming files.
- Saving files.
- Copying files and disks.
- Deleting files.
- Creating directories or folders.
- Finding files on a network or disk, or in directories or folders.
- Backing up files.
- Printing documents.
- Installing and removing software.
- Accessing a network.
- Customising the computer setup through control panels and settings.
- Protecting the computer from viruses and hackers.

Adding hardware

Windows will detect installed hardware and configure it with the appropriate drivers.
This works with a range of older hardware together with hardware that is known as 'plug and play'.

To install new hardware, double-click the **Add New Hardware** icon in the Control Panels folder. This runs the Add New Hardware Wizard that takes you through the installation steps. As part of the process, Windows will search for any new hardware. Once it is detected, the hardware installation will be completed by Windows, finishing with a message of successful completion.

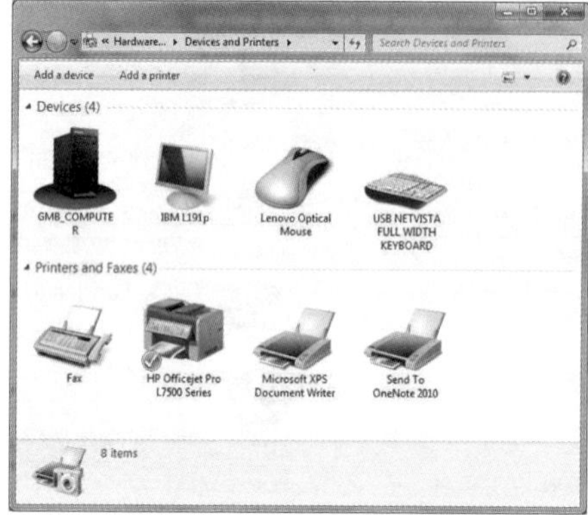

Adding hardware in Windows

Windows

Intel-based computers can operate with any one of Microsoft Windows, DOS (**disk operating system**), Unix or IBM OS/2. Apple Macintosh computers have their own proprietary operating system software, but some of them can also run with Windows or Unix. The most popular operating systems are those that use Microsoft Windows.

Microsoft Windows is an example of an operating system that has a graphical user interface (GUI). It uses pull-down menus, **icons** to represent files and directories, and a mouse or pointing device to activate commands by pointing and clicking or double-clicking. Most of the features of the operating system can be carried out using different systems, but Windows is illustrated here because of its widespread use.

In Windows, disks, files and **folders** are displayed as icons. Icons are selected by clicking on them. A selected icon is highlighted. Double-clicking an icon starts an action: opening a folder or starting an application, for example.

Each window has a number of menus. If you want to access a menu, click on the menu title and then move down the list of options to choose an action.

Each window has a number of characteristics that are the same:

- To close a window, click in the **Close** box at the top right of the window.
- To minimise a window, click in the **Minimise** box at the top right (the left-most icon of the three icons).
- To restore a minimised window, click on the icon button representing that window on the task bar.
- To move a window, click in the title bar, hold down the button and drag the window to the new location and then release the button.

- To resize a window, click in the bottom right corner of the window (the cursor changes to an arrow with a point on each end) and drag the corner to the new position.
- If not all the files or folders are displayed in a window, scroll bars appear that can be used to scroll through the window from top to bottom or left to right.

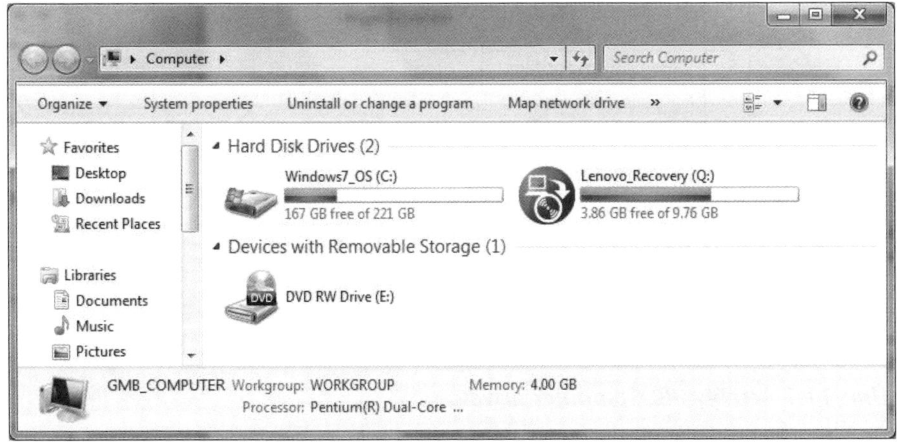

Windows 7 interface

Unit 11.1 Activity 8A: The active desktop

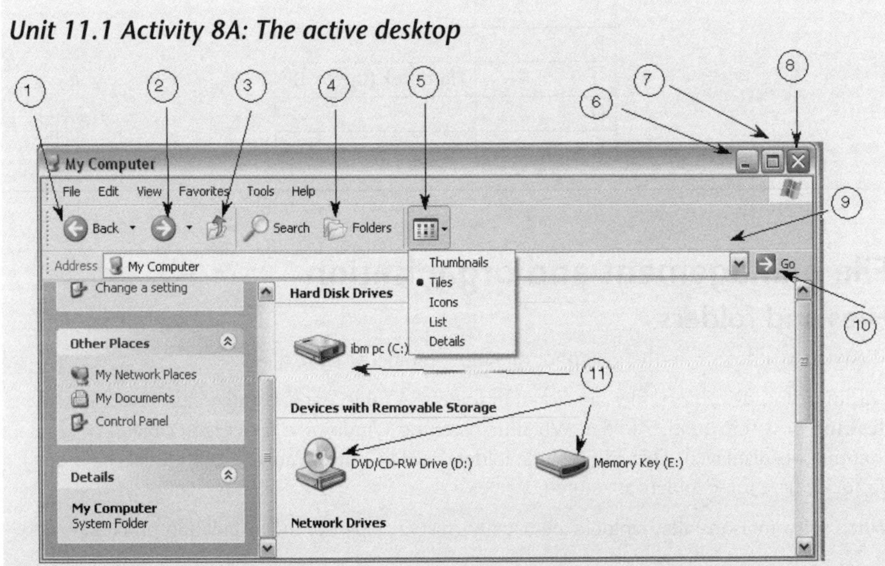

Identify the numbered items in the graphic above. What would you use each of the items (as they appear in this window) for? Complete the table on the next page.

	Item	Used for
1	Back button	
2	Forward button	
3	Up (folder) button	
4	View folders	
5	View options for files	
6	Minimise window	
7	Maximise window	
8	Close window	
9	Address bar	
10	Go button	
11	(C), (D) and (E) drives	

Unit 11.1 Activity 8B: Computer drives

On a computer with the Windows operating system, the following show the default names of computer drives. What do the drives represent?

Drive name	Default disk
A	
B	
C	Hard disk (internal)
D	
E	

File management and organisation

Files and folders

Microsoft Windows uses the metaphor of a filing cabinet to store files.

Within that filing cabinet, files are stored in folders. A folder can be stored either on the **desktop** or within another folder. When first starting Windows, a folder icon called My Computer is displayed. This will include folders called Control Panel and Printers. The user decides where these folders are stored.

When software is installed, folders are usually created as part of the installation process.

Folder names should be meaningful to make them easier to identify. File and folder names can be up to 255 characters in length. Some older software may not recognise names of this length and will truncate them.

To open a folder, double-click on the folder, or right-click and then select **Open** from the menu that appears.

Why use folders?

Folders are used to help the user organise files so that they can be found easily when they are needed. For example, all current files could be stored in a folder called My Documents. Another folder could be used for backups.

New folders

To create a new folder, move to the area in which the folder will be stored and choose **New Folder** from the ribbon across the top. A new folder, called New Folder, is created and the name can be immediately changed by typing over the current name.

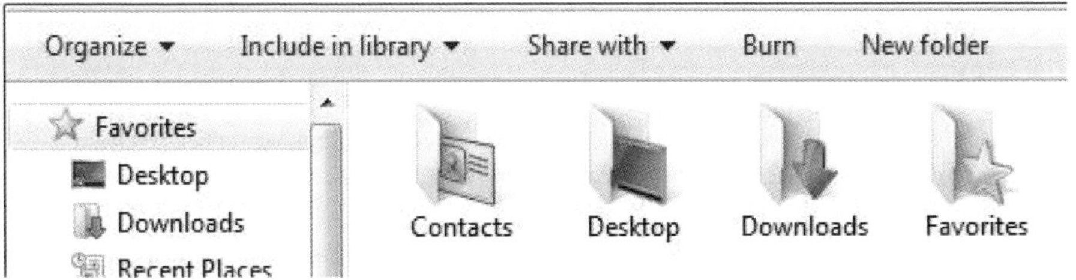

*Use the **New Folder** command to create a new folder*

Default folders

Most software will have folders into which files that are created are stored by default. You need to be aware of the location of stored files. You can create your own folders and ensure files are stored in these, or use the defaults with care.

Some applications allow you to alter the default folder for storing files.

The Libraries command provides some default folders including:

- Documents.
- Music.
- Pictures.
- **Video**.

Libraries in Windows

Copying files and folders

To copy a file or folder from one disk to another, select the file or folder with the left mouse button and drag it to the destination disk and then release the mouse button. The file or folder will then be copied to the disk.

The **Copy** and **Paste** commands may be used to copy files or folders. Select the file or folder to be copied. Click the right mouse button on the selected file or folder and choose the command **Copy** from the menu that appears. Move to the destination folder and again click the right mouse button and choose the command **Paste** from the menu. The file or folder will be copied into the destination folder.

The left mouse button can also be used to copy files and folders. Select the file or folder to be copied, hold the left mouse button down and also hold down the **CTRL** key, drag the file or folder to its destination and then release the mouse button and the **CTRL** key. The file or folder is copied into the selected destination.

Changing the name of a file or folder

A file or folder may be renamed by right-clicking on the file or folder and then choosing **Rename** from the drop-down menu that appears. A rectangle appears around the name that is highlighted, and the cursor appears in the box. A new name can then be entered.

Deleting files

Files may be deleted using the Explorer. Select the file to be deleted and choose **Delete** from the **Organize** menu. A confirmation of the deletion must be made.

Finding files

Files and folders can be found from the **Start** menu. Enter the file or folder name (or part of the name) in the Search box at the bottom left of the screen. The results of the search are shown immediately above the search box.

Finding files in Windows

Viewing files

Files in a folder may be viewed in a number of different ways: they can be sorted by name, type, size or date. This is accessed from the **Arrange Icons** command on the **View** menu.

Using the Explorer, the files can be viewed with details about the file size, type and date created by choosing the **Details** command on the **View** menu. In this form, the files can be sorted by name, size, type or date modified, by clicking on the name in the toolbar of the window.

Full details of a file can be obtained by selecting the file and choosing **Properties** from the **File** menu. This gives details about the file size, location, name, and the creation and modification dates.

Unit 11.1 Activity 8C: File handling with Windows

Describe how to carry out the following functions on a computer using the Windows operating system. For some tasks there will be more than one method of carrying it out.

1. Format a USB flash drive.
2. Copy a document from a hard disk to a USB flash drive.
3. Copy a document from a USB flash drive to a hard disk.
4. Rename a document.
5. Make a copy of a file on the hard disk.
6. Create a new folder (directory).
7. Move a document from one folder (directory) to another.
8. Delete a document from a hard disk.
9. Create a shortcut for a document.
10. Find the date of creation for a document.

Application software

Application packages are designed to meet the needs of a significant number of users. Application packages include:

- Word processors, such as Microsoft Word, Apple Pages.
- Spreadsheets, such as Microsoft Excel, Apple Numbers.
- Databases, such as Microsoft Access, FileMaker Pro.
- Presentation, such as Microsoft PowerPoint, Apple Keynote.
- Graphics and image manipulation, such as Corel Draw, Canvas, Adobe Photoshop.

Some of the above software is grouped into integrated packages, such as Microsoft Office and Apple iWork.

Choosing the most useful software for a task requires knowing both the task to be performed and the capabilities of the software. In some cases, different types of application software may be used for the same task. In other cases, it is evident that one particular software type is the most appropriate. An advertising flyer could be produced using page layout software, a word processing package or a graphics package. A 32-page magazine, however, would be best produced using desktop publishing software.

Application software is usually installed in the Program Files folder.

Application software types can include:

- Word processing.
- Spreadsheet.
- Accounting.
- Communication.
- Computer-aided design (CAD).
- Database management.
- Desktop publishing.
- Music composition.
- Multimedia authoring.
- Graphics.
- HTML authoring and website management.
- Programming.
- Electronic mail.

Some software types are used in conjunction with others. Text may be prepared in a word processor for importing into a desktop publishing program. Information in a database may be exported and merged with a form letter prepared using a word processing package.

Microsoft Word is able to embed cells from a Microsoft Excel spreadsheet into a document. The spreadsheet may be updated from within the word processor.

Starting programs

An application can be started by choosing **Programs** from the **Start** menu. A second menu shows the list of applications installed. A shortcut can be created by dragging the icon representing an application onto the Start button. That application is now included in the top section of the Start menu and can be accessed directly. This shortcut is useful for applications that are regularly used.

In a similar way, files can be opened using the Start menu. Choose **Documents** from the **Start** menu. A second menu shows a list of recently used files.

To remove shortcuts from the taskbar, click on the **Start** button and choose **Settings**. Now select the **Start Menu Programs** tab and then the **Remove** button. A list of items is displayed. Select the item and then choose **Remove** to remove it from the Start menu.

Unit 11.1 Activity 8D: Document files

Identify the following documents in the screen dump below. Write the name of the application that created the files next to the file icon.

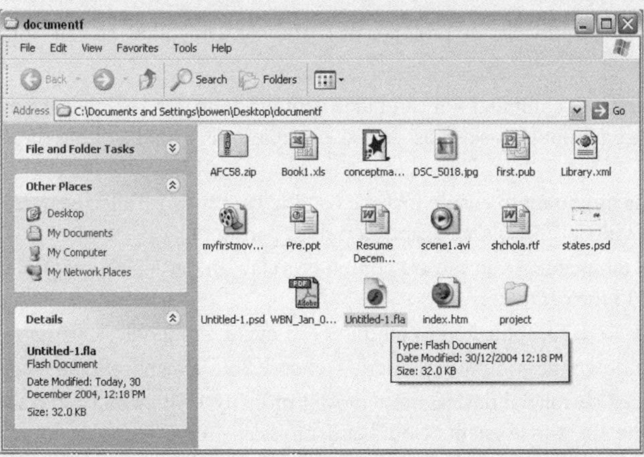

Care and appropriate use of hardware and software

Virus protection

A virus is a computer program that attaches itself to other computer programs. Once it is attached, it causes damage to files. A virus is spread when a disk containing a virus is inserted into the disk drive of a computer. The virus copies itself onto the hard disk of the computer.

Viruses can also be loaded from computer networks, including the World Wide Web.

A computer virus can damage files on a disc. This can be selective or it can affect every file. A virus can cause random system crashes and work can be lost. In some cases, a hard disk must be reformatted and all system software re-installed and user files also restored from backups. This is time-consuming and can be difficult. If backups are not current, important work may be lost.

To protect against the spread of viruses, virus protection software can be used. Virus protection software works by:

- Scanning: each time a disk is inserted, it is scanned to see if it has a known virus.
- Checking: running a virus-checking program regularly to check the files on a disk and take action if any viruses are found.

Other precautions to take include the following:

- Do not borrow disks from other people: whenever you borrow a disk you run the risk of infecting your computer.
- Be wary of public domain and shareware programs.
- Purchase and use only commercial software.
- Be aware when downloading software from the World Wide Web.
- Be aware that some games are a source of viruses.

Scanning software needs to be updated regularly. As new viruses are detected, the scanning software is altered to check for these viruses. Virus protection software will always lag behind the creation of viruses.

Hardware

Taking care of computer hardware prolongs its useful life. The following will help take care of the hardware:

- Dust can damage a computer – it can block vents and this can lead to overheating. Make sure that the environment is as dust-free as possible and clean dust from the computer regularly.
- Ventilation is important to ensure that the cooling fan can work effectively. Ensure that the vents are not blocked or placed against a wall or partition.
- Extremes of temperature can cause a computer to fail. In particular, overheating can be detrimental to the computer.
- Avoid fluids – a drink spilled on a computer can make it unusable.
- Always shut down the computer properly – choose Shut Down from the menu.
- Make sure that peripheral devices are removed properly. USB memory sticks should be ejected by the operating system before being physically removed.

Programs

Some files and file types for a personal computer are shown below.

File	Application	Type of document
.jpg	image editing	Joint Photographic Experts Group – image
.doc(x)	Microsoft Word	text – word processor
.xls(x)	Microsoft Excel	spreadsheet
.htm	browser	webpage
.pdf	Adobe Acrobat	Portable Document Format
.asp	Microsoft Access – query to database on the World Wide Web	webpage that accesses Microsoft Access database
.ppt(x)	Microsoft Powerpoint	presentation (multimedia)
.fp7	FileMaker Pro	database
.txt	Notepad	text file
.exe		program (executable file), eg Microsoft Word is winword.exe

.csv	Notepad	Comma-separated values
.html	browser	webpage
.gif	Adobe Photoshop	Graphic Interchange Format – image
.zip		
.swf	Adobe Flash	small web file – vector graphic, usually animation
.dwt	Adobe Dreamweaver	template page for website
.mov	Apple Quicktime	movie file (sound and or video)
.wav		
.rtf	Microsoft	Text – rich text format
.psd	Adobe Photoshop	image

Table 4 Different file types

Unit 11.1 Activity 8E: Using a computer

How are the following tasks performed on a computer?

1. Set the date and time.
2. Adjust the keyboard response rate.
3. Format a USB disk.
4. Back up a computer hard disk.
5. Check for a virus infection of a hard disk.
6. Install a printer driver on the computer.
7. Change the resolution of the screen display.
8. Find a file on the computer hard disk.
9. Check the fonts installed on the computer.
10. Alter the screen saver settings.
11. Alter the sounds that are used by the system software.
12. Explore the files on the computer by directories.
13. Copy a file from a hard disk to a USB key.
14. Install new hardware options for the computer.
15. Open an application software program.
16. Use the Help system.
17. Remove an application software program from a computer.
18. Adjust the energy-saving features of the monitor.
19. Find the size of a file on the hard disk.
20. Change the name of a file.

Unit 11.1 Activity 8F: Components of information systems

The following pictures represent components of information systems.

Identify the role of each in an information system.

Unit 11.1 Activity 8G: File extensions

The Windows operating system uses a period (full stop) and three-character filename extension to identify a document as an application and also a file belonging to an application.

Match the filename extension to the application that created the file.

Extension	Application software	Description of the application
.exe		
.doc	Microsoft Word	word processor
.xls		
.ppt		
.txt		
.pdf		
.isf		
.cws		
.rtf		
.avi		
.mov		
.bmp		
.pub		
.wmv		
.wav		
.jpg		

Unit 11.2 Word Processing

Topic 1: Introduction to word processing

Unit 11.2 deals with all aspects of word processing. Topic 1 provides an overview of word processing.

What is a word processor?

A **word processor** is computer software that deals with text-based material. It is possible to create a new document and then edit the text. The document may be stored on a local disk on the computer, on an external device, on a computer network or on the Internet. The document can be retrieved, modified, formatted and published.

Text that has been created by a word processor and stored in a file is referred to as a document. Using a word processor enables you to organise ideas and easily change the text.

The electronic copy that has been created on a computer (sometimes called 'soft copy') can be changed and formatted in many ways before printing. Material that is printed out is called 'hard copy'.

When text is published it may be done electronically or by printing on paper. Electronic publishing includes using:

- The World Wide Web.
- An organisation's intranet or network.
- A CD-ROM or DVD.
- A memory stick.

The most widely used **word processing** package is Microsoft Word and it is to this package that the text below refers.

Main features of a word processor

A word processor typically consists of the application itself, a dictionary for use with the spellchecker, a thesaurus, a help file and sample files.

A word processor can:

- Automatically move the cursor to the next line when the end of a line is reached (called 'word wrap around').
- Format the text using different fonts and styles.
- Move sections of text to a different position in a document (cut and paste).
- Copy a section of text and place it in a different position in a document (copy and paste).
- Copy text from a document and paste it into a different document.
- Check the spelling.
- Align text to the left or right margin.
- Set margins.

- Divide the document into separate pages for printing.
- Show the whole page on screen in a reduced view (Print Preview).
- Automatically number the pages.
- Find a particular word or phrase in a document (Find, Find and Replace).
- Provide online help.
- Offer choices for words by using a thesaurus.

Unit 11.2 Word Processing
Topic 2: Creating and saving a new document

Topic 2 explains how to create and save a new document (see Computer Studies Syllabus pp. 15–16). It covers:

- Starting Word.
- Getting familiar with the Word screen.
- Getting help.
- Creating a new document.
- Saving and opening a document.

Starting Word

Open **Microsoft Word** from the **Program** menu. The horizontal band that appears across the top of the screen is called the Ribbon. The Ribbon is divided into Tabs. The commands on the ribbon change each time a new Tab is selected.

The tabs include:

- File.
- Home.
- Insert.
- Page Layout.
- References.
- Mailings.
- Review.
- View.

Note: These tabs may vary in different versions of Word.

The tab is a method of providing top-level menu choices. A range of different commands is grouped underneath each tab. When the name of the Tab is clicked, a different range of commands appears.

The figure below shows the ribbon with the commands that are available when the **Home** tab is selected.

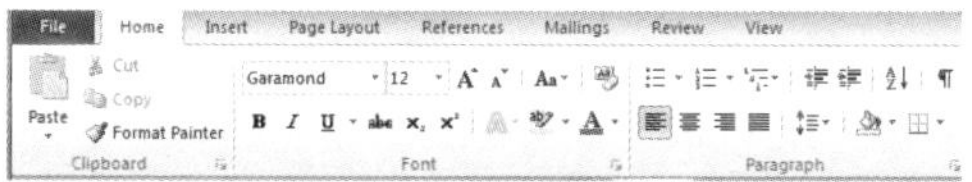

Ribbon in Microsoft Word showing Home tab

Getting familiar with the Word screen
Tabs on the Microsoft Word screen

Each tab in Microsoft Word provides a different set of commands.

For example, clicking on the **Insert** tab gives a range of commands involved with inserting text, images and formatting options. These commands are grouped; in this case the groups are:

- Pages.
- Tables.

- Illustrations.
- Links.
- Header & Footer.
- Text.
- Symbols.

Within the Pages groups, there are three options:

- Cover Page.
- Blank Page.
- Page Break.

Many of these commands are discussed later in this chapter.

Note that in the figure below, the **Insert** tab has been selected and a different set of commands appears.

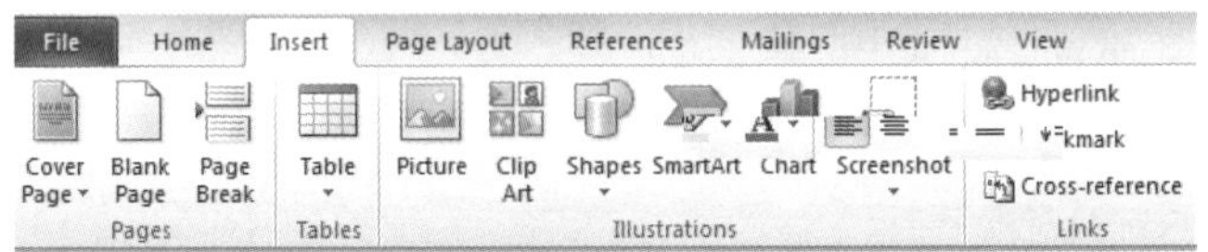

Ribbon in MS Word showing part of the Insert tab

Shortcuts in Word

There are many shortcuts in Microsoft Word that enable you to operate efficiently. These include:

- Right mouse click: Clicking anywhere within a document using the right mouse button provides a range of shortcuts including Cut and Paste.
- **Ctrl** key: The Ctrl key in combination with another key (or keys) provides a range of shortcuts, eg **Ctrl-C** for Copy, **Ctrl-X** for Cut, **Ctrl-V** for Paste, **Crtl-S** for Save.

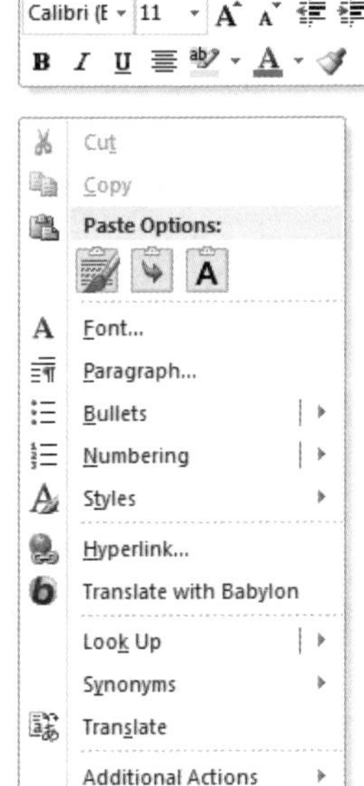

Shortcuts available by using the right mouse click

Getting help

To get help with Microsoft Office, click on the **Help** icon that is on the far right side of the ribbon.

Help icon

The window that appears depends upon whether or not you are online.

If you are offline, the window below appears. You can browse topics by clicking on a topic or you can enter a question in the dialog box.

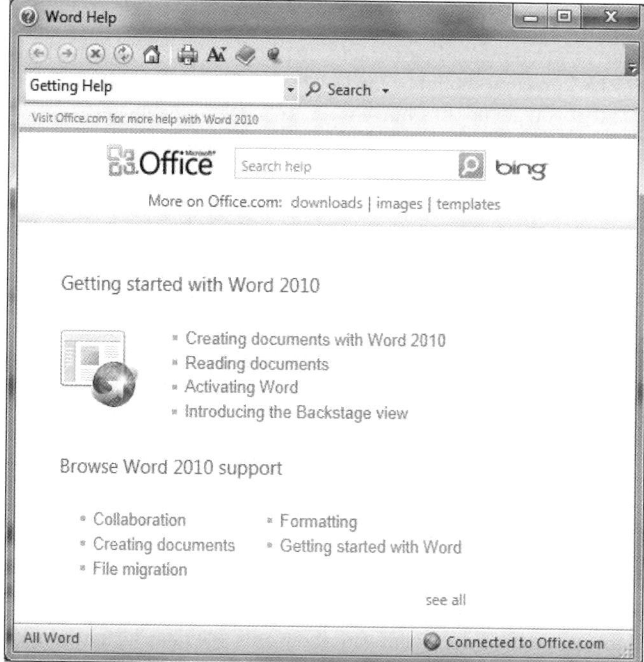

Getting help

Creating a new document

To create a new document:

- Open **Microsoft Word** from the Program Menu; or
- Select **New** from the **File** menu, if already in Word.

When starting a new document, treat the computer screen like a blank sheet of paper on which the main points are to be written. Enter the main points as a list on the screen, pressing the **Enter** key between each one. In the beginning there is no need to form sentences or paragraphs.

Unit 11.2 Activity 2A: Writing with a word processor

This exercise requires you to compose text using the keyboard.

Topic: What I like doing best.

1. Make a list of the five main points (single words only) you want to include. Give the document a name and save it.
2. Form the list into an order.
3. Form the words into sentences.
4. Form the sentences into paragraphs.
5. Print a copy of the document.

Saving a document

Documents should be saved regularly, especially after important changes have been made. At the end of a session a backup copy should be made. Always allow enough time at the end of a session to be sure that you are not in a hurry when saving your documents.

To save a document:

- Choose **Save As** from the **File** menu.
- Enter a name at the dialogue box.
- Click **Save**.

Once a document has been saved and given a name, it can be saved once changes are made. To do this:

- Choose **Save** from the **File** menu; or
- Use the shortcut **Ctrl-S**; or
- Click on the disk icon at the top left of the screen.

The disk icon can be used to save a document

Note that the **Save** command writes over (replaces) the previously saved version of the document.

Using the Save command

When starting a new document, the Save command can be used to save a new document. In this case, the name of the document given by Word is taken from the first sentence in the text.

For example, if the user starts a document with the words 'My new document' and then clicks **Save**, the default name is 'My new document'. This can be changed by entering a new name over the highlighted name.

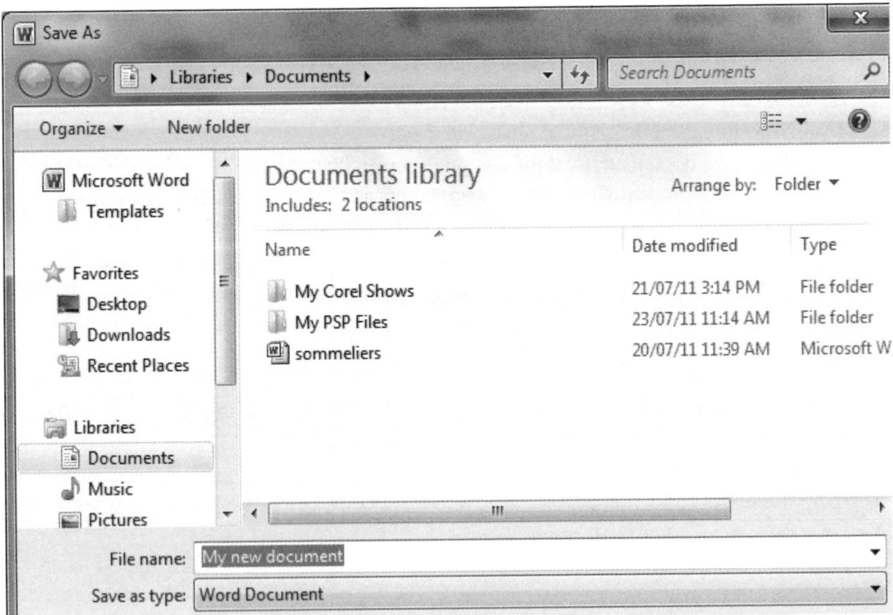

Saving a document

Save another copy of the document

To save another copy of a document, you should:

- Use the **Save As** command to save the document with a different name; or
- Use the **Save As** command and navigate to a different folder or a different storage device.

Naming conventions

When a document is saved, give it a name that is related to its contents. For example, if you are writing a letter to Joan, it could be named 'Joanlettermay2013'.

Saving automatically

Microsoft Word can be set to save documents automatically at a regular interval; for example, every ten minutes.

This is done using the **File** menu. Click on **Options** and choose **Save**. Note that the box next to **Save AutoReCover** needs to be clicked and the time interval can be altered.

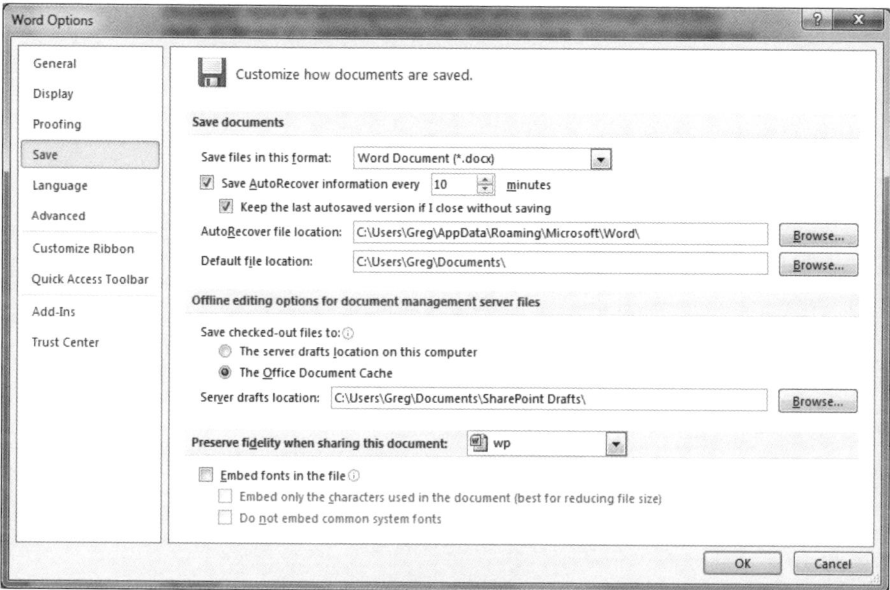

Setting the AutoSave

Unit 11.2 Activity 2B: Saving a document

1. Why is saving the document the most important step in the creation of a document? List two other important steps.
2. How do you set Microsoft Word to automatically save a document every 15 minutes?

Moving through a document

You can move around a document using:

- A mouse (the wheel on the top of the mouse can be used to scroll through a document).
- The arrow keys.
- The scroll bars.
- PgUp or PgDn keys.
- Function keys.

The **Find** command can be used to go to a particular piece of text, usually a word or phrase. The **Go To** command can be used to go to a particular page. These commands are on the **Editing** section of the **Home** tab.

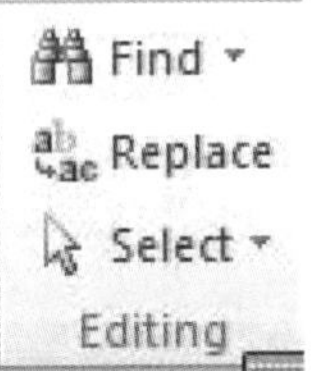

Editing section of the Home tab

Unit 11.2 Word Processing
Topic 3: Formatting documents

Topic 3 explores the various options available when formatting a document in Microsoft Word (see Computer Studies Syllabus pp. 16–17). It covers:

- Formatting characters.
- Formatting a paragraph.
- Formatting pages.

Text first, format later

With a word processor, **text** can be entered and then altered until the content and the layout are satisfactory. Generally it is best to enter the text first and format the document later.

Devote time and attention to keying in your ideas first. Pay less attention to typing and keyboard errors as they can be corrected later.

Referring to text in a document

Text means a character, word, line, sentence, paragraph or page.

What is a character?

A single key pressed on the keyboard will produce a character, such as:

- A lower case letter of the alphabet – for example, a, b.
- A number – for example, 7, 9.
- A punctuation symbol – for example, ?, /.
- A symbol – for example, &, *, ®.

The space bar should only be used to place a single space between words. Do not use it to format text.

What is a word?

A word is a character or group of characters joined together with a space either side. For example, 'a' and 'this' are both words.

What is a sentence?

A sentence is a group of words that makes sense on its own. A sentence starts with a capital letter and is completed by a full stop. The full stop is sometimes referred to as a 'period'.

What is a line?

A line is made of characters placed together on a row between the left margin and right margin. A line can be part of a sentence, part of a paragraph or a separate paragraph.

What is a paragraph?

A **paragraph** is usually defined as text followed by a 'return' character. The 'return' forces the insert point to the left margin on the next line. This type of 'return' is also referred to as a 'hard' return. Therefore a paragraph could be just a single line followed by a return character. The '¶' character often signifies this 'hard return'. The example below shows the line of text and a paragraph marker.

This·is·a·paragraph¶

Paragraph marker

The paragraph marker can be turned on and off on the **Paragraph** section of the **Home** tab.

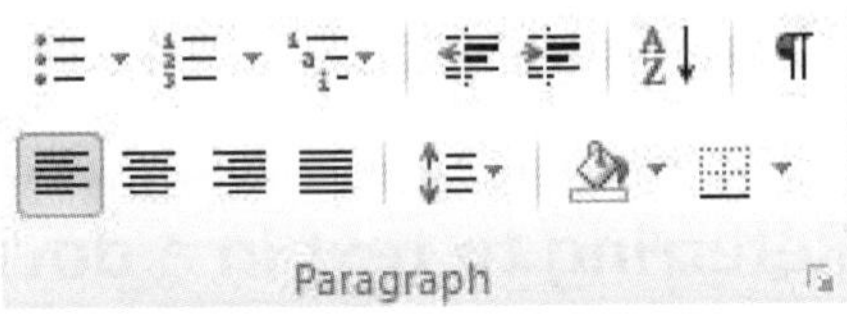

Turn the paragraph marker on or off on the Paragraph section of the Home tab

The final stage of document creation is formatting – that is, deciding how a document is to look. A range of fonts and settings can be tried before a document is completed.

Formatting refers to the way in which a document is arranged and is determined by the:

- Justification of lines.
- Alignment of lines.
- Amount of space between paragraphs.
- Use of fully blocked or indented paragraphs.
- Use of fonts and font styles.

Tips for consistent document formatting

The following will assist in formatting a document:

- If you use headings and subheadings, make sure that they are consistent.
- Try to keep to one or two fonts throughout your document, perhaps with use of **bold** and *italic* for emphasis.
- Use consistent line spacing throughout the text; this can then be changed to single spacing, line and a half, double or other spacing later.

Formatting characters

Changing fonts

A **font** is a type style used to represent a character. Each font's name refers to a family of characters. Many of the popular fonts have been used in the printing industry for hundreds of years.

Each family of fonts includes upper and lower case letters, special characters and a range of formatting options such as bold, italic and outline.

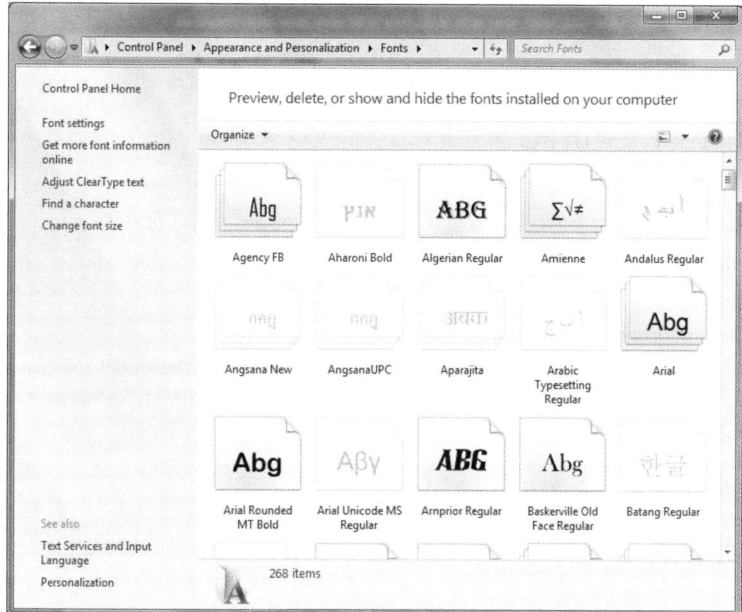

OpenType fonts

Microsoft Windows uses OpenType fonts. These display the same image on the screen as when printed on a compatible printer.

A number of OpenType fonts are part of the Windows operating system. Other fonts are supplied with printers and may be installed. Fonts can also be purchased and installed in the system.

Families of fonts are stored in the Control Panel. To see the fonts on your computer, open the **Control Panel** and choose **Appearance and Personalization**, then choose **Fonts**. This displays the fonts installed on your system. Other fonts can be added by copying the appropriate font file to this folder.

Most word processors are able to display a range of fonts on the screen. The size of a font is referred to in 'points'. A point is an old printing industry measure – one point equals 1/72 inch. For example, a font in 12 point would be 1/6 of an inch in height.

The font used in a document should be chosen to increase the legibility of the document. There are two options for typefaces: serif and sans serif. Serif fonts have additional strokes like small tails at the ends of the characters. The following are examples of three serif fonts (each is set in 14 point):

Times New Roman
Garamond
Palatino Linotype

Sans serif fonts do not have these finishing strokes. Following are examples of three sans serif fonts (each is set in 14 point):

Arial
Century Gothic
`Lucida Console`

This is how the main characters of the font 'Times New Roman' would appear:

abcdefghijklmnopqrstuvwxyz 123456789

This is how the main characters of the font 'Arial' would appear:

abcdefghijklmnopqrstuvwxyz 123456789

The font selected for a document will depend on the purpose of the document. The font 'Times' is suited to a formal document such as a report. 'Helvetica' is suited to less formal documents such as an advertising flyer or brochure.

Unit 11.2 Activity 3A: Differences in fonts

1. The letter k is shown in upper and lower case in the Times and Arial fonts (48 point size). What are the differences?

2. The following are examples of fonts. What differences can you note between them?

Arial
☠♏⬥ ✡□□&
`Courier`
Bookman

3. Do you like using different types of fonts? List three fonts that you like using.

Default font

The default font is part of the template that is being used. A new document will use the default font settings.

The default font can be changed at any time. To set a default font:

- On the **Home** tab, click the **Font Dialog Box Launcher**.
- Then click the **Font** tab.
- Set the options that you want.
- Click on **Set As Default** and then **OK** to make the change.

Formatting text

Varying font sizes can make headings stand out. The size of a heading can be set according to its importance in the document. An important heading would usually appear in a larger font size. Normal text font size is 10 or 12 depending on the type of font.

Variations of font style

The table below shows the variations in font characteristics offered by word processors.

Feature	Example	Use
Plain	This text is plain.	The default setting, this can be altered by the user.
Bold	**This text is bold.**	**Use for headings and important words in a document.**
Italic	*This text is italic.*	*Use for emphasis on words in a document.*
Underline	This text is in underline	Be careful with the use of underline as some letters such as y, g and j, which descend below the line, may be cut through by the underline.

Font characteristics

Different colours can also be applied to text.

Unit 11.2 Activity 3B: Formatting text

1. Key the following text into your word processor:
   My favorite dessert is vanilla ice cream covered in chocolate and nuts.
   Select the line and format the line in a font that has a 12 point size.
2. Copy the line and paste it back into the document to make three lines.
   a. Leave the first line formatted as plain text.
   b. Format the second line in bold.
   c. Format the third line in italics.
   d. Change the colour of the font.

Formatting a paragraph

Tips for setting out paragraphs

The following tips help make a document easier to read:

- Break text into paragraphs of reasonable length.
- Leave a line between paragraphs.
- Use subheadings within the text.
- Headings should be in a larger font size than body text.
- Use bold and italic for emphasis, not underline.
- Make the margins wide enough to allow comments to be easily written.

Alignment of lines and paragraphs

Text can be aligned in a document in a number of ways:

- Left aligned – each line will start on the left-hand margin. This is a normal default style for most word processors. This style will leave a ragged right margin.

  This text is left aligned.

  This text is left aligned. This text is left aligned.

  This text is left aligned. This text is left aligned. This text is left aligned.
- Right aligned – each line will finish on the right-hand margin. You may use this to give a story a dramatic effect on a particular line or lines. This style will produce a ragged left margin.

  This text is right aligned.

  This text is right aligned. This text is right aligned.

  This text is right aligned. This text is right aligned. This text is right aligned.
- Centred – each line will be placed an equal distance from the left- and right-hand margins. If the left and right margins are the same the line will be on the centre of the page. This style is often selected for headings so that they stand out. Never use spaces to try and centre text – always use the centre alignment button.

  This text is centred.

  This text is centred. This text is centred.

  This text is centred. This text is centred. This text is centred.
- Justified – each line will start on the left-hand margin and finish on the right-hand margin. The spacing between the words is altered to ensure that this occurs. This is most commonly adopted for books, where it is considered better to have the lines balanced.

  This text is justified at both left and right margins. This text is justified at both left and right margins. This text is justified at both left and right margins. This text is justified at both left and right margins. This text is justified at both left and right margins.

Alignment buttons

Each of these alignments may be set from the **Paragraph** section of the **Home** tab. Place the cursor anywhere within a paragraph and then click on the button for the desired alignment on the toolbar.

To apply the alignment to more than one paragraph, select multiple paragraphs and then click on the required button.

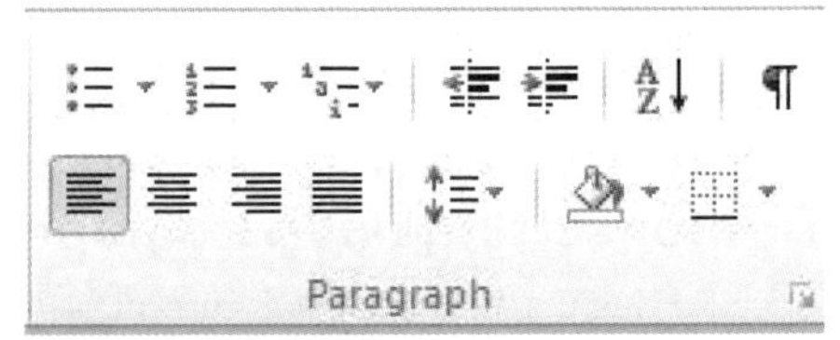

Alignment buttons

Unit 11.2 Activity 3C: Text alignment

1. Key in the following line:

   The white sails of the Sydney Opera House are like the sails of the yachts on the harbour.
2. Copy and paste the line into the document three times.
3. Format the first line as left aligned.
4. Format the second line as right aligned.
5. Format the third line as centered.
6. Format the fourth line as justified.
7. Compare your result with the lines below.

The white sails of the Sydney Opera House are like the sails of the yachts on the harbor.

The white sails of the Sydney Opera House are like the sails of the yachts on the harbor.

The white sails of the Sydney Opera House are like the sails of the yachts on the harbor.

The white sails of the Sydney Opera House are like the sails of the yachts on the harbor.

Creating indents

The ruler

The ruler provides a quick and easy way of setting document indents and tabs. It also shows the current settings. From the ruler you can see the document margins, left and right indents and any first-line indents.

The ruler can be displayed using the **View** tab; there is a checkbox for the **Ruler** to be displayed.

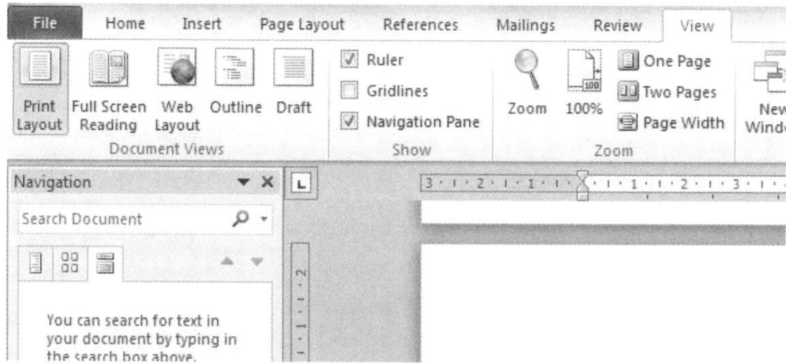

Show the Ruler on the View tab

There is a horizontal ruler and a vertical ruler.

Horizontal ruler

The indent marker on the ruler can be used to quickly set an indent for a document.

The ruler displays both a left and right indent. To change the indent, drag the indent marker to the required position.

Alternatively, the indent can be set on the menu using the **Indent** command on the **Paragraph** menu that is part of the **Page Layout** tab.

A first-line indent can be set on the ruler. A first-line indent is often used to indicate a new paragraph. To set a first-line indent, hold the **Ctrl** key down and drag the **First Line Indent** marker to the required position.

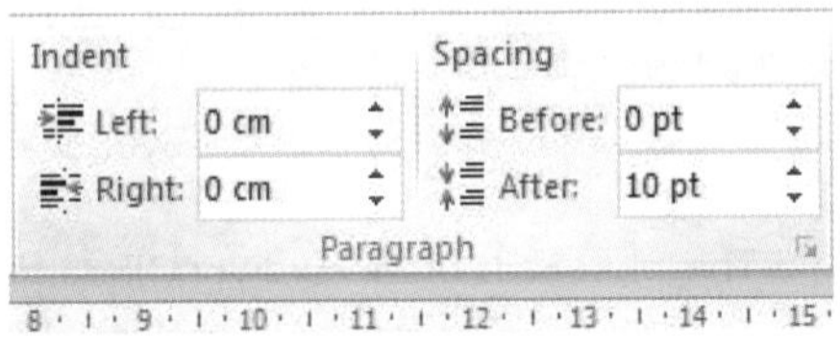

Indent dialog box

Hanging indent

A hanging indent is a paragraph that has all but the first line indented, ie the first line is on the left of the page and the remainder of the paragraph is indented.

To set a hanging indent, drag the **Hanging Indent** marker on the ruler to the required position.

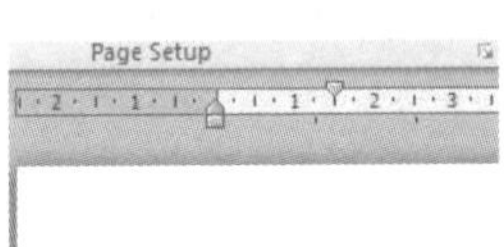

Hanging indent on the ruler

This is an example of a hanging indent. This is an example of a hanging indent. This is an example of a hanging indent. This is an example of a hanging indent. This is an example of a hanging indent. This is an example of a hanging indent. This is an example of a hanging indent. This is an example of a hanging indent.

A hanging indent

Bulleted and numbered lists

The **Paragraph** menu on the **Home** tab provides a range of formatting options for a paragraph.

Create a bulleted list

To create a bulleted list:

- Click on the **Bulleted List** icon.
- Enter your text.
- Press the **Enter** key to begin another bullet point.

To create a second level of bullets, click on the icon again.

Create a numbered list

To create a numbered list:

- Click on the **Numbered List** icon.
- Enter your text.
- Press the **Enter** key to begin another numbered point.

Clicking on the arrow next to the list icon in each case enables you to modify the icon or the number type.

Line and paragraph spacing

To adjust the line or paragraph spacing:

- Click on the **Line and Paragraph Spacing** icon on the **Paragraph** menu.
- Set the desired spacing.

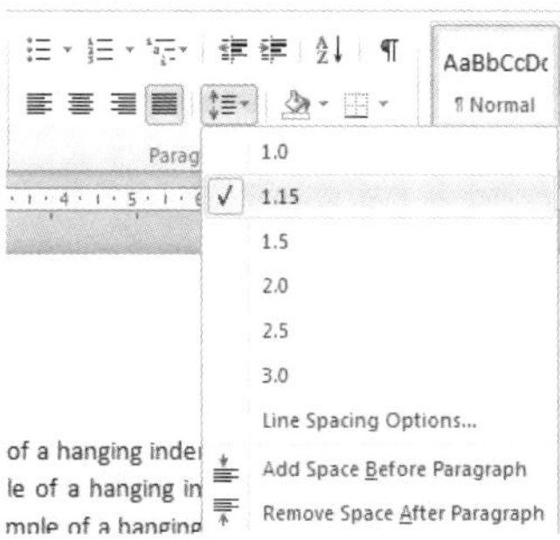

Line spacing option

Borders and shading

Borders and shading can also be added to a paragraph. The menu items **Shading** and **Border** are part of the **Paragraph** menu. To do this:

- Select the paragraph.
- Select the shading colour and intensity.
- Select the border type.

Using tab stops

When the tab key is pressed once, the cursor will move to a pre-set position on that line. **Tabs** are useful when setting out simple lists, tables and numbers in a document.

Tabs may also be used to exchange data within spreadsheets and databases.

Microsoft Word has default settings for:

- The position of the tabs: every 1.27 cm.
- The type of tab: a left tab.

Types of tabs

Microsoft Word has four types of tab stops:

- Left tabs: text aligns with the left edge of the tab stop.
- Right tabs: text aligns with the right edge of the tab stop.
- Centre tabs: text is centred on the tab stop.
- Decimal tabs: columns of numbers are aligned on the decimal point.

A tab can be set by:

- Selecting the type of tab at the left end of the ruler.
- Clicking in the required position on the ruler.

The icon representing the tab appears on the ruler.

A tab can also be set by:

- Selecting the **Paragraph dialog box** on the **Paragraph** menu that is part of the **Page Layout** tab.
- Choosing the **Tabs...** option from the dialogue box.
- Entering the tab setting and tab type in the **Tab** window.

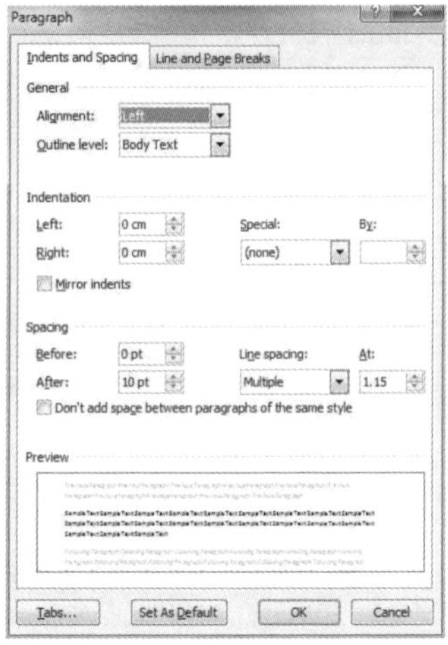

Paragraph dialog box and Tab option (bottom right)

Tabs may be altered after the text has been entered. Click on the tab and drag it to the new location. Once the tab is reset, the selected text will move to the new position.

A tab may be removed by clicking on it and dragging it down from the ruler into the document.

Formatting pages

Setting up your document

Microsoft Word has a number of default settings. A default setting is a value the software uses for a setting until the user changes it. When you start a new document, you start with those default settings.

A word processor may open with default settings for:

- Screen font and size.
- Page size.
- Measurement unit for ruler.
- Margins.
- Page number.
- Printer.

The **Page Layout** tab allows you to set up your page.

The **Page Setup** section of the tab allows you to set up:

- Margins.
- Orientation of the page – portrait or landscape.

- Size.
- Columns.
- Breaks.
- Line numbers.
- Hyphenation.

Set page margins, paper size and orientation

It is important to check the paper size so that the document can be set with correct margins. (The margins are the blank spaces surrounding the sides of the printed page.) For example, a standard paper size is A4. This is part of an internationally agreed convention on paper sizes. A4 paper is 210 mm wide and 297 mm long. Another common page size used is US Letter (United States letter). US letter size is 8.5 inches (216 mm) wide by 11 inches (279 mm) long.

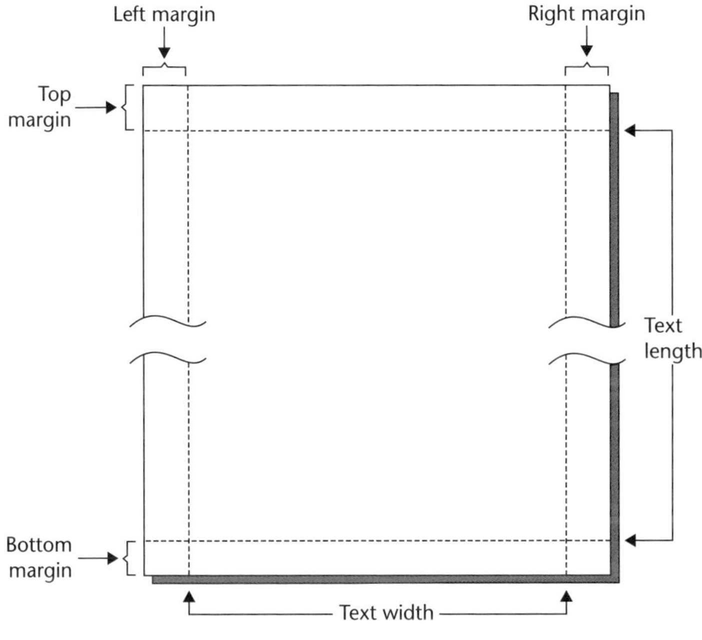

Document layout

The default margin sizes in Microsoft Word are:

- Top: 2.54 cm.
- Left: 2.54 cm.
- Bottom: 2.54 cm.
- Right: 2.54 cm.

As a general rule it is a good idea to have the left and right margins of equal width and the top and bottom margins of equal width. This means that the page will be horizontally and vertically centred on the paper when printed. A centred page looks balanced whereas unequal margins tend to distract the reader.

Creating page and section breaks

A page break can be inserted using the **Page Break** command on the **Insert** menu. This inserts a page break and the text continues on a new page.

A section break is used to change the layout or format of a document. A document might start with a single column and then change to a two-column layout. This can be done by creating a section break and applying different formatting rules. Different headers and footers can be created by using a section break.

The **Section Break** command is found on the **Page Layout** tab by selecting the **Breaks** menu item.

A page break can also be inserted from this menu.

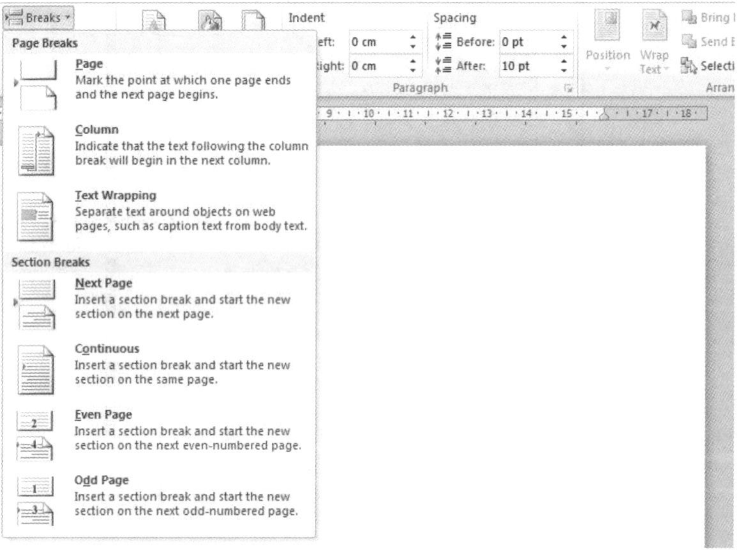

Breaks menu

Headers and footers

For a document with many pages, identifying information can be included on each page. Such information at the top of each page is called a header; at the bottom of the page it is called a footer. The **Header** and **Footer** commands are found on the **Header & Footer** section of the **Insert** tab.

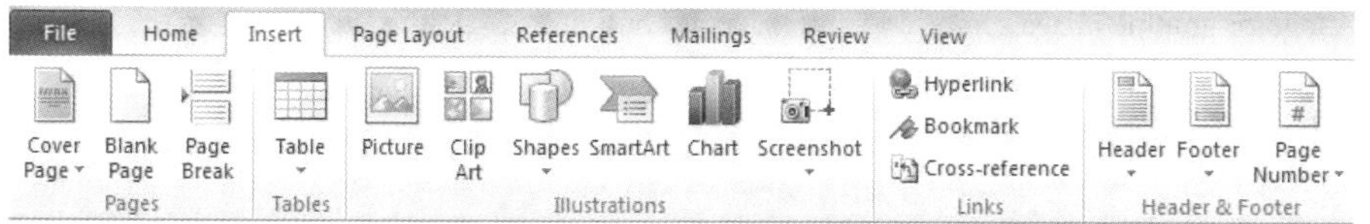

Header and Footer menu

To insert a header, click on the **Header** icon on the **Header & Footer** menu. This will provide a drop-down list of different types of header.

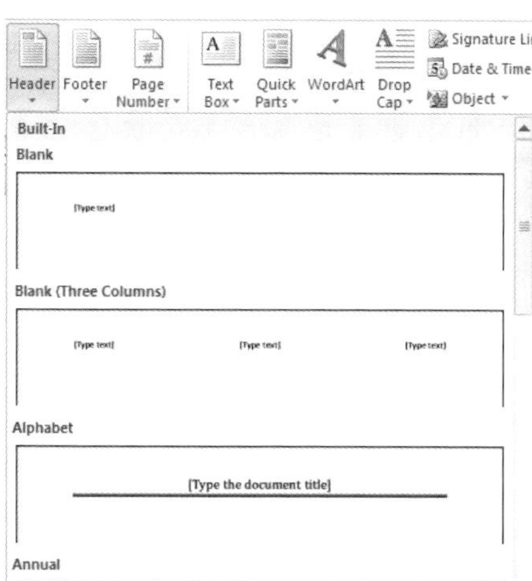

Some of the header options

Text can be entered into the chosen header. When complete, click the **Close** button on the menu.

The header as entered will appear at the top of each page.

The process for entering a footer is exactly the same except that the **Footer** icon is chosen rather than the **Header** icon.

Close Header and Footer button

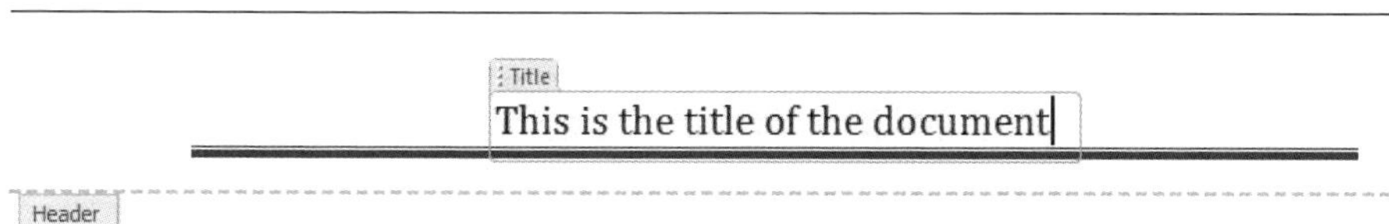

Example of a header

When editing a header or footer, the editing tools allow the option of a different first page or different odd and even pages.

A logo or graphic image can be added to a header or footer. To do this, when editing the header or footer, go to the **Insert** tab and click on the **Picture** icon. This allows you to select an image to go in the header or footer.

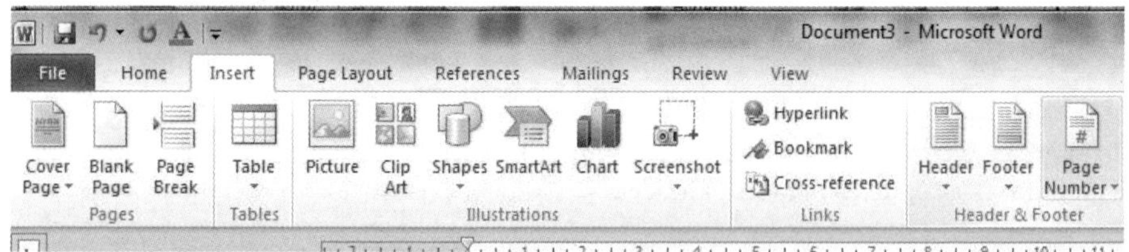

See the Picture icon on the Insert tab

A page number is usually put in a header or footer. To do this:

- Select the **Insert** tab.
- Choose the **Page Number** icon and select the position of the number.

Page numbering

Unit 11.2 Activity 3D: Formatting a document

1. What is a header?
 a. How is a header created?
 b. How can it be modified?
 c. How do you add page numbers?
 d. Set up a header for an assignment.

2. Set up a footer that automatically enters the date. How would you save the details so you could adapt it to another assignment later?

3. You notice that the page breaks in a long document are not in appropriate places. How can you insert a page break?

4. List the default settings of the version of Microsoft Word you are currently using. Check the margins, the paper size and the font name and size.

5. A friend has a printer that is using US Letter paper. How can you set up your document to print to this size paper?

6. What settings do you prefer to use for Word? Why?

Unit 11.2 Word Processing

Topic 4: Editing text

Topic 4 deals with editing text and viewing documents (see Computer Studies Syllabus pp. 17–18). It covers:

- Automating text options in Word.
- Inserting, overtyping and deleting text.
- Selection techniques.
- Moving and copying text.
- Page views.

Automating text options

Microsoft Word provides options that automate spelling and grammar. There is also an option to automatically complete words.

These options are managed on the **File** tab by selecting the menu item **Options**. Selecting **Proofing** provides a range of options that can be selected.

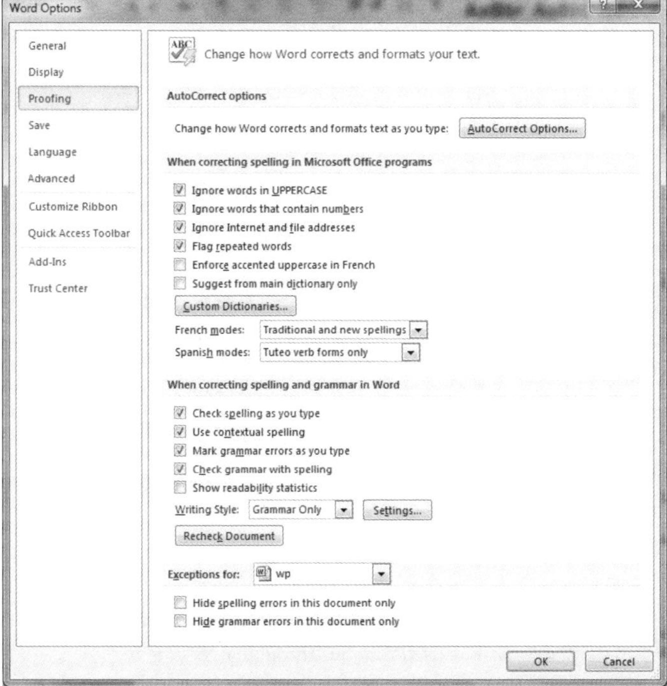

Proofing options

AutoText

The **AutoText** option allows you to add text automatically by typing only a few characters. This is useful if there are phrases that are regularly used.

AutoCorrect

The **AutoCorrect Options…** provides further options that allow you to customise the way in which you wish to use Microsoft Word. This option can be enabled or disabled using the check box at the bottom of the window.

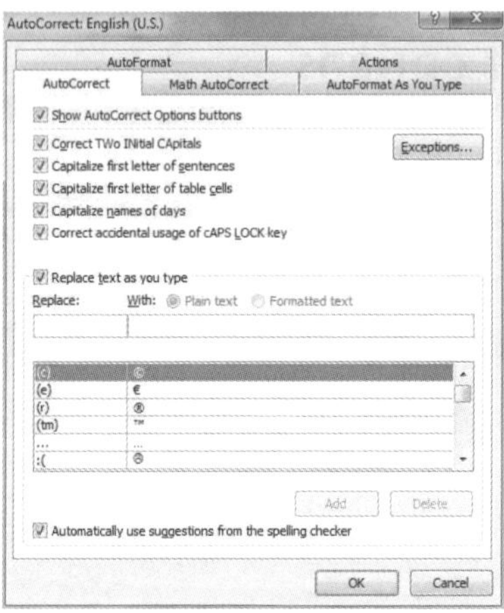

AutoCorrect figure

Inserting, overtyping and deleting text

The cursor

The cursor is a point of light that appears on the computer screen. The onscreen cursor shows the current position at which text may be entered. The cursor usually flashes to make it easy to locate on the screen.

There are a variety of ways in which the cursor will appear on the screen. The most common way is as a flashing line.

If the cursor changes shape, this may indicate a change in the function that can be performed. If the cursor becomes:

- An I beam – the cursor has moved from its current insertion point.
- An arrow – in the scroll bar it is used to move through a document.

Inserting text

To insert text in a document, move to the position in which the text is to be entered, click in that position and enter the text.

The standard rules for entering text with a word processor are:

- Use the **Enter** key at the end of a paragraph. Let 'word wrap around' put words onto the next line within a paragraph.
- At the end of a sentence, enter a full stop and then leave a single space before starting a new sentence.
- Do not use a hyphen at the end of a line unless it is part of a name or word.
- Use the space bar to insert a single space between words. Do not use the space bar to format text.
- Check the upper case or **Shift** key setting. Ordinary text should be entered in lower case, capital letters in upper case.

Word wrap around

When a line on the screen is full, words are automatically moved to the next line. It is only necessary to press the enter key at the end of the paragraph. Word wrap around is useful if the document is to be formatted again at a later date. For example, if the margins are changed the line length will automatically fit the new margins.

Date and time

The date and time can be inserted in a document. This is done using the **Date & Time** icon in the **Text** section of the **Insert** tab.

Note that there is a range of date and time formats that can be used. The date and time are taken from the computer in use. These are set using the **Date and Time** menu item in the **Control Panel**.

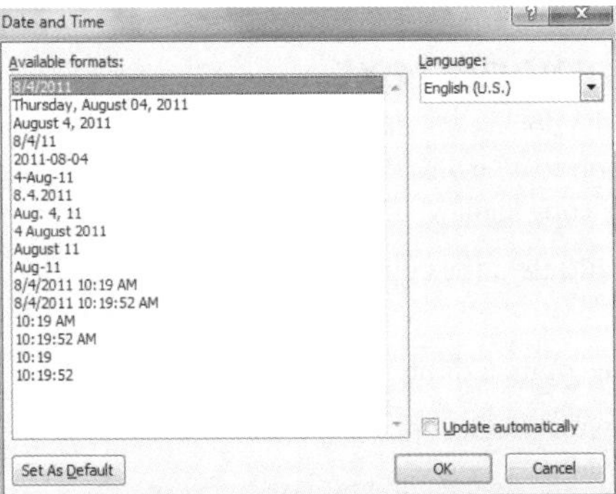

Date and Time options window

Overtyping text

When using the overtyping option, text is typed over rather than inserted. The **Insert** key on the keypad turns this option on and off. However, it may need to be enabled in Word options. Choose the **File** menu, then **Options** and then **Advanced**.

Deleting a single character

If the cursor is a vertical line, place it to the right of the character to be deleted and press the **Backspace** key. To delete the character to the right of the cursor, press the **Del** key.

Selecting and deleting a block of text

If text is to be edited it has to be selected. To select text, place the cursor at the start of the text, then:

- With the left mouse button held down, drag to the end of the text to be selected; or
- Hold down the shift key and move the cursor to the end of the text to be selected.

Selected text is highlighted by a colour on the screen. For example, the following line has been selected:

Selected text shows as reversed on the screen

Selected text

To delete a block of text, select the block and then press the **Backspace** key.

Other ways of selecting text include:

- Selecting a word: double-click on that word.
- Selecting a line: move the mouse to the left margin and click when it changes to an arrow.
- Selecting a sentence: hold down the **Ctrl** key and click anywhere in the sentence.

Moving and copying text

Text can be moved around a document after it has been entered. To 'cut and paste' means to move text from one position to a new position. To 'copy and paste' means to make a copy of the original text and place the copy somewhere else in the document.

When text is highlighted and then the copy or cut command is used, the text is placed in the Clipboard.

The **Cut**, **Copy** and **Paste** commands are shown on the **Home** tab on the Ribbon.

Another way of moving text is to select it and the drag the text to its new position.

The figure on the next page shows the cut and paste process.

Original text	Word processors, like other computer software, can 'cut' and 'paste' material. Remember that most software has an 'undo' function that can reverse the most recent action. A selected piece of text can be moved to another position.
Text to be moved is selected using the cursor	Word processors, like other computer software, can 'cut' and 'paste' material. Remember that most software has an 'undo' function that can reverse the most recent action. A selected piece of text can be moved to another position.
Selected text is cut	Word processors, like other computer software, can 'cut' and 'paste' material. A selected piece of text can be moved to another position.
Selected text is pasted at the end of the sentence.	Word processors, like other computer software, can 'cut' and 'paste' material. A selected piece of text can be moved to another position. Remember that most software has an 'undo' function that can reverse the most recent action.

Cut and paste of text

A selected piece of text can be moved to another position. Remember that most of the software has an 'undo' function which can reverse the most recent action.

Selected text is cut using the **Cut** command on the **Clipboard** section of the **Home** tab. It is pasted into the new position using the **Paste** command on the same section.

Selected text can be copied and placed elsewhere in the document using the **Copy** and **Paste** commands on the Clipboard tab. This may be done a number of times with text placed in a number of different positions.

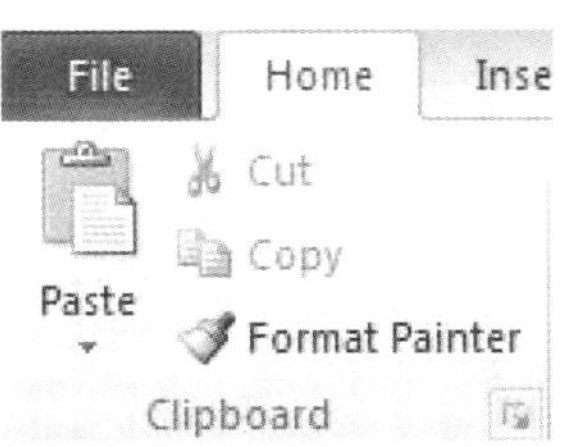

The Clipboard commands on the Home tab

Unit 11.2 Activity 4A: Cut, copy and paste

1. Enter the following lines of text. Do not press the enter key at any stage.

   The best thing about the holidays was the weather. It was terrific every day. The sun was shining through the early morning mist and the wind was very light.

   At what point did the text run on to the next line?
2. Save a copy of the document. Call the document by your given name and add 'Example 6' after it. For example, if your name is Marika you could name the document 'Marika Example 6'. Microsoft Word will add the extension '.doc' that is used to identify the type of file.
3. Enter the text in the 'Cut and paste of text' figure above called 'Original text' (paragraph 1).
4. Using Cut and Paste change the paragraph to the same as paragraph 4.
5. How do you select the following when using Microsoft Word:
   a. Character
   b. Word
   c. Line

   d. Paragraph
   e. Entire document?
6. What is the difference between 'cut and paste' and 'copy and paste'?
7. This exercise requires you to have more than one document open at the same time.
   a. Open two documents you have created.
   b. Select a paragraph of text from one document and copy it.
   c. Move to the other document and paste the text into it.

The clipboard

The **Clipboard** is a useful and important aspect of word processing. When text is cut or copied, it is stored in the Clipboard. When the **Paste** command is used, it places the contents of the Clipboard into the document wherever the cursor is located.

In Microsoft Word, the Clipboard can contain up to 24 different items. It can contain different types of data, including images, and can be used to copy data:

- Within documents.
- Between documents.
- Between applications.

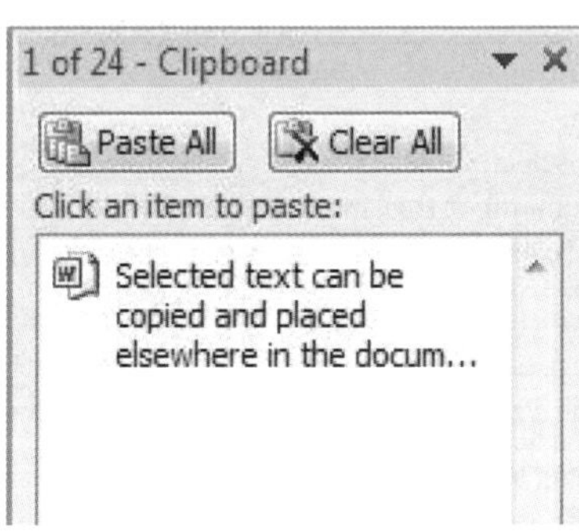

The Clipboard in Microsoft Word

The contents of the Clipboard can be viewed using the **Clipboard** command on the **Home** tab.

Drag and drop editing

Another way to cut and paste or copy and paste text is to use 'drag and drop'.

To cut and paste, select the text and then place the cursor on the text. Now drag the cursor to the new position and release the mouse button. The selected text is moved to the new insertion point.

To copy and paste, select the text and then place the cursor on the text and hold down the **Ctrl** key. Now drag the cursor to the new position and release the mouse button. The selected text is copied to the new insertion point.

Unit 11.2 Activity 4B: Working with a document

1. Complete each task before moving on to the next task. Save the document at the end of each step.
   a. Call the document 'Holiday' and include your name or initials in the document name.
   b. List the places where you would like to go for a holiday. Press **Enter** at the end of each place name to move to a new paragraph.

c. List the places in order of preference. Use the **Cut** and **Paste** commands to re-order them.
d. Next to each place, provide a one-sentence reason why you would like to go there. The reason is to be contained in the same paragraph.
e. After you have entered the reasons, check the order of places. Use cut and paste if you wish to change the order again.
f. Print a copy of the document.
g. Copy the material for the first five choices, create a new document and copy the material to it. Save the new document.

2. Refer to online help and write down how you can move the cursor to the beginning and end of a word, line, sentence, paragraph, screen, page and document.
3. Key in the following line:

   This is line number

   a. **Copy** the line.
   b. **Paste** the line into the document three times. There should now be four lines.
   c. Add the numbers at the end of each line so that they appear as below:

      This is line number 3

      This is line number 4

      This is line number 2

      This is line number 1

   d. Using **Cut** and **Paste** (or **Drag** and **Drop**) select the lines and put the lines in the correct order, numbers 1 to 4. How many cut and pastes does it take to do this?

Page views

Word has a number of different ways of viewing a document. These views are available on the **Document Views** menu item that is on the **View** tab.

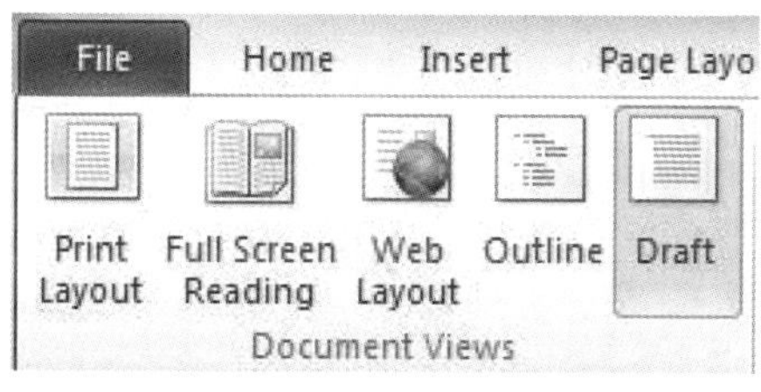

Document Views menu item

- The **Normal** or **Draft** view enables you to edit the text quickly but does not show some elements such as headers and footers.
- The **Web Layout** view shows the document as it would appear if it was a document on the World Wide Web.
- The **Print Layout** view shows the document as it will print out, including page breaks and headers and footers.
- The **Outline** view shows the document in outline format and makes the outline tools available.
- The **Full Screen Reading** view shows the document on the whole screen with very limited commands available. It is used for reading the document.

Unit 11.2 Word Processing

Topic 5: Finalising and printing a document

Topic 5 deals with finalising and printing a document (see Computer Studies Syllabus p. 18). It covers:

- Proofing your document.
- Previewing and printing.

Proofing a document

When a document is in its final stages it needs to be carefully edited. Editing involves checking:

- Spelling.
- Grammar.
- Punctuation.
- Paragraph organisation.
- Position of the page breaks in the document (called pagination).

Checking the spelling

If a word in a document is incorrectly keyed in or incorrectly spelt it may be found by using a spelling checker or spellchecker. Some dictionaries are based on American spellings, others are British and some are Australian. For example:

American dictionary	British dictionary
color	colour
centering	centring
defense	defence

A dictionary has two parts, the main dictionary and a user dictionary or Custom Dictionary. The main dictionary is usually selected when the software is installed. However, a word used on a regular basis but not recognised by the main dictionary can be added to the Custom Dictionary. Names of people and place names do not usually appear in a dictionary and would need to be included in the Custom Dictionary.

A spelling checker can:

- Find a word that it considers to be spelt incorrectly.
- Suggest alternatives for the word.
- Add words to the user dictionary.
- Replace the word with the correctly spelt word.

Using the dictionary

Microsoft Word provides a number of ways of accessing the dictionary and correcting the spelling.

One option is to check your spelling as you type. When a word appears to be incorrectly spelt, it is underlined in red. Placing the cursor anywhere within the word and then clicking on the right mouse button brings up a list of alternative spellings from which to select.

A second option is to click the **Spelling and Grammar** button on the **Review** tab. This starts checking the spelling from the current position of the cursor.

Spelling icon on the Review tab

Note that words can be spelt correctly but used in the wrong context, eg *there* and *their*, *hear* and *here*. A dictionary cannot pick up the incorrect spelling in cases such as these.

Unit 11.2 Activity 5A: Checking spelling

For the following exercises, check your answers with a partner if you need to.

1. Does the dictionary for the word processor you are using have a name? Is it British or American? How many words are in the dictionary?
2. Are the following words contained in the dictionary you are using?
   - **a.** user-friendly
   - **b.** dork
   - **c.** AIDS
   - **d.** yuppie
3. Suggest and find words that are relatively new to the language but not included in the word processor dictionary.
4. Key your family name into a word processing document and apply the spelling checker. What is the result? Can you add your name to the dictionary? If so, how?
5. Each of the following sentences contains an error that would not be picked up by a spelling checker. Find the error.
   - **a.** The boat was tied to a boy.
   - **b.** Wear is the pencil?
   - **c.** The car is parked over their.
   - **d.** The plain flew in the air.
6. Type a sentence that includes the same word twice in a row and check the spelling. Does the spelling checker pick up the duplicate word?
7. How many meanings do the following words have in your printed dictionary: set, run, go, open, strike, school, self? What do you think are the three most common uses of each word?
8. Find the meaning of 'green' in your dictionary. Does the dictionary meaning reflect what the word means today?
9. Does the term 'user-friendly' appear in your dictionary? What does the term mean? Give an example of how you would use the term.

Print preview

The **Print Preview** command on the **File** menu in Microsoft Word enables you to see how each page will look before it is printed. This view is a reduced-size view. It is very useful for checking where page breaks occur and adjusting them when necessary.

Non-printing characters

Many of the characters used to format a document are not printed. These are called non-printing characters and include the following:

- Spaces: pressing the space bar.
- Tabs: pressing the **Tab** key.
- Carriage returns: pressing the **Return/Enter** key.

In Microsoft Word, these characters may be displayed on the screen by pressing the **Show/Hide** button near the right-hand end of the **Paragraph** menu items on the **Home** tab. This button toggles the characters on and off.

Printing a document

Printing a document at the best quality is carried out at the end of the document's creation. The final copy should be printed when:

- Page breaks have been set correctly.
- Headings are all formatted correctly.
- Spelling and grammar have been checked.

It is usually advisable to print a draft copy of a document for checking before printing the final copy. Inkjet printers often offer the option of printing a document out more quickly rather than at the highest quality.

Before trying to print a document, make sure that the printer is connected and turned on. Also ensure that the correct printer driver has been chosen. The default printer is selected in the **Printers** folder.

What identifying information should be included in an assignment?

When submitting an assignment, the following details should be included:

- Date.
- Teacher's name.
- School name.
- The nature of the task (eg homework, assignment).
- Student's name.
- Student's year level and home group or class.
- Name of the task.
- Name of the subject.
- Due date.

Unit 11.2 Activity 5B: Printing

1. Make a draft copy and a final copy printout of a document. What are the differences regarding:

  a. The print quality?

  b. The time taken to print?

2. What information would you record for an assignment you currently need to complete and hand in for assessment?

Unit 11.2 Word Processing

Topic 6: Working with tables

Topic 6 deals with working with tables and lists (see Computer Studies Syllabus pp. 18–19). It covers:

- Creating tables.
- Managing tables.
- Formatting.
- Performing calculations.

Tables are used to present data in an organised manner. They are built with columns and rows, like a spreadsheet. Different types of data can be inserted into a table including text and graphics.

Creating a table

To insert a table:

- Select the **Insert** tab on the ribbon.
- Click on the **Table** icon.
- Move the cursor across the table representation to select the number of rows and columns required.
- These rows and columns are reflected in the Word document.
- Word adds the table to the document.

Data is entered in each cell of the table. Each cell may contain text, numbers or an image.

The column and row heights may be easily altered. Borders and shading assist in making a table an excellent way of presenting data in a document.

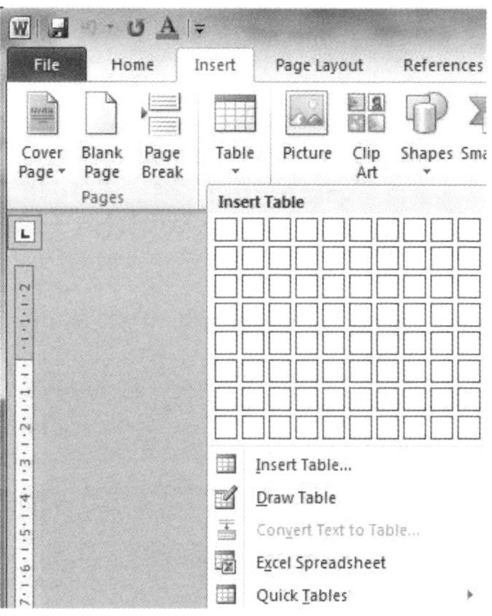

Creating a table

Entering data

Click inside a cell to enter data in that cell. Use the **Tab** key to move between cells or click in a different cell to enter data in that cell.

Lake	Province	Size (ha)
Murray	Western	64,700
Chambri	ESP	21,600
Wisdom	Madang	8,592
Khanda-Szaga	Western	7,840
Kutubu	SHP	4,924
Dakataua	WNB	4,920
Yonki	EHP	2,120
Aesake Lagoon	Western	2,120
Sirinumu	Central	4,100
Bossett	Western	1,680

An example of a table; note that the first column is selected

Inserting graphics

To add a graphic element to a cell:

- Click in that cell.
- Move to the **Insert** tab on the ribbon.
- Select the **Picture** menu icon.
- Select the image from your **Pictures Library**.

Managing tables

Managing tables involves selecting part of a table and then carrying out the required action.

Selecting a cell, row, column or entire table

To select a cell:

- Place the cursor in the cell and click the mouse button.

To select a row:

- Place the cursor to the left of the row (it changes into an arrow).
- Click the left mouse button.

To select a column:

- Place the cursor above the column (it changes to an arrow pointed downwards).
- Click the left mouse button.

To select an entire table:

- Place the cursor at the top left corner of the table (the cursor changes to a cross with an arrow on each end).
- Click the left mouse button.

Changing column width

To change a column width:

- Click and hold the mouse on one of the vertical lines on the boundary of the column.
- Drag the column to the desired position.

  or

- Click in the column.
- Right-click on the mouse and select **Table Properties...**.
- Choose the **Column** tab and set the width.

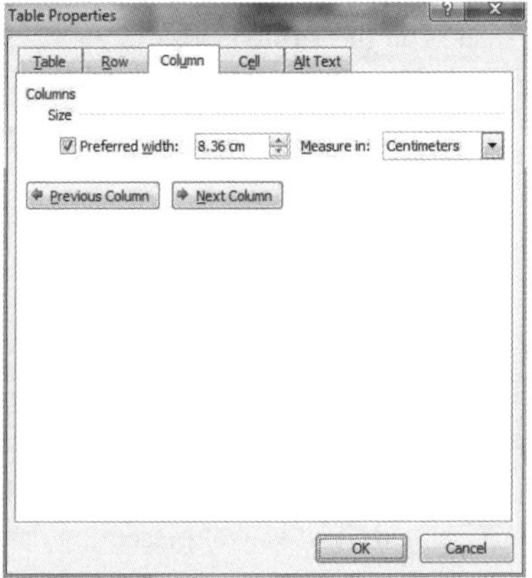

Changing the column width in a table

Changing row height

To change a row height:

- Click and hold the mouse on one of the horizontal lines on the boundary of the column.
- Drag the row line to the desired position.

  or

- Click in the row.
- Right-click on the mouse and select **Table Properties...**.
- Choose the **Row** tab and set the width.

Using the Table Tools tab

When the mouse is clicked inside a table, the **Table Tools** tab appears on the ribbon. This has two tabs:

- Design.
- Layout.

The **Design** tab enables a range of formatting and style options including:

- Table styles.
- Shading.
- Borders.
- Pen size and colour.

Design tab

The **Layout** tab provides a range of options including setting the width and height of cells and inserting rows and columns as well as deleting them.

The **Height** and **Width** commands can be used to ensure that the size of the cells is uniform.

Inserting rows or columns in a table

Another method of inserting rows or columns is to:

- Click in a cell.
- Click the right mouse button.
- The **Insert** menu item gives five options:
    - Insert Columns to the Left.
    - Insert Columns to the Right.
    - Insert Rows Above.
    - Insert Rows Below.
    - Insert Cells.

Table formatting

The **Design** tab on the **Table Tools** tab allows quick formatting that can give a table a very different look. For example, the following table can be easily changed:

Lake	Province	Size (ha)
Murray	Western	64 700
Chambri	ESP	21 600
Wisdom	Madang	8592
Khanda-Szaga	Western	7840

Lake	Province	Size (ha)
Kutubu	SHP	4924
Dakataua	WNB	4920
Yonki	EHP	2120
Aesake Lagoon	Western	2120
Sirinumu	Central	4100
Bossett	Western	1680

Simple table

Applying the **Light Shading** menu item from the **Design** tab transforms the look of the table.

Lake	Province	Size (ha)
Murray	Western	64 700
Chambri	ESP	21 600
Wisdom	Madang	8592
Khanda-Szaga	Western	7840
Kutubu	SHP	4924
Dakataua	WNB	4920
Yonki	EHP	2120
Aesake Lagoon	Western	2120
Sirinumu	Central	4100
Bossett	Western	1680

Table with formatting applied

Performing calculations in a table

Calculations can be carried out in a table by inserting a formula. This is done by clicking in the appropriate part of the table and accessing the **Layout** tab on the **Table Tools** tab. Now select the **Formula** command.

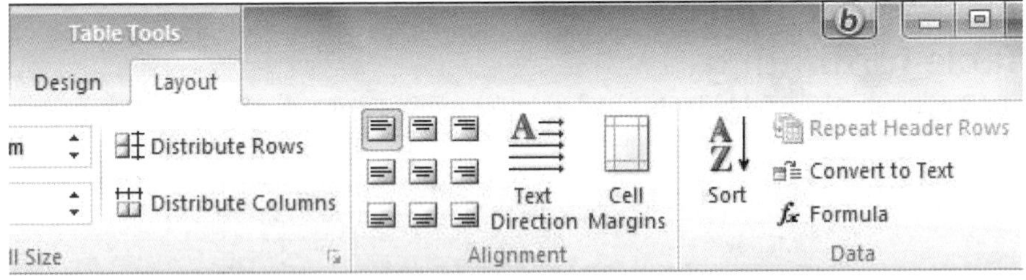

Table Tools tab includes Data menu with a formula

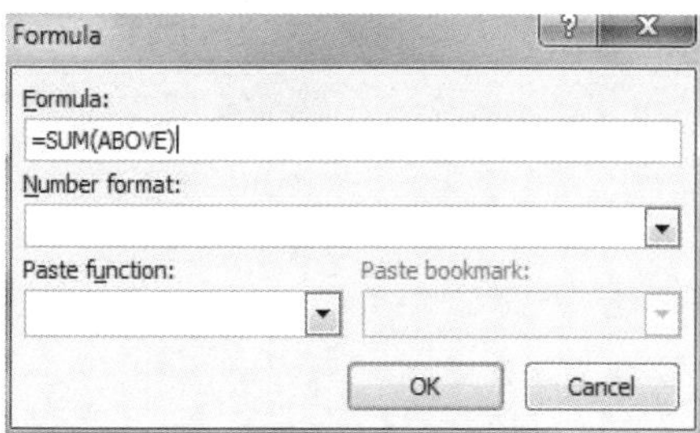

Formula for a table

By inserting the formula **=SUM(ABOVE)**, the total size is added to the table above.

Lake	Province	Size (ha)
Murray	Western	64 700
Chambri	ESP	21 600
Wisdom	Madang	8592
Khanda-Szaga	Western	7840
Kutubu	SHP	4924
Dakataua	WNB	4920
Yonki	EHP	2120
Aesake Lagoon	Western	2120
Sirinumu	Central	4100
Bossett	Western	1680
TOTAL AREA		122 596

Table with a calculation

Note that these formulae do not automatically reflect changes in the value of the data. If the data changes, you must choose the **Update Field** option, which is available by right-clicking the field.

Quick tables

The **Quick Tables** command enables you to insert a table template, ie a table that is already formatted and can then be modified by the user.

This is found on the **Insert** tab using the **Table** command.

For example, a calendar template can be used to quickly create a calendar.

MAY

M	T	W	T	F	S	S
	1	2	3	4	5	6
7	8	9	10	11	12	13
14	15	16	17	18	19	20
21	22	23	24	25	26	27
28	29	30	31			

A calendar created using Quick Tables

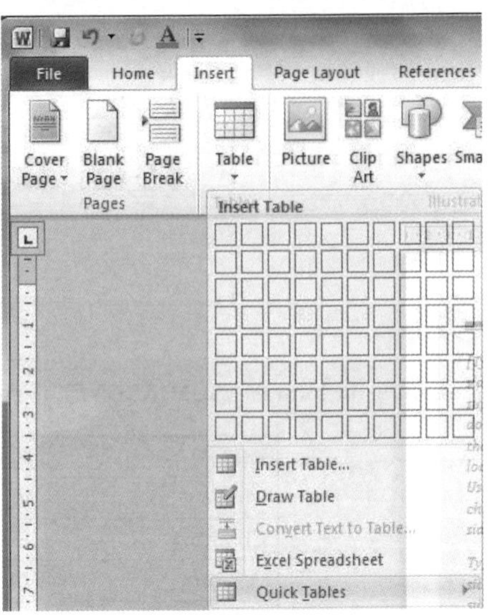

Quick Tables option

Unit 11.2 Activity 6A: Creating tables

1. Create a table in Word that reflects your school timetable.
2. Use the Quick Tables function to create a calendar for next year.

Unit 11.2 Word Processing

Topic 7: Working with graphics

Topic 7 deals with working with graphics (see Computer Studies Syllabus p. 19).
It covers:

- Inserting and formatting text boxes.
- Adding AutoShapes.
- Inserting pictures and WordArt.
- Creating a watermark.

Inserting and formatting text boxes

A text box is an object that can be inserted in a Microsoft Office document. The text box, like other objects, can be moved around the document to the desired position.

The **Text Box** icon is found on the **Text** section of the **Insert** tab, near the right-hand end.

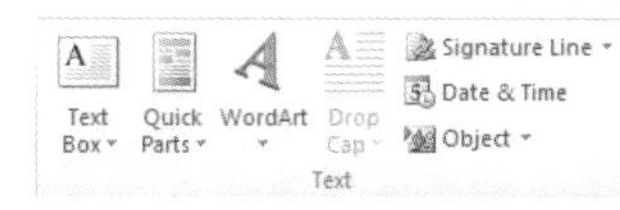

Text Box icon on Text section of the Insert tab

Inserting a text box

To insert a text box, click the **Text Box** icon. This gives a range of options for the type of text box you would like to use.

Once the text box is created, enter the text. When working with the text, the **Drawing Tools** tab becomes available.

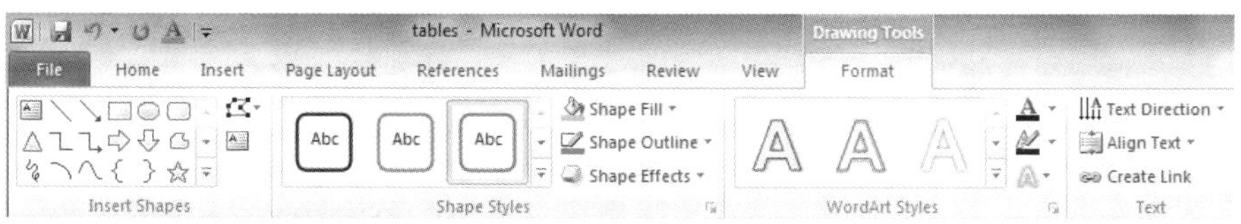

Drawing Tools menu item

Formatting a text box

These tools can be used to modify the look of the text box, including:

- Colour and type of text.
- The shape outline.
- The fill inside the text box.

The usual formatting changes to the font can be made using the **Font** menu on the **Home** tab on the ribbon.

When the text box is selected, the cursor changes to a cross with arrows on each end. This cursor can be used to drag the text box around the document.

> *[Type the sidebar content. A sidebar is a standalone supplement to the main document. It is often aligned on the left or right of the page, or located at the top or bottom. Use the Drawing Tools tab to change the formatting of the sidebar text box.*
>
> *Type the sidebar content. A sidebar is a standalone supplement to the main document. It is often aligned on the left or right of the page, or located at the top or bottom. Use the Drawing Tools tab to change the formatting of the sidebar text box.]*

Example of a text box – one of the options provided by Word

AutoShapes

Word has a large number of **AutoShapes** that can be added to a document and modified to suit.

These are accessed on the **Insert** tab, choosing the **Shapes** command, which displays a range of different shapes to use.

To insert a shape:

- Select the shape from the drop-down menu.
- Note that the cursor changes to a cross.
- Drag across your document to insert the shape.

With the shape selected, you now have access to a **Shape Styles** menu that enables the shape to be modified.

Shape Styles menu

The shape fill, outline and effects can be modified. The figure below shows two different versions of the same shape.

Two versions of the same shape

Clip art, pictures and SmartArt

Pictures and clip art can be inserted from the **Illustrations** menu on the **Insert** tab.

Inserting a picture from the Clip Art gallery

To insert clip art, choose **Clip Art** from the menu and the images are displayed on the right side of the screen in a clip art list. Word provides a range of images and further images are available at Word.com.

To insert the image, double-click it and then move it to the appropriate place in your document.

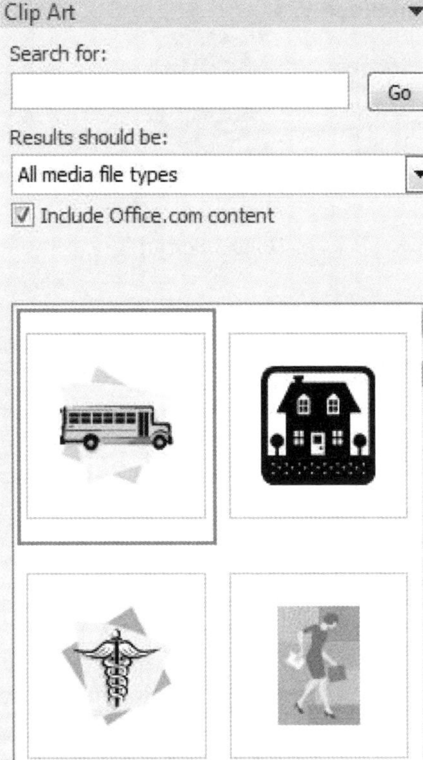

Clip Art gallery

Inserting a picture from another file

A picture can be inserted by choosing the **Picture** menu item and then selecting the image. This can be a photograph you have taken or an image you have created. You will need to navigate to the image.

SmartArt

SmartArt can be used to insert a different type of graphic image, eg a flowchart or an organisation chart or processes. You are able to add text to the images to give them meaning.

To do this, choose **SmartArt** in the **Illustrations** menu on the **Insert** tab.

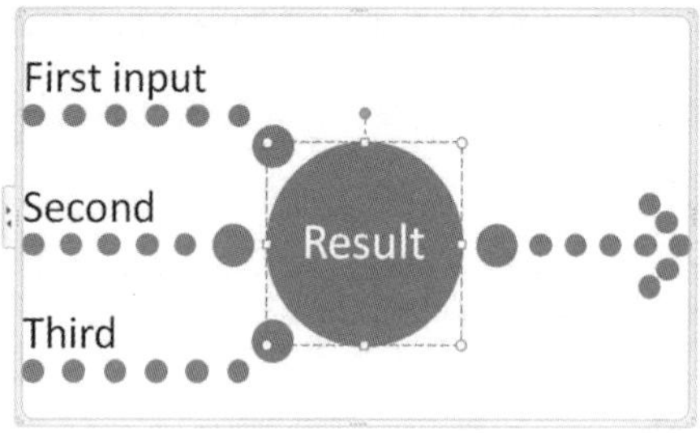

Using SmartArt

Watermarks

A watermark is text or graphics that appears in the background of a page or pages. For example, a document might be 'CONFIDENTIAL' or 'DRAFT'.

To insert a watermark, go to the **Page Layout** tab and choose the **Watermark** command from the **Page Background** section of the tab.

Word provides a number of default types that you can use as a watermark. You have the option of modifying the text or adding a graphic watermark if you choose the **Custom Watermark...** option.

Custom Watermark option

Unit 11.2 Activity 7A: Working with graphics

1. When you insert a picture, you may need to modify it.
   a. How do you resize the picture?
   b. How do you crop the picture?
   c. How can you add a border to the picture?
2. How do you insert a chart into a Word document?
3. Create a document that has a watermark labelled 'Draft' across it.

Unit 11.2 Word Processing

Topic 8: Working with styles and templates

Topic 8 explains how to work with styles and templates (see ICT Syllabus p. 13).
It covers:

- Creating and applying a character style.
- Creating and applying a paragraph style.
- Copying styles between documents.
- Modifying and deleting a style.
- Creating a document from a template.
- Creating and modifying a document template.

Styles

Word has a collection of pre-set **styles**. These styles can be used to ensure consistency within a document. They can easily be applied to either a word or a paragraph.

Styles can be accessed on the **Home** tab on the ribbon using the **Styles** command at the right end of the ribbon. A style is applied to a paragraph. Clicking in the paragraph and then on a style applies that style to the whole paragraph.

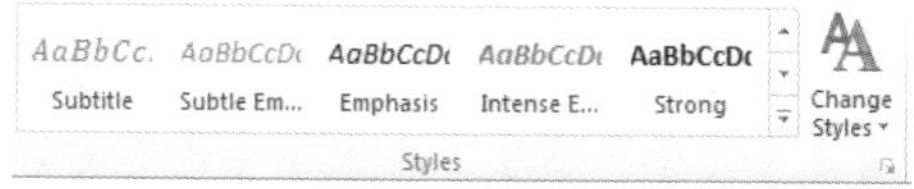

Styles from Home tab

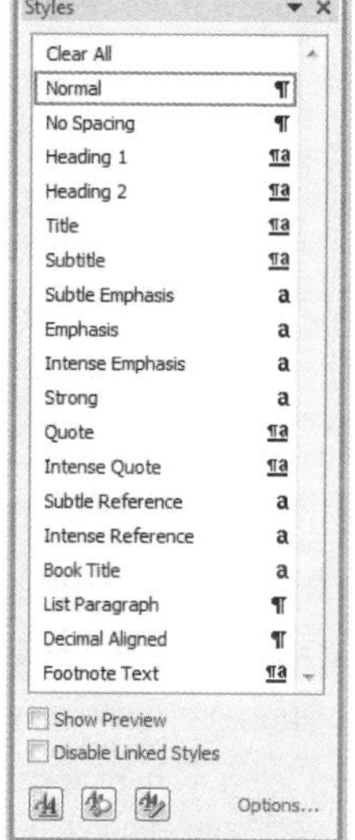

Style list

Creating and applying a character style

A character style applies formatting to a character – font name, size, colour, emphasis, etc. These styles to do not apply to the whole paragraph, just to a character, word or selected text.

To see the pre-defined styles in Word, click the **Styles Dialog Box Launcher** (the diagonal arrow under the **Change Styles** command) and the styles are displayed. The paragraph styles are marked with the paragraph marker ¶. Those that are a character style are marked with the letter **a.**

Creating a character style

To create a new quick style:

- Format the text as desired.
- In the **Styles** section of the **Home** tab, click on the **More** button.
- Select **Save Selection as a New Quick Style**.
- To make it a character style, click on the **Modify...** button and select the **Style Type** as being **Character**.
- The new style now appears in the Styles menu.

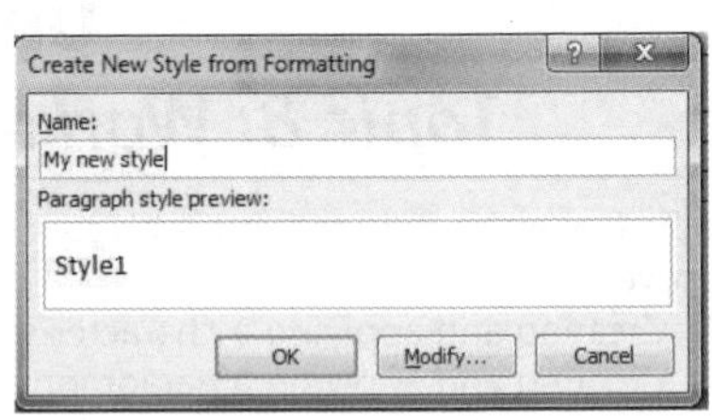

Insert the styles naming window

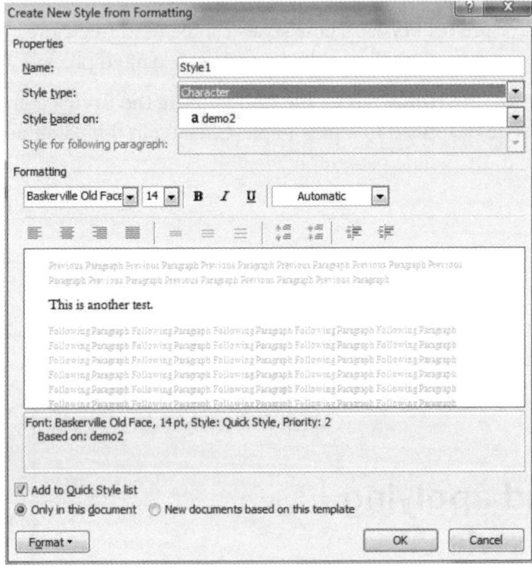

Creating a Style Type

Applying a character style

To apply a character style:

- Select a character or characters and click on the style name. The style is applied to the selected characters.
- Place the cursor within a word and click on the style name. The style is applied to the word.

Creating and applying a paragraph style

A paragraph style works in a similar manner to a character style but it applies to the whole paragraph.

To create a new quick style, do the same as for a character style. However, ensure the **Style Type** is selected as being **Paragraph**.

Applying a paragraph style

To apply a paragraph style:

- Click anywhere in the paragraph and click on the style name. The style is applied to the paragraph.

Copying styles between documents

Styles can be copied between documents using the **Manage Styles** option in the **Styles** dialog box.

The **Import/Export** function allows styles to be imported or exported to a template or another document.

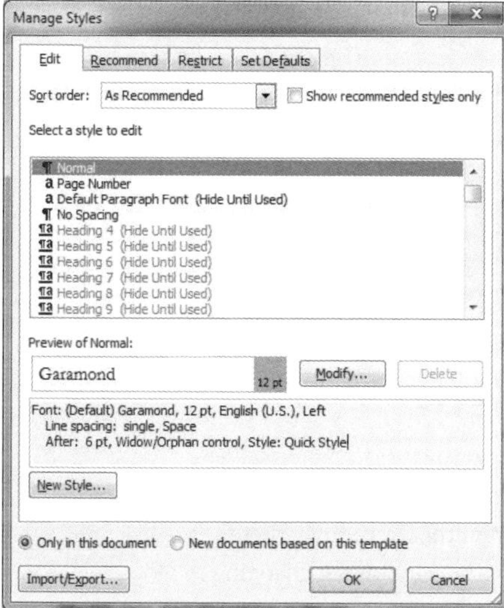

Manage styles window

Unit 11.2 Activity 8A: Styles

The example below shows the characteristics of the style called Heading 2.

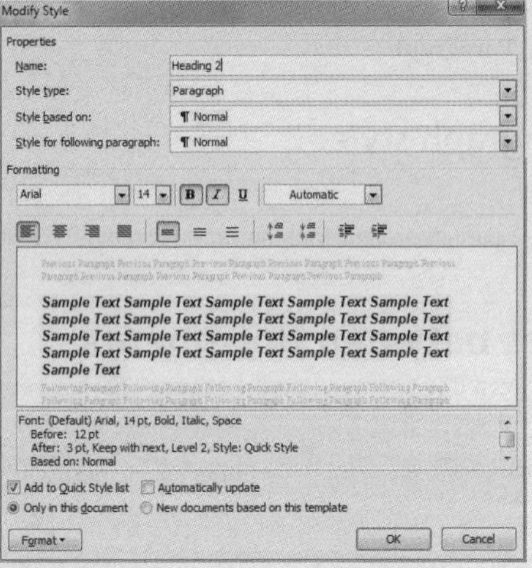

The style Heading 2

1. What is the name of the font?
2. What is the font size?
3. What formatting has been applied to the font?
4. How would you change the font to 28 point size?
5. How do you apply the style to a paragraph?
6. How can you change the colour of the style?

Modifying styles

A style can be modified by:

- Right-clicking on the style name.
- Selecting **Modify...** from the drop-down menu.
- Making the changes in the window, eg changing the font.
- Clicking **OK** to put the changes to work.

What is a template?

A **template** in Microsoft Word is a document that stores various styles, formats and preferences. Templates are used to create standard formats and styles so that a consistency in document appearance can be achieved.

A document that is used repeatedly with minor modifications should be set up as a template.

Microsoft Word documents that are templates are stored with the '.dotm' extension. When a template is opened, the document is not named and will need to be saved with a different name when used.

Microsoft Word uses a file called NORMAL.DOTM that is used as a template for new documents, unless the user chooses differently. Clicking the **New** button on the toolbar opens a blank document based on the normal template.

Using templates

To use a template, choose **New** from the **File** menu and click on the required tab in the dialog box. Now select the template that you wish to use.

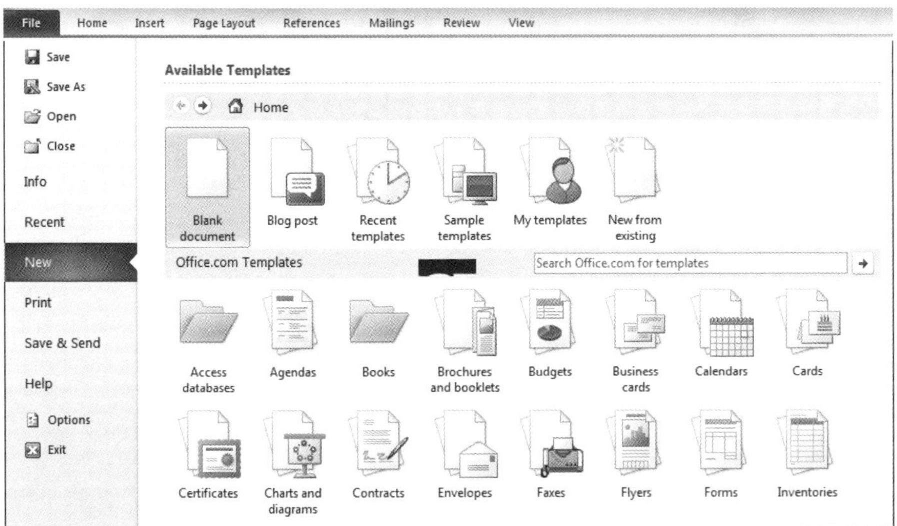

Some of the templates available in Microsoft Word

Unit 11.2 Activity 8B: Templates

1. **a.** Set up a template that contains your name, address and contact details that you can use for your own letterhead.
   b. Use clip art to insert an image.
   c. Save your letterhead as a template.
2. Create a template for a single page, two-column newsletter for a rugby club.

Unit 11.2 Activity 8C: Margins and paper size

Open a new, blank document. Choose **Page Setup** from the **File** menu.

1. What is the paper size?
2. What are the values for the top and bottom margins?
3. Alter the paper size and then click the **Default** button.
4. Alter the top and bottom margins and then click the **Default** button.
5. Start a new document and see if your changes are reflected in that blank document.

Unit 11.2 Word Processing

Topic 9: Creating mail merge and labels

Topic 9 explains how to create a mail merge and labels (see ICT Syllabus pp. 13–14). It covers:

- Selecting the document type.
- Selecting the starting document.
- Selecting the recipients.
- Adding records to the data source.
- Creating and previewing the letter.
- Performing a mail merge.
- Printing the letters.
- Customising and enhancing the mail merge.
- Creating mailing labels.

Mail merge is used to personalise form letters and print addresses on mailing labels and envelopes. A mail merge is an important tool for many businesses and organisations in the communication process with customers and members.

Mail merging involves the merging of a main document – the one containing the standard information that is the same in each letter – with a data source. The data source can be a Word document or another file such as a spreadsheet or database.

In Microsoft Word, the process involves:

- Creating the main document.
- Creating or identifying the data source.
- Inserting the field names in the main document.
- Carrying out the merge.

The menu items relating to mail merges are on the **Mailings** tab on the ribbon.

Selecting the document type

The first task is to select the document type. This is done on the **Start Mail Merge** section of the **Mailings** tab.

The choices of type are:

- Letters.
- Email messages.
- Envelopes.
- Labels.
- Directory.
- Normal Word document.

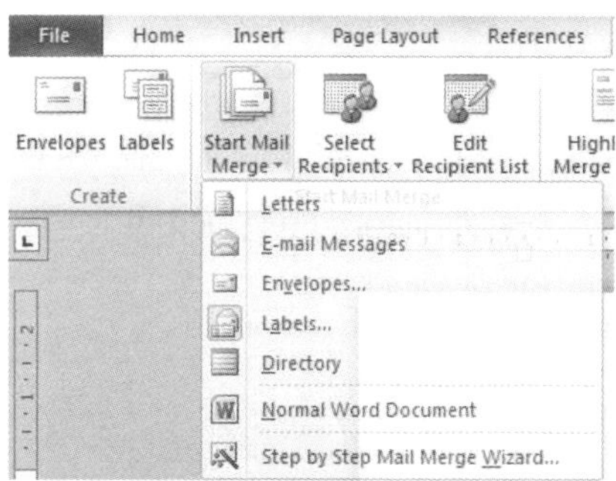

Starting a Mail Merge

Selecting the starting document

The starting document can be:

- One you have already prepared, eg a Word document.
- A new document that is prepared at the start of the process.

Once the document is open, the data source needs to be identified.

Selecting the recipients

The recipients can be selected using the **Select Recipients** menu item in the **Start Mail Merge** section.

The recipients can be selected by:

- Entering a new list.
- Identifying a data source.
- Using Outlook addresses, if these are set up on your computer.

If you choose to enter a new list, Word provides a blank table into which you can enter the data. It has a number of different fields that can be used but these may be modified or deleted.

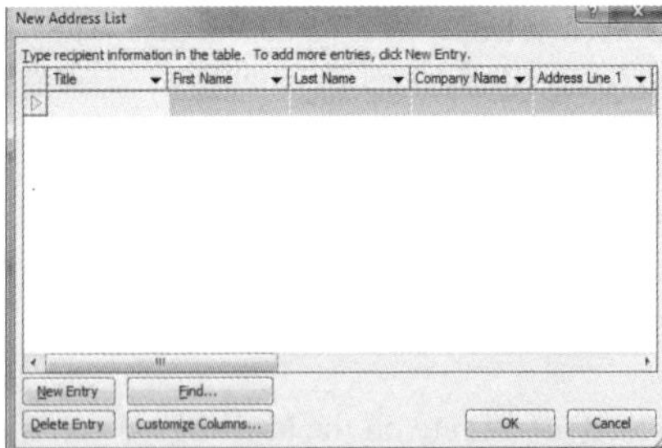

Field names

Adding records to the data source

Fields can be added or deleted using the **Customize Columns...** command in the address list window. Field names can also be changed using this command.

Names can be entered using the **Tab** key to move between fields.

Once the data is complete, the data source needs to be saved and given a name. Click the **Close** button to go through this process.

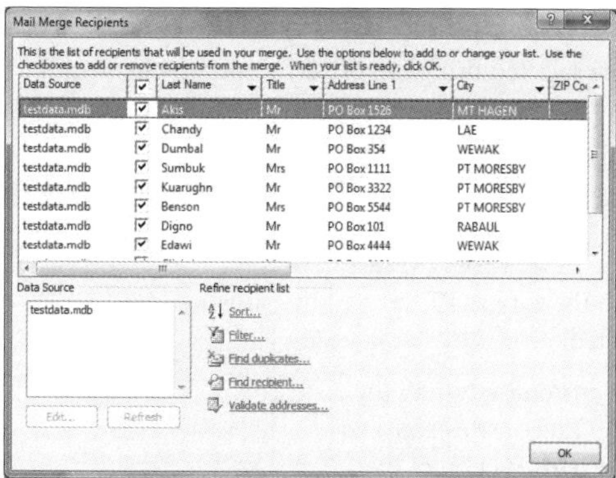

Completed data source

Records can be added by choosing **Edit Recipient List** and then adding the new record using the **New Entry** command.

Creating the letter

Field names must now be added to the main document. Open the main document and click and hold down the **Insert Merge Field** button. This will provide a list of the field names from the data source. Place the cursor in the appropriate position in the main document and then select the field name from the menu. The field names are shown enclosed in special characters.

Note that a space is entered between each merge field on the one line.

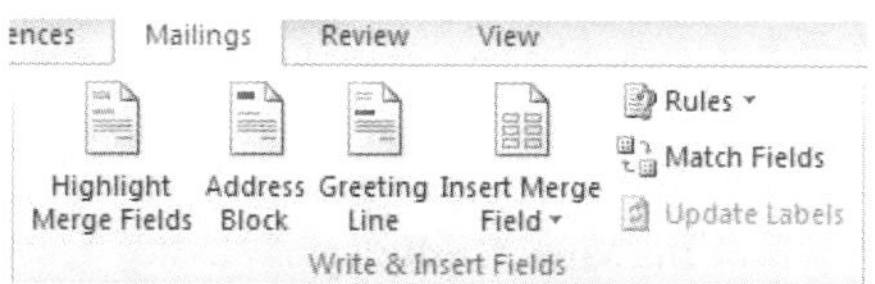

Inserting merge fields

Previewing the letter

To preview the results, click on the **Preview Results** button in the **Preview Results** section of the **Mailings** tab.

This will show the letter with the data from the first record inserted. To view further records, click on the arrow to move through the recipient list.

Performing a mail merge

Once you are happy with the preview results, click the **Finish & Merge** button. Choosing the **Edit Individual Documents** menu item enters the entire merge document into one Word document. This document should then be saved and printed.

Customising and enhancing the mail merge

Particular records can be selected using the **Filter…** option when editing the **Mail Merge Recipients.**

For example, in the figure at right, the records are filtered with the rule:

City is Equal to PT MORESBY

Only those records with the City as PT MORESBY will be selected.

Note that letters can be customised using the **If … Then … Else** rule. Rules are established in the **Write & Insert Fields** section of the **Mailings** tab.

Choose Rules gives a number of options, including **If … Then … Else**.

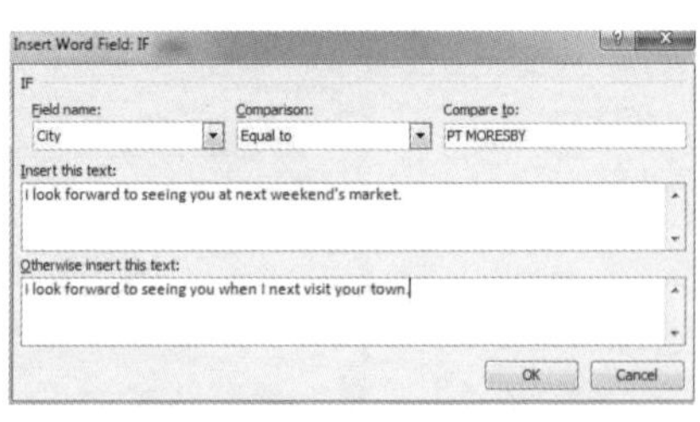

Mail Merge Recipients Selection

The figure above gives an example of a rule with one sentence of text being inserted if the rule is true and another if it is not true.

Mailing labels

Mailing labels can be produced in a similar manner to the mail merge described above. To produce a mailing label merge document:

- Select **Labels** then choose **Start Mail Merge.**
- Select the **Label vendor** and then the **Product number** for the labels.
- If the gridlines for the labels do not show, go to the **Table Tools** tab, select **Layout** and check the **View Gridlines** box.
- Use **Select Recipients** to choose your data source.
- Choose **Address Block** from the **Write & Insert** tab to insert the address (this can be modified if necessary).
- Now choose **Update Labels** from the same tab. This enters the fields for each label.

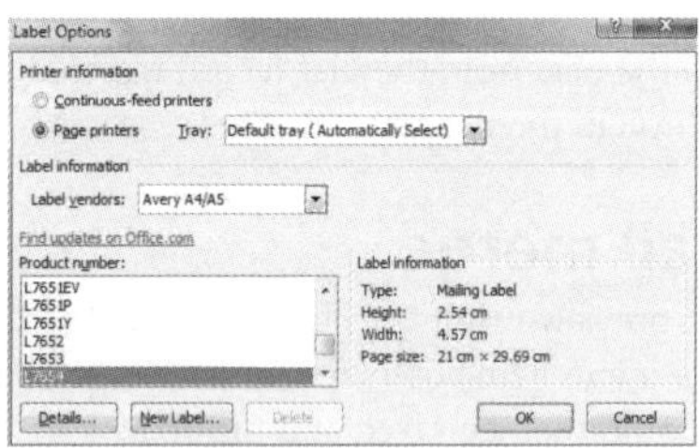

Selecting a label type

- Select **Preview Results** to check the merge.
- If it is correct, choose **Finish & Merge**.

«AddressBlock»	«Next Record» «AddressBlock»	«Next Record» «AddressBlock»
«Next Record» «AddressBlock»	«Next Record» «AddressBlock»	«Next Record» «AddressBlock»

A mail merge document for labels

Unit 11.2 Activity 9A: Create a mail merge letter

1. Create the data table below and use it for a mail merge.

Mailingname	Title	Given	Family	No	Street	Town
Mr B J Bauer	Mr	Brian	Bauer	13	New St	Goroka
Ms T Y Carruthers	Ms	Tonia	Carruthers	233	Thompsons Rd	Port Moresby
Mr D P Balley	Mr	David	Bailey	16	Henry St	Wewak
Mrs R J Elijah	Mrs	Ronnie	Elijah	58	Normanby Rd	Rabaul
Mr F D Hang	Mr	Frank	Hang	17	Bradley St	Lae
Ms S P Thom	Ms	Susie	Thom	53	Andrew Ave	Goroka
Miss L E Stewart	Miss	Leonie	Stewart	491	Burke Rd	Mt Hagen
Mr I Pavlic	Mr	Ian	Pavlic	78	Richardson St	Port Moresby

2. Use the information in the table above for a mail merge for a social gathering you are going to hold. Include a map of where the gathering is to be held and include that in the letter.
3. Add two more people to the list above.
4. Create a set of mailing labels from the data.

Unit 11.2 Word Processing

Topic 10: Working with columns

Topic 10 explores working with columns (see ICT Syllabus p. 14). It covers:

- Creating columns for an entire document.
- Creating columns for part of a document.
- Creating columns for an existing document.
- Changing the number of columns.
- Changing the width of columns.
- Adding vertical lines between columns.

Creating columns for an entire document

Columns can be created in Word using the **Columns** command on the **Page Setup** menu items section of the **Page Layout** tab.

To create a new document with multiple columns, start a blank document. Choose **Columns** and choose the number of columns from the drop-down menu.

If the three-column option is chosen, three columns are set up. By default, this sets up three equal columns. Text flows down the first column and, at the bottom of the page, into the second column at the top.

Creating columns within an existing document

To create columns within a document, select the text that you wish to place into columns and then choose the **Columns** command and select the number of columns. The columns are applied to the selected text.

For an existing document, the whole document can be selected and the **Columns** command used to create the desired number of columns.

Formatting columns

The **Columns** command also allows you to:

- Modify the width of the columns.
- Add a vertical line between columns with a check box.

Choose the **More Columns...** menu item when using the **Columns** command to achieve this.

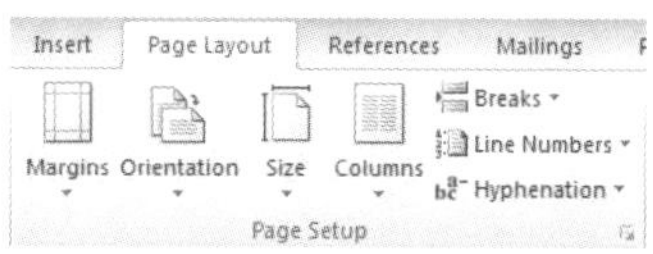

Columns icon

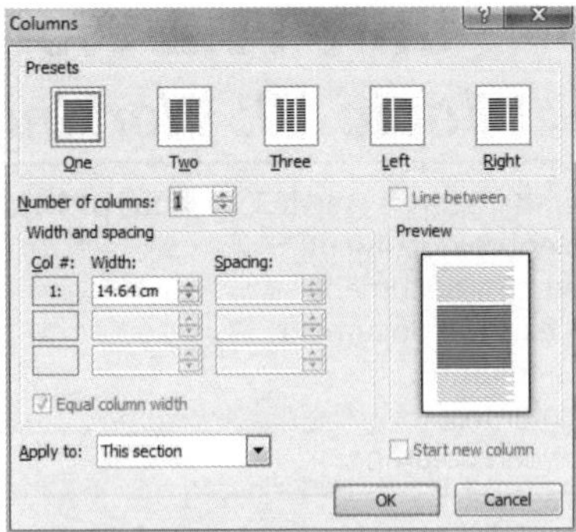

Columns options

Unit 11.2 Word Processing

Topic 11: Working with outline and long documents

Topic 11 deals with working with outline and long documents (see ICT Syllabus p. 14). It covers:

- Creating footnotes and endnotes.
- Creating and updating a table of contents.
- Organising a document in outline view.

Footnotes and endnotes

Footnotes and endnotes are used to:

- Add extra comments or explanations by the author.
- Give references to sources of information or quotations.

A footnote is printed at the bottom of the page. An endnote is printed at the end of the document. Attention is drawn to the note by a number or symbol in the document.

Microsoft Word allows you to add footnotes and endnotes. It provides automatic settings and allows you to create your own settings.

If you insert a footnote in a document, Word will automatically:

- Number the footnotes in order through the document.
- Format the footnote so that the text is in 10 point size in the font you normally use.
- Provide a reference mark with a font size of 10 points and a 3 point superscript.
- Print the footnotes at the bottom of the page of the document with a line separating them from the text.

The menu items are on the **Footnotes** section of the **References** tab.

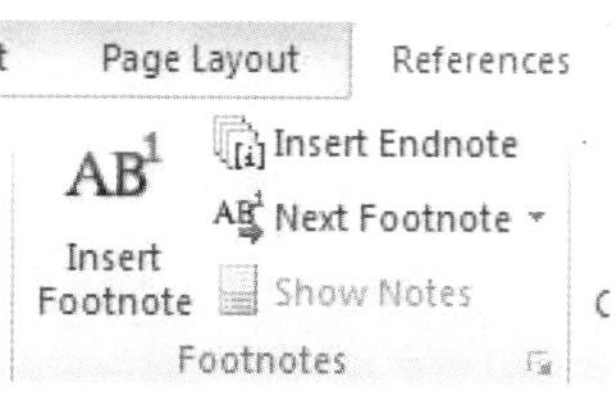

Footnotes menu

Inserting a footnote

To insert a footnote:

- Select the **Insert Footnote** command on the **References** tab.
- Enter the text for the footnote at the bottom of the page.

Inserting an endnote

To insert an endnote:

- Select the **Insert Endnote** command on the **References** tab.
- Enter the text for the endnote at the end of the document.

Converting footnotes to endnotes

To convert footnotes to endnotes:

- Go to the **Footnote and endnote** dialog box (click on the diagonal arrow at the bottom right corner of the **Footnotes** section of the **References** tab).
- Choose the **Convert...** option.
- Then check the **Convert all footnotes to endnotes** menu item.

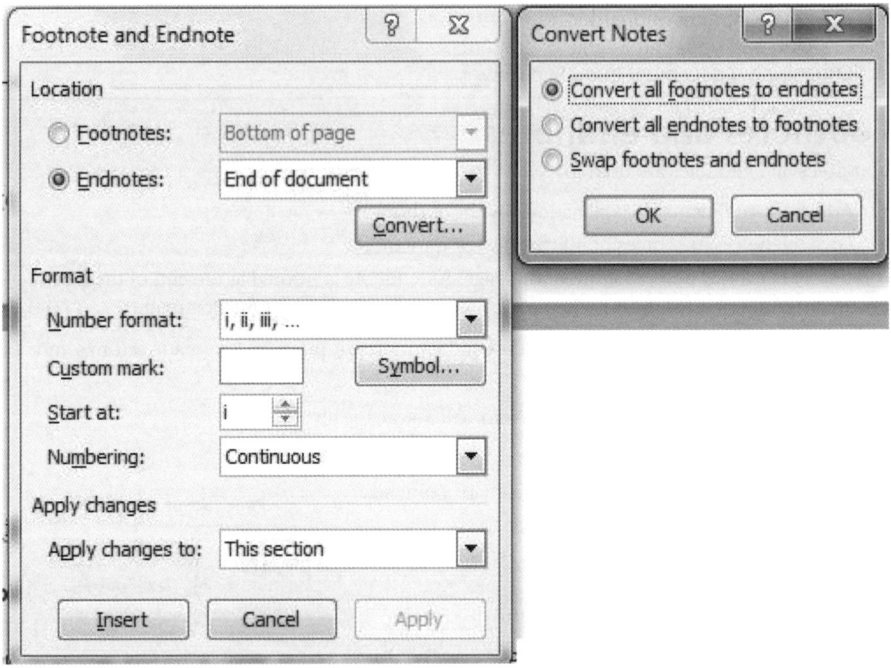

Converting footnotes to endnotes

Table of contents

Microsoft Word can generate a table of contents based on the styles that have been used in the document. These styles appear on the **Home** tab.

Creating a table of contents

The **Table of Contents** command is located in the **Table of Contents** section on the **References** tab.

To create a table of contents, click at the location that you wish to use for the table of contents (usually at the start of the document).

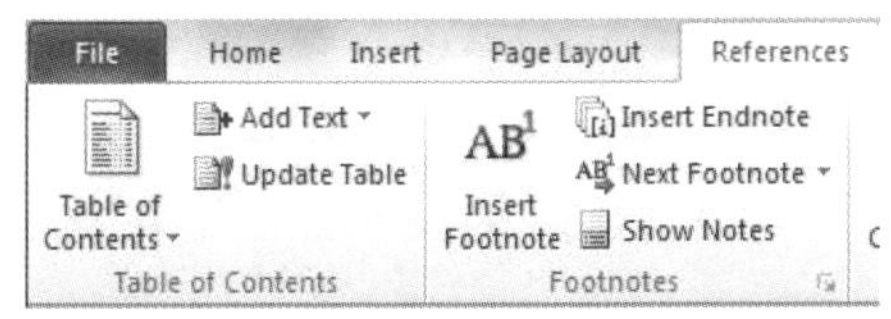

Table of Contents icons

Now click on the **Table of Contents** icon. Word gives you the choice of automatic tables based on the styles – typically Heading 1, Heading 2 and Heading 3. If you select one of the automatic tables, the table of contents is generated including the page numbers.

The figure below shows a typical table of contents generated in this manner.

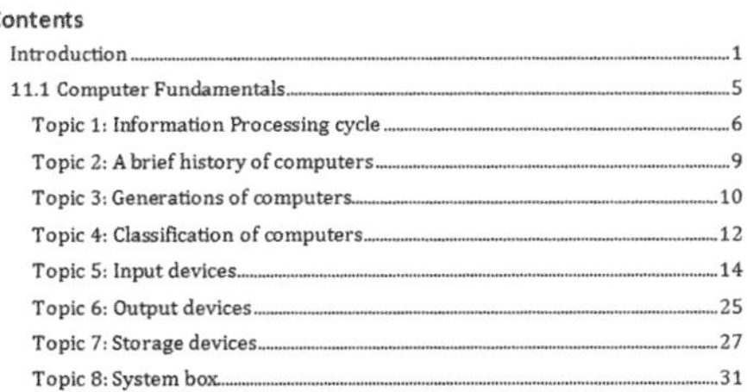

Contents

Introduction 1
11.1 Computer Fundamentals 5
Topic 1: Information Processing cycle 6
Topic 2: A brief history of computers 9
Topic 3: Generations of computers 10
Topic 4: Classification of computers 12
Topic 5: Input devices 14
Topic 6: Output devices 25
Topic 7: Storage devices 27
Topic 8: System box 31

A table of contents

Updating a table of contents

If headings are added or removed, the table of contents can be updated using the **Update Table** command in the **Table of Contents** section.

Organising a document in outline view

If a document is created using a structure built on headings, subheadings and body text, the **Outline** view can be useful in making changes to the structure of the document.

The **Outline** view is available on the **View** tab.

This shows the document with a navigation panel down the left side and a range of outlining tools on the **Outlining** tab.

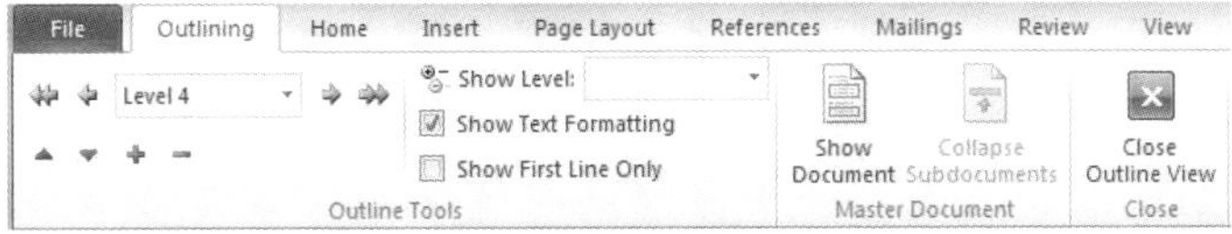

Outlining tab

The arrows on the Outlining tab can be used to change the style of the selected text.

The navigation panel can be used to move quickly through the document. It can also be used to move blocks of text around.

Clicking in one of the headings and dragging it to a new position moves all the text under that heading to the new position. This enables you to quickly change the order of sections in a large document.

Unit 11.2 Word Processing

Topic 12: Sharing information with other programs

Topic 12 explains how to share information with other programs (see ICT Syllabus pp. 14–15). It covers:

- Using word processing with spreadsheets and Power Point.
- Working with object linking and embedding.

Microsoft Office allows the sharing of information between its different components.

Including a spreadsheet in a word processing document

There are two different ways of using a spreadsheet in a Word document:

- As a spreadsheet inserted in the document that can access the Excel commands.
- As a spreadsheet copied from Excel and linked to Excel so that changes in the external spreadsheet are reflected in the document.

Inserting a spreadsheet

On the menu for **Insert Table** in Word, one of the options is to insert an **Excel Spreadsheet**.

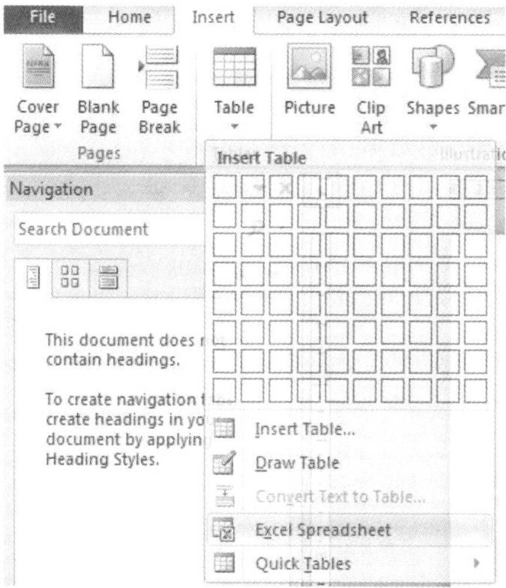

Insert an Excel spreadsheet

Selecting this inserts an Excel workbook into the document. This workbook accesses all the Excel commands and can be manipulated in the same way as a spreadsheet. Double-clicking in the worksheet allows it to be edited and displays the menu items.

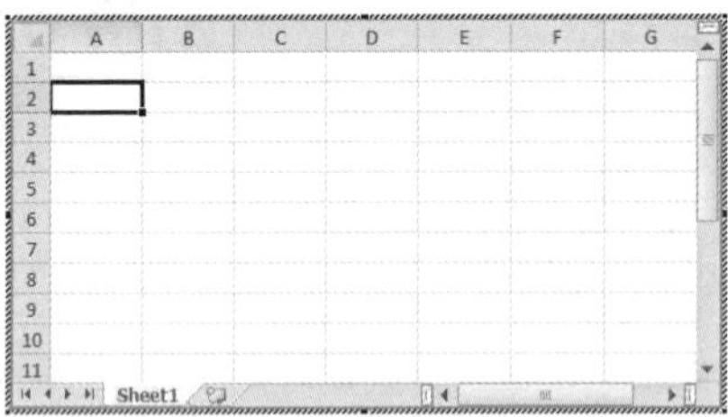

Worksheet inserted into a document

Part of a spreadsheet can be copied and pasted into Word. To do this:

- Select and copy the cells in Excel to be copied.
- Move to the Word document.
- Choose the **Paste** option to link the file.

When the spreadsheet file is updated and saved, it is linked to the Word document and the changes are reflected in the Word document.

Using a spreadsheet as mail merge data source

A spreadsheet can be used as the data source for a mail merge with a Word document. The process is similar to that of a mail merge within Word but the data source is identified as a spreadsheet document.

To use a spreadsheet as a data source, do the following:

- Create the document to be used in the mail merge.
- Choose **Select Recipients** from the **Start Mail Merge** section of the **Mailings** tab.
- Select **Use Existing List** from the menu.
- Note that the default assumption is that the first row of data contains column headers. These column headers are the field names to be inserted in the document.

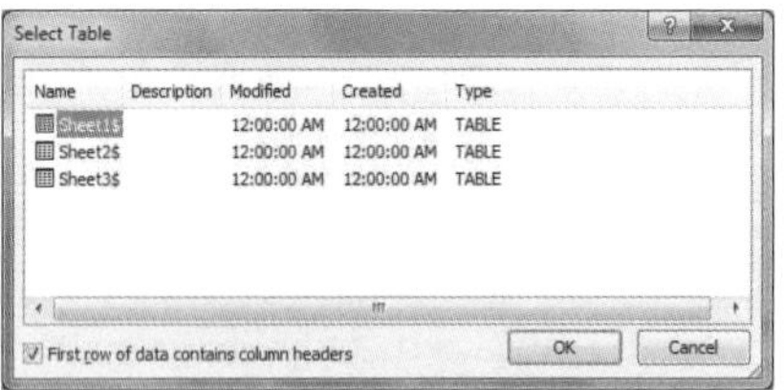

Selecting a worksheet for a mail merge

- Select the **Insert Field Names** option and place the field names in the document.
- Preview the results.
- Finish the merge and print the document.

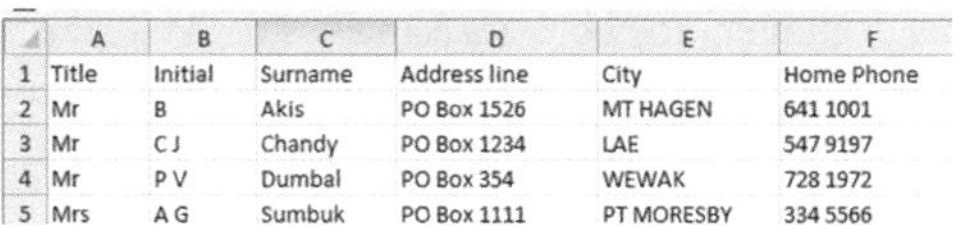

	A	B	C	D	E	F
1	Title	Initial	Surname	Address line	City	Home Phone
2	Mr	B	Akis	PO Box 1526	MT HAGEN	641 1001
3	Mr	C J	Chandy	PO Box 1234	LAE	547 9197
4	Mr	P V	Dumbal	PO Box 354	WEWAK	728 1972
5	Mrs	A G	Sumbuk	PO Box 1111	PT MORESBY	334 5566

Worksheet with field names for a mail merge

Creating a presentation

A PowerPoint presentation can be created from a Word document. To do this, the Word document must have used different level headings as styles.

To do this in PowerPoint:

- Create a new slide using the **New Slide** command on the **Home** tab.
- Select the item **Slides** from **Outline...** from the drop-down list.
- Select the Word document you wish to use.

The hierarchy of headings is imported from the Word document into PowerPoint and the slide or slides are created.

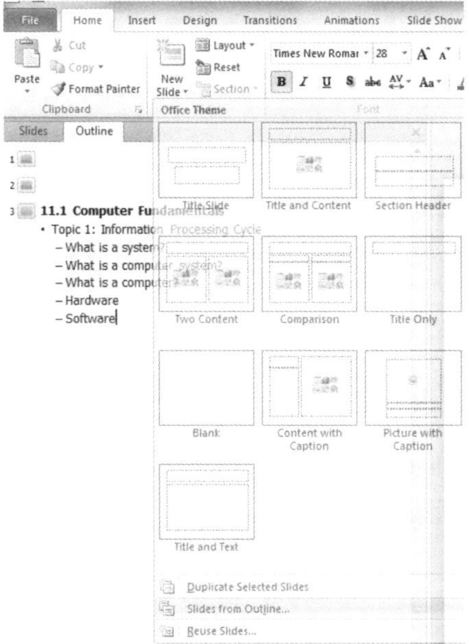

Creating PowerPoint slides from an Outline

Object linking and embedding

Objects such as a spreadsheet, image or a presentation can be placed in a Word document using the **Object** command on the **Text** section of the **Insert** tab.

These objects can be either *linked* or *embedded* in the document. In Microsoft terms, the three-letter acronym **OLE** refers to **Object Linking and Embedding**.

If an object is linked in a document, the object is actually stored outside the document. The contents of the object are displayed in the Word document. If the contents of the object are changed, this is reflected in the Word document.

If an object is embedded in a Word document, it becomes part of that document. The object can be edited by double-clicking on it – this starts the program that was used to create the document and allows the editing to take place.

To insert and object in a Word document, do the following:

- Select the **Insert** tab.
- On the **Text** section of the tab, choose **Object** and select **Object**.
- To select an object from another file, choose **Create from File**.
- Choose the file.
- To insert the file so that it is linked, click in the **Link to file** box.
- To insert the file so that it is embedded, click **OK**, leave the **Link to file** box empty.

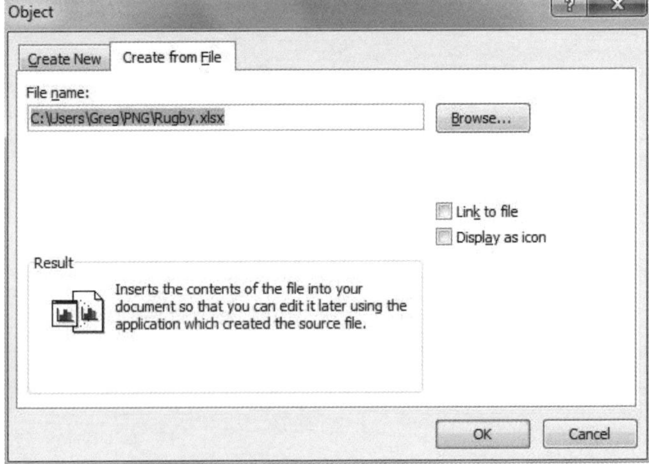

For example, inserting the spreadsheet 'Rugby prices' in a Word document could look like this:

Rugby Prices

	Rugby at	Soccer at LFA Oval
Transport	2.45	1.85
Ticket	10.95	7.85
Food	2.25	5.75
Drink	2.50	3.25
Total	15.70	16.85

If the spreadsheet is linked, changes made in the spreadsheet will be reflected in the Word document.

If the spreadsheet is embedded, changes are made by double clicking on the object and then editing it.

Unit 11.2 Word Processing

Topic 13: Sharing information with other people

Topic 13 explains how to share information with other people (see ICT Syllabus p. 15). It covers:

- Creating documents with restricted permission.
- Protecting document from unauthorised changes.

Creating documents with restricted permission

Documents can be created with restricted permission. By default, anyone can open and change a Word document. However, this can be managed on the **File** tab using the **Info** menu item.

The **Protect Document** menu item gives four different options:

- Mark as Final.
- Encrypt with Password.
- Restrict Editing.
- Add a Digital Signature.

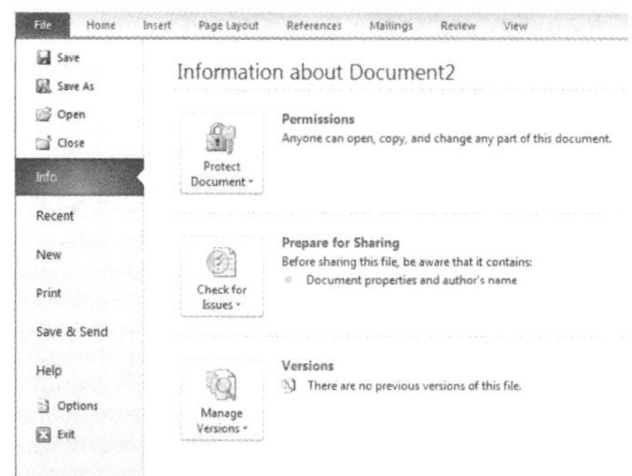

Permissions in Word

Mark as final

Choosing this option means that the document becomes read-only. If you are sharing it with other people, they know that it is a final document and it cannot be changed. It means that people cannot inadvertently or mistakenly make changes to the document.

Encrypt with password

The Encrypt with Password option allows you to set a password for the document. The document can then be opened only by entering the password. When the password is set, it needs to be confirmed by typing it a second time. Passwords are case-sensitive and you must ensure that the Caps Lock is turned off. Passwords cannot be retrieved – if you forget the password you will not be able to access the document.

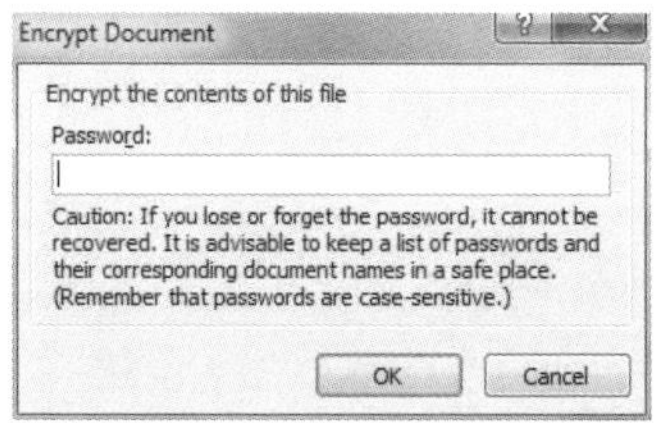

Password protection for a document

Restrict editing

This option allows you to restrict who can edit a document and what type of changes these people can make.

You can limit people to:

- Making formatting changes.
- Editing the document, or parts thereof.

You are able to specify the users either on your network or by creating a list of users.

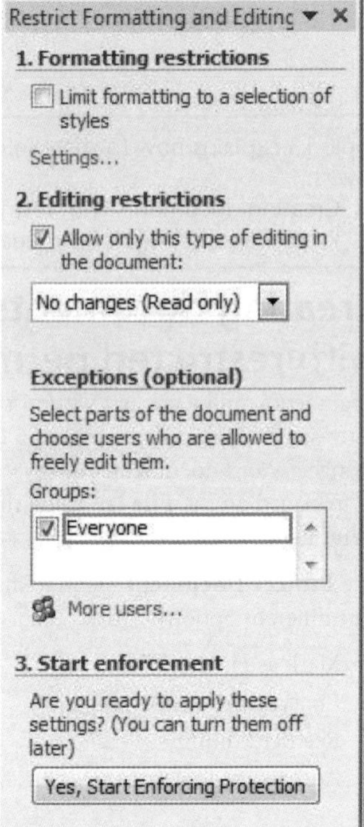

Editing restrictions in Word

Digital signatures

A document can be protected with a **digital signature**. The purpose of a digital signature is to give an assurance that the document is authentic. They are often used for financial transactions or documents involving contracts. The laws regarding digital signatures vary between countries, with particular differences between the USA and Europe.

Microsoft can provide a digital signature for a Word document.

Unit 11.2 Word Processing

Topic 14: Working with online forms

Topic 14 explains how to work with online forms (see ICT Syllabus p. 15). It covers:

- Creating an online form.
- Inserting form fields.
- Preparing the form for distribution.

Creating an online form

Online forms are used for collecting data. An online form has two parts:

- The main document containing information and questions.
- Fields that are to be completed by the user.

Additionally, an online form will usually have some protection built in to prevent users from altering the form and allowing them to enter only the required information.

The creation of an online form requires the **Developer** tab. This tab is not necessarily available on the ribbon. If the Developer tab is not on the ribbon:

- Go to the **File** menu and choose **Options.**
- From the menu on the left, choose **Customize Ribbon**.
- On the right side of the window make sure that the **Check Box** next to the main tab **Developer** is ticked and click **Reset** if necessary.

Now set up the main document with the questions you are going to ask, if it is to be a survey.

Note that you will need to use tools in the **Controls** group on the **Developer** tab to insert fields into a document.

Inserting form fields

Text field

You can start by finding out the name of the respondent. To do this, choose the **Plain Text Content Control** icon:

Aa

The field is inserted in the document and you now select the **Properties** icon. This icon allows you to set options about the field and its content. Enter a name for the field – *Name* – and then click **OK**.

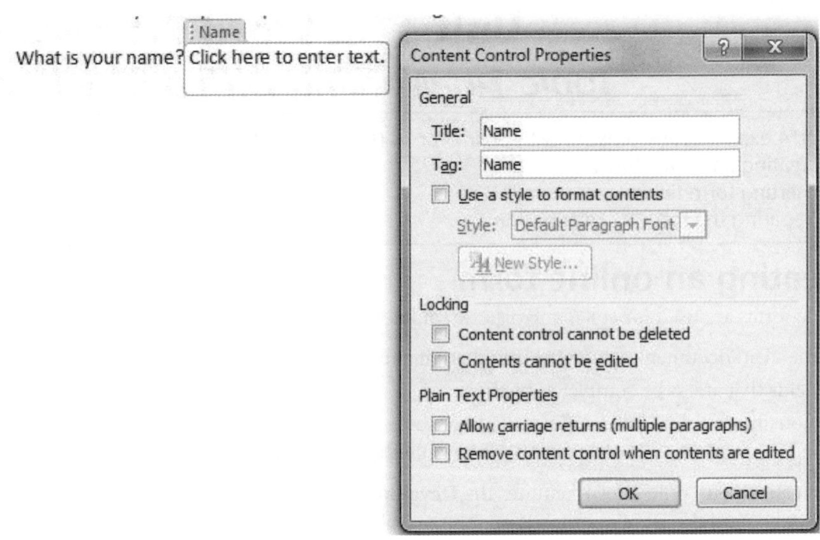

Creating a text field

Date field

You may like to capture the date of attendance at a movie. Dates can be entered in many different ways by users, but the date field option allows the user to select a date from a calendar and ensures that the format is consistent between users.

Use the **Date Picker Content Control** icon to enter this as a date field:

Date Picker Content Control icon

Once again choose **Properties**, and notice that you have a range of date formats that you can choose. If you are happy with the default format, click **OK**. The form now brings up a calendar for the user to select the date.

Drop-down number form field

You might like to capture how often a person attends the movies. This can be done using a drop-down list showing only numbers. To do this, choose the **Drop Down List Content Control** icon:

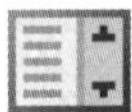

Drop Down List Content Control icon

As before, choose **Properties**, give the field a name and then some values by clicking **Add...** and entering the required vales. When complete, click the **Content Control** check box so that values cannot be altered by the users.

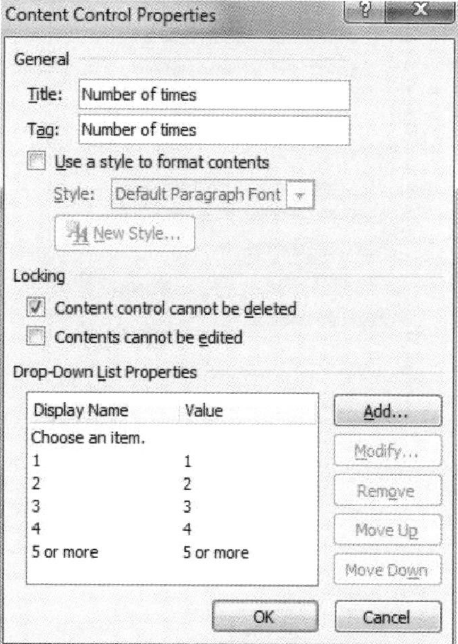

Setting the content for a drop-down list

Note that the values in the drop-down list can be text. The same method can be used to capture text fields by creating a list.

Note that help text should be added to the main document to ensure the questions are meaningful.

Check box

Using a check box is another method of collecting data. The **Check Box Content Control** icon is used to create a check box:

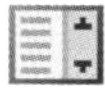

Check Box Content Control icon

As with the other fields, the **Properties** icon allows access to modifying the field.

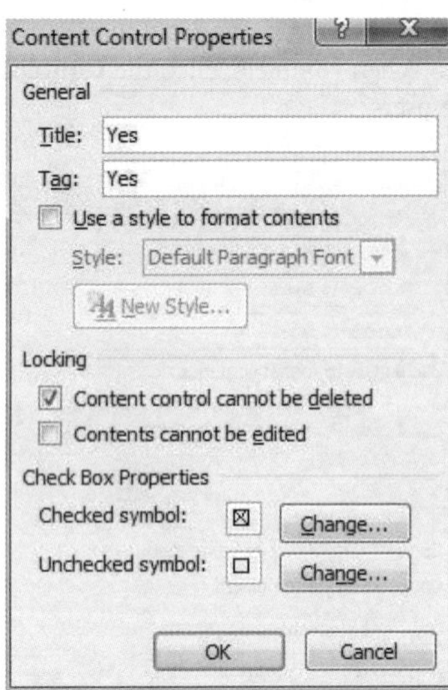

Configuring a check box

For example, the symbol to be used in the check box can be altered. A Yes/No check box could look like this:

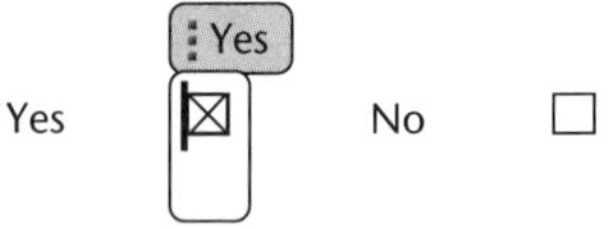

Example of a check box

Preparing the form for distribution

Protecting a form in Word

The document can be protected using the **Protect** menu items in the **Developer** tab. Editing restrictions can be set that only allow the filling in of fields on the form. Starting enforcement requires a password. If the password is lost or forgotten, the document cannot be edited.

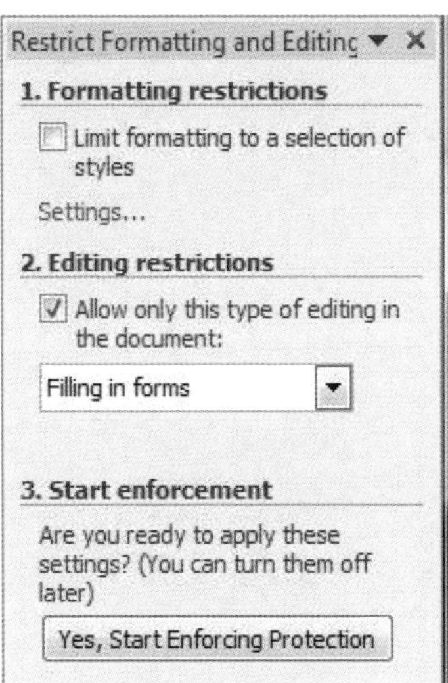

Protecting an interactive form

When the document is distributed, it can be completed by filling in the form, then saved and printed in the normal manner.

Unit 11.3 Computers and Society

Topic 1: Impacts on society

Unit 11.3 explores the role of computers in society. Topic 1 in this Unit explores the impact computers have had on society (see ICT Syllabus pp. 16–17 and Computer Studies Syllabus pp. 20–1). It covers:

- Computers in business, communications, education, entertainment, home, medical world, military and national security, scientific research.
- Employment and career opportunities.

Changing technology brings increasing rates of change in society with consequences both expected and unexpected. The challenges for information systems are to meet the needs of society, to be easy to use, and to allow people to use these systems in a secure and responsible manner.

People increasingly obtain information, make decisions and purchase goods and services by interacting with computers and information systems.

These information systems can impact upon us as individuals through:

- Education, including skills update and training.
- Employment, both what we do and how we do it.
- Communication.
- Electronic commerce.
- Leisure activities.

Developments in online technology have changed our relationships with time and space. It is now commonplace to communicate with people in diverse areas and to carry out transactions without necessarily knowing where those transactions occur.

Understanding information technology and systems in our society sometimes seems beyond the reach of people who do not have the technological skills of those who design and operate the systems. But information technology and systems are used to solve problems for individuals and society and do not exist for their own sake.

Societies must accommodate the needs of all people and the challenge for information technology professionals is to create systems, large and small, that are simple and easy for people to use.

Significance of information systems

Information systems affect the society in which we live. They have an impact upon:

- Political systems.
- Legal systems.

- Economic systems.
- Social structures.

These systems and structures are dependent upon information and communication. Decisions made on the basis of information available today will develop and create the society we live in tomorrow.

Computers in business

In order to maintain a competitive edge and to adhere to government regulations, it is important for organisations to continue to successfully implement and maintain ICT systems.

ICT systems within business are critical to the day-to-day operation and long-term success of the business.

Businesses have developed a range of information systems that operate both internally and externally. Some of the internal functions of the systems used by businesses are:

- Manage their staff with human resource systems.
- Manage their budgets with financial packages including:
    - Accounting packages.
    - Sales.
    - Payroll.
- Manage control of stock for sale.
- Provide a source of up-to-date information about the company.
- Provide tools for staff to collaborate using a company's intranet.

Computers are embedded within many organisations and have become vital components of the running of those organisations.

Many businesses deal with customers and the general public through external systems. These include:

- **Websites** providing information about the company and its services.
- Online transactions for sales and services.
- Tracking goods that are in transit.
- Quotations for products and services.

Large businesses now have dedicated ICT departments to meet their organisation's needs. Many new businesses have emerged to meet these needs. There are also many industries that have been changed significantly by the use of computers.

Online retailing

Amazon.com was founded in 1994 and went online in 1995. It was the first significant online retailer. Amazon has profoundly changed the nature of retail sales.

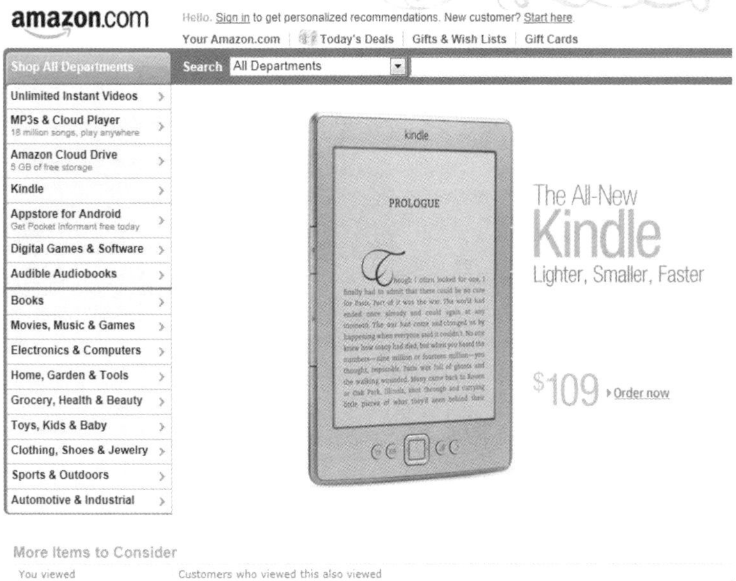

Amazon.com – online retailing

Amazon initially sold only books but quickly diversified into a large range of goods including CDs, DVDs, electronics, sporting goods and clothes.

Amazon has centres around the world to fill orders. These centres are based in the USA, Canada, Europe and Asia.

Amazon became profitable for the first time in 2001. Amazon has acquired a number of other companies and it also hosts and operates online retail sites for other organisations.

Amazon works in the following manner:

- New users create a login.
- Users log in with a user name and password.
- Amazon attempts to personalise the shopping experience and it recommends items that the user might be interested in based on past purchases.

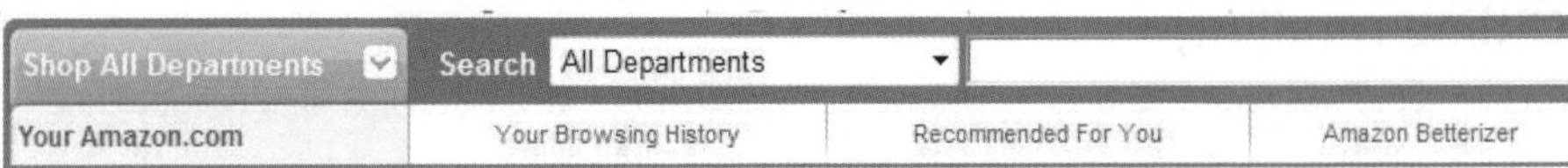

Greg, Welcome to Your Amazon.com (If you're not Mr Greg Baker, click here.)

Today's Recommendations For You

Here's a daily sample of items recommended for you. Click here to **see all recommendations**.

Secrets of the Sommeliers: Ho... (Hardcover) by Rajat Parr
(18) $20.79
Fix this recommendation

Yquem (Hardcover) by Richard Olney
(5) $43.96
Fix this recommendation

MOS 2010 Study Guide for Mi... (Paperback) by Joan Lamb...
(10) $26.99
Fix this recommendation

Personalised recommendations from Amazon

- The user browses the catalogue.
- Items are added to a shopping cart.
- When finished, the user proceeds to the checkout.
- Shipping details are entered and a shipping method is selected.
- Payment is made using a credit card or debit card.

Amazon keeps the purchaser informed of the progress of the sale by email and also offers the opportunity to track the parcels.

Many retail organisations have had to change how they operate to compete with Amazon. Many other online sales organisations have been created.

Amazon operates around the world and transactions can take place at any time of the day or night.

Travel

Computer technology and the Internet have also changed the way in which people book travel throughout the world.

For many years, travel bookings were made exclusively through travel agents or directly with airlines. The new technology has given consumers the opportunity to take responsibility for making their own travel arrangements. Travel agents have lost much of their traditional business and have had to change the way they operate and the services they offer.

Air Niugini offers the opportunity to book online

Other online travel organisations offer flights, hotel bookings, hire cars and travel advice around the world.

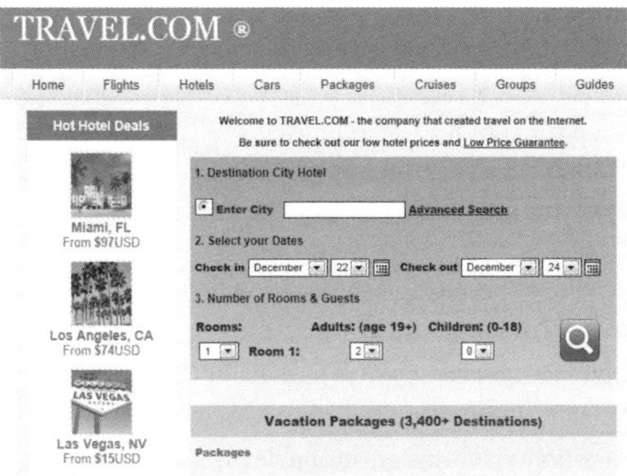

Travel.com offers a range of travel options around the world

Share broking

Stocks and shares on the stock market were previously sold through stockbrokers who charge fees for each transaction.

Online share broking has changed the way in which stockbrokers operate. The cost of individual transactions has dropped and the consumer has been able to perform many of the functions that were previously carried out by stockbrokers.

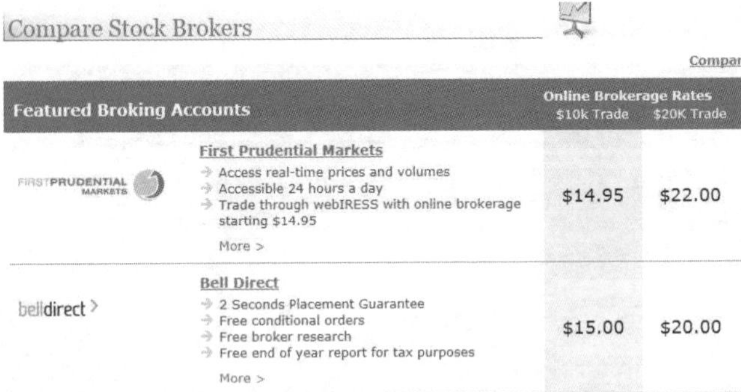

Some online stockbrokers

Communications

Computers and networks are fundamental tools in communication systems. At home, at work and in leisure activities, a range of different communication activities take place. These include:

An Internet Protocol telephone

- Email is now a fundamental way of communicating between individuals and within organisations.
- Internet Protocol (IP) telephony is widely used across computers and networks. IP telephones have a range of features not available on the public switched phone networks.
- Products such as Skype are used to communicate across the Internet using both voice and images. Skype allows users to reduce the cost of long-distance and international calls.
- Instant messaging and text messaging have become popular as quick and relatively inexpensive methods of communicating.
- Social media including Facebook, YouTube and Twitter are widely used to facilitate communication.

Many of these communication platforms are available on mobile devices such as smartphones and iPads as well as computer systems.

In summary, the number of communication devices has increased significantly. The methods by which people are able to communicate have also increased. Many people are now available to communicate 24 × 7, ie 24 hours per day, every day of the week.

Air Niugini uses Facebook and YouTube

However, some of the communication methods and devices can become annoying and intrusive. Many clubs and organisations ban the use of mobile phones inside their premises. Listening to another person's telephone conversation on a PMV can be annoying. Mobile telephone calls can interrupt face-to-face discussions.

Many people value the different methods of communication for the immediacy of the communication and the ease with which they can stay in contact.

Education

When computers were first introduced into schools, they were accompanied by specialist subjects with a heavy emphasis on programming. Students were taught about computers and learnt methods of computer programming.

When software applications such as word processors, spreadsheets and databases became commonly available, general subjects, often called Computer Studies, were developed.

Keyboarding is now needed at all year levels. Computer competency is integrated across the curriculum. Students are increasingly developing information literacy skills for use with online Internet services.

Changes in the curriculum in this area are ongoing. This reflects the changes in the general levels of skill students have, and the changes in technology caused by increasingly sophisticated software and hardware.

One-to-one computing

In the mid-1990s one-to-one computing was first introduced into some Australian schools. This involved each student having a personal notebook computer that he or she brought to school every day and used at home.

A lot of the activities were based on Seymour Papert's research at the MIT Media Laboratory in the USA. It involved a theory of learning where students learn by doing and creating knowledge. It is led by skilled teachers and challenged the then traditional role of the teacher in front of the classroom.

Using computers in a classroom

The Australian model of one-to-one computing schools has been adopted by many states in the USA and some European countries. The development of the Apple iPad and other similar devices has further accelerated the movement to one-to-one computing for students in schools throughout the world.

One-to-one computing enabled the technology to become embedded into classroom practice and computer usage became embedded in the curriculum.

Role of the teacher

Information technology thus had an impact on the role of the teacher and the educational institution. Rather than being reservoirs of knowledge, in many schools, teachers have become more involved as facilitators and mentors for the students.

Students are working in teams to complete projects using methods closely reflecting those used in the workplace. Teachers act as guides and advisors.

This concept has been challenging for many teachers. They needed continued training in the use of hardware and software and had to develop new skills.

As the technology evolves, teachers have had to continually learn to adjust and adapt to use that technology in an effective manner.

Distance learning

Educational institutions, where there is emphasis on individual responsibility and self-directed learning, are competing for students on an international scale rather than within a country. Many courses will be promoted and conducted using online services.

Many universities throughout the world are offering online courses at both the undergraduate and graduate levels. The universities have developed software that allows some social interaction with other students whilst allowing students flexibility in when and where they learn.

The universities accept students from anywhere in the world.

Online Courses: Distance Education at Harvard

Harvard online courses at the Extension School

Study from anywhere in the world. We offer more than 150 Harvard online classes, available in 2 formats, in fall and spring semesters.

Harvard University in the USA offers online courses

Materials and resources online

The volume of information available online is increasing at a rapid rate. The quality varies depending on the source of the information. The information is more detailed and enables investigation of areas that once required detailed evidence-gathering and research. Scrutiny of resources takes time and an understanding of how useful it might be for the purposes of study.

Encyclopaedias have been replaced by online resources such as Wikipedia.

Online information has also changed the way school libraries operate. Many libraries now offer a great variety of digital information as well as traditional books.

Modes of assessment

Assessment by written examination may be phased out as the skills these examinations require are supplanted by the use of computers in the classroom. As students increasingly use computers in their daily school life, the assessment of their studies with handwritten responses seems to contradict the purpose of acquiring computer skills. However, some people are concerned at the impact on students' handwriting skills.

Resources for computing

To equip schools with the latest technology requires significant funds, both to set up the equipment and to continue to maintain and improve it. Funds need to be provided for such things as:

- Computer hardware and peripheral devices.
- Networking and cabling.
- Organisation of fixtures and fittings.
- Software with appropriate licensing.
- Power for computers, printers, scanners.
- Technical and maintenance staff.

Schools require additional funding and government support to keep up with the latest developments. In some countries governments have provided significant funding, while in others the burden has been borne by the local school communities.

The continued professional development and training of teachers is also of critical importance.

The classroom of tomorrow

The classroom of tomorrow will be quite different from the traditional classroom of desks and chairs with the teacher at the front of the class.

Classrooms will allow for:

- Individual curriculums suited to a student's needs, interests and abilities.
- Flexible and different learning styles.
- Students learning at different rates.
- Students collaborating on tasks and projects.
- A range of different devices for teaching and learning, including personal handheld devices connected to the school's network.

The modes of assessment will also change to allow different skills to be assessed and in different ways.

Entertainment

Computers and the Internet have provided many different forms of entertainment for individuals and groups. Some of the ways in which computers are used for entertainment are listed below.

Games for individuals

The computer industry has seen the development of games for all ages. They range from simple games that simulate the use of cards, such as Solitaire, to more complex games.

Simulations that can be played over a period of time have been very popular. For example, SimCity simulates the building of a city over time and allows the user to make decisions about the type of development that takes place and the infrastructure needed for that development. This is an example of an open-ended simulation.

SimCity – a popular simulation

After the success of SimCity a number of other simulations were developed, including SimTower and The Sims. A number of other game products have been developed and there are online communities.

Most computer operating systems come with a small number of games.

Games for multiple players

Games have been developed that allow people to compete against each other using the Internet. One very successful game of this type is Microsoft's Age of Empires series. These are strategy games that started out being based on the Roman Empire.

Age of Empires can be played as a stand-alone game or in a community of users.

Age of Empires strategy game

Online games

There are many online games available from sites such as www.games.com. Some of these games are played online, while others will need to be downloaded.

Free Online Games from Games.com

Games.com is home to over 2,400 Free Games and Premium Downloads.

Ice Breakers

35 levels of puzzle matching excitement only on Games.com!

Play Ice Breakers

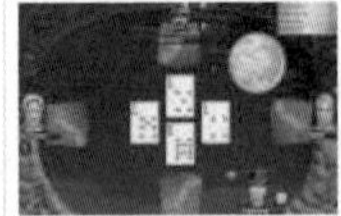

Hearts

Shoot the Moon if you're feeling brave.

Club 300 Bowling

All the fun of bowling without the lame shoes.

Word Zen

Word puzzle & Mahjong in one great game.

Broke

Try this new take on the classic Breakout game.

Online games

Care needs to be taken when using online games. In some cases, people create different aliases and attempt to entrap people into doing foolish things.

Games can also be a source of viruses.

Online gambling is another form of entertainment, but this can be very dangerous for unsuspecting people to use.

Entertainment centre

The computer can be used as an entertainment centre. Activities include:

- Listening to music.
- Downloading music.
- Watching videos, either online or on a DVD.
- Downloading movies.
- Creating and accessing photograph albums.

The YouTube site at http://www.youtube.com/ is a popular source of online videos and allows users to post videos.

Care needs to be taken by users to ensure that copyright restrictions on music and video are adhered to at all times.

ICT in the home

High-definition television set

Computing devices are becoming a central part of life at home. In particular:

- Many homes have wireless networks that connect multiple devices.
- The use of the Internet in the home enables communication and collaboration.
- In the future, Internet-ready devices will be installed in homes. An example of such a device is a refrigerator that will allow the user to control it remotely from a computer or a handheld device.

The emergence of digital television sets is seeing the convergence of devices in the home. Digital television provides:

- High-quality images.
- A larger range of television channels than that provided by the analog television sets.
- The ability to record multiple programs and to replay them easily.
- High-quality surround sound.

ICT in the medical world

The use of **ICT** is having a profound impact on the medical world.

In medical practices, management software is being widely used to allow the efficient and effective management of the business. Typical software packages include a number of modules, including:

- Appointment scheduling and management.
- Medical billing and integration with government systems.
- Patient records, including notes.
- Medical imaging, including storage and retrieval.
- Management of prescriptions.

Medical imaging

Computers are being used in medical imaging. In these applications, images of parts of the body are created for diagnosis of injuries or to reveal damaged or diseased organs.

The types of techniques used include:

- X-ray.
- Magnetic resonance imaging (MRI): powerful magnets are used to create images.
- Ultrasound: high-frequency broadband sound waves are used to create images. These are often used in managing pregnancies.

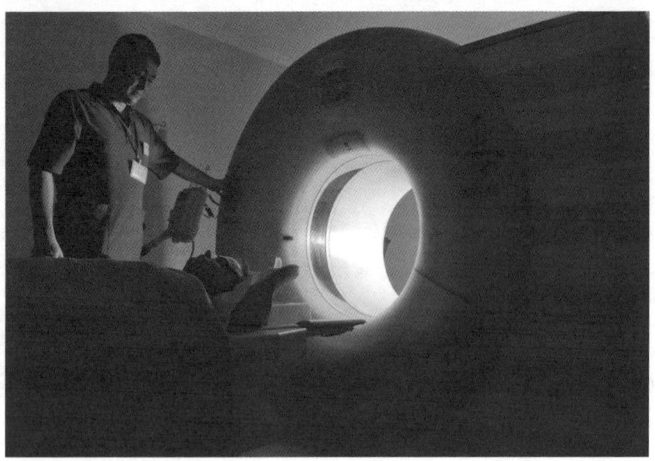

A magnetic resonance imaging system

Online medical services

Online medical services can provide:

- Information about medical conditions and drugs.
- Access to medical experts.
- Online learning and reference materials for medical professionals.

Services such as these can provide continuing education for medical practitioners.

Remote medical services

Remote medical services can be provided using the computer and Internet technology. These services can be provided for patients in remote areas that are difficult to reach, or in emergencies.

The technology enables access to a doctor experienced in telemedicine when an incident occurs in an isolated environment and when people are under stress.

There are companies that specialise in the provision of such services.

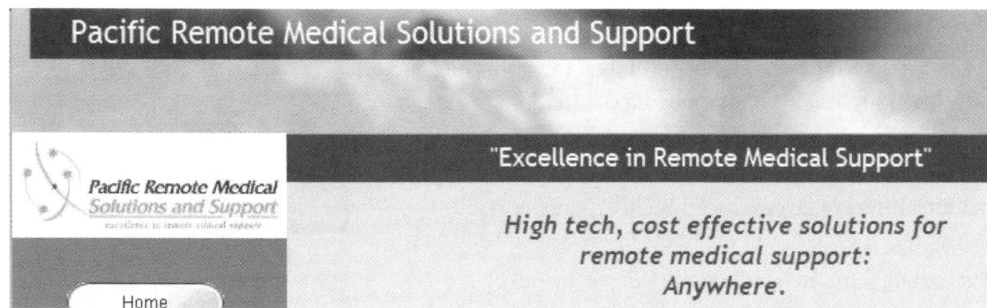

An example of a company providing remote medical support

ICT in the military and national security

Military and national security are areas that have driven research and development of ICT systems and devices.

National security refers to the survival of the state using economic, political and military power. Nations rate national security as a very high priority and thus large amounts of funds are spent in this area.

Some of the areas in which ICT is of great importance are:

- The use of intelligence services to detect, avoid or defeat threats to the state.
- The provision of effective and efficient armed services.
- The detection of internal threats using intelligence services.
- Implementing measures in times of national emergency and disaster.

The terrorist attacks in the USA on 11 September 2001 highlighted the importance of the role of intelligence services in detecting threats.

Since that time, much effort and large amounts of funds have been devoted to the improvement of such services. One particular focus has been on the integration of separate databases spread among many of the different agencies. Hence, systems integration has become important.

Intelligence services use a range of technologies including:

- Satellites that circle the Earth recording images and radio signals that are then analysed.
- Databases that track the movement of people and that identify likely areas of concern.
- Communication systems that track the movement of funds around the world.

A satellite circles the Earth

Weapons systems

Weapons systems have highly developed range-finding and target-seeking ICT systems embedded into them.

Armed servicemen and servicewomen use computers in the field for communication and weapons guidance. Computer manufacturers have developed highly robust portable computers for the use of members of the armed services.

The military and national security departments of governments are prolific users of technology. Many of the significant developments that have become commonplace at home started out as military applications. There are many more applications of ICT within the military services.

A serviceman in the field

Scientific research

Scientists, engineers and researchers are able to use ICT facilities to put together and analyse vast amounts of data. The scientists can concentrate on the theories and use the processing power of the modern computers to test those theories.

Solving mathematical equations

Many scientific problems require the solving of complex mathematical equations to verify and test solutions. Software programs have been developed that remove the human error in these complex calculations and are able to provide answers to these calculations.

Some examples of the software in use are:

- Mathematica, developed by Wolfram Research.
- MATLAB, for use with technical computing for scientists and engineers.
- Maxima, for the manipulation of mathematical expressions.

Prediction modelling

Computer models are developed to investigate how data might appear in the future. These models are used to predict things such as changes in climate, how a newly engineered product might behave, and the effects of medications on people.

Australian Synchrotron

The Australian Synchrotron opened in Melbourne, Australia, in 2007 and is a significant research facility for the scientific community. It was funded by both the Australian government and the State of Victoria.

These state-of-the-art facilities have ICT resources embedded into the operation to assist the research capabilities of scientists from Australia and its near neighbours.

The Australian Synchrotron in Melbourne

Employment and career opportunities

Technology and changing skills

Technology changes the way work is performed. Businesses use new technology to seek a competitive edge, to reduce costs and to remain competitive.

Employees need skills that reflect the tasks they are required to perform in their employment.

Although the effect of technology on the business depends on the type of business, there is continued change in all work places. A business cannot expect to be operating tomorrow the way it was operating yesterday.

Introduction of technology means that the skills required to carry out particular tasks need to be evaluated. In some cases, new technology affects the employment task itself.

Deskilling

Deskilling occurs when workers' skills are replaced or partly replaced by automation. This means that the skill level of the worker is reduced. If human skills are no longer required, then job losses could occur.

Multiskilling

Many employers find it desirable for employees to have skills in more than one area. The employees' chances of remaining in the same industry are enhanced if they are able to perform a wide range – rather than a narrow range – of tasks.

Redundancy

If a job is replaced by new technology, then the worker faces losing that job. Sometimes many jobs of a particular type may disappear.

Banks, for example, have dramatically reduced their employment levels, particularly the number of bank tellers, as new technologies have changed the way they operate. The use of automatic teller machines and online banking has reduced the need for bank tellers in branches.

Reskilling

Reskilling occurs when the worker acquires skills additional to those already possessed. Skills essential to one technology may change as a new technology is introduced. Skills in photography, for example, change if the process moves from 35 mm film to digital cameras. The manner in which photographs are edited and used changes in this process.

Training

Ongoing training is required for most occupations today. The pace of change in the workplace requires employees to be up to date with the changes taking place and to be aware of the implications for their workplace and the daily tasks they perform.

Training staff in the use of new technology is a significant cost for employers. But if the training is not done, the cost may be greater through low productivity, errors and wasted time.

Changing patterns of work

Changing patterns in working hours can to some extent be attributed to the changing shape of information technology and information systems.

For example, current trends in workplace management include:

- Increasing part-time work.
- An increasing number of women in the labour force.
- The increasing use of short-term contract labour and consultants rather than full-time employees.
- The shifting of work hours outside traditional business working hours.

Telecommuting

Telecommuting is defined as working from home using a computer and telecommunications equipment to link to the employee's place of employment. Data is transmitted to and from the place of employment without the employee being physically present.

Telecommuting requires equipment including:

- Telephone access.
- Computer: a desktop if working from home, a notebook computer if moving around.
- Reliable and fast access to the Internet.
- Access to a multifunction device that provides printing, scanning and copying.
- Secure access to the employee's network.

Advantages of working from home

The advantages of working from home for some employees include:

- Saving the time, energy and expense used in commuting.
- Less disruption and distraction from other workers.
- Easier sharing of life between work and family.
- The possibility of flexible hours of work.

For organisations, the advantages include:

- Cost savings, with the employer able to make savings on facilities including office space and equipment.
- The ability to offer valued employees flexibility in their working arrangements.
- The productivity of an employee working at home can be greater than at work.

Disadvantages of working from home

The disadvantages of working from home include:

- The need for clearly defined work areas at home.
- Possible interruptions from family, neighbours and friends.
- Lack of immediate technical support.
- Lack of personal communication and interaction with fellow employees.

For organisations, the disadvantages include:

- Possible lack of supervision and also collaboration of the employee's work.
- Security issues are increased with secure network access required.
- Loss of the ability to 'brainstorm' or discuss ideas and concerns.
- The possible erosion of the corporate culture.

Telecommuting has become a popular way of working for many employees who are looking for flexibility and independence while doing their work.

Call centres

People interact with organisations and government by a variety of methods, including by letters, facsimile, live chat, email and telephone.

A call centre

A telephone call centre is a centralised workspace that an organisation uses to handle telephone calls to and from customers. Call centres usually have a significant amount of computer automation. Call centres can handle large volumes of calls. They are able to screen the calls and a call can be forwarded to the most appropriate person.

The computer automation and tracking allows the organisation to obtain a lot of information about the calls and their effectiveness.

Call centres are used by telemarketing companies, customer help desks and large organisations that sell a high volume of products and services. In times of emergencies, governments will establish call centres to manage the high number of calls.

Some call centres use automated systems to direct calls. The caller is presented with a range of options and uses the keypad to select the correct option or options. Some call centres use voice recognition software to respond to calls or to direct the call appropriately.

The establishment and growth of call centres has provided flexibility for the workforce. A lot of casual and part-time work has become available and many women have taken roles in such organisations.

Call centres can be set up in countries other than the one in which the call originates. Some organisations have used call centres in different countries to reduce their operational costs.

E-commerce

Electronic commerce (e-commerce) is buying and selling goods and services using digital networks.

Usually the transactions are carried out across the Internet. Increasingly transactions are being carried out using handheld devices such as a smartphone.

An e-commerce transaction usually has the following steps:

- The customer accesses a website and identifies the goods or services required.
- The purchase is usually done using a shopping cart application.
- Payment is made using a credit card or some other electronic payment method.

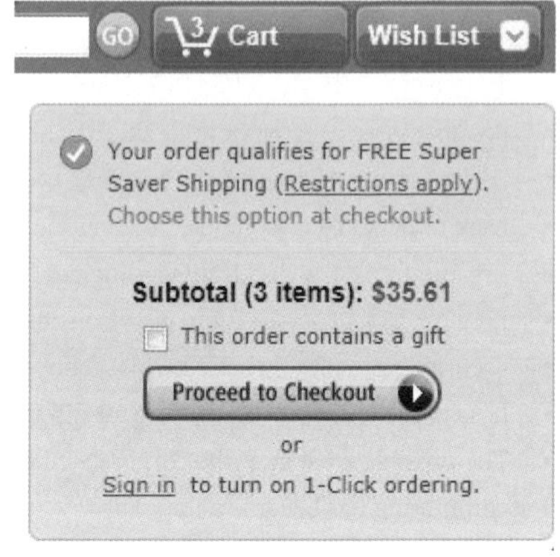

This shopping cart has three items

Some e-commerce sites require the purchaser to create an account with a user name (often an email address) and a password.

E-commerce must use 'secure' sites and ensure the transaction takes place in a secure environment, often identified by a 'https' in the web address and a 'padlock' icon in the browser. This means the transactions are encrypted.

E-commerce stores do not need a shop-front business, often called a 'bricks and mortar' business, for customers to physically visit. Goods are packaged at warehouses and distributed through the postal service or other delivery channels.

Service businesses are particularly suited to e-commerce, such as:

- Banking.
- Travel and accommodation.
- Share trading.
- Retail, including books, whitegoods and clothes.

The transactions are documented electronically with invoices and documents that can be printed if required. Customers with accounts can log in to the e-commerce site and view their transaction history.

Some traditional retailers are concerned that online businesses are reducing their share of the market and undercutting the prices of goods.

E-commerce purchases do not always attract local taxes. In Australia, some online purchases avoid the goods and services tax. In the USA, many state sales taxes are not paid.

Advantages of e-commerce

There are a number of advantages of using e-commerce. These include:

- Business can trade 24 hours a day, 7 days a week.
- Customer purchases and interests can be recorded and used in marketing. This technique was pioneered by Amazon.
- Niche and specialist product markets can be catered for and developed by businesses.
- Producers of goods and services can deal directly with customers.

Disadvantages of e-commerce

- Purchasers need to be careful that they are dealing with a real business and ensure that the goods and services will meet expectations.
- There may be no opportunity to physically inspect the goods before purchase.
- Where goods and services are purchased overseas, the terms and conditions of sale and laws that apply to the transaction may differ.
- Stolen credit cards and credit card information may be used in fraudulent transactions.
- Packing and shipping goods can be expensive.

E-commerce applications have allowed new types of companies and organisations to operate. To an extent, they can be operated outside local trading conditions and can provide a wide range of goods and services.

eBay is a widely used e-commerce site

Online or phone banking

A banking transaction is an exchange of information. The value of all transactions conducted using notes and coin currency is small compared to the value of transactions conducted electronically.

Banks and financial institutions have enabled clients to conduct financial transactions using websites. A user name and password access provides access to a wide range of banking services. Some banks provide confirmation of the transfer of funds by the use of a text message to a mobile phone.

Shop-front banks are required less by clients and some banks actively discourage these with fees that only apply when a client visits a bank.

The staff required in bank branches has declined. However, the staff for networks and security and information system infrastructure has increased.

Some banks use call centres to manage customer requests and some of these call centres are offshore. Some banks also outsource some of their ICT development to countries other than where the banks are physically located.

Cloud computing

Cloud computing refers to the hosting of a service to an organisation or an individual via the Internet. Cloud computing services have three characteristics:

- The services are sold on demand and the user can pay by the minute or the hour.
- The services are elastic; the user decides how much of the service is to be used.
- The provider of the service takes full responsibility for the operation and management of that service.

Many individuals use cloud services from vendors such as Microsoft, Google and Yahoo. For example, Google services include Google Mail (Gmail) and Google Docs. Google Docs includes word processing, spreadsheets and presentations. The documents are stored on the Internet (in 'the cloud') and can be accessed by any computer that is connected to the Internet. There is no need to have individual versions of the application software stored on the computer.

Some organisations use cloud servers for:

- Computer servers.
- Running applications.
- Storage.

The users of the services have little or no control over the geographical location of where the data is stored or where the services actually take place.

Founded in 1999, Salesforce.com is one of the leading providers of cloud services to organisations. The services it provides include:

- Sales force automation.
- Marketing tools.
- Social networking tools.
- A platform for building and hosting websites.

Transform your business with the trusted leader in cloud computing and CRM.

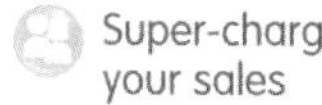

Super-charge your sales

Sales Cloud
The world's #1 sales application
View demo | Pricing

Data.com®
B2B sales and marketing account and contact data
View demo | Pricing

Deliver amazing service

Service Cloud
Customer service for the social enterprise
View demo | Pricing

Remedyforce
The leading ITIL-based help desk, now in the cloud
View demo

Join the conversation

Chatter
A secure, private social network for your business
View demo | Pricing

Radian6
Social media monitoring and engagement
Learn more

Build killer apps

Force.com
The cloud platform for custom application development
View demo | Pricing

Database.com
The trusted cloud database
View demo

Heroku
The platform to build social and mobile apps on Ruby and Java
Learn more

Some of the services offered by Salesforce.com

Unit 11.3 Activity 1A: Working from home

1. Would you like to work from home?
   - **a.** List the advantages of working from home.
   - **b.** List the disadvantages of working from home.
   - **c.** Would you need to rearrange the fixtures, fittings and furniture at home to be able to work successfully?

2. Interview a person who predominantly works from home. Some general questions you could ask include:
   - **a.** Is the person self-employed or an employee?
   - **b.** Why did the person decide to use his or her home as the place of work?
   - **c.** What changes did the person need to make to the home to equip it adequately for work?
   - **d.** How does working from home differ from having a separate place of work?
   - **e.** What forms of communication to the workplace from home are the most important?
   - **f.** Are interruptions and distractions to work more likely in a workplace or at home?
   - **g.** Would the ability to work at home be an important consideration if the person changed jobs?
   - **h.** Has the person become a better employee or worker?

Unit 11.3 Computers and Society

Topic 2: Measures to protect computers and data

Unit 11.3 explores the role of computers in society. Topic 2 in this Unit focuses on the various measures needed to protect computers and data (see ICT Syllabus p. 17 and Computer Studies Syllabus p. 21). It covers:

- Protection of data.
- Identification and access.
- Safety requirements – user and equipment.

Protection of data

There are many threats to information systems used by organisations and individuals on computer systems. Threats can be grouped into external or internal threats. Threats can be accidental or deliberate.

External threats

Examples of external threats are:

- Theft of equipment and/or files.
- Theft through industrial espionage.
- Damage to systems and information by a virus.
- Damage to systems and information by hackers obtaining unauthorised access.

Where an organisation has portable computers and devices accessing a network, the data on these devices is very susceptible to theft. Portable storage devices such as flash memory drives can also hold large amounts of valuable data.

Internal threats

Examples of internal threats are:

- A disgruntled employee may damage or erase data files; sometimes this may involve unauthorised access within a system.
- Employees may accidentally damage or lose files.
- An employee may provide confidential data to an outside organisation.

Accidental threats

Examples of accidental threats are:

- Fire, water or smoke damage.
- Power loss and power surges.
- Incompatibility of software and hardware which may cause data loss.
- System and hardware failures that occur on an irregular basis.

Backup procedures

A **backup** is a copy of an original file that is kept on a storage medium. Backups are kept so that they can be used if anything happens to the original file or files.

Organisations keep backups to ensure that a system can be restored in case of failure.

Types of backups

The types of backups are:

- Full backup: every file is copied to an appropriate storage medium. This can take a long time and other activity on the computer should be stopped to ensure the task is completed.
- System backup: copies only the system files so that the operating system can be recreated but user data is not backed up.
- Incremental backup: only those files that have changed since the last backup will be done. Specialist software is used to do this task.
- Selective backup: the user selects particular files to be backed up.

Making backups

Most organisations will have formal procedures for backing up their systems. They will typically use specialist software to carry out the backups.

They will use a combination of:

- Regular full backups, perhaps weekly.
- Incremental backups, perhaps daily.

They may replicate data across the organisation's network. A tape system as described in Chapter 1 may be used for data storage. RAID systems will be used to help ensure the integrity of the data.

Many organisations will:

- Store backup tapes off site; or
- Replicate backup data across the network to different physical locations.

Some organisations will use backups in the cloud, as described in Unit 11.1.

The backup procedure needs to account for:

- What: what data and/or system files will be backed up?
- When: at what time will it be backed up and how long will it take?
- Who: who makes sure that the backup occurs and takes responsibility for the backup?
- How: how will the backup be saved and how will it then be physically stored safely?

Testing of backup strategy

It is necessary to check that a backup strategy is working to plan. A test environment should be set up with checks to ensure that the backup is correct and can be restored to equipment.

Symantec Backup Exec is a commercial product that is widely used

Individual users can back up files on a Windows computer using the backup utility that is available in the **Control Panel**.

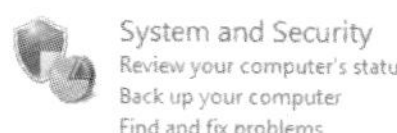

Backups can be carried out from the Control Panel

Data security

In most information systems, the data is shared by many people. This makes the data vulnerable to improper access or use.

Security measures need to be put in place to ensure:

- Accuracy.
- Integrity.
- Timeliness.
- Security.

Factors affecting data security

Factors that affect data security include:

- Procedures for updating the information system: additions, deletions, modifications of data.
- Security to ensure that only appropriate, authorised users have access to certain data.
- Security to ensure that only appropriate users have modification rights: user privileges.
- Backup procedures to ensure that the integrity of the data is not affected when the computer system fails: regular backups, off-site backups, disk shadowing, redundant systems, failsafe systems.
- Protection against external factors: hackers, viruses, power failures, disasters.

Threats to data and files

Backups are needed to protect against loss if any or all of the following occur:

- Power surges or power failures can cause the computer to shut down suddenly. If this occurs when the disk is being accessed, the disk may be damaged and need repair. Most organisations will use a universal power supply (UPS) to minimise the effects of power failures by enabling controlled shutdown using backup battery power.
- A fault in the system software can cause the files to be damaged. Causes of this include software conflicts, alterations to the system software when new software is installed, and errors in the software. No application is error-free. Errors are called 'bugs'. Software companies can provide updates so that serious problems can be resolved.
- Computer viruses can cause files to be damaged. Organisations and individuals use anti-virus software to protect computers but these are not always successful and can be difficult to keep up to date.
- Hardware malfunction: a physical error in the computer hardware may cause a computer to malfunction. Software may need to be re-installed after a computer is repaired.
- Damage to the hard disk can be caused by knocking or moving it when it is in use. If the disk has to be replaced or reformatted, backup files will be required.
- Files can be accidentally deleted from a hard disk. This is usually done in error by a user. If an important file is mistakenly deleted, it may need to be restored from a backup file.
- A file can be changed by the user who could then decide the original file is needed.
- If a computer is lost or stolen, backup disks can be used to recreate lost files on another computer.

Storage

Data needs to be safely stored for easy retrieval when needed. Data is stored on:

- Hard disks.
- Optical disks.
- Tapes for backup.
- Flash memory.

In systems that have very high data integrity needs, disk shadowing is used to keep up-to-date copies of the data on more than one disk.

Secure and reliable backup procedures are needed to ensure the ongoing integrity of the data.

Storing documents for the future

The longevity of a document as a means of communication depends upon:

- The technology used to produce the document.
- The storage medium used to store the document.

Paper has until recently been the predominant medium for communicating and storing information. A digital document may perhaps only exist as a computer file, but is required to be kept.

Recreating a document from a computer file

The ease with which the document can be retrieved and recreated depends on:

- The computer operating system.
- The software used.
- The format in which the document is saved.
- The technical demands of any compression or encryption scheme that may be applied to the file.

Identifying a document

A document prepared using a computer is distinctively recognised by the operating system and the software used to produce the document.

A newsletter, for example, could be produced using Microsoft Word 2011 and Publisher 2011 with a computer using the Windows operating system.

The document could be archived on a CD. This information would be the minimum required for another person to access the document without having to use trial and error.

Disk storage formats

If a document is to be accessed in the future, perhaps five, ten or 20 years from now, the storage medium used to archive the document is a factor in determining whether the document can be recreated. If the document was on a CD, for example, will the computer have a disk drive and will the drive be able to read the disk format?

What is the longevity of the storage medium, for example how long will a CD last, and what are the storage conditions that are optimal for longevity?

The floppy disk was invented in 1971. It is a magnetic storage device on a thin and flexible medium. It was initially created in an 8-inch (200 mm) format, then a 5.25-inch (133 mm) format and finally in a 3.5-inch (89 mm) format. From the 1970s to the 2000s, most personal computers were made with a built-in floppy disk drive and floppy disks were used for external storage. However, they have now been superseded by other forms of storage such as flash memory. Data stored on floppy disks can now only be accessed using outdated computers.

Opening a document in the future

Although a document can be stored in a variety of storage media, there is no guarantee that the document will be retrievable in the format in which it was originally stored. If, for example, the appropriate software or translators are missing, the document will be difficult to open. The following factors may limit the ability of a computer to recreate the document:

- Changes in operating systems of computers.
- Changes in application software (software that is not successful in the marketplace disappears).
- Changes in standards for storing information.
- Encryption schemes associated with the storage.
- Use of compression schemes.
- Less than optimum storage conditions for the storage medium, such as a disk, which may fail.

As Microsoft Word has evolved, Word documents have changed in format. The current version of Word will open documents created with older Word versions but not vice versa.

For long-term archival purposes, documents need to be stored in formats that will be accessible in the years and decades ahead.

Disasters

A disaster is an event that occurs suddenly, generally with little warning, and causes significant damage. For ICT systems, a disaster is something that renders an organisation's computer resources and/or network inoperable.

Natural disaster

A catastrophic event such as a natural disaster like flood, cyclone, earthquake or fire could destroy buildings and all the equipment. This may require an information system to be rebuilt from scratch.

The task would be to enable the organisation to get to the same position as it was prior to the disaster occurring.

Technical failures

Other man-made or technical failures may lead to a significant interruption to services. These could include the loss of services from a telecommunications company, eg telephone or network services, that could prevent an organisation from operating normally. Other technical failures could include key **switches** failing, important servers failing and wireless technology failing.

Disaster recovery plans

Disaster recovery plans are created to allow organisations to recover from events that prevent the organisation from operating normally. A key requirement is to allow businesses to continue to operate normally or to resume normal operation in a reasonable time.

A disaster recovery plan will include:

- Key areas of vulnerability that will affect the organisation.
- Definition of what the organisation regards as a disaster.
- Identification of the disaster recovery team and the roles of the members of that team.
- Communication protocols for the organisation including external partners.
- Full description of the backup and restore policies.
- Description of the hardware and software that may need to be recovered.
- The location of off-site facilities including alternative processing capacity and storage.
- Contact details for all key personnel.
- Steps to be taken in different scenarios, eg in case of fire.
- Processes for damage assessment.
- Processes for recovery of systems or services.

Disaster recovery plans involve a risk assessment and organisations must decide what risks they can afford to take.

Some organisations maintain disaster recovery sites-off site that are managed by another vendor. For example, vendors such as IBM maintain highly secure data centres that organisations can use to replicate systems. Other organisations are beginning to use cloud services to replicate their systems and data.

Disaster recovery measures can be quite costly to implement and may never be used. However, the lack of such measures may be extremely costly in times of an unplanned and unpreventable disaster.

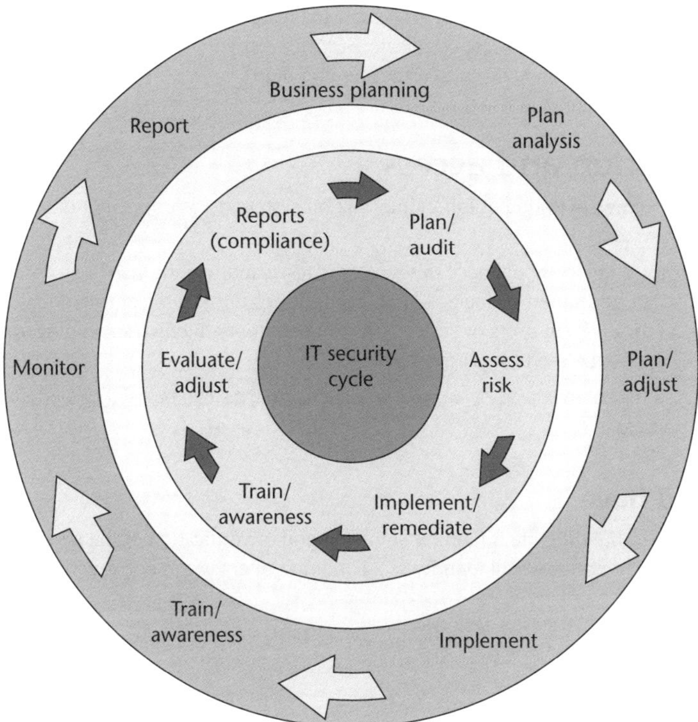

Disaster recovery plans

> ***Unit 11.3 Activity 2A: Disasters***
>
> List four types of disaster that could cause an information system to completely shut down.

Encryption

Data **encryption** is a method of preventing unauthorised access to data that is being transmitted on a network. Encryption encodes data and renders it unreadable if it is intercepted. The United States government has set up a Data Encryption Standard that it uses to evaluate the effectiveness of encryption.

Cryptography uses a key that both the sender and the receiver possess. The sender transmits the message; it is encoded and can only be decoded if the receiver has the appropriate secret decryption key. This method identifies legitimate senders and receivers and prevents the alteration or interception of the message.

Many websites use the Secure Sockets Layer (SSL) to transmit data privately. Many transactions are carried out using the HTTPS protocol to ensure security.

SSL is a standard security layer for creating encrypted transactions on the Internet. SSL ensures that data transmitted between a browser and a web server is encrypted. To be able to create an SSL link, the web server requires an SSL certificate. Security companies such as Verisign sell and maintain SSL certificates and help organisations install them and use them.

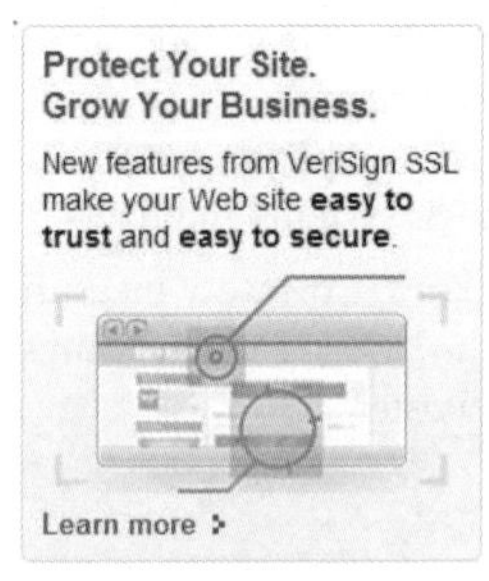

SSL certificates from Verisign

Identification and access

Maintaining a secure environment for an information system helps to prevent unauthorised access to such systems.

Physical security is one component of this: access is restricted to authorised personnel. Doors and buildings can be secured by locks. Many organisations use key systems that have different levels of access for different users or smart cards to open doors. Biometrics, eg fingerprints or retina scans, can also be used for access.

The access systems are managed by computer systems. Alarms can be used to alert authorities to out-of-hours access.

What you have

Gaining entry to a building often requires some method of verification of the person's right to enter the building. Verification of identity as a condition of entry can occur with:

- Keys.
- ID cards, usually with a photographic image.
- Smart cards.

Keys

Most organisations use keys to secure buildings. Keys can be arranged on a hierarchical basis with a master key system. A master key gives access to a number of different locks within an organisation. At the highest level, a master key will open every lock in a building.

Keys provide a first level of security. Most people are familiar with keys and they are relatively easy to use. However, for organisations requiring many buildings or rooms to be locked, the process of issuing and managing keys can be complex and time-consuming.

The loss or theft of a key can cause significant difficulty to an organisation. If a master key is stolen, the organisation's buildings are made insecure. To resolve the problem, an organisation may need to:

- Change every lock that the master key could access.
- Recall and replace all the keys that use those locks.

A process such as this is expensive and time-consuming.

Electronic keys

There are systems that use electronic keys, ie keys that are connected to a central keying system via a network. Keys are issued to users and the locks to which users have access depend upon the organisation's policies and the users' needs.

The advantages of such systems are:

- In the case of loss or theft, a key can be disabled quickly and a new one issued to the user.
- The use of keys can be monitored, which can be useful when there is suspected unauthorised access.

The disadvantages are:

- Cost: the capital cost of acquiring the system.
- Infrastructure: the need to have all of the locks accessible on a network.

Many organisations use key management systems

Identification cards

Identification (ID) cards are useful in providing physical identification of members of an organisation. These allow people to see quickly whether or not a person is authorised to be in a building.

Photo identification cards are used in many organisations, such as:

- Hospitals and medical centres.
- Schools and universities.
- Businesses.
- Public events.

They provide increased security, as it is difficult to use someone else's card undetected. Photo identification can help to reassure people that they are dealing with a legitimate member of an organisation.

ID cards can also incorporate electronic access cards. These cards operate in conjunction with electronic access systems and can be centrally controlled.

The ID card can be:

- A proximity card that is used with a special card reader to gain access.
- A swipe card with a magnetic strip that is used with a reader.

What you know

Personal identification number

A **personal identification number (PIN)** is a code used by an individual to identify that individual. Banks use PINs to authorise financial transactions, eg when withdrawing cash from an automatic teller machine.

A PIN can be used for access into a building or to set or turn off an alarm on a building. Many security systems use a PIN to operate alarms. Some people use a PIN on a mobile phone.

Individuals using a PIN should never:

- Disclose the PIN to another person.
- Write down the PIN on paper.
- Give out the PIN in reply to an email request.

Passwords

A **password** is a series of characters, usually letters, numbers and other characters. A password is associated with a user name.

A password is an important security measure. Passwords are used to identify users and to ensure that they have the correct levels of access to computer and information systems.

Most organisations have rules about passwords in terms of the length, the characters to be used, and how often it should be changed.

Typical rules include:

- Passwords to be changed regularly; perhaps every 90 days.
- Minimum number of characters in the password and the inclusion of numbers and other characters.
- Not allowing a password to be reused after it has been changed.
- Locking out a user after a number of unsuccessful attempts.

People should not use passwords that can be guessed, eg someone's name, a telephone number or a football team.

Unit 11.3 Activity 2B: Passwords and their use

List five systems that require you to have a password or PIN to access. Can you modify the password or PIN? If so, how?

Unit 11.3 Activity 2C: Setting a password

Maintaining security on a computer system is fundamental to the operation of the computer and also the network.

Alistair is required to provide a password to access a network. The following are possible suggestions for his password. Alistair thinks about possible passwords and is attempting to choose one that will be easy for him to remember. He lives in Madang, was born on 21 June 1978 and his wife's name is Betty. Alistair has a dog called Basil.

Comment on each password and give each password a score from 1 to 10.

1. riatsila
2. dog
3. madang
4. 21061978
5. betty
6. J23arGk1
7. Acme
8. Alistairlovesbetty
9. password
10. 23
11. June6
12. Basil
13. Alistair78
14. charles

Scoring system:

Score	Comment
10	Alistair would need to remember this password and keep the password secure.
9	Reasonably secure
8	Offers protection
7	Would offer protection against random attack and inside knowledge
6	Would offer protection against random attack
5	No apparent connection to Alistair; random attack may reveal
4	Requires some knowledge about Alistair to work it out; externally satisfactory, internally not
3	Not satisfactory
2	May as well leave it on a Post-it note attached to the monitor
1	No real thought, anyone with a little time could discover it
0	Why bother

Unit 11.3 Activity 2D: Forgetting a password

Choose three of the following examples and investigate what will happen if the passwords are forgotten.

1. Password to an Internet mail account, such as Hotmail or Yahoo mail.
2. PIN to a bank account using an automatic teller machine.
3. Password to a notebook computer.
4. Password to a document created in Microsoft Word.
5. Password to a computer network.

Digital signatures

A digital signature is an electronic signature that is used to authenticate the sender of a document or the person who signs a document.

A number of organisations, including Microsoft, can provide users with a digital signature. An organisation provides the user with a private key and the document is forwarded to the receiver in an encrypted form. The receiver uses a key to decrypt the message.

A digital signature is useful for ensuring the validity and authenticity of electronic transactions. However, there are costs involved and time must be taken to set up the process.

CoSign Desktop Digital Signature Software

The CoSign® digital signature solution helps you cut costs and expedite business processes by automating your formal approvals affordably.

CoSign Desktop is ideal for individuals or small organizations with up to 10 signers. Learn more about the differences between CoSign Desktop and CoSign Central.

CoSign Desktop digital signature software is priced at **$9.95 per user per month**, paid annually ($119.40/year). The price includes email support, maintenance, software upgrades, user license, and a web-trusted certificate.

Cosign is a provider of digital signatures

Who you are: biometric devices

People are unique and their personal characteristics can be used to identify them. **Biometric recognition** devices such as fingerprint scan, iris scan or voice recognition are used to verify identity. These systems are very complex and expensive but are used where high levels of security are required.

Some notebook computers offer a fingerprint scan as a method of logging on to the computer.

A fingerprint reader with a USB connection

Malware

Malware is short for malicious software: software that is designed to cause damage to computer systems. Malware includes computer viruses, worms, Trojan horses and spyware.

Computer virus

A computer **virus** is a piece of software that often attaches itself to genuine programs on a computer system. It has the intention of causing damage to the computer.

The virus might attach itself to a word processing program and run every time the word processor is activated. The virus replicates and attaches itself to other programs. A computer virus can make a computer unusable.

A very common method of spreading computer viruses is as an attachment in an email program. If the attachment is opened, it can run the virus that can infect the computer.

Each different virus has its own definition.

How are computer viruses distributed?

Computer viruses are spread between computers using either media that is infected or network connections that are disguised as legitimate files or messages. Thus viruses have been spread by:

- Disks with viruses installed that are used on multiple computers.
- Emails that are sent with attachments and include viruses.
- Software with viruses attached that is downloaded from the Internet and installed on a computer.

Why worry about a virus?

A computer virus can damage files on a disk. It can be selective or it can affect every file. A virus can cause random system crashes and work can be lost.

In the worst case, a computer can become completely inoperative.

What can be done to combat the spread of viruses?

Use virus protection software that can combat the spread of viruses. Computers often include **anti-virus** software when they are purchased. This software works by:

- Scanning any files copied to the computer.
- Running a virus-checking program.
- Checking existing files on start-up.
- Running in the background and continually checking files.

Other precautions to avoid a virus include:

- Not borrowing flash disks or accepting files from other people; whenever you borrow a disk you run the risk of infecting your computer.
- Being wary of public domain and shareware programs.
- Purchasing and using only commercial software.

- Taking care when downloading files from the Internet and bulletin boards; being particularly careful of games that can be a source of viruses.
- Not opening attachments on email messages unless you know the sender of the email and are confident of the authenticity of the attachment.

Note that virus protection software needs to be updated regularly. As new viruses are detected, the software is altered to check for these viruses. However, virus protection software is always going to lag behind the creation of viruses.

Most virus software is updated automatically on the Internet.

Worms

A **worm** is a malicious computer program that replicates itself across a computer network. It usually performs actions that cause damage to the computer's operating system, including shutting down the system or using the computer's resources.

A worm is usually installed by a person inadvertently opening an email attachment that contains the malicious script. A worm will generate further email messages and can flood a network. In some cases, it can lead to a denial of service, making the network inoperable.

Trojan horses

'A **Trojan horse** is a program that claims to rid your computer of viruses but instead introduces viruses to your computer.' (*Webopedia*)

A Trojan horse application looks to be useful and benign. This type of application may allow remote users access to a computer and allow the logging of keystrokes or the capturing of passwords, PINs and other important information.

Spyware

Spyware is software that covertly obtains information about a computer system using the Internet. This is done without the user's permission or knowledge. Spyware is often hidden in software that is downloaded from the Internet. When it is installed it tracks the activity of the user and sends that information to someone else. Spyware can be used to:

- Collect email addresses.
- Monitor passwords.
- Find out credit card details.
- Use someone else's Internet bandwidth.

Anti-spyware

There is a range of tools that can be used to guard against spyware attacks.

This type of software will detect spyware software on your computer and attempt to remove it. Some of the software packages will detect the attempt to load software onto a computer in real time and will prevent that from happening.

The detection and removal of spyware is becoming more complex and **anti-spyware** programs can be left behind in detecting new threats.

Phishing

Phishing is the act of sending an email to someone, falsely claiming to be another person. Someone using phishing replicates the email address of a legitimate sender.

The users of phishing are attempting to get people to provide them with sensitive or personal information that can be used for identity theft. The email can be seeking credit card or banking details. It may try to get the user to log on to a bogus website to provide such information.

Cleaning agents

A cleaning agent is software that is used to help keep your computer operating effectively. A cleaning agent will remove unwanted files and folders from your computer.

The agent usually gives you configuration options about which files are to be cleaned, eg log files and temporary folders. By removing unwanted files, it can free up disk space on the computer and will make it easier to carry out file defragmentation and speed up other disk-intensive activities.

Computer hard drive cleaning software

Cleaning Agent is a **computer hard drive cleaning software.** It is a handy disk utility that cleans your disks of unwanted files and folders fast. It lets you configure what items to clean - such as log files, cache files, temporary folders - and then removes them quickly with a click anytime you need.

An example of cleaning agent software

Unit 11.3 Activity 2E: Computer virus timeline

Listed below are ten computer viruses regarded by some as being in the top ten. Find out details of the virus and the year they were identified.

Virus	Description	Year	Details
Conficker	Time bomb		
Elk Cloner	Boot sector virus		
ExploreZip	Virus through zip file attachment		
I Love You	Email with malware attached		
Klez	Spoof email addresses		
Melissa	Spamming of email systems		
MyDoom	Email and address books, denial-of-service attacks		

Virus	Description	Year	Details
Nimda	Email, network and information system vulnerabilities		
Sasser	Exploited computers that had not installed the latest security updates		
Storm	Malware disguised as a file, such as video		

System failures

Computer system failures happen in two different ways:

- Hardware failure.
- Software failure.

Hardware failure

A hardware failure is when a component in the hardware fails and causes the computer to fail. Typical failures include:

- Hard disk failure: the hard disk is a physical device and the performance degrades over time.
- Failure of the mainboard.

A hard disk can be replaced, but to return the computer to the state it was in, backups need to have been carried out and be up to date. A mainboard can easily be replaced.

Most computers are purchased with a warranty provision from one to three years. The warranty will repair hardware. Depending on the terms of the warranty, the computer will be repaired on-site or it may need to be returned to either the place of purchase or a service centre.

Many hardware failures do not result in the loss of data. However, a hard disk failure may well result in the loss of data.

Software failure

Software failures are usually related to the corruption of the operating system software. These will often require re-installation of the operating system.

If the operating system has failed, the computer will need to be restarted using a floppy disk, a flash disk drive or an external disk that has a valid operating system attached. If the system can be restarted in this manner, most of the data on the hard disk should be able to be recovered.

Some computer vendors provide utility programs that help with the restoration of the operating system in the case of a failure.

One type of failure that is difficult to recover from is BIOS failure. This is the input–output system chip. If the BIOS password is changed it may be impossible to restore the computer to a usable state. If there is an interruption to a BIOS update it might also cause the computer to fail.

Unit 11.3 Activity 2F: Hardware failure

1. The newspaper story below refers to a chemical leak in Newcastle, NSW, Australia. What caused the fault?
2. What could have been done to prevent the fault occurring?
3. What problems would Orica need to deal with as a result of this leak?

COMPUTER CARD RESPONSIBLE FOR ORICA LEAK

A failed computer card was behind the latest chemical leak at Orica's Newcastle plant, the company says.

About 20,000 litres of weak ammonium nitrate solution overflowed from a tank during pumping operations at the Kooragang Island plant on Wednesday afternoon, the Environment Protection Authority (EPA) said.

Orica site manager Sean Winstone said an investigation by the company found that the spill was primarily the result of a failed computer card.

"The failure of this computer card meant that the control system did not shut down the plant before the overflow occurred," Mr Winstone said in a statement on Thursday.

Computer theft and vandalism

Computer theft is a significant problem for individuals and organisations. There are two issues concerned with computer theft:

- Physical replacement of the computer, including cost.
- Loss of data that can be difficult to recover.

Associated with this is the potential for unauthorised access to private and personal data. *The Australian* newspaper reported on 11 June 2011 that:

> A computer containing details of high-flying board members was stolen when thieves broke into the Australian Institute of Company Directors' office.
>
> The PC hard disk contained 66 000 records, including names, addresses, phone numbers and birth dates of 28 000 members. The rest belonged to clients.
>
> Some records had the names of personal assistants and their email addresses.

In fact, the physical cost of replacing a computer may well be very small compared to the cost of restoring data and the risks associated with the unauthorised access to data.

Notebook computers are particularly vulnerable to theft. Notebook computers left in a visible position in vehicles can easily be stolen. Students carrying notebook computers to and from school are also vulnerable to mugging and theft.

Some companies have installed tracking devices in notebook computers, making the computer difficult to dispose of without detection. The careful choice of user names, passwords and other biometric protection can render a stolen computer useless.

Some of the steps that can be taken to reduce the possibility of notebook theft are:

- Never leave the computer in a visible position in a vehicle.
- Carry the computer in a nondescript bag, not an obvious computer bag.

- Do not leave a notebook computer in a meeting room if you need to leave the room.
- Install a cable lock on the notebook computer.
- Make sure that your user name and password are hidden.
- Back up the data and keep the backups separately from the computer.

Vandalism is malicious damage to a computer. Vandalism can be prevented by ensuring other people do not have access to the computer. The steps above for preventing theft are also useful in the prevention of vandalism.

Unit 11.3 Activity 2G: Protecting data in the workplace

Adline Pty Ltd is an advertising agency with 20 employees. There are 15 computers that are networked. Three people work in reception, which is also the main office. Jane and Frank are full-time employees; Gail works three half-days per week. Jane mainly operates the accounting software. Frank operates the switchboard and does general office duties. Gail provides technical support including hardware installation and software support.

Advise on the following practices and comment on how each of them could be improved.

1. Jane is the only person who knows how to back up the accounting software. This is not a problem as she works full-time.
2. Jane currently backs up the accounting software once per week.
3. Jane backs up the accounting program as well as the data files on a 100 MB disk.
4. Jane locks the 100 MB backup disk in the office safe which is in reception.
5. Frank enters meeting times in the calendar which is accessed by the employees. Frank makes a backup of the meeting files at irregular intervals.
6. Frank, on one occasion, worked from a backup copy stored on the hard disk which did not have the current week's entries.
7. Frank is a novice computer user and reads computer magazines and manuals at work to find out how to use a computer.
8. Frank logs all deliveries to the office in a database created by Gail. The database is still a work in progress and Gail will complete it when she has time. Sometimes Frank will enter the same delivery twice.
9. Frank, from time to time, creates letters to send to clients. He does not usually name the letter file until he saves the letter after it has been printed. Sometimes the computer freezes as the letter is being printed.
10. Gail recently installed new browser software on the computers in reception when working late one evening. Both Jane and Frank are mystified about the changes when they turn on their computers the next morning.
11. Jane, at the end of the day, turns her computer monitor off and leaves the CPU running. Sometimes the cleaner requires the same power point and disconnects the computer.
12. Frank sometimes works at home on work documents. When he returns to work he continues working on the documents on the flash drive only.
13. Jane also creates letters for clients. She simply adds a new letter to a single document which contains all the letters for a particular month for all clients. She says it is easy to copy and paste the address details from one letter to the next.

14. For important office memos Frank does not keep an electronic copy of the memo, but rather prints the memo and files it in the filing cabinet.

15. Gail purchased a single copy of a new database management program. She installed a copy on two computers at work and also her home computer so she could learn the package for work purposes.

16. Frank has been given a shareware program downloaded from the Internet by his best mate. He wants to try the software on the work computer.

Unit 11.3 Activity 2H: Network password tasks

1. Why would a network administrator insist that personnel change their passwords on a regular basis?

2. In a work environment, how often should passwords be changed?

3. How do you remember the passwords you use?

Unit 11.3 Computers and Society

Topic 3: Environmental, social and ethical issues

Topic 3 explores the environmental, social and ethical issues related to computers and computing (see ICT Syllabus pp. 17–18 and Computer Studies Syllabus p. 21). It covers:

- Moral and ethical issues.
- Environmental problems.
- Social problems.

Moral and ethical issues

Any society develops a set of rules to set the boundaries of accepted behaviour within that society.

These moral codes are not necessarily written down or stated literally in the laws of that society. The moral code, however, is an important part of the underlying value system of the society and is reflected in the laws.

For example, it is regarded as immoral to kill and take the life of another human being. Most people do not need the law of murder and subsequent penalty for them to understand and appreciate that it is wrong.

Ethics

Ethics are the beliefs we hold about what is right and wrong. There are social norms that exist in a society about what we can and should do, or not do, in our everyday life. For example, telling a lie, stealing or cheating would be regarded as unethical. How we decide what is ethical could be affected by:

- The set of values experienced in the family and community when we are young.
- The influence of our peer group, role models and leaders in our social, sporting, business and political systems and the general community.
- Religion.
- Life experience.

Work ethics

In the workplace there are many relationships that need to be managed with attention to standards of ethical behaviour.

Stakeholders in a business are those affected by the business operations. They have an interest, direct or indirect, in the success of the business. Business behaviour and the way an organisation conducts business, including how its employees make decisions and interact with others, are influenced by ethics daily.

Organisations have rules and expectations about how people use computers and information systems in the workplace. Many of these rules and expectations are explicitly stated, but some are unwritten.

In general, organisations provide computers for users so that they can carry out the mission or business of the organisation in a manner that meets the organisation's goals and is consistent with its ethics.

Acceptable use policy

Most organisations will have an **acceptable use policy** for the use of computers and associated infrastructure.

An acceptable use policy describes what users are allowed to do with the IT resources of the organisation and what they are not allowed to do. It will often define what sanctions are put in place if there is a breach of the policy. The policy will also provide for audits of user activity.

Policy on Acceptable Use of Electronic Resources

Summary

This policy defines the boundaries of "acceptable use" of limited University electronic resources, including computers, networks, electronic mail services and electronic information sources, as detailed below. It includes by reference a self-contained compilation of specific rules that can be modified as the electronic information environment evolves.

The policy is based on the principle that the electronic information environment is provided to support University business and its mission of education, research and service. Other uses are secondary. Uses that threaten the integrity of the system; the function of non-University equipment that can be accessed through the system; the privacy or actual or perceived safety of others; or that are otherwise illegal are forbidden.

Part of the acceptable use policy of the University of Pennsylvania in the USA

Most organisations will try to strike a balance between what is reasonable and unreasonable private use. Some of the issues that need to be dealt with include:

- Personal privacy and whether employers may track employee emails and Internet usage.
- The use of work email for private use.
- The use of illegal copies of software.
- Unauthorised copying of software.
- Training people to understand privacy laws and how to deal with personal information.
- Using colleagues' user names and passwords.
- The role of employees in maintaining security of data in the workplace as well as small portable storage devices (such as laptops and USB flash drives) that may contain valuable data.

The privacy and responsible use of data is of concern in all organisations. The University of Pennsylvania forbids:

> Unauthorised access, possession, or distribution, by electronic or any other means, of electronic information or data that is confidential under the University's policies regarding privacy or the confidentiality of student, administrative, personnel, archival, or other records …
>
> Source: http://www.upenn.edu/computing/policy/aup.html

Users within an organisation have different information needs and will therefore have different requirements for access to an organisation's databases. It is the responsibility of the organisation to ensure that the user's level of access is appropriate to the user's needs. It is the responsibility of the users to ensure that they access only that which is appropriate to their needs.

Privacy breaches can have significant implications for organisations.

SONY OVERHAULS PLAYSTATION SECURITY

Sony has overhauled the security of its PlayStation network as the company begins to get the network back online, days after the system was hacked.

On Friday, Sony confirmed its PlayStation network had been hacked and an "illegal and unauthorised person" gained access to the personal details of 77 million users including passwords, names, addresses and dates of birth.

The network had been compromised a week before and as a result Sony shut down the PlayStation network as it tried to address the security breach.

Sony announced on Sunday it would restore the network in phases "shortly," beginning with PlayStation's gaming, music and video services.

In the past week the company has been advised by expert information security firms and has overhauled its security measures to ensure greater protection of personal details.

Issues affecting society

Information systems and computers provide people with opportunities to use computer systems to carry out illegal activity.

Computer crime

Computer crime refers to illegal activity involving computers and networks. These fall into two categories:

- Those that target computers or networks directly.
- Those that use computers or networks to carry out crimes.

Crimes that target computers and networks include:

- The proliferation of viruses.
- Denial-of-service attacks.
- The spread of malware.

Crimes that use computers include:

- Fraud and identity theft.
- Phishing.
- Cyber-bullying.

The significance of networks and the ubiquitous access to the Internet have sparked the rise of cybercrime.

HIV and AIDS

HIV and AIDS are significant issues in all societies. Computers, networks and the Internet can be a source of advice and support for many people.

Social networks can be used to develop online communities that offer support and counselling for those afflicted with the virus.

Hackers and crackers

It is common to call anyone who has unauthorised access to a network a '**hacker**'. The distinction drawn between a 'hacker' and a '**cracker**' is that the 'cracker' has a criminal motive over and above the unauthorised access.

Hackers usually operate as individuals and aim to access a network to gain information that is normally not available to them. In some cases it can be just for a thrill and to see how far they can penetrate the network security.

The hacker may also seek acceptance within groups of like-minded people who exist in loosely organised groups.

Crackers access networks and indulge in activities such as:

- Damaging the data on a network.
- Stealing information such as personal information and credit card details.
- Stealing data to commit identity fraud.
- Causing computers to crash.
- Using scripts and automatic programs to cause system malfunctions.

Pornography

Pornography is a picture or movie that is designed to get people sexually aroused.

The Internet has provided a very easy method for people to distribute and access pornography. Accessing pornographic sites using computers or networks supplied by an employer is usually a breach of the acceptable use policy of that organisation.

Accessing pornographic sites is regarded by many as being socially unacceptable. Filters to block access to pornographic sites are available. Of particular concern is ensuring adolescents and children do not have access to such sites.

Identity theft

Identity theft is a type of fraud that involves pretending to be someone else and using that other person's identity to steal money or goods. The perpetrator usually gains access to some of the victim's personal details such as date of birth, credit card number and PINs and uses these to steal money or goods.

Many of the phishing schemes are attempts at gaining enough personal information to carry out identity theft.

In the US, social security numbers are sought after by criminals. A number of US universities and colleges have had significant problems caused by hackers accessing their information systems and stealing social security numbers and other personal data.

Identity thieves don't discriminate!

Identity theft is a rapidly increasing white-collar crime that affects more than 10 million Americans annually. Identity fraud, which includes identity theft cases, costs the USA over $52 billion each year.

Identity theft can cause a lot of damage. For example, a woman in California was a victim of identity theft when her drivers licence was stolen. The female thief used the licence as identification to draw out $15,000 from the victim's bank account. The thief also opened several credit card accounts under the victim's name and ran up bills of a further $9000.

Identity theft in the USA costs over $52 billion

A stolen wallet or purse will contain significant documents that can be used for identity theft: a driver's licence, credit and debit cards and, perhaps, PINs. It is important to be able to stop the use of credit cards in the case of theft or loss.

Similarly, mail theft can be used to access personal and financial documents and information.

Mining the trash is where thieves go through trash cans and remove personal and financial documents that have been discarded. These documents can be used for identity theft. Some organisations have also been guilty of discarding private and financial information about clients and customers in a manner that allows thieves to access the data. Such access can be prevented by shredding discarded documents.

Telephone solicitation

Some organisations use call centres to seek new business. These provide the opportunity for some people to pretend to be representatives of a well-known and reputable organisation.

These people may use excuses to try to get personal information from the person who responds to the call. In these cases, it is important to not disclose a PIN or password to such a person. Reputable organisations will not ask for these.

Cyber-bullying

Cyber-bullying is when a child, pre-teen or teen is tormented, threatened, harassed, humiliated, embarrassed or otherwise targeted by another child, pre-teen or teen using the Internet, interactive and digital technologies or mobile phones. It has to have a minor on both sides, or at least have been instigated by a minor against another minor. Once adults become involved, it is plain and simple cyber-harassment or cyberstalking.

(Source: http://www.stopcyberbullying.org/what_is_cyberbullying_exactly.html)

Cyber-bullying is a significant problem in many societies. It has come about with:

- The popularity of social media sites such as Facebook and Twitter.
- The increased use of mobile telephones.
- The ease with which compromising photographs can be taken and posted.
- The proliferation of text and instant messaging.

The immediacy of the technology, the ready availability of networks and the possibility of anonymous posting of comments on websites all contribute to this significant issue.

Many organisations have been created to deal with cyber-bullying. They provide advice to users and encourage the responsible and ethical use of hardware, software and networks.

Economic issues: changes in the workplace

Careers and career change

Changing technology is a contributing factor to changes in careers. Workers today can expect to have a number of careers during their working life. Many new jobs will be created in the next ten years which reflect the development of technology.

Even if people remain in the same job for a lengthy period of time, it is likely that the job will change and they will be doing it differently.

How has an accountant's role changed?

Accounting software packages have fundamentally altered the job of an accountant. Accountants and bookkeepers kept the accounting records for many businesses using double entry accounting. The skills to do this manually are specialised and require extensive training.

Accounting software has removed much of the complexity of this process, providing a person knows how to use the software and has appropriate document recognition skills so that the information can be entered correctly.

Most businesses now use accounting software and record the financial transactions as they occur. Accountants now provide businesses with:

- Training in the operation and use of accounting software.
- A chart of accounts for the business type.
- Advice on taxation and preparation of taxation returns.
- Monitoring of financial stability.
- Long-term financial planning.

Online services

Increasingly, transactions are made using **online** services. This may bring sellers of goods and services closer to the buyers of goods and services. It may affect those who act as intermediaries in the production and distribution process.

Some examples of businesses acting as intermediaries include:

- Real estate agents.
- Travel agents.
- Stockbrokers.
- Insurance brokers.

People who know exactly what they want may deal directly with the provider of the service. For example, they can buy an airline ticket online and receive a seat allocation at the same time.

If a person is not completely sure of the differences between alternatives offered by different suppliers, then an intermediary, eg the travel agent, may be used for advice and guidance.

Environmental problems

Hardware

The hardware to support ICT is made by sophisticated manufacturing processes in a variety of countries. The rate of technological change has been increasing; products have a limited lifespan and there is limited opportunity to reuse equipment as it becomes obsolete.

When hardware fails it is often cheaper to replace the item than to attempt to repair it.

Consumables

Printer cartridges for laser printers contain toxic chemicals and require sophisticated recycling plants to reuse some parts or recycle the remainder.

Disposal of by-products (e-waste management)

Disposal of old equipment and recovery of materials of value, such as metals, is very labour-intensive and often done in countries where the cost of labour is low. Some countries also do not have environmental safeguards that protect the environment and people from unsafe processes.

Disposal of old computers and equipment by just burying in landfill is not socially or environmentally acceptable. These items are not biodegradable, may never break down, and therefore contaminate the earth. It has been proposed by some that the price of new computer equipment should include a charge whereby the manufacturers have a responsibility to be involved in the recycling and proper disposal of equipment when it is no longer useful.

Some local government authorities manage e-waste

Social problems

Gambling

It is easy for people to become involved in online gambling. The Internet offers access for people to gamble using credit on a wide range of events such as sporting events as well as games of chance.

There is limited government control on many of these activities and people can lose substantial amounts of money through gambling.

Gambling applications have now been developed for handheld devices making it even easier to participate.

Governments are concerned about the ease with which people can gamble on the Internet. One commentator noted:

> You can now lose the home without leaving home.
>
> (Attributed to the Reverend Tim Costello)

Stress

Reliance on technology, computers and mobile devices is increasing as society becomes more complex. Working with computers can become very stressful. Unplanned outages, damage or loss of files can contribute to stress.

The failure to understand new software or inadequate training can also contribute to stress and frustration. Unrealistic expectations of what a computer system can deliver can be frustrating.

Careful planning, regular backups and appropriate training can significantly reduce the stress on individuals.

Fussing with computers

Some people become so fascinated with computers and with using them that they become preoccupied and addicted. In particular, they may crave access to the Internet.

People who do become addicted:

- Make use of their computer every available moment.
- Neglect their family responsibilities.
- Use computers when they should be doing other things, such as at school or work.
- Interact online in the virtual world to the neglect of the physical world to which they belong.

Social networking

The rapid rise and popularity of the social networking site has proven to be a powerful way for people to meet and interact.

Some social networks such as Facebook enable people to communicate easily as well as attract others to the network and link to them. Some networks such as LinkedIn have the same purpose but exist in a narrower realm of business. Many social networking sites do not charge for membership and this has encouraged people to join.

Twitter provides an immediacy that many find interesting

Risks associated with social networking sites

Longevity of information

Once information is posted on the Internet on a social network site it is likely to exist online forever and be beyond the control of the person who posted the information.

A person may regret posting personal information as the nature of their relationships change. Future partners, employers and the community in which the person lives may form an opinion of a person based on what is posted online, even though that person has changed.

Ownership of information

Members of social networking sites have, on joining, agreed to a comprehensive list of rules. These rules are complex and it is not easy to fully understand their effect and significance at the time of joining.

Rules and management of sites

The owners of sites can and do change their rules of operation and this may affect the 'privacy' of the information posted.

Information overload

Society today has access to more information than at any time in human history. Some factors contributing to this are:

- Technology such as the Internet and digitisation of information means the amount of information is increasing at an increasing rate.
- Increasingly information is available in 'real time' and then updated continually.
- The variety of methods of accessing and transferring information – for example, phone (voice and text), email and messaging – have expanded.
- The duplication and reworking of existing information have become easier.

This can mean that individuals feel overwhelmed by the volume of information and have difficulty in developing their knowledge as they feel distracted by the constantly changing state of information.

Email in particular poses a threat to organisations and people because of the amount of time that it takes for people to deal with it.

Unit 11.3 Computers and Society

Topic 4: Government controls and laws on ICT

Topic 4 explores the government controls and laws related to computers and computing (see ICT Syllabus p. 18 and Computer Studies Syllabus pp. 21–2). It covers:

- Impact of copyright laws.
- Internet ethics and objectionable materials.
- Government controls and laws on ICT.

Copyright law

Copyright law is designed to protect the rights of the creators of intellectual property. Intellectual property can exist in many forms including music, art, movies, television programs, literature and computer software.

Software **copyright** is used by companies to prevent unauthorised copying and use of their software. Software is typically sold with a software licence. These licences specify the conditions under which the software can be used, copied and distributed.

Companies take precautions to prevent copyright infringements. In some cases, large penalties can apply for the unauthorised use of software.

Open-source software allows users to modify the software under certain conditions. If the software has been available in the public domain it may not be subject to any copyright conditions.

Copyright law in the digital age

In the digital age it is relatively easy to both copy and distribute the works of others in a digital form. Students, researchers and authors need to ensure that content is of their own creation. If not, then they must acknowledge the source of the content.

Many images and movies are available on the Internet for purchase. These are subject to copyright laws and conditions of use will be provided by the site. Some images may be purchased and are then royalty-free, ie they can be used without the payment of royalties provided they have been legitimately purchased.

Some software will include the source of material copied from the Internet. The example on the right shows an entry copied from *Wikipedia* into Microsoft's OneNote, which includes the source of the material.

Kevin Hughes (www) - Wikipedia, the free encyclopedia

Tuesday, 13 December 2011
8:41 AM

Kevin Hughes was one of the pioneers of the World Wide Web in the United States, while a student at Honolulu Community College (HCC). He is one of only six inductees in the World Wide Web Hall of Fame announced at the first international conference on the World Wide Web in 1994.[1][2]
He developed the "imagemap"[3] and created one of the first campus web sites, including novel (at the time) ideas such as a virtual tour of a campus museum. Hughes later developed seminal technologies for numerous commerce web sites. He also designed the original public domain icons that come with the Apache HTTP Server.[4]

Inserted from <http://en.wikipedia.org/wiki/Kevin_Hughes_(www)>

An entry from Wikipedia *in OneNote*

Internet ethics and objectionable materials

The Internet enables a great range of different content to be available on sites. It can be accessed without the traditional forms of classification that applied to music, movies, television and printed materials. Distribution of pornography and movies can bypass the safeguards that society puts in place such as banning material or only allowing limited access, including restricted classifications for movies. Printed materials and books can be banned if they contain material that does not meet the expected standards of the society.

Through blogs, wikis, chat rooms, forums, social networking sites and normal websites people are able to post comments and have them published. This can give rise to religious, cultural, racial and political vilification, often where comments are posted under the apparent anonymity of the Internet. The careless use of such social networking sites can cause unwanted distress and harm.

Many sites that allow comments to be posted are administered by a 'moderator' who can remove offensive material. Most sites have rules and online protocols to give guidelines about content. 'Flaming' occurs when derogatory and offensive comments are made in response to a post; they are often directed at the individual rather than facilitating the conversation that the forum or blog is designed to do.

Internet filtering is used by governments in some jurisdictions but this requires considerable resources to ensure that all materials it may wish to restrict are in fact prevented from access. Businesses and organisations such as schools will have filtering to prevent objectionable materials, spam emails and junk mail from penetrating their firewalls. At times, however, Internet filtering can prevent access to legitimate and useful sites.

Government controls

The Australian government has a range of whole-of-government policies relating to the use of information and communications technologies.[1] These policies relate to:

- ICT Strategy & Governance.
- ICT Service Improvement & Delivery.
- ICT Security & Authentication.
- ICT Better Practice & Collaboration.
- ICT Infrastructure.
- ICT Investment Framework.
- ICT Procurement.

Governments around the world now make a lot of information available on the Internet. At the time of writing, the website for the Papua New Guinea parliament was under construction. The link http://www.parliament.gov.pg/ could be explored in the future.

Privacy

Governments around the world have made laws regarding the privacy and protection of personal information.

Organisations have responsibilities to ensure that data is:

- Accurate.
- Up to date.
- Protected from intrusion.

[1] See the Australian Government Department of Finance at www.finance.gov.au/e-government/index.html.

- Able to be restored in the case of failure.
- Available only to appropriate persons within the organisation.

Privacy is a complex area of government and many states and territories have legislative approaches that are sometimes in conflict. Most governments have a security policy that applies to all their departments and agencies.

Most organisations have privacy policies for dealing with their customers. Telstra is an organisation that provides voice and video services in Papua New Guinea. A copy of Telstra's privacy policy is available on its website.

Telstra Corporation Limited

Protecting your privacy

We are committed to providing you with the highest levels of customer service. This includes protecting your privacy.

Set out below is information that we are required to communicate to our customers. We recommend that you keep this information for future reference.

The start of the Telstra privacy policy: http://telstra.com.au/privacy/privacy-statement/

Unit 11.3 Activity 4A: Breaches of privacy

Telstra Australia mistakenly made available on the Internet the user names, account details and passwords of a number of users.

1. List the concerns that users might have with this breach of privacy.

2. Could such details be used for identity theft?

Unit 11.3 Computers and Society

Topic 5: Ergonomics in ICT

Topic 5 explores the importance of ergonomics in ICT (see ICT Syllabus p. 18 and Computer Studies Syllabus p. 22). It covers:

- Design of furniture.
- Placement of equipment.
- Keyboarding techniques.
- Work routine.
- Total work environment.
- Design of software.

Design of furniture

Desk design

Computer desks have adjustable heights for working areas, for example, the keyboard area.

The mouse should be the same height as the keyboard. A keyboard height in the range of 58–71 cm is suitable for most users.

Chair design

The seat height and back support should be adjustable. The height should be adjustable so the feet rest flat on the floor, and the hands address the keyboard correctly.

Placement of equipment

Screen position

The top of the screen should be at or slightly below eye height. The user distance from the screen should be in the range of 45–71 cm. If the monitor has controls for brightness and contrast these may need adjustment.

Lighting

Poor lighting and glare can give rise to headaches and blurred vision when looking at a computer screen. Sunlight directly in front of the monitor can affect the amount of glare and reflection.

Reflections should be avoided by placing the monitor to the side of light sources. Do not have a direct, external source of light on the monitor, eg have the back of the monitor to a window.

Working constantly with monitors can bring about eye strain. Frequent short breaks should be taken.

Keyboarding posture and technique

Posture is how you place your body. Correct posture can mean tiring less easily and preventing undue stress on your body. You will be able to work more effectively if you are relaxed when using a keyboard. Get into the habit of adopting good posture and keyboarding technique at the start of each keyboarding session.

Posture and technique can be divided into two main areas:

- How to sit on the chair and address the keyboard and screen.
- The position of the arms, hands and fingers on the keyboard and the technique for pressing the keys.

The feet should be flat on the floor, about two shoe-widths apart. Ensure your weight is transferred down the seat back evenly. Sit reasonably upright without being stiff. Your shoulders should be relaxed without dropping or being stiff. Your head should be held up in line with your body, not forward of the body line.

Your arms should hang along the side of your body. The forearms should be parallel to the floor and the line of the thighs. The wrists should be straight, parallel to the floor and the line of the thighs. If necessary, the hands can be slightly higher than the elbows (within 0 to 20 degrees above horizontal). The fingers should be relaxed with a gentle curve, almost 180 degrees to the keyboard.

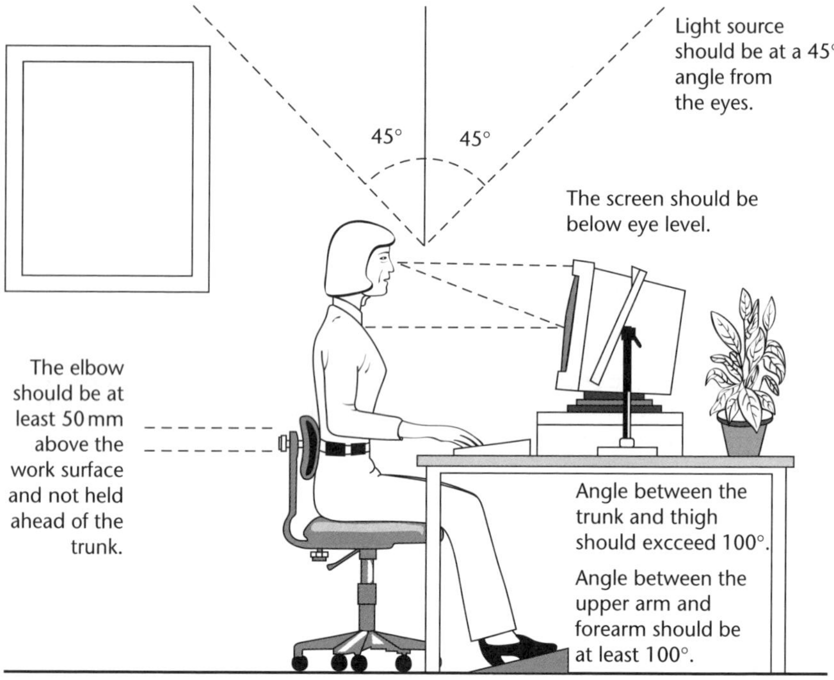

Using a workstation correctly

Using a keyboard and a mouse

Quickly glance at the keyboard and check the position of your fingers before you start typing. You should see the G and H keys in the space between your hands.

Work routine

Organisations have to develop procedures and work practices to make the workplace safe and healthy for workers. Although there are costs involved there are benefits of increased productivity if workers are able to perform their tasks safely with a feeling of well-being.

Occupational overuse syndrome

There has been much research into the effect of posture and technique on keyboarding, particularly in regard to 'occupational overuse syndrome'. Occupational overuse syndrome covers a range of pains and discomfort associated with the soft tissue, tendons and muscles. This syndrome is also referred to as RSI (repetitive strain injury).

If a keyboard is used to enter information at high speed for long periods of time without breaks there is a danger of injury.

Keyboard operators should take regular breaks from keyboarding and carry out other tasks.

Design of software

Software can be produced in many different situations and in response to differing needs.

A program could be produced commercially by a major software company, such as Microsoft, or custom-built by programmers to meet specific requirements, such as software for a bank.

Software on a personal computer

Software on a personal computer is generally classified as:

- An operating system, eg Microsoft Windows, Mac OSX.
- Utilities, eg virus protection.
- Applications, eg word processing, spreadsheet.

Unit 11.3 Activity 5A: Choosing software

The following are examples of tasks commonly performed using a computer. For each task indicate the software type you would use. If you choose an integrated package, state which module of the package you would use. For some tasks there could be more than one software type that could be used.

1. Write a letter.
2. Create a budget for your next holiday.
3. Organise your personal finances for the coming year.
4. Connect to the World Wide Web.
5. View a page on the World Wide Web.
6. Send a message to another person.
7. Create an image to use on a newsletter.
8. Manipulate an image taken with a digital camera.
9. Design a new layout for a garden.

10. Organise your daily events for the next three months.

11. Play a music CD from your computer CD drive.

12. Create a system to organise your CD collection.

13. Decompress a file downloaded from the Internet.

14. View a video file from a CD.

15. View a PDF file.

16. Compose a web page.

17. Record a sound as a digital file.

18. Make a presentation to accompany a talk.

19. Communicate with a computer by speaking.

20. Create a sophisticated newsletter with three columns.

Unit 11.3 Activity 5B: Software ownership

From a personal computer you have access to, list five different types of software. Find the maker and version of the software and the nature of the software licence.

	Name of the software	Maker	Software Version	Software media (eg pre-installed, disk, download, subscription, cloud)	Software licence (eg commercial, educational, shareware)	Price
1						
2						
3						
4						
5						

Complexity of technology

Software complexity

Software today is more sophisticated than that which accompanied the first personal computers. The tasks we perform with software are more complex and require more training for a user to be proficient with that software. For example, accounting software packages now perform many tasks that were previously done by bookkeepers and accountants. On the other hand, software generally has become more user-friendly.

Computer skills are regarded as essential for many jobs today and are often listed as requirements in job advertisements. Ongoing training in the workplace is a major issue for all employers as employees need to update skills when new software is introduced.

Many businesses and organisations are reluctant to introduce new versions of software until they have been tested with existing systems, and training needs have been considered.

Software sophistication

Increasingly, software is used to provide training simulations where computer-modelled environments simulate real-world situations. Flight simulators for airline pilots were an early example of this use. Pilots could gain a sense of what it would be like to land a plane at an airport they had never been to.

The use of computer models to simulate real-life experience is often referred to as 'virtual reality'. By using sensors such as gloves and helmets, people can experience different scenarios and possibilities and allow interaction with various environments and situations.

Virtual reality has important implications for:

- Science.
- The military.
- Education.
- Medicine.
- Architecture.
- Design.
- Education and training.

Development of software

The major software companies spend a large amount of time and money developing software.

When personal computers first came into use, all the instructions needed to be entered by the user. This was called the command line interface.

The development of the graphical user interface and its introduction with the Apple Macintosh computers in the 1980s transformed the way computers were used.

The graphical user interface (GUI) allowed the user to operate devices to interact with images rather than commands. The main features of the GUI are:

- A pointer on the screen that changes shape depending on the context and allows movement and selection.
- A pointing device, usually a mouse.
- A desktop with icons.
- Drop-down menus for user commands.

Since that development, all major software types have continued to improve the interface.

Software designers will continually release new versions of software that:

- Rectify faults (bugs) in the original software.
- Add new features requested by users.
- Change the user interface to make it easier to use.

Users have the opportunity to test the software during the software development cycle.

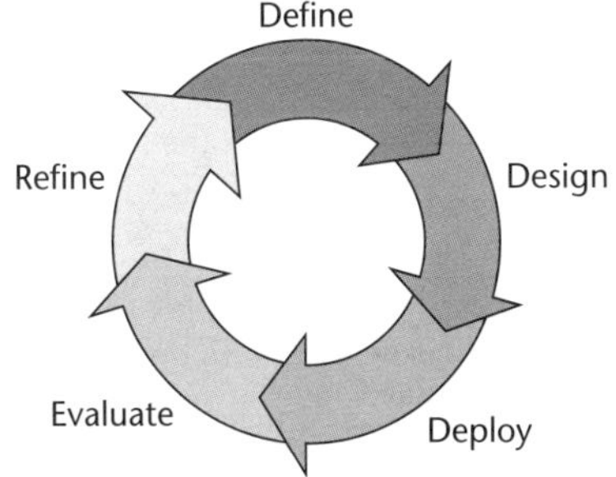

Software development cycle

'Beta testing' is the term used for giving users the opportunity to test a piece of software before its release. Beta testers give feedback on:

- Issues with the product, eg software malfunction.
- Ease of use.
- Suggestions for improvements.

Individuals and organisations can become beta testers for software developers. Microsoft provides the opportunity for people to become beta testers

Unit 11.3 Activity 5C: Upgrading to new software

Software should be upgraded from a previous version in a way that minimises problems and ensures immediate resumption of work.

Listed below are a variety of tasks that may be performed when upgrading software. The example assumes that the software is downloaded from the Internet.

Place the tasks in the correct order to provide the best upgrade process.

	Task	No.	Comment
1	Record the serial number of the software		
2	Check if documents created by earlier versions are compatible with the upgrade; check if the upgrade 'forces' the document to be converted to the newer file format or allows the option of remaining as the previous version		
3	Decide if it is necessary to upgrade to the new version of the software		
4	Check if there is sufficient hard disk space to allow the installation		
5	Back up documents created by earlier versions of the software		
6	Check to see if the earlier version of the software will be removed by the upgrade		
7	Check if the version number of the upgrade is the correct version		
8	Register as a user of the software		
9	Decide in which directory the software is to be installed		
10	Ask a technician or other users about their experience with the software upgrade		
11	Check the licence provisions for the upgrade		

	Task	No.	Comment
12	Decide on an appropriate time for the upgrade to take place		
13	Test-run the software on existing and new documents		
14	Print a document using the software		
15	Read any 'Read Me' files contained with the installation		
16	Read the user manual regarding installation		
17	Find hardware requirements to support the software upgrade		
18	Restart the computer		
19	Virus-check the installation files		
20	Suspend virus-check software on computer if required for installation		

Unit 11.4 Spreadsheets
Topic 1: What is a spreadsheet?

Unit 11.4 explores spreadsheets. Topic 1 in this Unit gives an introduction to spreadsheets.

What is a spreadsheet?

A **spreadsheet** is a rectangular working area onto which numbers and text are entered in rows and columns. The area where each row and column meets is called a **cell**. Each cell can contain numbers or text.

The most common program used to create spreadsheets is Microsoft Excel.

Almost any type of calculation that can be set up in rows and columns can be done with a spreadsheet. A spreadsheet is made up of many individual cells. The number of columns and rows in Microsoft Excel varies depending upon the version of Excel. In total, there are many millions of cells in each worksheet.

An Excel file is called a **workbook**. Each workbook is made up of a number of **worksheets**. A Microsoft workbook often opens up with three worksheets. Extra worksheets can be added and others deleted.

A worksheet is the area in which numbers and text are entered. Rows are numbered from 1 to 65 536 and columns are identified by letters from A to Z then AA, AB–AZ, BA, BB–BZ and so on. The last column is labelled IV.

Each cell can contain a:

- Number, eg 45, 99.43, –887.
- Piece of text, eg Gillian Jones.
- Formula, eg =A1*2, which multiplies the value in cell A1 by 2.
- Function, eg =SUM(A1:A12).

Why use a spreadsheet?

A spreadsheet is a very good way to solve problems that involve calculations. It is also useful for displaying data that is arranged in a table. Some examples of typical uses for a spreadsheet are:

- Finding out how much interest can be earned over a period of time with a particular investment.
- Preparing a budget.
- Working out how much money must be repaid when taking out a loan.
- Keeping track of the value of a portfolio of shares.

How is a spreadsheet organised?

The location of a cell is referred to by the letter representing the column and then the number of the row. For example, cell B5 refers to the cell in column B, row 5.

The term 'active cell' refers to the cell that is being worked on at that instant. The contents of the active cell appear in the formula bar. The names along the top of the window are the various menus that contain commands to be used with the spreadsheet.

Unit 11.4 Activity 1A: Reading a spreadsheet

	A	B	C	D	E	F
1			Gina's Profit Report 2011			
2						
3		1st Qtr	2nd Qtr	3rd Qtr	4th Qtr	Total
4						
5	Revenue	12,345	13,580	12,901	13,543	52,369
6	Costs	8,944	10,285	9,874	10,565	39,668
7	Profit	3,401	3,295	3,027	2,978	12,701

A sample spreadsheet

1. A cell in a spreadsheet has a cell reference of A1. What is the column and what is the row in the reference?
2. Write down what is contained in the following cells of the sample spreadsheet:
   a. B5
   b. E6
   c. F3.
3. Looking at the sample spreadsheet, write down the cell references for:
   a. 2nd Qtr
   b. Total
   c. 12,701
   d. Gina's Profit Report 2012.

Moving around a spreadsheet

The screen can display only a part of the worksheet at any one time. This display is called a window. Any part of the worksheet may be displayed in a window by moving the cursor. The cursor may be moved by using:

- The arrow keys.
- The mouse.
- The tab key.
- The **Go To**… command on the **Find and Select** menu.

You can also move around the worksheet using:

- The scroll bars.
- The **PgUp** and **PgDn** keys.

However, the cursor does not move using these methods unless you click in a cell to make it the active cell.

Getting help

The **Help** icon at the top right of the screen allows access to Excel Help.

Help icon

Entering data in the help area provides answers to some queries. Access is also available online.

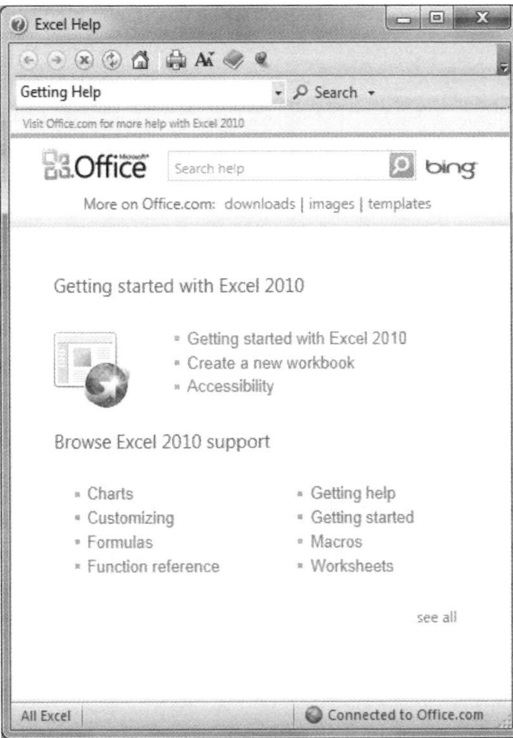

Help window

Unit 11.4 Activity 1B: Moving around a worksheet

1. Use the Office Help to find all the ways you can move around a worksheet.
2. Open a new worksheet and use each of these ways to move the cursor around the screen. Move to the last row, then the last column. What is the cell reference of the cell in the last row and last column?
3. Move the cursor to the cell G110 and write down what you did to get there.

Entering text

Text is used to provide meaning to the worksheet with headings and labels for cells, rows and columns. Labels help explain what the numbers in a cell represent.

Text is entered in a cell by making that cell active then using the keyboard to enter the text. Once the text is correct, press the enter key to accept it.

A cell is made active by clicking in it.

Example: Going to the rugby

This example uses a worksheet to work out the cost of going to the rugby.

The costs might include transport to the ground, the ticket, and food and drink at interval or after the match.

First, set up the headings:

- Create a heading in the first row of the second column, cell B1.
- In the first column, starting at A3, enter labels for each row: transport, ticket, food, drink.
- In A8, enter the label 'TOTAL'.

The worksheet is shown below.

The width of a column may need to be changed to ensure that all the text can be displayed. To change the width of a column, move the cursor to the line between the columns until it changes to a double-headed arrow, then double-click the left button. This adjusts the column width to fit all the text.

	A	B	C	D	E	F
1		**Cost of Going to the Rugby at SCRUM Oval, Lae**				
2						
3	Transport					
4	Ticket					
5	Food					
6	Drink					
7						
8	**TOTAL**					

Going to the rugby spreadsheet

Unit 11.4 Activity 1C: Creating different types of spreadsheets

1. Enter the text in the 'Going to the rugby' example and save the worksheet, calling it 'Rugby'.
2. Use a worksheet to enter your school timetable. It should look something like the example below. Print the worksheet when it is complete.
3. For each of the following, create row and column headings that would be needed to solve the problem.
   a. Work out the total cost of buying a new car. Costs will include the purchase price, dealer charges, stamp duty, registration, insurance and extra items such as an air conditioning unit.
   b. Create a worksheet that compares the prices of four different cars. Use advertisements from a newspaper to find the names and models of the cars. Use a column heading 'Price' with a row for each type of car you identify.
   c. Create headings in a worksheet that will keep track of your results for assignments and tests in your subjects at school. You will need to enter suitable headings and the names of the subjects you are studying.

	A	B	C	D	E	F
1			**Julia Chan's Timetable**			
2						
3		Monday	Tuesday	Wednesday	Thursday	Friday
4						
5	1	English	Biology	Science	History	Chinese
6	2	Maths	Communication	Phys Ed	Technology	English
7	3	History	Maths	Chinese	Music	Art
8	4	Music	Technology	Maths	English	Science
9	5	Chinese	Media Studies		Maths	Biology
10	6	Technology	History	Communication	Chinese	Maths
11	7	Science	Art	English	Science	Communication
12	8	Phys Ed	English	Biology	History	History

A school timetable

Unit 11.4 Activity 1D: Formatting a spreadsheet

1. How is text in a cell aligned by default?
2. How is number in a cell aligned by default?

Entering numbers

Numbers can be entered in a cell by making that cell active and using the keyboard to type in the number. Press the **Enter** key once the number has been entered.

Example: Going to the rugby

The costs of transport (K3.00) ticket (K7.75), food (K2.95) and a drink (K1.95) give the following spreadsheet.

	A	B	C	D	E	F
1		**Cost of Going to the Rugby at SCRUM Oval, Lae**				
2						
3	Transport	3.00				
4	Ticket	7.75				
5	Food	2.95				
6	Drink	1.95				
7						
8	TOTAL					

Going to the rugby spreadsheet

Note that the width of column A has been altered to show all the text.

Unit 11.4 Activity 1E: Entering numbers

1. Enter the numbers in the 'Going to the rugby' example into your 'Rugby' spreadsheet.
2. For each of questions 3a to 3c in Activity 1C, enter the costs and amounts of money you have found in the appropriate cells.

Formatting numbers

Numbers are displayed by the worksheet in a variety of ways. The number 765 could be entered and formatted as:

- An integer (whole number): 765.
- A decimal number with a specified number of decimal places: 765.00.
- Money: K765 or K765.00.
- A percentage: 76500%.

A spreadsheet represents a date as a number. In Microsoft Excel, when a number is formatted as a date, the number 1 refers to 1 January 1900, 2 is 2 January 1900, 3 is 3 January 1900, and so on. Thus 366 is 31 December 1900 (1900 was a leap year). The number 41 044 is the date 15 May 2012.

Unit 11.4 Activity 1F: Formatting numbers

1. Look at the **drop-down menu** on the **number tab** and write down how many different ways it allows you to format numbers.
2. The following data types can be entered in a spreadsheet. How would you enter the data and how could you then use the spreadsheet to format the display of the data to make it easier to understand and read?
    - **a.** A number.
    - **b.** An amount of currency.
    - **c.** A date.
    - **d.** A time.
    - **e.** A percentage.
3. Enter today's date in a worksheet. What number does Excel use to represent that date? Enter your birthday in a worksheet. What number does Excel use to represent your birthday?

Naming cells

Cells can be given meaningful names rather than referring to them as A1, B23 etc.

To name a cell:

- Select the cell.
- Select the **Define Name** command on the **Define Names** section of the **Formulas** tab.
- Excel will show a suggested name – this can be selected or modified.

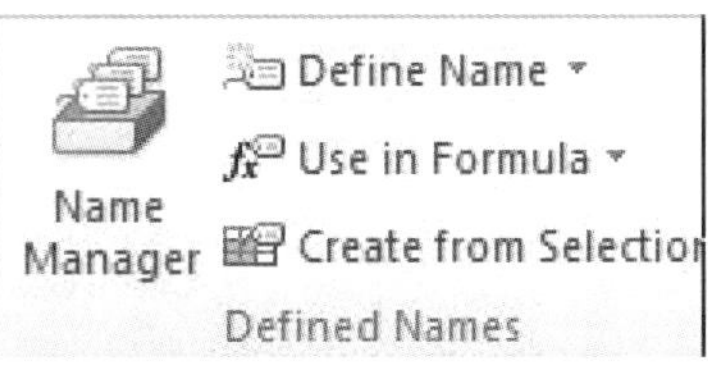

Defining names

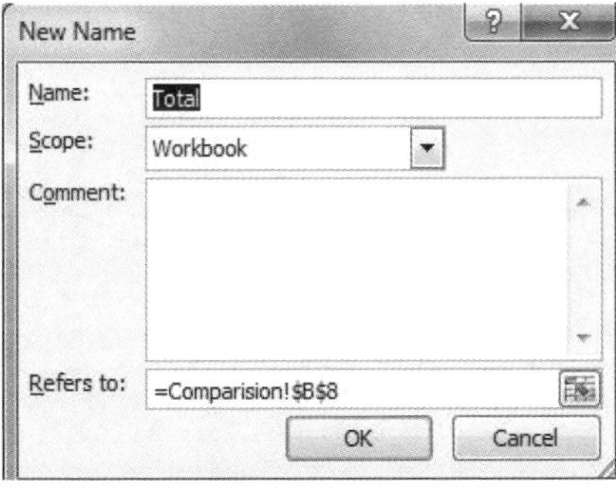

Entering a name

The name of the cell is displayed in the Name Box and this can be used for navigation.

Cell name in Name Box

Unit 11.4 Spreadsheets

Topic 2: Formulae

Topic 2 explains formulae and how they are used in spreadsheets.

What is a formula?

A **formula** is used for making calculations. It consists of:

- An '=' sign.
- One or more cell references and operators such as '+' for addition or '–' for subtraction.

The formula '=A5+1' means that 1 is added to the value stored in cell A5 and the result is placed in the active cell. The figure below shows the value 45 in cell A5 and the formula '=A5+1' in cell A6, which has the value 46.

	A
1	
2	
3	
4	
5	45
6	46

	A
1	
2	
3	
4	
5	45
6	=A5+1

Using a formula in a spreadsheet

In calculating the cost of going to the rugby, cell B8 will need a formula to work out the total cost. The results are shown below.

	A	B
1		**Rugby**
2		
3	Transport	3.00
4	Ticket	7.75
5	Food	2.95
6	Drink	1.95
7		
8	**TOTAL**	**15.65**

	A	B
1		**Rugby**
2		
3	Transport	3
4	Ticket	7.75
5	Food	2.95
6	Drink	1.95
7		
8	**TOTAL**	**=B3+B4+B5+B6**

The cost of going to the rugby

Cell B8 contains the formula '=B6+B5+B4+B3'. The formula is entered by typing an '=' sign followed by the cell references. Another method is to enter the '=' sign and then click on each of the cells to be added together, putting a '+' sign between each reference. The formula is shown in the second figure above.

BODMAS rules

BODMAS rules tell you the order in which calculations are to be done.

BODMAS stands for: **B**rackets
Of
Divide
Multiply
Add
Subtract

For example:

(9–7)*3 do the brackets first
= 2 * 3 then multiply
= 6

Excel follows the same rules.

Unit 11.4 Activity 2A: Working with formulae

	A	B
1	Purchase price	350,000
2	Stamp duty	6,100
3	Lawyer's fees	850
4	Bank fees	1,245
5	Removalist	455
6	TOTAL	358,650

1. Key in the worksheet above and save it as 'House'.

2. Modify the spreadsheets you have created in Activity 1C on page 229 to include simple formulae for the totals.

Using a function

Another way of doing additions is to use a **function**. A function is made up of:

- An '=' sign.
- A function name.
- Brackets or parentheses.
- An argument: usually a range of cells to be used in the calculation.

Thus, B6 in Activity 2A could contain the function '=SUM(B1:B5)'. In this case:

- The function name is 'SUM'.
- The argument or range refers to all the cells from B1 to B5 inclusive.

Microsoft Excel has a large range of functions. Another useful function is 'AVERAGE', which calculates the average of the numbers in the specified range. For example, the figure below shows the runs scored for six cricketers, with the average calculated in column F.

	A	B	C	D	E	F
1	Name	Scores				Average
2						
3	Taylor	25	65	101	3	48.50
4	Ponting	15	165	21	32	58.25
5	Hussey	104	0	0	63	41.75
6	Clarke	58	78	101	24	65.25
7	Waugh, S	99	2	26	14	35.25
8	Hayden	25	1	2	88	29.00

Worksheet showing average runs scored by some former and current Australian cricketers

The figure below shows the same worksheet with the function for the average in column F.

	A	B	C	D	E	F
1	Name	Scores				Average
2						
3	Taylor	25	65	101	3	=AVERAGE(B3:E3)
4	Ponting	15	165	21	32	=AVERAGE(B4:E4)
5	Hussey	104	0	0	63	=AVERAGE(B5:E5)
6	Clarke	58	78	101	24	=AVERAGE(B6:E6)
7	Waugh, S	99	2	26	14	=AVERAGE(B7:E7)
8	Hayden	25	1	2	88	=AVERAGE(B8:E8)

Worksheet showing the function in column F

Unit 11.4 Activity 2B: Sum activity and average function

1. Modify the worksheet you saved as 'House' to use the 'SUM' function to work out the total cost.
2. Use a worksheet to enter the points scored by each National Basketball League team last weekend (or use the results from another sport that interests you) and use the 'AVERAGE' function to calculate the average score.

What happens if a cell value is changed?

What happens to the cost of going to the rugby if the price of the ticket goes up but you spend less on food and drink? Entering the changed numbers in the worksheet cell results in an instant recalculation of the result, as shown below.

	A	B	C	D	E	F
1		**Cost of Going to the Rugby at SCRUM Oval, Lae**				
2						
3	Transport	3.00				
4	Ticket	10.95				
5	Food	2.95				
6	Drink	2.75				
7						
8	**TOTAL**	**19.65**				

Going to the rugby after some price changes

Example: Buying a house

What happens if the purchase price of the house is changed? Entering a new value in that cell immediately results in a new value in cell B6.

	A	B
1	Purchase price	425,000
2	Stamp duty	6,100
3	Lawyer's fees	850
4	Bank fees	1,245
5	Removalist	455
6	TOTAL	433,650

Changing the cost of buying a house

Unit 11.4 Activity 2C: Buying a house

1. Enter the new amounts in your worksheet called 'House' and check the value of the total.
2. Alter the figures in your worksheets from Activity 1C on page 229 and note what happens to the results.

Copying cells

Text, numbers and formulae can be copied from one cell to another, just like using a word processor.

Example: Buying a house

What happens if you wish to compare the cost of two different houses? Create a second column by adding the new numbers plus a heading in cell C1. The 'TOTAL' cell for the new column can be created by copying it from B6. Select B6, copy it, move to cell C6 and paste it. The worksheet below is the result.

	A	B	C
1	Purchase price	425,000	535,000
2	Stamp duty	6,100	7,100
3	Lawyer's fees	850	1025
4	Bank fees	1,245	1,450
5	Removalist	455	555
6	TOTAL	433,650	545,130

Comparing the cost of two houses

The formula is copied from cell B6 to cell C6 and is shown below.

6	TOTAL	=B1+B2+B3+B4+B5	=C1+C2+C3+C4+C5

Copying formulae

Example: Comparing the rugby and the soccer

Compare the cost of going to the rugby with the cost of going to the soccer.

Select cells B3 to B8, copy them and paste them into cells C3 to C8.

Now, alter the text in cell C1 and the numbers in cells C3 to C8. The new result appears in cell C8, as shown here:

	A	B	C
1		**Rugby at SCRUM Oval**	**Soccer at LFA Oval**
2			
3	Transport	3.00	1.50
4	Ticket	10.95	8.00
5	Food	2.95	5.95
6	Drink	2.75	3.50
7			
8	**TOTAL**	**19.65**	**18.95**

The formula is also copied from cell B8 to cell C8, as shown below.

8	Total	=B3+B4+B5+B6	=C3+C4+C5+C6

Copying formulae

Unit 11.4 Activity 2D: Using worksheets for comparison

1. Alter your 'Rugby' worksheet to compare the cost of going to the rugby and going to the cricket.
2. Alter your 'House' worksheet to compare the cost of two different houses.
3. Alter your worksheet comparing the cost of different cars to add a column showing the cost of last year's model.

What is a relative reference?

The formula for calculating the total cost of going to the movies in cell B8 is '=B6+B5+B4+B3'.

Stored in B8 is a formula which says: 'Add the value of the cell two cells up and the value of the cell three cells up and the value of the cell four cells up and the value of the cell five cells up'. Thus, when it is copied to cell C8 it works correctly, adding up the numbers in column C.

These are called **relative cell references** because they refer to cells by their position compared to the active cell. Figure 9.18 shows relative references.

	A	B
1		**Rugby**
2		
3	Transport	3
4	Ticket	10.95
5	Food	2.95
6	Drink	2.75
7		
8	**TOTAL**	**=B3+B4+B5+B6**

Relative references

Filling cells quickly

Text, numbers and formulae can be quickly copied into a range of cells.

This is done by selecting a range of cells and then clicking on the period (full stop) at the bottom right of the selection and then dragging down. To create a list of numbers from 1 to 10:

- Enter 1 in A1.
- Enter 2 in A2.
- Select cells A1 and A2.
- Click and drag on the period on the corner of cell A2. Note that the cursor changes to a '+'.
- Drag down to cell A10.

The figure below shows the results.

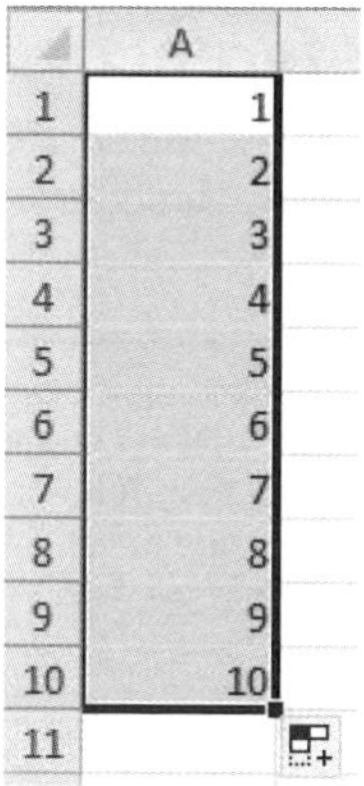

	A
1	1
2	2
3	3
4	4
5	5
6	6
7	7
8	8
9	9
10	10
11	

This method can also be used to enter a formula in a range of cells. For example:

- Enter 1 in A1.
- Enter the formula "=A1+1" in cell A2.
- Click and drag the period in the corner of cell A2.
- The series of numbers is created and the formula is copied into each cell.

The number 1 is entered into cell A1 and the formula '=A1+1' in cell A2.

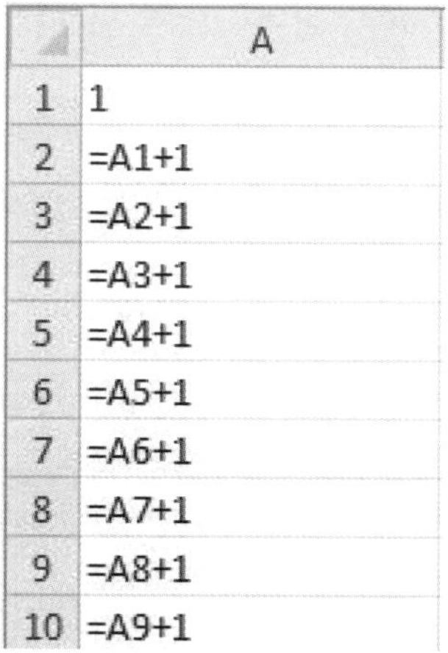

	A
1	1
2	=A1+1
3	=A2+1
4	=A3+1
5	=A4+1
6	=A5+1
7	=A6+1
8	=A7+1
9	=A8+1
10	=A9+1

Unit 11.4 Activity 2E: Simple calculator

1. Enter the number 1 in Cell A1. Enter the formula '=$A$1' in Cell A2 and fill down from A2 to A10.
2. Enter the text 'times' in Cell B1 and fill down from B2 to B10.
3. Enter the number 1 in Cell C1. Enter the formula '=C1+1' in Cell C2 and fill down from C2 to C10.
4. Enter the text 'equals' in Cell D1 and fill down from D2 to D10.
5. Enter the formula '=A1*C1' in Cell E1 and fill down from E1 to E10.
6. Change the number in cell A1 to 55. What happens?
7. How much does it cost to buy 7 spare parts at K46.69?

What is an absolute reference?

When you want to store a reference to a cell that will not change with the copy or fill command, you must refer to the **absolute cell reference**. This is done by using $ signs in the cell reference.

Example: Increasing the price

A trader decides to increase the price of each item of stock by 10%. Five items of stock are affected by this price increase. The value 10% is entered in cell C1. This will be used to work out the increase in the price of each item. Item A has a price of $50.00 (cell B4). The price increase is calculated by multiplying the value in cell B4 by the value in cell C1. The result, $5.00, is stored in cell C4. To get the new price, add cells B4 and C4 and store the result in cell D4.

	A	B	C	D
1	Percentage increase		10%	
2				
3	Stock Item	Old Price	Increase	New Price
4	Item A	50.00	5.00	55.00
5	Item B	123.00	12.30	135.30
6	Item C	38.00	3.80	41.80
7	Item D	45.55	4.56	50.11
8	Item E	258.00	25.80	283.80

Calculating a percentage price increase

The formula that is entered in cell C4 is '=B4*$C$1'. This formula means that to get the price increase in cell C4, you multiply the contents of cells B4 and C1. The formula for cell D4 is '=B4+C4'.

This process is repeated for each item. For item B, multiply the values in cells B5 and C1, and store the result in C5. Then add cells B5 and C5, and store the result in cell D5.

The $ sign shows that when the formula is created by copying to the cells below it always refers to the cell C1. That is, $C$1 is an absolute reference. This is shown below.

	A	B	C	D
1	Percentage increase		0.1	
2				
3	Stock Item	Old Price	Increase	New Price
4	Item A	50	=B4*$C$1	=B4+C4
5	Item B	123	=B5*$C$1	=B5+C5
6	Item C	38	=B6*$C$1	=B6+C6
7	Item D	45.55	=B7*$C$1	=B7+C7
8	Item E	258	=B8*$C$1	=B8+C8

Actual cell references

Unit 11.4 Activity 2F: Spreadsheet terminology

1. Write a short definition of the following terms that are used in spreadsheets:
   - **a.** Function.
   - **b.** Formula.
   - **c.** Label.
   - **d.** Value.
   - **e.** Number.
   - **f.** Result.
2. Explain the difference between an absolute and relative cell reference.

Unit 11.4 Activity 2G: Class mark analysis

1. Students in a class have just received the following marks in a test. The test was out of a total of 50 marks.
   What functions would you select to calculate the following?
   - **a.** The top mark gained.
   - **b.** The lowest mark gained.
   - **c.** The total marks gained divided by the number of candidates.
   - **d.** The number of candidates who sat for the test.

2. For the above, show the actual formula that would appear in the cell. What would be the best chart to show the results in a graphical form?

A	B	C
1	Student A	43
2	Student B	36
3	Student C	39
4	Student D	32
5	Student E	12
6	Student F	43
7	Student G	11
8	Student H	29
9	Student I	14
10	Student J	34
11	Student K	16
12	Student L	24
13	Student M	37
14	Student N	24

'What if' analysis

When important data in a worksheet is changed, a new result is immediately calculated. This is called **'what if' analysis**. For example, what if the rate of increase in the product price was 15% instead of 10%? Entering 15% in cell C1 causes the worksheet to recalculate the results.

'What if' analysis is used to check what happens when figures change. It is particularly useful when working out figures that involve money.

Unit 11.4 Activity 2H: 'What if' analysis

1. What is the purpose of a 'what if' analysis that is often conducted using a spreadsheet? Explain how it could be used in relation to currency exchange rates.
2. Create the worksheet on page 230, making sure that cell C1 contains an absolute reference. Change the value in cell C1 to 15%, 20% and 5%, and write down the new prices in each case.
3. Create the worksheet on the next page, which calculates the value of a house over time. Assume that the property purchase price is K340 000 and that the house will increase in value at the rate of 5% each year. Note that the formulae in column B refer to an absolute reference for cell B2. Change the values of B1 and B2 to answer the following questions:
   a. What would the value of the house be after 10 years if the inflation rate is 10%?
   b. What would the value of the house be after 10 years if the inflation rate is 7%?
   c. What would the value of a house that cost K450 000 be after 10 years if the inflation rate was 4%, 6% or 10%?

	A	B
1	Initial house value	350,000
2	Inflation rate	3%
3		
4	Year	House value
5		
6	0	350,000
7	1	360,500
8	2	371,315
9	3	382,454
10	4	393,928
11	5	405,746
12	6	417,918
13	7	430,456
14	8	443,370
15	9	456,671
16	10	470,371

a Screen display

	A	B
1	Initial house value	350000
2	Inflation rate	0.03
3		
4	Year	House value
5		
6	0	=B1
7	1	=B6+B6*$B$2
8	2	=B7+B7*$B$2
9	3	=B8+B8*$B$2
10	4	=B9+B9*$B$2
11	5	=B10+B10*$B$2
12	6	=B11+B11*$B$2
13	7	=B12+B12*$B$2
14	8	=B13+B13*$B$2
15	9	=B14+B14*$B$2
16	10	=B15+B15*$B$2

b Actual cell references

4. A new car depreciates in value each year; that is, the value of the car decreases by a certain percentage. Set up a worksheet that includes a cell for the original value of the car, the depreciation rate and the value of the car after each year for six years. Start with a car of value K31 000 and a depreciation rate of 25%. Remember to use an absolute value when referring to the cell with the depreciation rate.

Unit 11.4 Activity 2I: Planning a holiday

Draw up a budget for a family holiday to China. Use a spreadsheet to work out costs for a family of four including:

1. Travel
2. Accommodation
3. Car hire
4. Living expenses
5. Souvenirs
6. Cost of trips and excursions, eg trip to the Great Wall of China.

You should investigate costs of different travel, accommodation and car hire to ensure that you have the best price.

Unit 11.4 Activity 2J: Comparing house prices

Compare house prices in Papua New Guineas. Use the median prices for towns that are available in the weekend newspapers or on the Internet.

Use a spreadsheet to answer the following questions:

1. Which town is the most expensive?
2. Which town is the least expensive?
3. Which town had the largest increase in value in the last 12 months?
4. Which town had the smallest increase in value in the last 12 months?
5. Have the prices dropped in any towns in the last 12 months?

Unit 11.4 Spreadsheets
Topic 3: Printing a worksheet

Topic 3 explains how to print a worksheet.

Small worksheets are easily printed on one page of paper. However, large worksheets may take several sheets of paper and care must be taken to ensure that they are printed out in the correct order, and that page breaks are in appropriate places.

Microsoft Excel allows the user to set the area of a worksheet to be printed. This is done by:

- Selecting the range of cells to be printed.
- Choosing the **Set Print Area** command on the **Page Layout** tab.

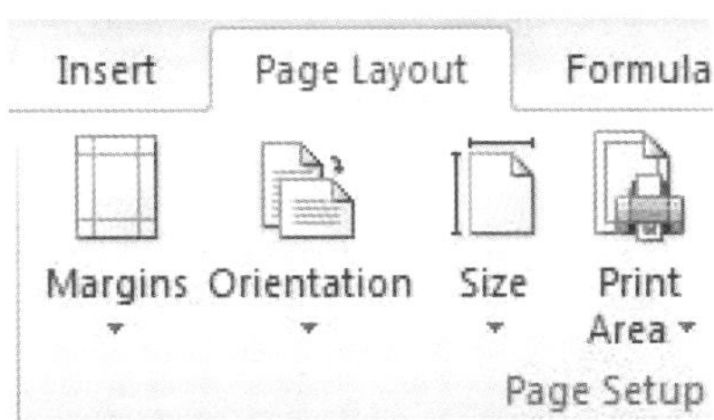

Setting the print area

The **Print** command, also on the **File** tab, provides a preview of each page. It is useful for ensuring that page breaks are in the correct place.

Excel allows a lot of flexibility in printing. The page can be printed in either portrait or landscape mode. Other options include printing with or without gridlines and with or without column and row headings. Headers and footers displaying page numbers, date, time, document title and other information may also be included. Top, bottom, left and right margins may be adjusted. These options are all accessed from the **Page Layout** tab.

Unit 11.4 Spreadsheets

Topic 4: Charts

Topic 4 gives an overview of charts as they are used in spreadsheets.

Cells of a worksheet may be selected and a chart created by Excel. These charts are very useful for displaying information. Excel chart types include:

- Column.
- Pie.
- Bar.
- Area.
- Line.

The charts are accessed on the **Chart** section of the **Insert** tab.

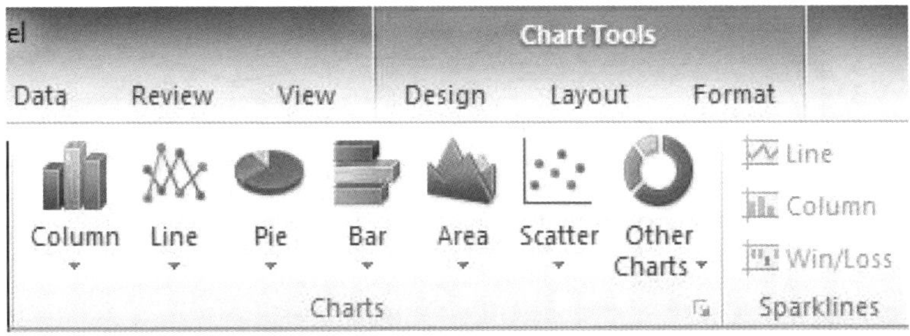

Excel chart types on the Insert tab

The worksheet below tracks the price of BHP Billiton shares at the end of the week over an eight-week period.

	A	B
1	**BHP Share Prices**	
2	15/07/2011	42.89
3	22/07/2011	43.43
4	29/07/2011	41.42
5	5/08/2011	38.12
6	12/08/2011	38.21
7	19/08/2011	37.50
8	26/08/2011	38.64
9	2/09/2011	39.04

BHP Billiton share price over an eight-week period

Example: line graph

These prices can be represented on a line graph as shown in the figure below. To create this graph, take the following steps:

- Select the cells to be represented on the chart.
- Choose the **Line** menu from the **Charts** section of the **Insert** tab.
- Choose the line graph from the menu.
- Add a chart title using the **Chart Title** command in the **Chart Tools** tab.
- Turn off the legend on the right of the chart using the **Legend** command.

The labels for the horizontal (x-axis) and vertical (y-axis) axes are generated by Excel.

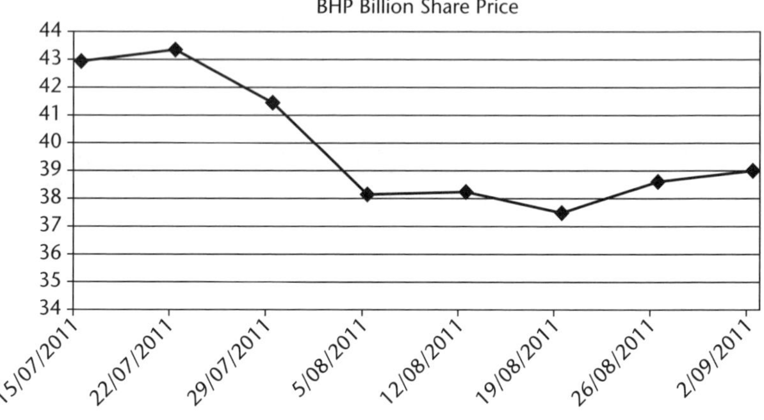

A line graph of share prices

Pie charts

Pie charts are useful for representing data such as a budget so that the contribution of each item can be shown.

Example: pie chart

Carrying out the following steps using the 'Rugby' worksheet could create a pie chart of these figures.

- Select the cells of the worksheet to be used: that is, A3 to B6.
- Choose the **Charts** menu from the **Charts** section of the **Insert** tab.
- Choose the chart type (the one with a 3D visual effect).
- Enter a chart title.

The result should look something like this:

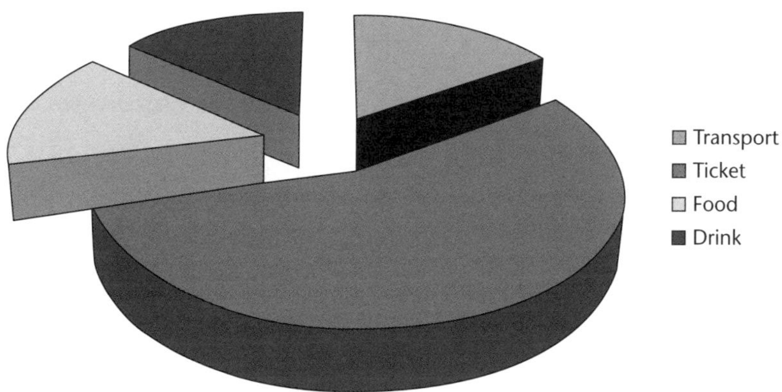

Pie chart showing the cost of going to the Rugby

Bar charts

Bar charts are used for making comparisons. For example, the chart below compares the costs of going to the rugby and going to the soccer. Note the addition of a legend on the right side of the chart.

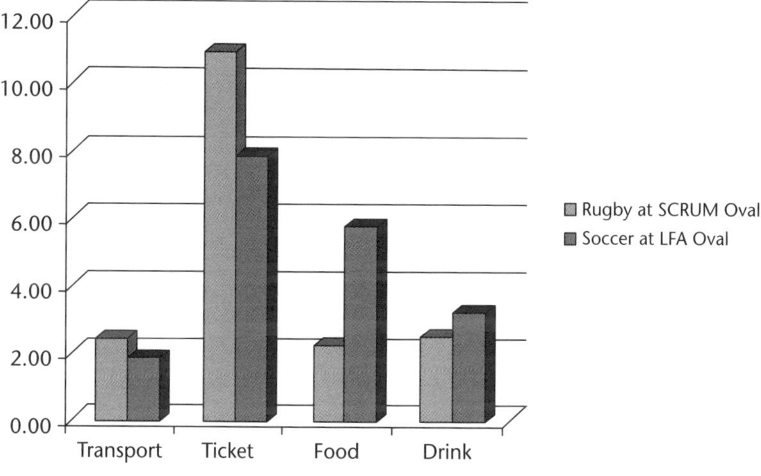

Bar chart comparing costs

Unit 11.4 Activity 4A: Extension exercises

1. Use the figures on the preceding pages to create worksheets and draw the charts shown in the figures. In each case, alter the figures and note the changes to the charts.
2. Find out the prices of ten different items in the supermarket. Enter the prices on a worksheet and use a bar chart to show the comparison.
3. Use a worksheet to work out the cost of purchasing a personal computer. Include the cost of the computer, software, DVDs, a printer and a cable modem.
4. Create a worksheet to work out the profit for a month's trading by a service station. The income is made up of petrol and oil sales of K39 563, labor charges of K13 445 and spare parts sales of K4503. The expenses are made up of salaries K12 000, rent K6500 and the cost of goods (petrol, oil, spare parts) K19 766.
5. Compile a list of 15 different items that may be purchased at a supermarket. Use a worksheet to list the items. Find out the prices of the items from two different supermarkets, enter them on the worksheet and compare the total prices.
6. Create a worksheet to work out the annual salaries of a company following a pay rise. Use cell A3 to contain the pay rise percentage and use an absolute reference in the formula you create. Try the spreadsheet with the following figures:

Surname	Initials	Old Salary	New Salary
Carey	P J	45 000	
Peters	R F	33 000	
Rowland	K M	49 950	
Cobb	J J	22 450	

7. The Apple Computer Company share price over a period of 10 days was (in $US):

07-Sep-11	$ 383.93
06-Sep-11	$ 379.74
02-Sep-11	$ 374.05
01-Sep-11	$ 381.03
31-Aug-11	$ 384.83
30-Aug-11	$ 389.99
29-Aug-11	$ 389.97
26-Aug-11	$ 383.58
25-Aug-11	$ 373.72
24-Aug-11	$ 376.18

Use a worksheet to enter this data and draw it as a chart. Save the chart as a web page and open the chart using a browser. Open the table of data using a browser.

Unit 11.4 Spreadsheets
Topic 5: Using advanced functions

Topic 5 in this Unit deals with some of the more advanced functions of spreadsheets (see ICT Syllabus pp. 19–21). It covers:

- Working with advanced formatting.
- Working with multiple worksheets and workbooks.
- Using advanced functions.
- Creating pivot tables and analysing data.

Advanced formatting

Excel has a range of different number **formats** built into the system. The formats include:

- Currency.
- Accounting.
- Date.
- Percentage.

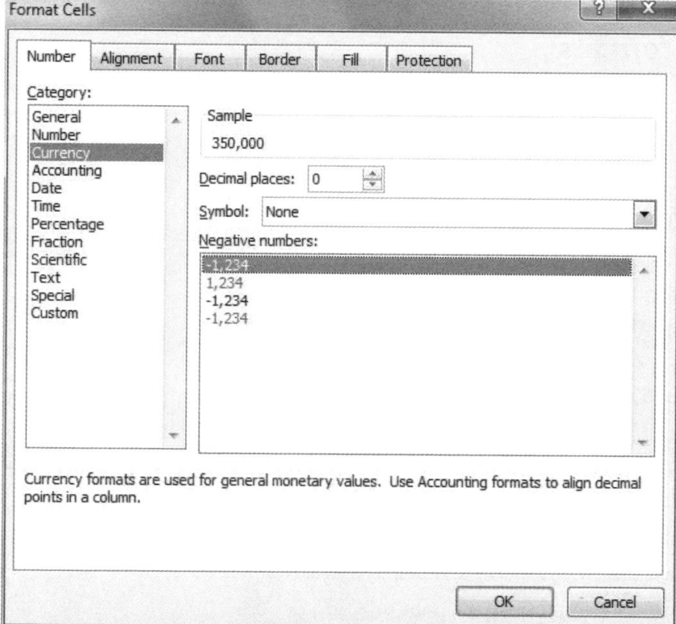

Format cells window in Excel

Each of these standard formats can be adjusted to suit your preference.

The **Currency** format can be set to:

- Modify the number of decimal places – you may not require decimal places for large numbers.
- Change the currency symbol – a wide range is available from the drop-down menu.
- Display negative numbers with a minus (-) sign or display them in red.

The **Date** format has a range of ways to format the date.

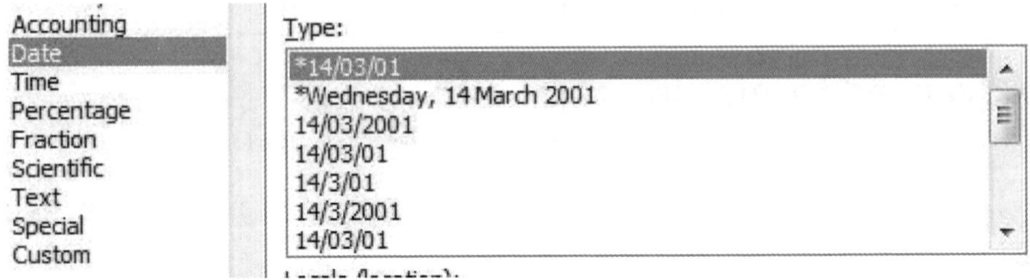

Some of the date formats available

Custom formats

The **Custom** category in the **Format Cells** window can be used to create your own number formats. You can use codes to define how you display digits, decimal places, dates and currency symbols.

Number format codes

0 can be used as a placeholder for digits in a number:

- The format 0.00 will display the number 4.5 as 4.50.
- The format 0.000 will display the number 4.5 as 4.500.
- The format 00.000 will display the number 4.5 as 04.500.

This type of format can be used to display precisely the number of digits you require on either side of the decimal point.

can be used as a significant placeholder for numbers. It will only display significant (non-zero) digits:

- The format #.## will display the number 4.5 as 4.5.
- The format #.## will display the number 4.56 as 4.56.
- The format #.## will display the number 4.567 as 4.57.
- The format #.## will display the number 0.45 as .45.

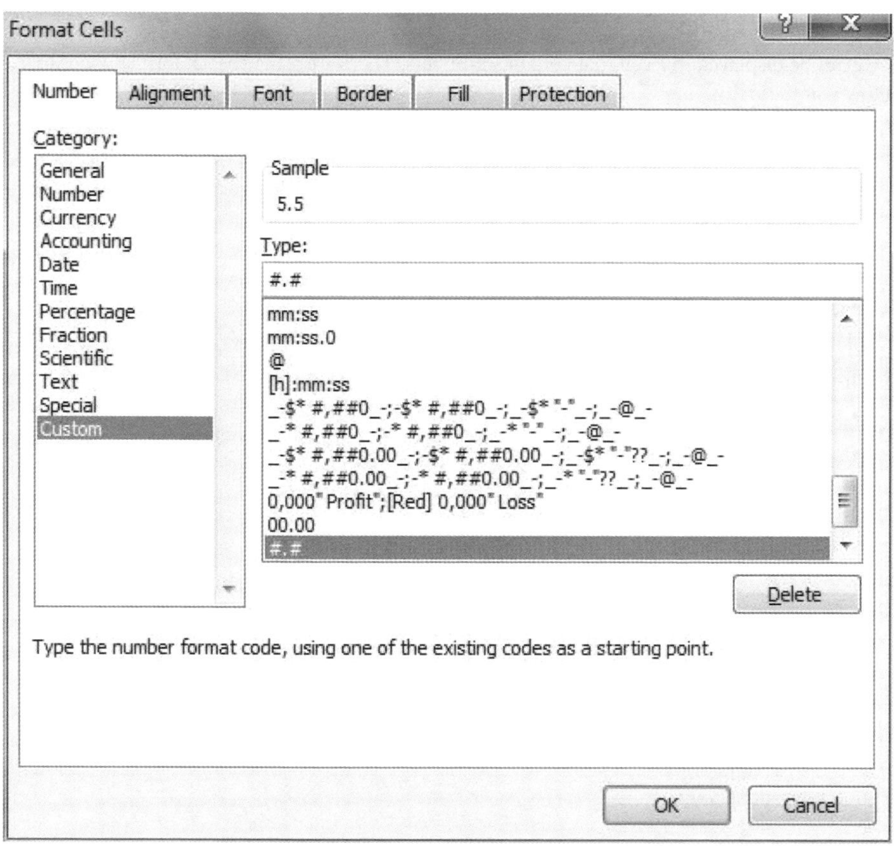

Custom number formats

Date formats

You can create your own custom date formats. Days, months and years can be combined in many different ways:

- The format dd/mm/yy displays 10 March 2012 as 10/03/12.
- The format dd/mm/yyyy displays 10 March 2012 as 10/03/2012.
- The format dd-mmm-yy displays 10 March 2012 as 10-Mar-12.
- The format dd-mmmm-yyyy displays 10 March 2012 as 10-March-2012.

In a similar way, different formats for times can also be created.

Text format codes

Text can be displayed in a cell that contains numbers. There are some special format codes that allow you to do this.

To add text to a number, create the number format with the text in quotes, including a space to separate the text from the number.

The format:

- 0,000 "Profit";0,000 "Loss" displays:
  - 10,000 as 10,000 Profit.
  - -10,000 as 10,000 Loss.

A colour can be added by changing the code to:

- [blue] 0,000 "Profit";[red] 0,000 "Loss" displays:
  - 10,000 as 10,000 Profit in blue.
  - -10,000 as 10,000 Loss in red.

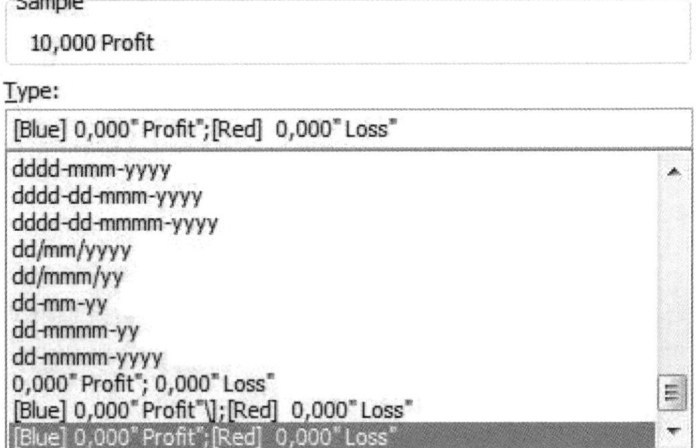

Custom number format with text

Conditional formatting

Conditional formatting allows users to see important aspects of the data in a worksheet.

Conditional formatting is where Excel applies special formatting to particular cells. The formatting is applied only to cells that meet a certain condition. The special formatting is usually colours, borders and backgrounds.

The **Conditional Formatting** command is found on the **Styles** section of the **Home** tab.

Conditional formatting can be used to highlight particular cells. For example, the figure on page 235 showed the scores of some Australian cricketers and their averages.

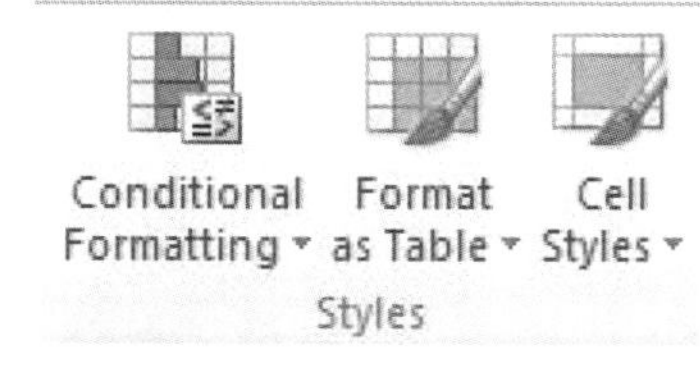

Conditional formatting menu

To highlight the averages above 40, do the following:

- Select the column with the average scores.
- Go to the **Conditional Formatting** command.
- Choose **Highlight Cells Rules**.
- Then choose **Greater Than**.
- The following window appears, which allows the criteria to be entered.

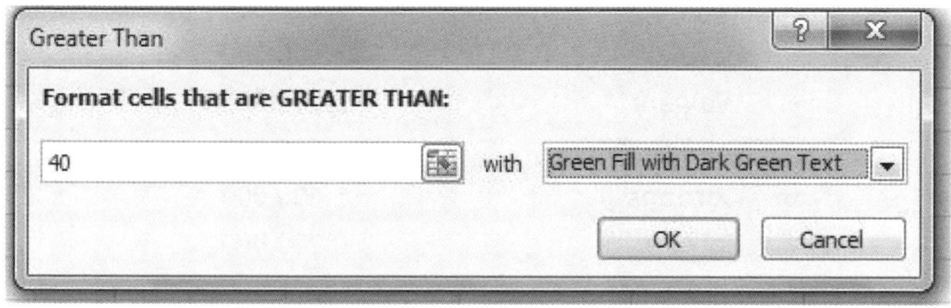

Entering the criteria

In this example, the cells where the average is greater than 40 will have a **Green Fill with Dark Green Text**, as shown in the drop-down menu.

The worksheet now has those cells highlighted.

Name	Scores				Average
Hayden	25	101	65	3	48.50
Slater	15	44	27	72	39.50
Langer	0	2	58	13	18.25
Waugh M	106	12	44	19	45.25
Waugh S	74	3	52	141	67.50
Ponting	0	55	2	4	15.25

Cells highlighted have an average greater than 40

The conditions can also be based on text values. In the figure below, asking-prices for properties around Port Moresby are shown.

Port Moresby Properties for Sale

Location	Price (K)
Korobosea	1,300,000
Touaguba Hill	1,980,000
Brampton	1,400,000
Gerehu	350,000
Boroko	1,500,000
Gerehu	400,000
Tokarara	600,000
Boroko	2,500,000
Waigani	2,800,000
Garden Hills	750,000
Gordons	1,400,000
Boroko	3,200,000

Prices for properties around Port Moresby

To highlight those properties in Boroko, for example, set up the rule:

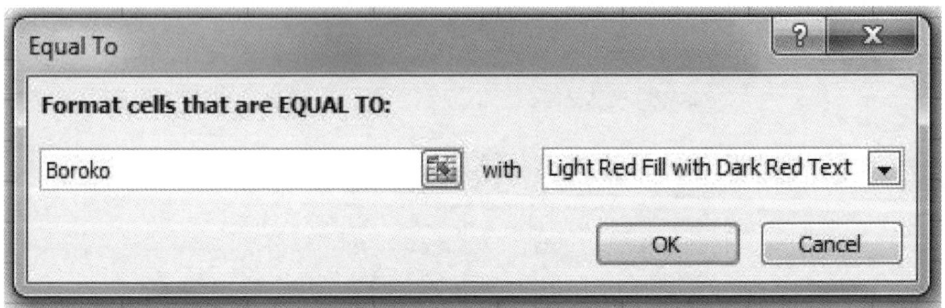

Rule to highlight properties in Boroko

The conditions can be based on calculations. The following rule highlights those prices that are above average in the list:

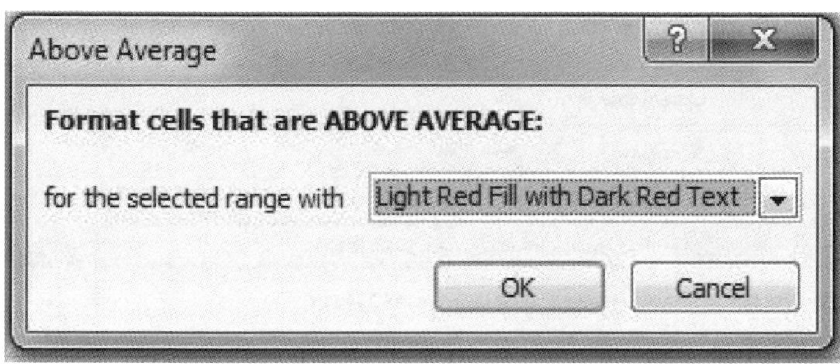

Formatting cells that are above average

The result is shown in the figure below.

Port Moresby Properties for Sale

Location	Price (K)
Korobosea	1,300,000
Touaguba Hill	1,980,000
Brampton	1,400,000
Gerehu	350,000
Boroko	1,500,000
Gerehu	400,000
Tokarara	600,000
Boroko	2,500,000
Waigani	2,800,000
Garden Hills	750,000
Gordons	1,400,000
Boroko	3,200,000

Cells that are above average

Managing the rules

Rules can be managed on the **Conditional Formatting** menu. Rules can be:

- Added.
- Modified.
- Deleted.

The **Manage Rules…** command provides a window that shows rules to be modified.

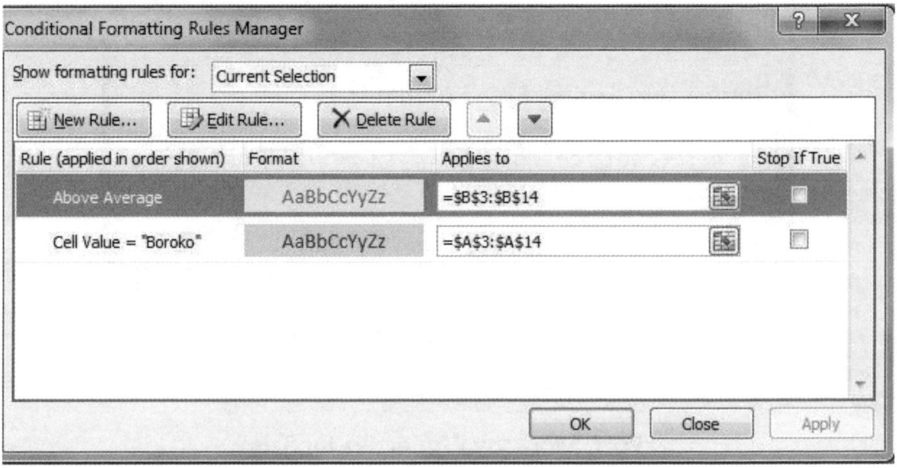

Managing rules

Using conditions

A condition can be used as part of a number format. The condition is contained in brackets. Each condition is separated by a semicolon.

For example, the number format:

- [<50] "Fail";[>=50] "Pass"

will enter the text "Fail" in the cell if the number is less than 50 and will enter the text "Pass" if it is 50 or more.

A telephone number can be formatted so that if it is longer than 7 digits, those digits before the 7 digits are treated as an area code. For example, the following condition:

- [<9999999]### ####;(###) ### ####
  - Formats the number 4542244 as 454 2244
  - Formats the number 624542244 as (62) 454 2244.

Using styles

Excel has a range of pre-defined styles that can be used in a worksheet. The styles can be seen on the **Home** tab by accessing the **Styles** command and then selecting **Cell Styles**.

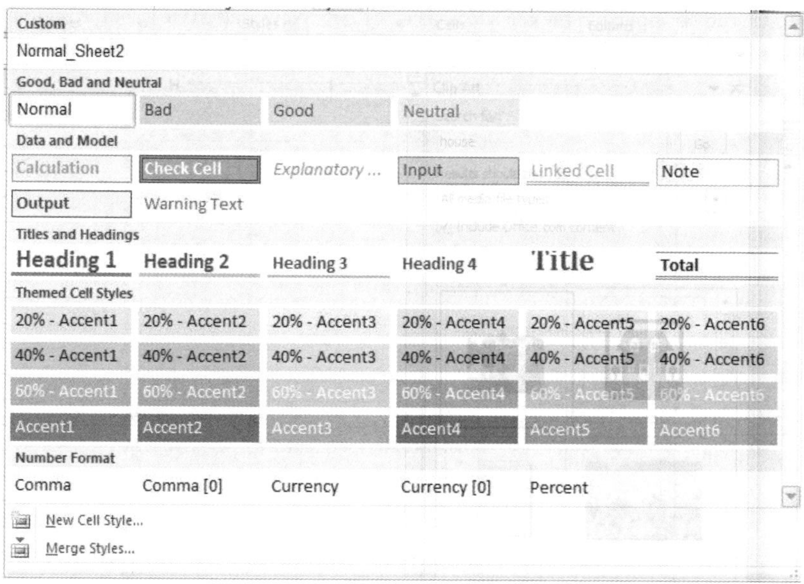

An example of the cell styles

These cell styles are available as themes on the **Page Layout** tab.

To apply a style:

- Select the cells to which the style will be applied.
- Choose **Cell Styles** on the **Styles** section of the **Home** tab.
- Select the cell style, eg 'Heading 2'.

Styles allow the user to develop a consistent set of font types, sizes and colours.

When a different theme is applied from the **Page Layout** menu, the various styles are then applied to the worksheet, including any charts.

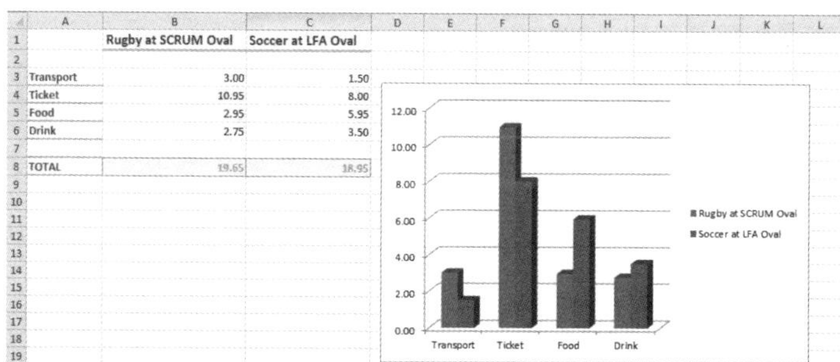

A worksheet with styles defined and a theme applied

A new style can be applied in the cell styles sheet. Choose **New Cell Style ...** at the bottom of the window. This brings up a style window that allows the attributes to be set.

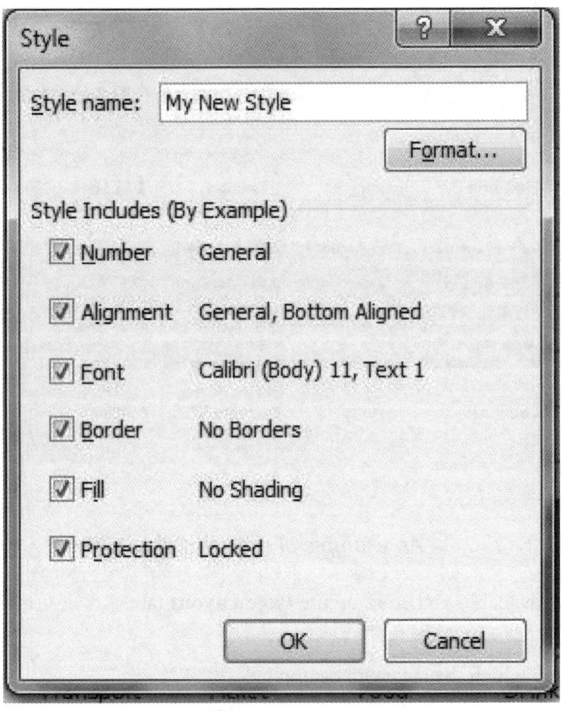

Creating a new style

The user needs to:

- Give the style a name.
- Modify the attributes, eg font, alignment, etc.
- Click **OK**.

The new style now appears in the style sheet window.

To modify the style:

- Open the style window.
- Right-click on the style name.
- Choose **Modify...**
- Make the appropriate changes.

To delete a style:

- Open the style window.
- Right-click on the style name.
- Choose **Delete**.

To merge styles from another worksheet:

- Open the worksheet from which you wish to copy the styles.
- Select **Cell Styles** from the **Styles** section on the **Home** tab.
- Choose **Merge Styles…** from the bottom of the window.
- Select the open worksheet.
- Click **OK** to copy the styles.

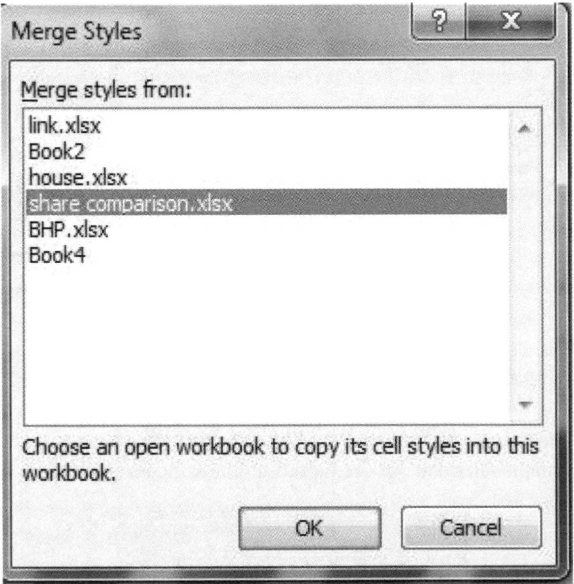

Merging styles

Working with multiple worksheets

It can be useful to have a workbook that is composed of identical worksheets for each month or quarter and to have a summary worksheet that collects data from each of those worksheets.

It is important that each worksheet has the same arrangements of rows and columns. For example, a workbook can be set up with costs for each month of the year with each worksheet named Jan, Feb, Mar etc.

	A	B	C	D
1	**Summary Results**			
2				
3	Gross Sales	80,570.00		
4	Costs	52,414		
5	Net Revenue	28,156		
6				
7				
8				
9				
10				
11				
12				
13				
14				
15				

Summary / Jan / Feb / Mar / Apr / May / Jun

Workbook with multiple worksheets

Each worksheet contains sales data for the month, in the same format:

	A	B
1	Gross Sales	10,558
2	Costs	6,541
3	Net Revenue	4,017

Sales figures for one month

The summary sales figures can be worked out on the first worksheet (named Summary) by entering the following formula:

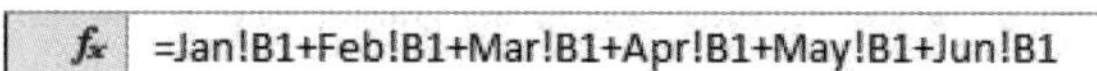

Formula takes numbers from different worksheets

Note that the part of the formula 'Jan!B1' means cell B1 on the worksheet named Jan.

Another method is to use the SUM function. In this case the syntax is:

Using a function across worksheets

The function adds the values in cell B1 in the worksheets in the range Jan to Jun. The results are shown below.

	A	B
1	**Summary Results**	
2		
3	Gross Sales	80,570.00
4	Costs	52,414
5	Net Revenue	28,156

Summary results from a range of worksheets

The summary worksheet could be maintained in a separate workbook. The functions in this workbook are shown below.

	A	B
1	**Summary Results**	
2		
3	Gross Sales	=SUM([ThreeD.xlsx]Jan:Jun!B1)
4	Costs	=SUM([ThreeD.xlsx]Jan:Jun!B2)
5	Net Revenue	=B3-B4

Summary worksheet

Note that the name of the Workbook 'ThreeD.xlsx' is now part of the function.

Combining worksheets and data

Moving worksheets

A worksheet may be moved from one workbook to another. To do this:

- Right-click on the name of the worksheet.
- Select **Move or Copy...**
- In the window that appears:
  - Select the name of the workbook to which the worksheet is to be moved.
  - Select the position into which the worksheet will be moved.
- Click **OK**.

The worksheet is then moved to the chosen location.

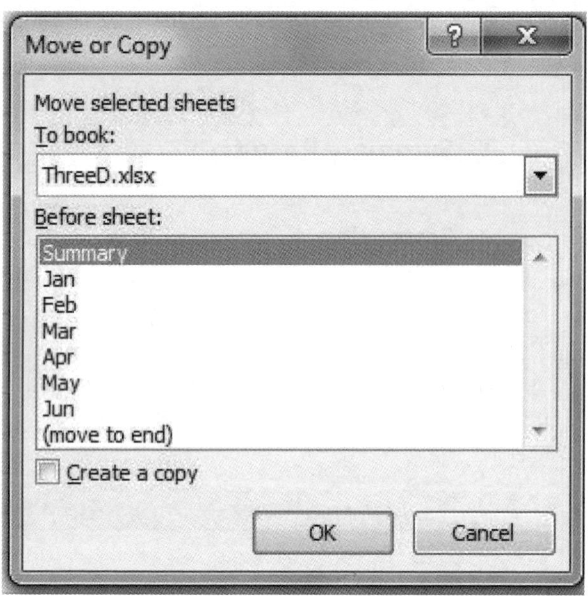

Moving a worksheet

Copying worksheets

A worksheet may be copied to another workbook. To do this, follow the above procedure but also click in the box labelled **Create a copy**. This will copy the worksheet to a different workbook but will also leave the original workbook intact.

Using advanced functions

Using financial functions

PMT is a financial function that enables you to calculate the monthly repayment on a loan amount with a fixed interest rate over a fixed period of time.

The function is of the form: **PMT(rate,nper,pv,fv,type)**

- Rate is the interest rate, eg 6% pa.
- Nper is the number of periods over which a loan is to be repaid.
- Pv is the amount of the loan.
- Fv is the final value of the loan at the end of the repayment period; this is set to zero if it is left out of the formula.
- Type indicates when the payments are made, ie at the start or end of each period. The default value is at the end of each period.

Generally, the values for fv and type are omitted and the default values are used.

For a house that has a loan of K300 000 with an annual interest rate of 6% and repayments made monthly, the calculations are shown in the figure below.

18	**House Repayment**	
19		
20	Value of Loan	300,000
21	No. of years	20
22	No. of periods	240
23	Annual interest rate	6%
24	Monthly interest rate	1%
25		
26	Monthly repayment	-2149.29

Loan repayment

Note the following calculations:

- No. periods = no. of years * 12.
- Monthly interest rate = annual interest rate / 12.

18	**House Repayment**	
19		
20	Value of Loan	300000
21	No. of years	20
22	No. of periods	=12*B21
23	Annual interest rate	0.06
24	Monthly interest rate	=B23/12
25		
26	Monthly repayment	=PMT(B24,B22,B20)

The formulae used

This calculation could use cell names to make it more meaningful. In this case, the formula would look like this:

```
fx =PMT(Monthly_interest_rate,No._of_repayments,Value_of_loan)
```

PMT function

Unit 11.4 Activity 5A: Buying a house

1. Create a worksheet to calculate the repayments on a loan for a house where:

a. The amount of the loan is K250 000.

b. The annual rate of interest is 5.5%.

c. The period of the loan is 20 years.

2. What happens to the repayment if:

a. The amount of the loan is increased to K275 000?

b. The annual interest drops to 4.75%?

c. The period of the loan is changed to 17 years?

d. The amount of the loan is changed to K220 000 and the interest is 5.75%?

Using the ABS function

The ABS function returns the absolute value of the number, ie the number without a sign. For example:

- ABS(12) = 12.
- ABS(-12) = 12.

The absolute value is useful in measuring *errors* in predictions. Consider measuring the accuracy of sales forecasts against actual sales. The forecasts may vary significantly – both positive and negative errors are possible.

To consider the accuracy of the forecast, you need to know the actual sales versus the forecast sales and the error.

In the figure below, the forecast versus actual sales show up as no error over a period of six months but if you take the absolute value of the error it is 10%. That is, sales forecasts have an average error of 10%, either above or below the forecast.

	A	B	C	D	E	F	G	H	I
1	Sales Forecast Accuracy					Sales Forecast Accuracy Using ABS			
2									
3		Forecast	Actual	Error			Forecast	Actual	Error
4	Jan	2550	2875	325		Jan	2550	2875	325
5	Feb	2900	3025	125		Feb	2900	3025	125
6	Mar	3250	3750	500		Mar	3250	3750	500
7	Apr	4500	3450	-1050		Apr	4500	3450	1050
8	May	5000	4900	-100		May	5000	4900	100
9	Jun	5250	5450	200		Jun	5250	5450	200
10	TOTAL	23450	23450	0			23450	23450	2300
11			% Error	0				% Error	10%

Using the ABS function

Using logical functions

Logical functions are used in worksheets to help make decisions.

The IF function checks whether a condition that is described is TRUE and returns one value. It returns another value if the condition described is FALSE. Its format is:

- =IF(Condition,Value_if_true, Value_if_false).

A logical condition or test might be:

- B6>0.
- D8= “South”.
- E9>=D9.

For example, the following function =IF(B6>0,50,0) would mean: ‘If the value in cell B6 is greater than 0 then 50, otherwise 0.’

Returning a text value

The IF function can be used to return a text value. For example, a list of examination scores can be examined so that:

- If the score is greater than or equal to 50, the value ‘Pass’ is returned.
- Otherwise, the value ‘Fail’ is returned.

The function is:

```
=IF(score>=50,"Pass","Fail")
```

IF function returns a text value

An example of the worksheet is shown below. Note that the range B2:B6 has been given the name ‘score’.

	A	B	C
1	**Name**	**Score**	**Result**
2	John	45	Fail
3	James	50	Pass
4	Peter	21	Fail
5	Ingrid	75	Pass
6	Elizabeth	80	Pass

Results of using the IF function

Returning a numeric value

The IF function can also be used to return a numeric value. This value can be the result of a calculation.

For example, many organisations pay salespeople commission based on the revenue generated. Commission could be paid on the following basis:

- If revenue is greater than K10 000 then the commission is 5% of the revenue.
- Otherwise, it is 3% of the revenue.

The function is:

```
=IF(Revenue>10000,0.05*Revenue,0.03*Revenue)
```

IF function returns a calculated value

An example of the worksheet is shown below. Note that the range B2:B6 has been given the name 'revenue'.

	A	B	C
1	**Sales Person**	**Revenue**	**Commission**
2	John	12,554	627.70
3	James	9,542	286.26
4	Peter	8,500	255.00
5	Ingrid	15,748	787.40
6	Elizabeth	6,502	195.06

Commission results using the IF function

Using a nested IF function

The IF function offers two possible results – either the test is TRUE and the first formula or text is used, or the test is FALSE and the second formula or text is used.

A nested IF function can be used to make further distinctions. In the examination score example on page 257, the score can be separated so that:

- Less than 50 is a 'Fail'.
- 50 to 69 is a 'Pass'.
- 70 and above is a 'Credit'.

To build the IF statement, do the following steps:

- Test for the first condition, ie if less than 50 then fail.
- If that condition is true, 'Fail' is the result.
- If that condition is false, test to see if the score is less than 70.
- If that is true, 'Pass' is the result.
- If that condition is false, 'Credit' is the result.

The IF statement has a second IF statement nested inside the formula:

```
=IF(score<50,"Fail",IF(score<70,"Pass","Credit"))
```

A nested IF function

The results are shown below.

	A	B	C
1	**Name**	**Score**	**Result**
2	John	68	Pass
3	James	49	Fail
4	Peter	21	Fail
5	Ingrid	75	Credit
6	Elizabeth	80	Credit

Using a nested IF function

Excel allows the user to nest up to 64 IF statements but they quickly become very complex. For example, the results could be further separated to provide that a score or 80 and above is regarded as a distinction. This is done using the following nested IF statement:

```
=IF(score<50,"Fail",IF(score<70,"Pass",IF(score<80,"Credit","Distinction")))
```

Another nested IF function

Using OR, AND and COUNTIF functions

The OR function is a logical test. The syntax is:

- =OR(logical1, logical2).
    - If either logical1 or logical2 is true, the value TRUE is displayed.
    - If either logical1 or logical2 is not true, the value FALSE is displayed.

For example, if a number is between 1 and 100, the following formula would display FALSE:

```
=OR(A27<0,A27>100)
```

The OR function

If the number was either less than zero or greater than 100, it would display TRUE.

27	25
28	FALSE

Using the OR function

The AND function is another logical test. The syntax is:

- =AND(logical1, logical2).
    - If both logical1 and logical2 are true, the value TRUE is displayed.
    - If either logical1 or logical2 is not true, the value FALSE is displayed.

For example, if a number is between 1 and 100, the following formula would display TRUE:

=AND(A24>0,A24<=100)

The AND function

And the worksheet shows:

24	25
25	TRUE

Using the AND function

The COUNTIF function counts the number of times that a particular criterion is met in a cell range. The syntax is:

- =COUNTIF(cell range, criteria)

The function can be used to count the number of occurrences in a table. The table below shows real-estate prices:

Location	**Price**
Gerehu	350,000
Boroko	2,500,000
Erima	550,000
Ensisi Valley	700,000
Gerehu	850,000
Gerehu	400,000
Tokarara	680,000
Tokarara	550,000
Morata	510,000
Tokarara	280,000

Using the COUNTIF function

If these are in an Excel worksheet then the function COUNTIF can be set up:

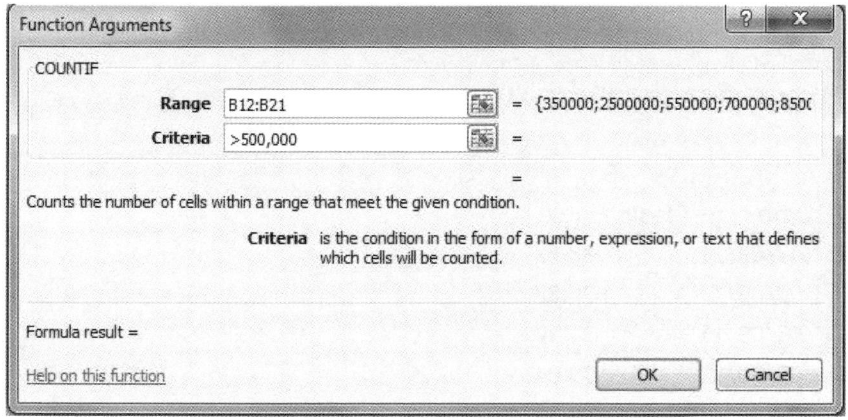

The COUNTIF function

These can give results such as:

24	No. houses > 500,00	7
25	No. Houses in Gerehu	3

Results using the COUNTIF function

Using lookup functions

A lookup function is used to look up values in a table in Excel.

VLOOKUP can be used in a vertical table or list. For example, the date and closing price of BHP Billiton shares can be listed in a table. A list such as this can be very long and can be difficult to look at.

The VLOOKUP function can be used to look up the price of the share on any given date that is in the list.

The function has the following format:

VLOOKUP(lookup_value, table_array, col_index_num, [range_lookup])

In this format:

- Lookup_value is the value that will be searched for, eg the date of the required share price.

	A	B
1	Date	Closing Price
2	07/09/11	38.23
3	06/09/11	36.88
4	05/09/11	37.70
5	02/09/11	39.04
6	01/09/11	39.87
7	31/08/11	39.74
8	30/08/11	39.35
9	29/08/11	39.15
10	26/08/11	38.64
11	25/08/11	38.61
12	24/08/11	38.21
13	23/08/11	38.21
14	22/08/11	37.53

Part of a table of BHP Billiton share prices

- Table_array is the range of cells that makes up the table to be searched, in this case the range A2 to B173.
- Col_index_number is the number of the column that contains the value that is being searched for, ie the share price on the given date.
- Range_lookup is either TRUE or FALSE. If the value is FALSE, an exact match is required.

	A	B	C	D	E	F
1	Date	Closing Price				
2	07/09/11	38.23				
3	06/09/11	36.88				
4	05/09/11	37.70				
5	02/09/11	39.04				
6	01/09/11	39.87				
7	31/08/11	39.74			Date	05/09/11
8	30/08/11	39.35			Closing Price	37.70
9	29/08/11	39.15				

Using the VLOOKUP function

In the example, the date is entered in cell F7 and the price is displayed in cell F8.

If the date is changed, the closing price is changed. For example, entering 22/08/11 returns 37.53.

The completed formula is shown in the next figure.

```
=VLOOKUP(F7,A2:B173,2,FALSE)
```

The VLOOKUP function

Using VLOOKUP in a different worksheet

The same process can be used to look up a value in a different worksheet. In this example, if the worksheet is named 'BHP', then the formula becomes:

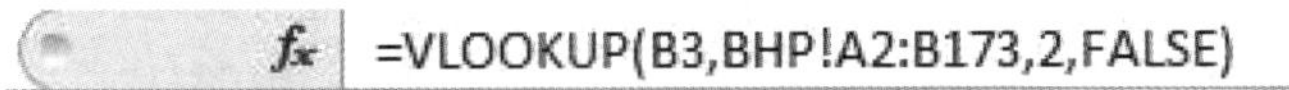

The VLOOKUP function in a different worksheet

Note that the range has become 'BHP!A2:B173' where BHP! refers to the worksheet name and the ! indicates that it is in a different part of the file.

Using VLOOKUP in a different file

In the same manner, data can be looked up in a different file and displayed.

In the following example, data for the BHP Billiton share price and for the NAB share price are stored in different files. The closing price for each share on a given day can be looked up and displayed by entering the date.

		BHP Billiton	NAB
1		**BHP Billiton**	**NAB**
2			
3	Date	11/02/11	
4	Closing Price	43.35	25.69
5			

The VLOOKUP function in a different file

Note that the formula for the range now includes the spreadsheet name in square brackets ie '[BHP.xlsx]' and '[nab.xlsx]' together with the worksheet name.

```
=VLOOKUP(B3,[BHP.xlsx]BHP!$A$2:$B$173,2,FALSE)    =VLOOKUP(B3,[nab.xlsx]Price!$A$2:$B$174,2,FALSE)
```

Looking up values in a different file

Using data outlining

Outlining data can be useful in providing summary information. For example, consider the spreadsheet on the right, which shows sales figures for a small business in three months (January to March) and in three different regions.

The data needs to be sorted and then it can be put into outline form and subtotals can be included.

The data needs to be selected, including the headings. The commands to be used are on the **Data** tab, in the **Outline** section on the right side end of the tab.

	A	B	C
1	**Month**	**Region**	**Sales**
2	Jan	North	1,500
3	Jan	South	2,500
4	Jan	East	1,400
5	Jan	West	1,325
6	Feb	North	1,655
7	Feb	South	2,345
8	Feb	East	1,775
9	Feb	West	2,356
10	Mar	North	2,255
11	Mar	South	1,126
12	Mar	East	1,589
13	Mar	West	1,998

Sales figures for a three-month period

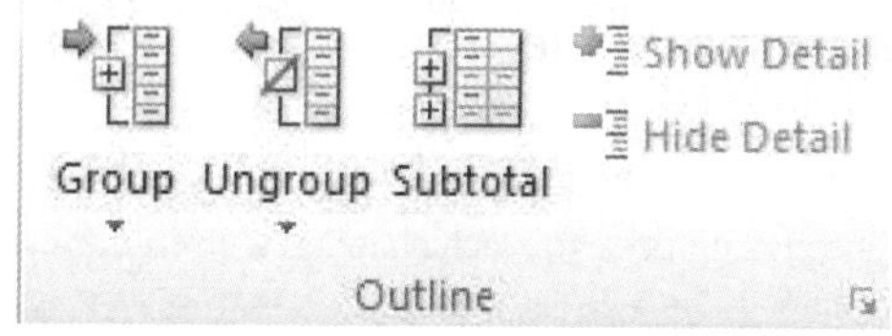

*The **Outline** commands*

Clicking the **Subtotal** command brings up the following window:

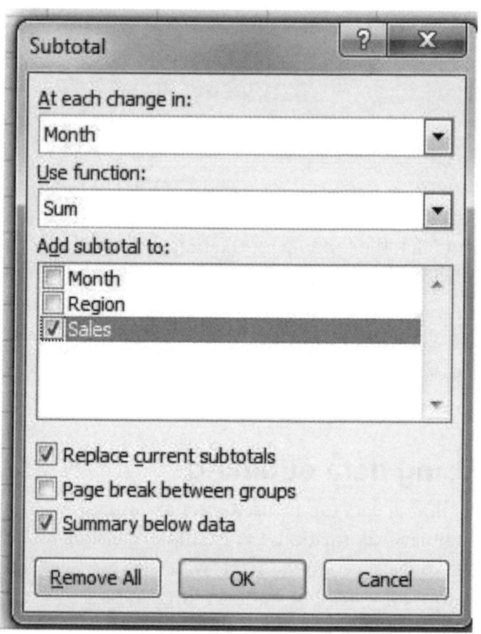

The Subtotal command

The window specifies three variables:

- The data will be grouped according to the month.
- The function SUM will be used; it will provide subtotals for each month.
- The subtotals will be based on the sales figures.

Note that the column headings are important in identifying each piece of data.

The subtotals for each month are automatically inserted into the worksheet and the grand total at the bottom. Note also that outline controls are added to the left of the row headings. These can be activated by clicking on them or by using the **Show Detail** or **Hide Detail** command in the **Outline** section of the **Data** tab.

Note that in the figure below, the summary data only is shown for Jan and Feb.

1 2 3		A	B	C
	1	**Month**	**Region**	**Sales**
+	6	**Jan Total**		6,725
+	11	**Feb Total**		8,131
·	12	Mar	North	2,255
·	13	Mar	South	1,126
·	14	Mar	East	1,589
·	15	Mar	West	1,998
−	16	**Mar Total**		6,968
−	17	**Grand Total**		21,824

Outline of data with subtotals and total

Note also that a formula has been inserted for the subtotals:

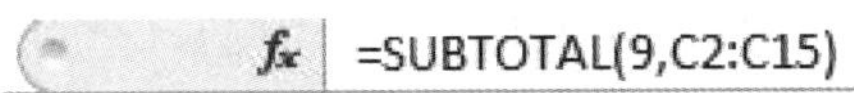

The SUBTOTAL function

In the formula, the digit '9' refers to the function that is being used and 'C2:C15' is the cell range.

Using a pivot table

A pivot table is a way of summarising data within an Excel spreadsheet. A PivotTable report allows the user to present data in a manner that is easy to read.

In particular, it allows the user to:

- Query large amounts of data.
- Subtotal data to provide meaningful reports.
- Filter and sort data.

To use a pivot table:

- Click in the table of data.
- Go to the **Insert** tab and choose **PivotTable** on the **Tables** section of the tab.
- Confirm the data range and click **OK**.

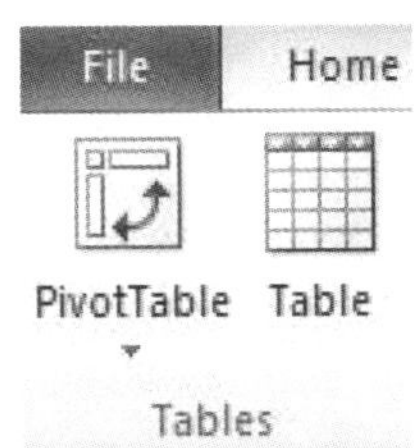

The PivotTable command

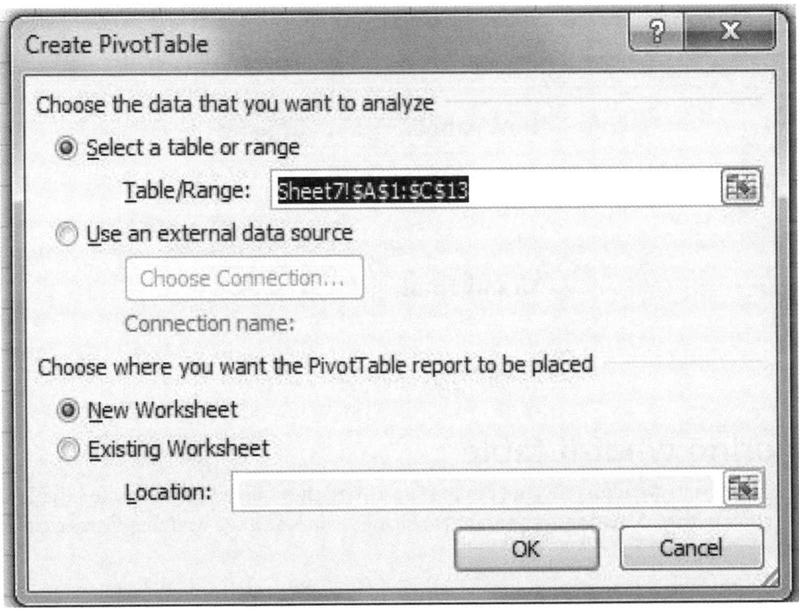

Creating a pivot table

- A pivot table field list appears on the right side of the window.
- Select the fields to be represented in the summary – in this case **Month** in the **Row Labels** and **Sales** for the summary in Σ **Values**.

Fields to be used in a pivot table

- A summary report appears in a new worksheet.

	A	B
1		
2		
3	**Row Labels**	**Sum of Sales**
4	Jan	6725
5	Feb	8131
6	Mar	6968
7	**Grand Total**	**21824**
8		

Summary report from a pivot table

Exploring what-if table

When spreadsheets were first invented in the late 1970s, they offered the ability to be able to quickly carry out recalculations. The ability to change values and see what happens became known as *what-if changes*.

These have become widely used in financial modelling. For example, the PMT function (discussed on pages 254–6) can be used to set up a what-if analysis when buying a vehicle using a loan.

The function calculates the payment on the loan where:

- The payment is the same for each period, say, each month.
- The interest rate is the same for the period of the loan.

The values that need to be input are:

- Rate: interest rate per period.
- Nper: number of periods for the loan.
- Pv: value of the loan.

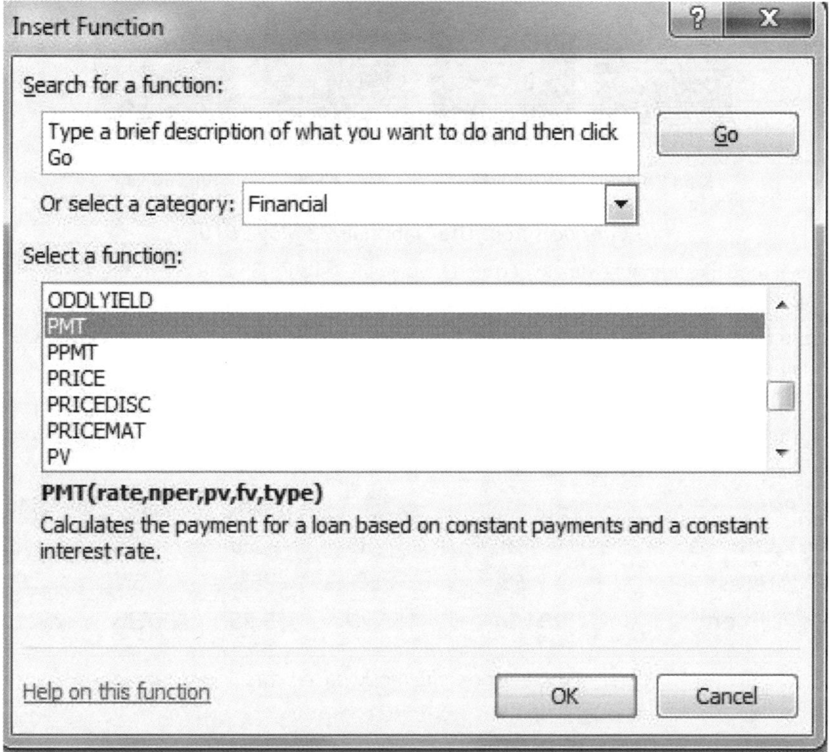

PMT function

For example, if a Toyota Hiace has a value of K6490, there is an interest rate of 5% and the repayments are to be made each month over a three-year period, the following values are entered in a worksheet:

- Cell B2: Price 6490.
- Cell B3: Term 36 months.
- Cell B4: Annual interest rate 5%.
- Cell B5: =PMT(B4/12,B3,B2).

The monthly payment is displayed in Cell A5.

	A	B
1		Toyota HiAce
2	Price	6,491
3	Term	36
4	Interest	5%
5	Payment	194.54

Payment value on a car valued at K6490

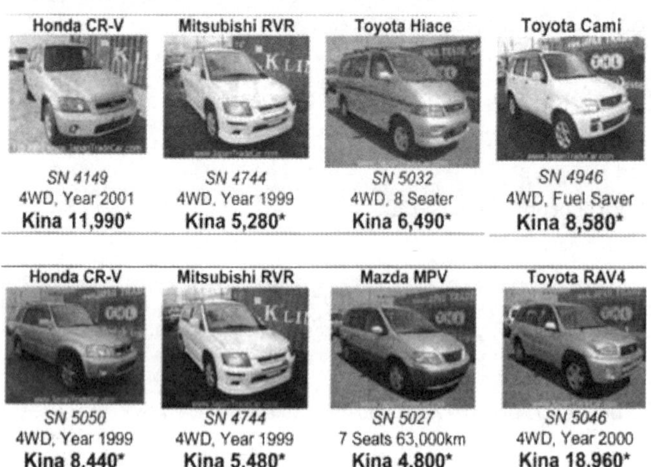

Car prices from The National, *28 May 2010*

A what-if model can now be quickly created by copying cells B2:B5 into cells C2:C5 and similarly into columns D, E, F …

The results are shown below with different car values entered. The model can be used to see what happens if the interest rate changes or if the number of repayment periods changes.

	A	B	C	D	E	F
1		Toyota HiAce				
2	Price	6,491	5,280	11,990	8,580	8,440
3	Term	36	36	36	36	36
4	Interest	5%	5%	5%	5%	5%
5	Payment	194.54	158.25	359.35	257.15	252.95

Payments on differently priced cars

Two variable what-if tables

Excel's **Data Table** command, found on the **Data Tools** section of the **Data** tab, can be used to extend the what-if analysis to two variables.

Using the example of the price of a car, a table can be established that displays a table of payments when:

- The price varies.
- The term or period of the loan varies.

This involves creating a table, starting with the cell B5 and with:

- A column of different prices in column B.
- A row of different terms in row 5.

The table below taking in cells B4:F12 is now selected.

	A	B	C	D	E	F
1	Price	9,000				
2	Term	36				
3	Interest	5%				
4	Payment	269.74	24	36	48	60
5		5000				
6		6000				
7		7000				
8		8000				
9		9000				
10		10000				
11		11000				
12		12000				

The table for the two-variable what-if is selected

Now select **Data Table** from the **What-if Analysis** command on the **Data Tools** section of the **Data** tab.

The **Row input cell** is the Price and the **Column input cell** is the Term.

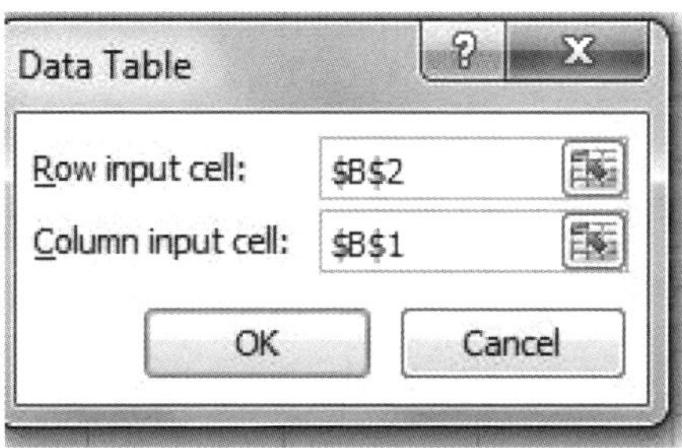

Entering the Row input cell and the Column input cell

The table of values is now created:

	A	B	C	D	E	F
1	Price	9,000				
2	Term	36				
3	Interest	5%				
4	Payment	269.74	24	36	48	60
5		5000	219.36	149.85	115.15	94.36
6		6000	263.23	179.83	138.18	113.23
7		7000	307.10	209.80	161.21	132.10
8		8000	350.97	239.77	184.23	150.97
9		9000	394.84	269.74	207.26	169.84
10		10000	438.71	299.71	230.29	188.71
11		11000	482.59	329.68	253.32	207.58
12		12000	526.46	359.65	276.35	226.45

Results of the two-value what-if table

To understand the table, cell C6 contains the payment for a price of K6000 over a term of 24 months.

Goal seek

Goal seek is used when you know the result that you want from a formula but do not know what input values you need to put into the formula to get that result.

For example, if you know that you can afford to repay K250 per month over a 36-month period for a car, what is the value of the car that you can afford? To work this out:

- Enter the term in cell B3.
- Enter the interest rate in cell B4.
- Enter the formula '=PMT(B4/12,B3,-B2)' in cell B5.

B5 fx =PMT(B4/12,B3,-B2)

car

	A	B	C	D	E
1		Vehicle Value			
2	Price				
3	Term	36			
4	Interest	5%			
5	Payment	0.00			

Worksheet for Goal Seek

Now, select **Goal Seek...** from the **What-If Analysis** menu item on the **Data Tools** section of the **Data** tab.

In the dialogue box enter:

- Set cell B5.
- To value: 250.
- By changing cell $B$2.

That is, the value 250 is to be achieved by changing the value in cell $B$2, where the result will be stored.

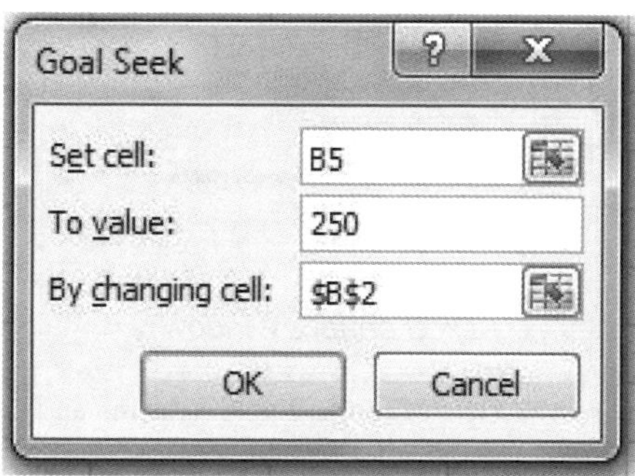

Setting the goal

Click **OK** and the result shows in cell B2:

	A	B
1		Vehicle Value
2	Price	8,341
3	Term	36
4	Interest	5%
5	Payment	250.00

Result of Goal Seek

Loading add-ins and using Solver

Solver is an add-in to Excel that is provided by another vendor. It is not usually available on the menus but it can be added in.

Solver is used in more complex what-if problems.

To install Solver, do the following:

- Select the **File** tab.
- On the left side of the window, select **Options**.
- When the Excel options window appears, select **Add-Ins**.

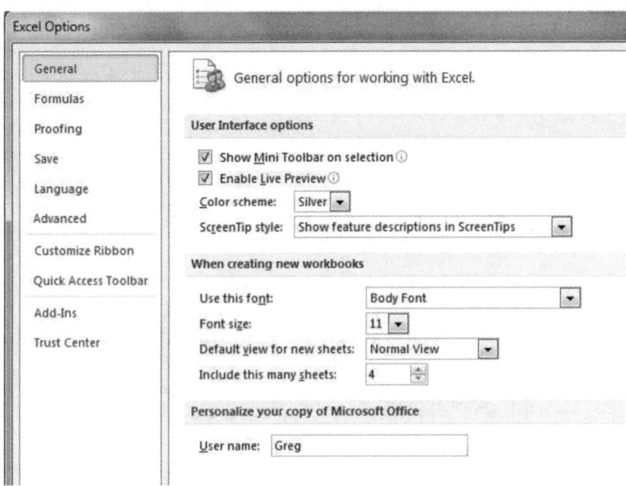

Excel options window

- At the bottom of the window, select **Manage: Excel Add-ins** and click **Go…**

Managing Excel add-ins

- Make sure that the **Solver Add-in** check box is ticked and then click **OK**.

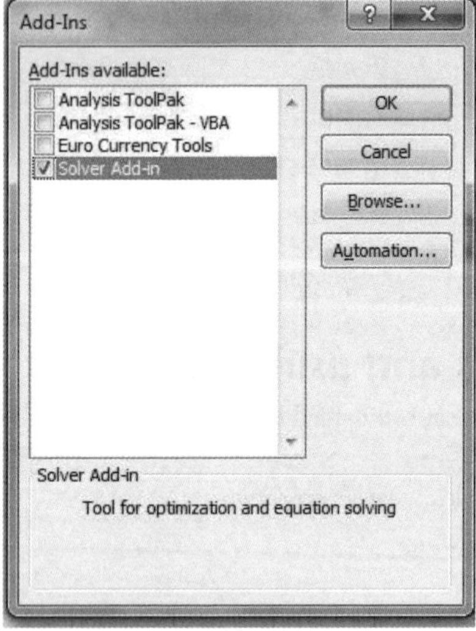

Solver add-in

Solver is now added as a new **Analysis** menu item as part of the **Data** tab.

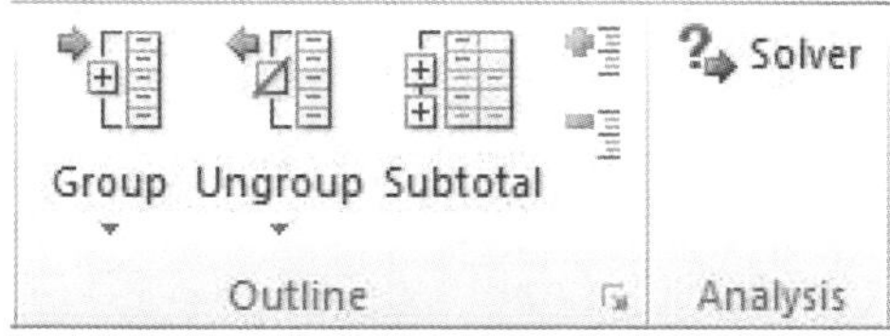

Solver is now found on the Data tab

Using Solver

Solver is a what-if analysis tool for solving complex problems.

It is used to find an optimum value for a particular cell, subject to a number of constraints, or limits on values, in other cells.

Solver is a third-party product created by Frontline Systems Inc. For examples of how to use Solver, go to the Solver website at www.solver.com.

Unit 11.4 Activity 5B: Goal seek exercise

Use the Goal Seek technique to work out how much you could borrow for a house if:

- The monthly repayment is K1500.
- The term of the loan is 15 years (180 months).
- The interest rate is 6.5%.

Unit 11.4 Spreadsheets
Topic 6: Integrating with other applications

Topic 6 in this Unit focuses on integrating with other applications (see ICT Syllabus p. 21). It covers:

- Copying data from other applications.
- Using the Text Import Wizard.
- Exporting data to another file type.
- Inserting objects.
- Exporting data to Excel workbook in another application.
- Getting specific information using a database query.
- Editing a database query.

Exchanging data in a table with Word

A table in Microsoft Word can be copied into Microsoft Excel. Similarly, Excel data can be copied into Word.

To copy a table from Word into Excel:

- In Microsoft Word, select the table.
- On the **Home** tab, choose **Copy**.
- Go to Excel and choose where you wish to paste the table.
- On the **Home** tab, choose **Paste.** By default, it will retain the formatting from Word.

	Lake	Province	Size (ha)
1			
2	Murray	Western	64,700
3	Chambri	ESP	21,600
4	Wisdom	Madang	8,592
5	Khanda-Szaga	Western	7,840
6	Kutubu	SHP	4,924
7	Dakataua	WNB	4,920
8	Yonki	EHP	2,120
9	Aesake Lagoon	Western	2,120
10	Sirinumu	Central	4,100
11	Bossett	Western	1,680

Example of a table copied from Word into Excel

To copy cells from Excel into Word:

- In Microsoft Excel, select the cells you wish to copy.
- On the **Home** tab, choose **Copy**.
- Go to Word and choose where you wish to paste the table.
- On the **Home** tab, choose **Paste.**

	Rugby at SCRUM Oval	Soccer at LFA Oval
Transport	3.00	1.50
Ticket	10.95	8.00
Food	2.95	5.95
Drink	2.75	3.50
TOTAL	19.65	18.95

A table copied from Excel into Word

Copying data to another file type

Copying an Excel chart into Word

To copy a chart from Excel into Word:

- In Microsoft Excel, select the chart you wish to copy.
- On the **Home** tab, choose **Copy.**
- Go to Word and choose where you wish to paste the table.
- On the **Home** tab, choose **Paste.**

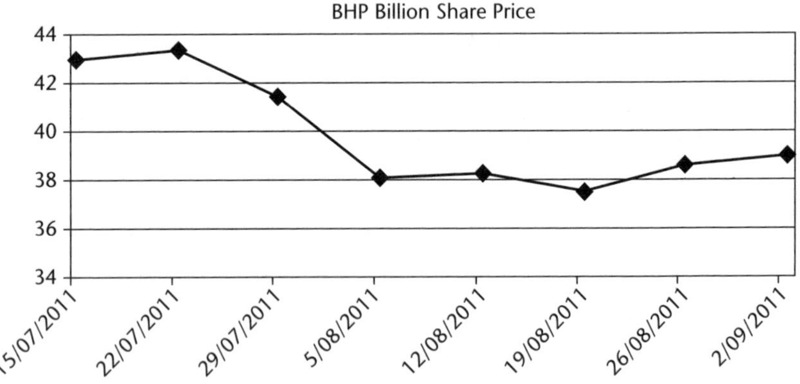

A chart copied from Excel into Word

Copying Excel data into PowerPoint

To copy data from Excel into PowerPoint:

- In Microsoft Excel, select the chart you wish to copy.
- On the **Home** tab, choose **Copy**.
- Go to PowerPoint and choose where you wish to paste the table.
- On the **Home** tab, choose **Paste**.

Copying an Excel chart into PowerPoint

To copy a chart from Excel into PowerPoint:

- In Microsoft Excel, select the chart you wish to copy.
- On the **Home** tab, choose **Copy**.
- Go to PowerPoint and choose where you wish to paste the chart.
- On the **Home** tab, choose **Paste**.
- Two of the **Paste** options allow you to link the data. Choose **Use Destination Theme & Link Data (L)**.

This pastes the chart into PowerPoint and creates a link to the worksheet. If the data in the worksheet is modified, that change is reflected in the chart.

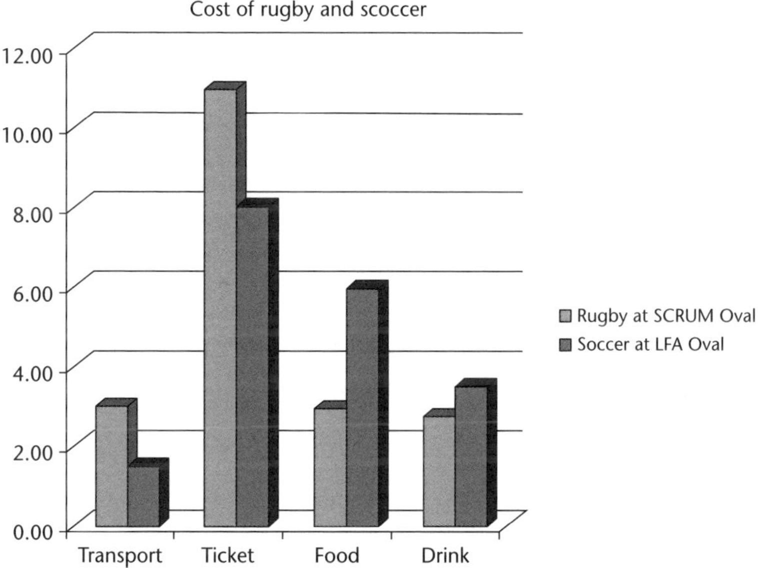

An Excel chart embedded in a PowerPoint presentation

Copying data from Access into Excel

To copy data from Access into Excel:

- In Microsoft Access, select the table you wish to copy.
- Select the cells in the table you wish to copy.
- On the **Home** tab, choose **Copy**.
- Go to Excel and choose where you wish to paste the data.
- On the **Home** tab, choose **Paste**.

Members

ID	Surname	First name	Address	Town	Telephone
1	Akis	Bernard	Moka Pl	MT HAGEN	542 1111
2	Herman	John	First St	LAE	479 8888
3	Jackson	Michael	Finch St	LAE	479 1111
4	Kabobo	Peter	Mokoraha Rd	PORT MORESB	555 2222
5	Masonga	Martin	Walnut St	LAE	479 3214
6	Faiwlok	Peter	Wahgi Pde	MT HAGEN	542 1234
7	Goodwin	Nick	Wopkai Rd	MT HAGEN	542 7890
8	Posu	Jim	Posu Rd	MT HAGEN	542 6666

Selecting data in Access

	A	B	C	D	E	F
1	**Members**					
2	ID	Surname	First name	Address	Town	Telephon
3	1	Akis	Bernard	Moka Pl	MT HAGEN	542 1111
4	2	Herman	John	First St	LAE	479 8888
5	3	Jackson	Michael	Finch St	LAE	479 1111
6	4	Kabobo	Peter	Mokoraha Rd	PORT MORESBY	555 2222
7	5	Masonga	Martin	Walnut St	LAE	479 3214
8	6	Faiwlok	Peter	Wahgi Pde	MT HAGEN	542 1234
9	7	Goodwin	Nick	Wopkai Rd	MT HAGEN	542 7890
10	8	Posu	Jim	Posu Rd	MT HAGEN	542 6666

Data from Access pasted into Excel

Exporting data

Data can be exported from Excel using the **Save As** command on the **File** tab. The **Save As** command gives a range of different formats in which data can be saved.

Clicking on the **Save as type:** command displays the list of data types.

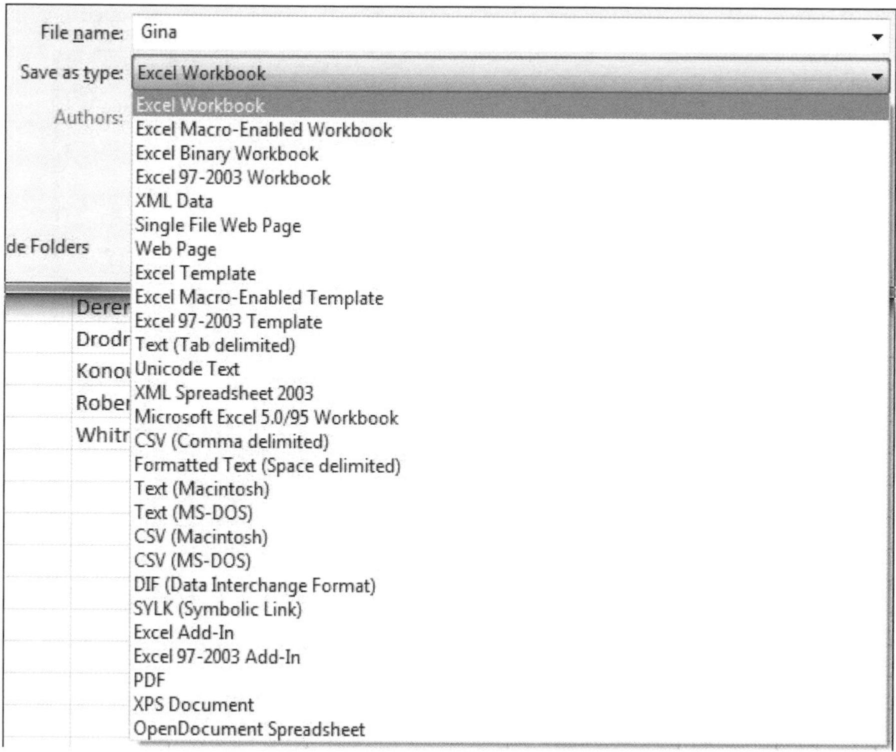

Different data types that can be used for export

The most commonly used file types for this are text and comma-separated values.

- Text files have the extension '.txt'. In this format, the text from each cell is separated by the tab character and each row is separated by the carriage return character.
- Comma-separated value files have the extension '.csv'. In this format, the values from each cell are separated by commas and each row is separated by the carriage return character.

Many other applications can open '.txt' and '.csv' files, including Word, Access and Outlook.

Importing data using the Text Import Wizard

Excel can open a variety of different file formats. It uses a Text Import Wizard to import text files. To be used in a spreadsheet, text needs to be either tab delimited or in comma-separated value (csv) format.

Select the **Data** tab and, in the **Get External Data** section, choose the **From Text** command. This brings up the Text Import Wizard.

The Text Import Wizard gives you the option to choose how the data has been formatted:

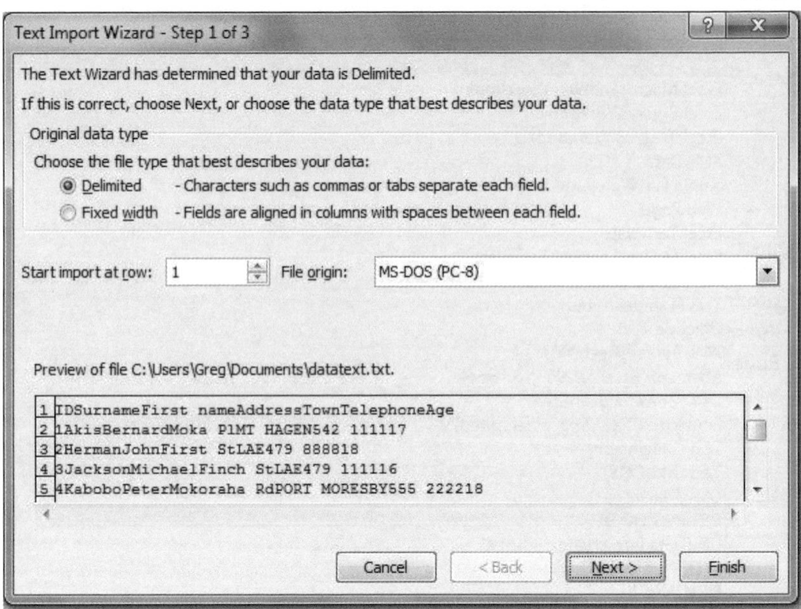

Importing text into a worksheet

The next part of the process allows the user to select the type of delimiter used:

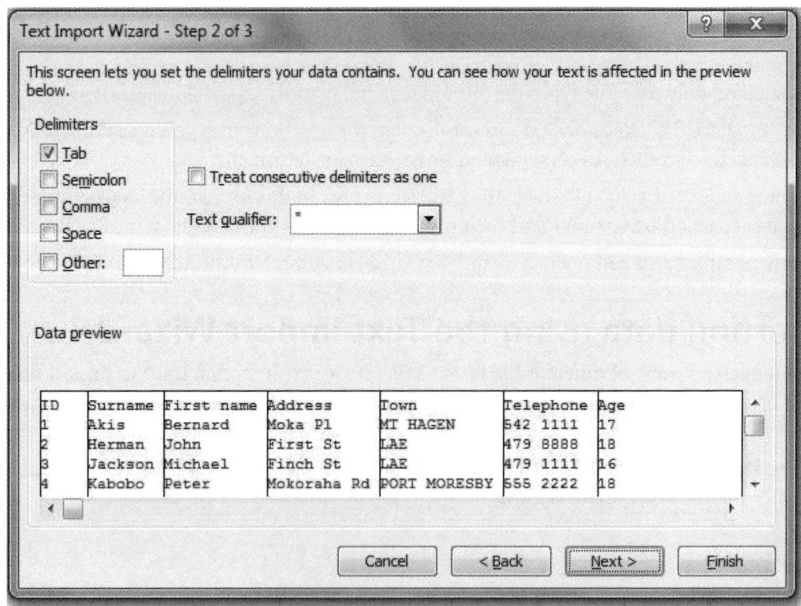

Choosing the field delimiter

The data is then imported into the worksheet.

Importing data from Access

Microsoft Access is the database management package that is part of the Microsoft Office suite. Data can be imported directly from Microsoft Access into Excel. This is set up in Access using the **Export** section of the **External Data** tab.

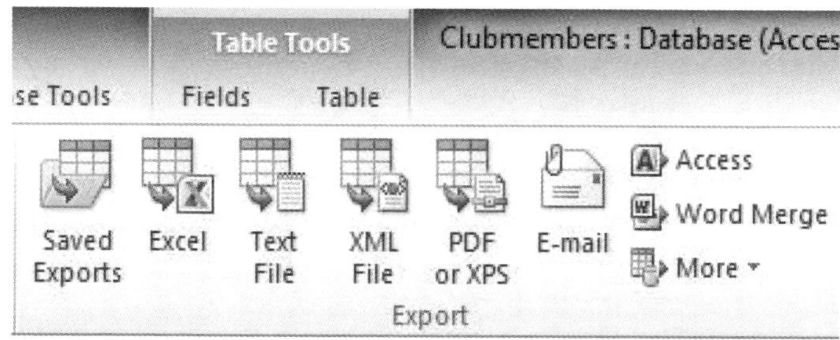

The Excel command can be used to export data from Access to Excel

The process allows you to:

- Select the destination worksheet.
- Save the steps used in the export process.

The destination worksheet can be an existing one, or a new one can be created. By saving the steps, it is possible to repeat the process easily in the future.

Inserting objects

Objects can be inserted into a worksheet from within Excel as well as from other applications. Pictures, clip art and shapes can be inserted into a worksheet. This is done using the **Illustrations** commands on the **Insert** tab:

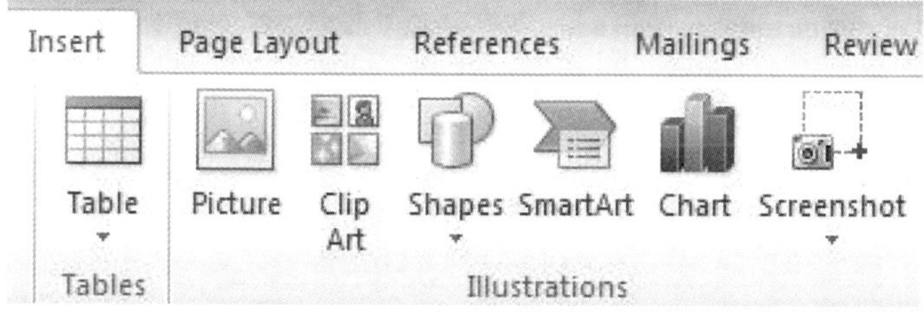

Images can be inserted into a worksheet

To insert a piece of clip art, do the following:

- Choose **Clip Art** from the **Illustrations** section of the **Insert** tab.
- Select the image from the window on the right.
- Double-click on the image or drag it onto the worksheet.

Part of the Clip Art window. Note that a search has been made for a house

Note that when the picture has been added to the worksheet, a **Picture Tools** tab appears that allows you to modify the picture. This is the same menu that appears in Microsoft Word when an image is inserted.

Part of the Picture Tools tab that is available when an image is inserted into a worksheet

The tools allow the user to resize or crop an image. It can be useful to reduce the file size of a picture as it can significantly increase the size of a worksheet.

To do this, choose **Compress Pictures** which is in the **Adjust** group on the **Picture Tools Format** tab.

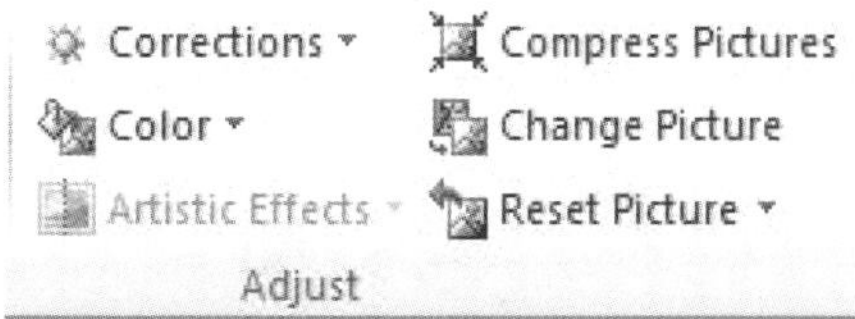

Compress Pictures option in the Picture Tools tab

Note that one of the compression options is to delete the cropped areas of pictures. When a picture is cropped, the part that is removed remains part of the worksheet but is not displayed. However, deleting the cropped areas of the picture will reduce the size of the image and the size of the worksheet.

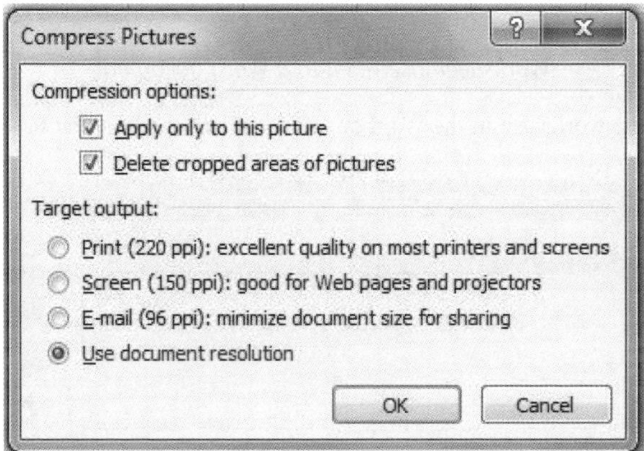

Compression options for pictures

The **Shapes** and **SmartArt** commands on the **Picture Tools Format** tab also give a range of possibilities for adding graphic images to a worksheet. Again, these are the same as in Microsoft Word.

Inserting and linking a spreadsheet in a Word document

Part of a worksheet can be copied and pasted into Word. To do this:

- Select the cells in Excel to be copied.
- Move to the Word document.
- Choose the Paste option **Link & Keep Source Formatting**.

When the spreadsheet file is updated and saved, it is linked to the Word document and the changes are reflected in the Word document.

House Prices

Purchase price	475,000	535,000
Stamp duty	6,100	7,100
Lawyer's fees	850	1025
Bank fees	1,245	1,450
Removalist	455	555
TOTAL	483,650	545,130

Worksheet inserted into a Word document

Right-clicking in the worksheet in the Word document shows the link that has been created:

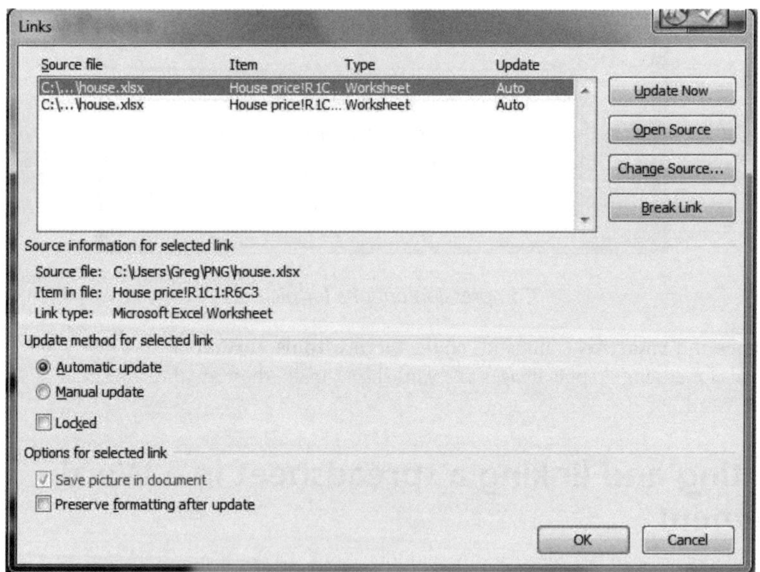

Note the link between the Word document and the worksheet

Unit 11.4 Spreadsheets

Topic 7: Protecting and auditing forms and templates

Topic 7 explains how to protect and audit forms and templates (see ICT Syllabus pp. 21–2). It covers:

- Creating a new workbook using a template.
- Protecting worksheet style, contents and elements.
- Protecting the worksheet from unauthorised user access.

Using a template

Built-in templates

Microsoft Excel has a number of built-in templates that allow the user to quickly create a workbook. To use a template:

- On the **File** tab, select **New** and see the available templates.

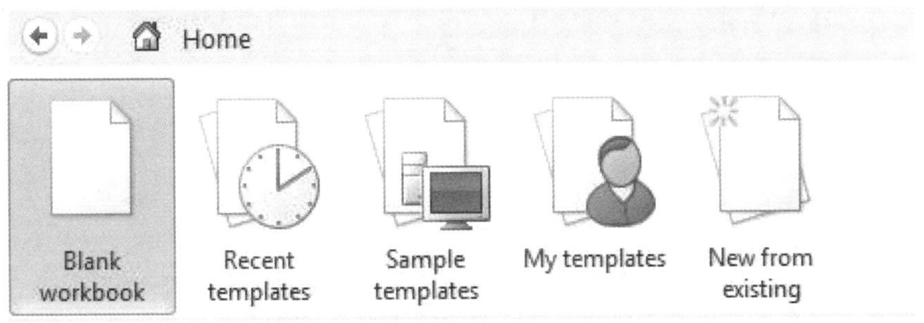

Excel templates

To choose a template, select the **Sample templates** icon and see the templates that have been set up. Some of these are shown below.

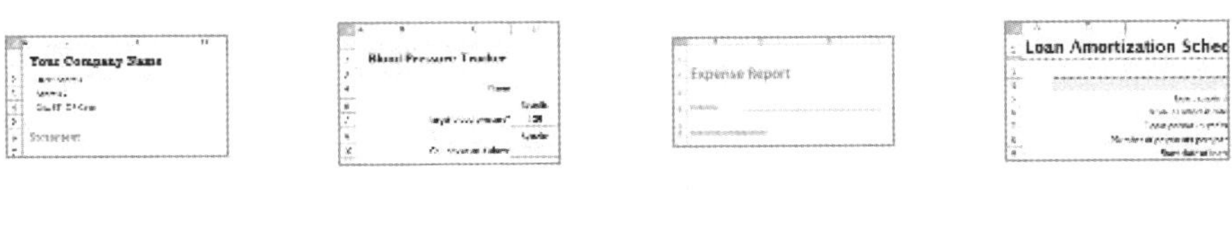

Sample templates ready to use

To use a template, double-click on the icon and then enter the required data. For example, double-clicking on **Loan Amortization** brings up a worksheet as shown below.

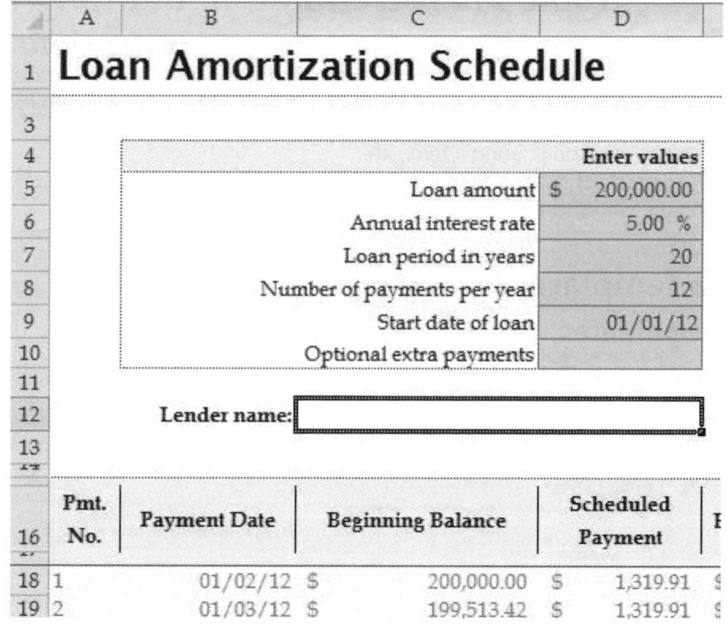

Loan amortization template

The template has a data-entry section and, once that is done, the calculations are completed using formulae that cannot be modified and the results are displayed.

Templates on Office Online

There is a much larger range of templates available at Office Online. These are also available through the **File** tab by selecting **New**:

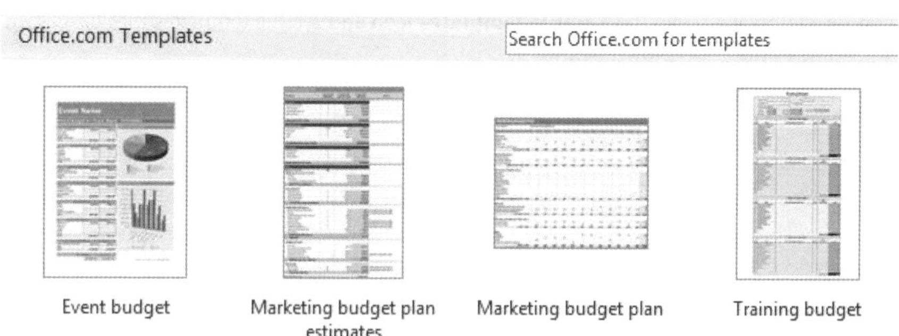

Some of the templates available on Office.com

Once the template is downloaded, data can be entered and it can be saved as a worksheet.

Creating a new template

Users can create a new template from a worksheet. To do this:

- Start a new worksheet.
- Create the items that you wish to enter into the worksheet.
- Choose **Save As** from the **File** tab.
- From the drop-down menu for **Save as type**, choose **Excel Template**.
- Enter a file name and click **Save**.

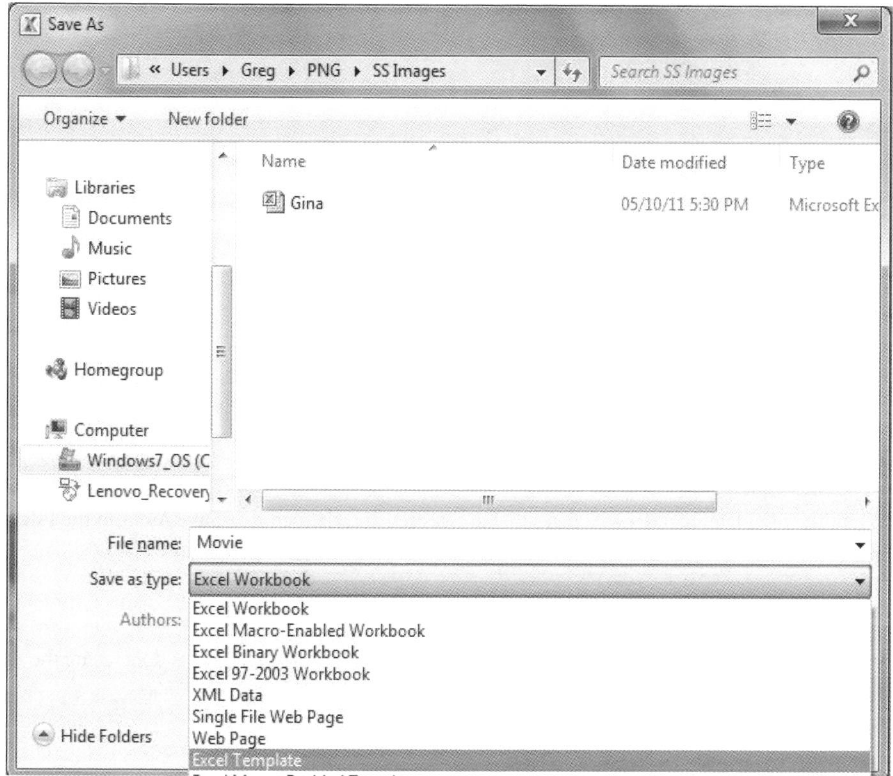

Saving a worksheet as a template

The template is saved and can now be accessed from the **File** tab, choosing **New** and selecting **My templates**.

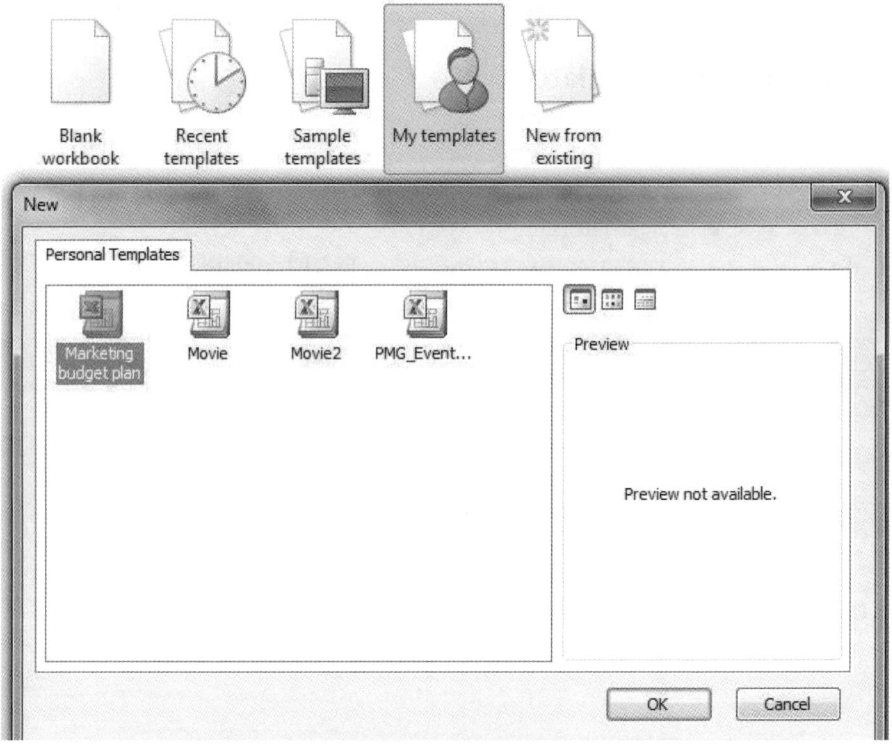
Blank workbook
Recent templates
Sample templates
My templates
New from existing
New
Personal Templates
Marketing budget plan
Movie
Movie2
PMG_Event...
Preview
Preview not available.
OK
Cancel

Using your own template

Once the template is opened, data can be entered in the worksheet and saved.

To edit the template, make the changes that are desired and then choose **Save As** from the **File** tab and make sure it is again saved as an **Excel Template**, overwriting the old template.

Protecting a worksheet

A workbook, a worksheet or cells within a worksheet can be protected. This is done using the commands on the Changes section of the Review tab.

Protect Sheet
Protect Workbook
Share Workbook
Protect and Share Workbook
Allow Users to Edit Ranges
Track Changes
Changes

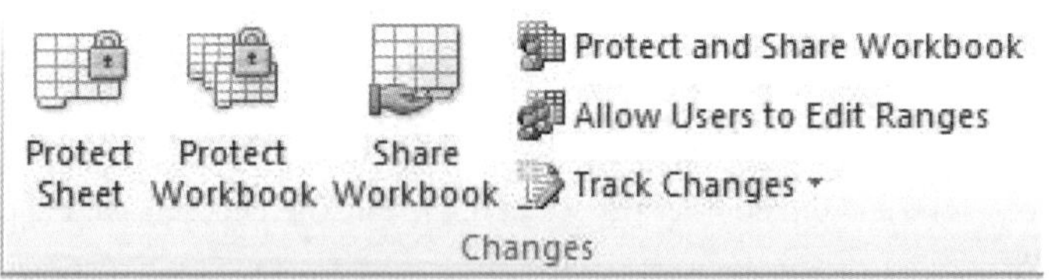

Changes section of the Review tab

To protect a worksheet:

- Choose **Protect Sheet** from the **Changes** section of the **Review** tab.
- Select any changes you would like others to be able to make.
- Enter the password (twice).

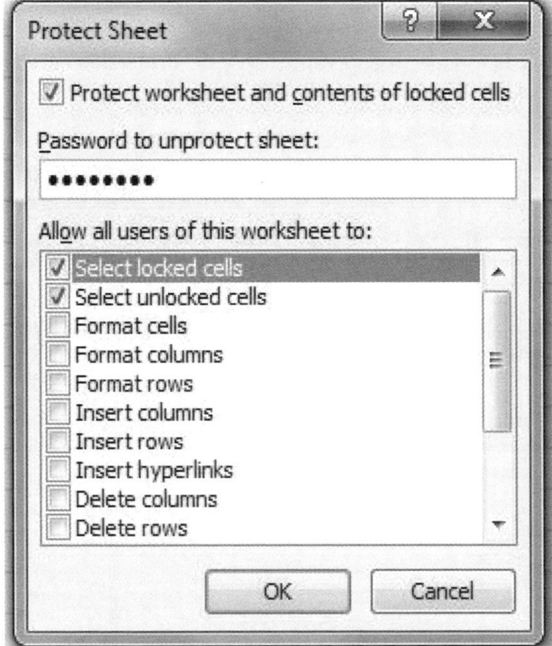

Protecting a worksheet

Changes can now not be made without removing the protection.

To unprotect a worksheet:

- Choose **Unprotect Sheet** from the **Changes** section of the **Review** tab.
- Enter the password and click **OK**.

Cells can be unlocked for editing in a protected worksheet using the **Allow Users to Edit Ranges** command from the **Changes** section of the **Review** tab.

The worksheet and cells can also be locked using the **Format** command on the **Cells** section of the **Home** tab.

Hiding cell formulae

The formulae can be hidden from view in a protected worksheet. When this is done, the formula no longer displays in the formula bar.

There are two steps to doing this:

- Use the **Home** tab to select the cells whose formulae you wish to hide.
- Use the **Review** tab to ensure the formulae are hidden.

On the Home tab:

- Go to the **Cells** section of the tab and choose **Format**.
- Select the **Format Cells** command – it is the last command on the menu.
- In the **Format Cells** window that appears, choose the **Protection** tab and make sure the **Hidden** check box is selected.
- Click **OK**.

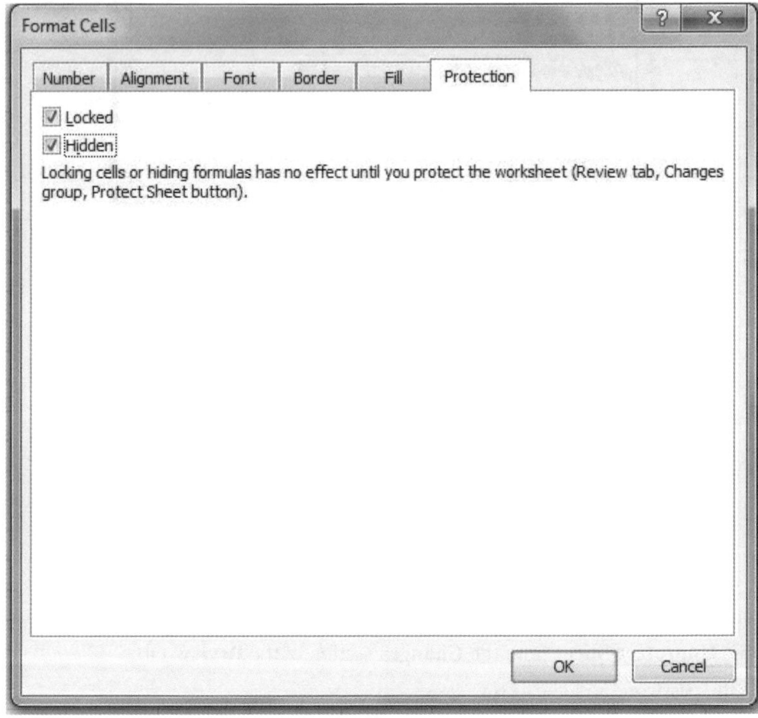

Setting hidden cells

Now, go to the **Review** tab.

- On the **Changes** section of the tab, select **Protect Sheet**.
- The **Protect Sheet** window asks for a password.
- Make sure the **Select locked cells** checkbox is ticked.
- Click **OK**.

The formulae are now not displayed in the formula bar.

Allowing users to edit a worksheet

On the **Review** tab, in the **Changes** section, the **Allow Users to Edit Ranges** command allows the setting up of user privileges.

First, select the range of cells that users will be allowed to edit.

Setting up a worksheet for users to edit

Give the range a title and then select the range:

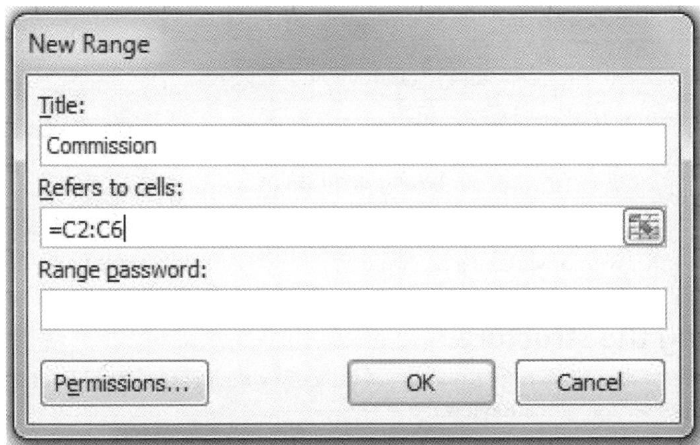

Setting the range for editing

Now select the **Permissions…**

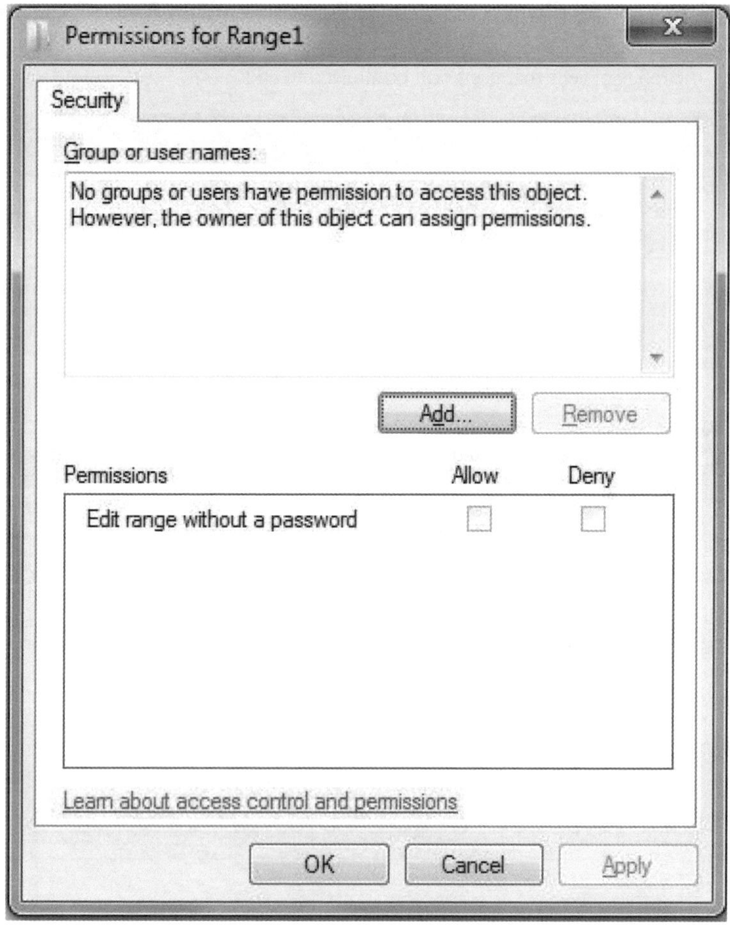

Setting permissions

The groups or users are selected from the network. Note that permission can be set to edit a range of cells either with or without a password.

Protecting the structure

The structure of a workbook can be protected by choosing the **Protect Workbook** command on the **Changes** section of the **Review** tab.

Protecting the structure means that worksheets cannot be added, deleted or moved around.

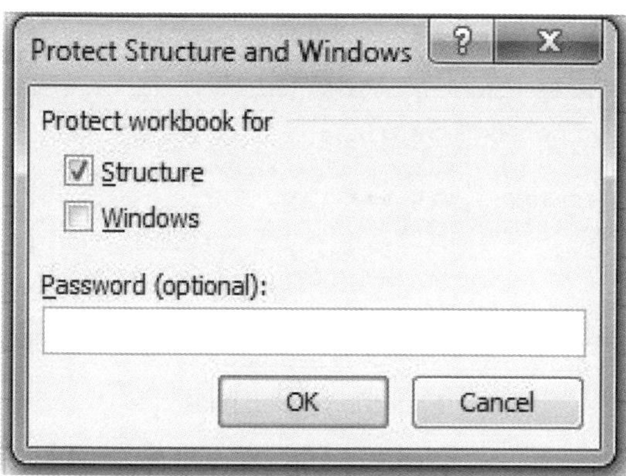

Setting a password

Entering the password (twice) sets up the protection.

To unprotect the workbook structure, again choose the **Protect Workbook** command. If the workbook is protected, the icon is highlighted. Entering the password and clicking **OK** unprotects the workbook.

Protecting a workbook from unauthorised access

A workbook can be protected from unauthorised access by setting a password to open it. This is done on the **File** tab by selecting the menu item **Info**.

Permissions on a workbook

Clicking the **Protect Workbook** icon and choosing **Encrypt with Password** allows a password to be set up – again, the password needs to be confirmed.

Now, when the workbook is opened, it requires the password.

Protecting a workbook

The password can be removed by going to the **Encrypt with Password** command and deleting the password, ie leaving it blank and then saving the changes.

Unit 11.4 Activity 7A: Spreadsheets revision

1. Investigate the functions DEC2BIN and BIN2DEC. These convert decimal numbers to binary and binary to decimal. Use the functions to complete the following tasks:
   - **a.** Convert the following decimal numbers to binary:
     - **i.** 34
     - **ii.** 56
     - **iii.** 213
     - **iv.** 982
   - **b.** Convert the following binary numbers to decimal:
     - **i.** 1011
     - **ii.** 100001
     - **iii.** 101111
     - **iv.** 11001010
2. Use the Loan Amortisation template in Excel to investigate the repayments on a mortgage loan of K180 000 over 15 years at an interest rate of 6%.
3. Create a what-if table to identify the repayment costs of purchasing four different vehicles assuming an interest rate of 6% and a loan time of three years.
4. Create a worksheet that compares the costs of at least three different desktop computer systems. Include the cost of:
   - **a.** Computer and monitor
   - **b.** Printer
   - **c.** External USB hard disk storage
   - **d.** Microsoft Office

5. Students in a class have just received the following marks in a test. The test was out of a total 50 marks. The teacher would like you to use a spreadsheet for a range of calculations to analyse the results.

◇	B	C	D	E	F	G
1	**Name**	**Test Mark**	**Grade**		**Grades**	
2	Student A	43	A		**Mark**	**Grade**
3	Student B	36	B		0	E
4	Student C	39	B		10	D
5	Student D	32	B		20	C
6	Student E	12	D		30	B
7	Student F	43	A		40	A
8	Student G	11	D			
9	Student H	29	C			
10	Student I	14	D		**Marks Analysis**	
11	Student J	34	B		Maximum	50
12	Student K	16	D		Highest	
13	Student L	24	C		Lowest	
14	Student M	37	B		Total marks	
15	Student N	24	C		Average	
16	Student O	15	D			
17					Students	
18						
19						
20						
21						

Student mark worksheet

The teacher would like the worksheet to show:

- The top mark gained for this test.
- The lowest mark gained this test.
- The total marks earned by all candidates.
- The number of candidates who sat for the test.

a. Using an 'IF' statement, construct an expression that would enter the grade automatically based on the student mark.

b. Create the letter grade as above but using a 'LOOKUP' function.

c. Which is the better function to use?

d. Create a 'random' number in cells C2 to C16 that would demonstrate that the function is working as expected.

e. What cells should be 'protected' in the spreadsheet to prevent accidental entry?

6. Figure below shows the Apple share prices for the month of November 2011. It gives the date, the closing price and the volume of shares sold each day.
   a. Use a worksheet to show:
      i. The highest price for the month.
      ii. The lowest price for the month.
      iii. The average price for the month.
      iv. The average number of shares traded per day.
      v. The total number of shares traded for the month.
   b. Use the LOOKUP function to access the closing price on any date.
7. Go to the site: http://uk.finance.yahoo.com where you can access the Apple share prices. Download the share prices for three months.
   a. Use data outlining to work out the number of shares sold each month.
   b. Use a pivot table to work out the number of shares sold each month.

	A	B	C
1	Date	Close	Volume
2	30-Nov-11	$382.20	14,497,800
3	29-Nov-11	$373.20	13,423,400
4	28-Nov-11	$376.12	12,371,900
5	25-Nov-11	$363.57	9,098,600
6	23-Nov-11	$366.99	15,295,400
7	22-Nov-11	$376.51	14,607,900
8	21-Nov-11	$369.01	15,999,300
9	18-Nov-11	$374.94	13,283,500
10	17-Nov-11	$377.41	17,139,300
11	16-Nov-11	$384.77	12,449,900
12	15-Nov-11	$388.83	15,386,100
13	14-Nov-11	$379.26	15,460,900
14	11-Nov-11	$384.62	23,338,400
15	10-Nov-11	$385.22	26,598,300
16	09-Nov-11	$395.28	19,926,700
17	08-Nov-11	$406.23	14,278,400
18	07-Nov-11	$399.73	9,641,000
19	04-Nov-11	$400.24	10,772,400
20	03-Nov-11	$403.07	15,763,800
21	02-Nov-11	$397.41	11,691,100
22	01-Nov-11	$396.51	18,974,200

Apple share prices

Unit 11.5 Databases

Topic 1: Getting started

Unit 11.5 explores databases. Topic 1 in this Unit offers a general introduction to databases (see ICT Syllabus pp. 23–4). It covers:

- Understanding how a database works.
- Getting familiar with the database screen.
- Getting help and maintenance.
- Working with database objects.

What is a database?

Data is made up of recorded facts, figures, images and sounds about people, objects, events or many other items. Data is collected and stored in a **database**. Throughout this Unit, Microsoft Access is referred to as the database management package that is used to create and modify data.

Joanne Peters
8 Doyle St
Lae 411 Morobe
Papua New Guinea

Maria Lombardi
123 Okuk Hwy
Goroka 441 Eastern Highlands
Papua New Guinea

John Ataia
17 Toma St
Rabaul 611 East New Britain
Papua New Guinea

A database of names and addresses on cards

A database is made up of data that is arranged so that it can be searched, organised and selected, as shown in the figure on the right. Each item of data is related to each other item in some way.

Databases are used to provide information at home and in the workplace. Some examples of databases are:

- A telephone directory.
- The names of students attending a school.
- Video titles in a video library.
- Employees in a company.
- Books in a library.
- Passengers on an airline flight.
- Records of births kept by a state registry.

Why do we have databases?

Data on its own is not very useful. It needs to be organised and interpreted so that it has meaning. Sorting data helps to make the data easy to interpret.

People use databases to find information about goods, services and other people. Organisations use databases to provide information that helps people make decisions. Many organisations need databases to carry out their day-to-day business.

Databases kept by people

People create databases for use at home. The database might be stored on a computer or written in a book, on paper or on cards. Some examples are:

- Telephone numbers in a notebook.
- A list of valuable items that are kept at home.

- A street directory.
- A dictionary.
- A collection of recipes.
- A list of names and addresses for Christmas cards.

Databases kept by organisations

Businesses and organisations create and maintain databases as part of their everyday operation. Some examples are:

- A school keeps a database of all its students' names, addresses and telephone numbers.
- A supermarket has a database of all the items that it sells.
- A bank has a database of all its customers and their accounts.
- Libraries keep catalogues of books that are lent out.
- A tennis club keeps a database of its members.
- A video library uses a database to keep track of both its customers and its videotapes and DVDs.

Unit 11.5 Activity 1A: Databases in the local community

1. Think of the databases that you use at home and at school. These databases may be stored on a computer or written in a book or on cards.
   a. List five different databases that you use at home.
   b. List five different databases that you have your name recorded on at school.

2. List five different databases that are used by organisations that you come into contact with outside school.

3. You have been asked to keep track of members of your local tennis club and you have to create a database. Write down what information you think you would want to get from your database. What information would you need to keep?

The telephone directory

The telephone directory is a database. It stores names, addresses and telephone numbers for a large number of people and organisations (these are called subscribers). The entries in the White Pages telephone book are stored alphabetically.

Four typical entries are:

- Agua W J
  PO Box 1111 Pt Moresby
  Hunter St, PT MORESBY
  321 0000
- Smith J R
  PO Box 2222 Lae
  Sandpiper Rd LAE
  472 0000

- Numbai Security Service
  PO Box 3333 Wewak
  WEWAK
  475 0000
- Rabaul Volcanic Observatory
  PO Box 4444 Rabaul
  RABAUL
  982 0000

The telephone directory is made up of entries for:

- Individuals.
- Businesses.
- Government departments and organisations.

Unit 11.5 Activity 1B: Finding information in databases

1. Find the first page of the White Pages telephone directory that contains telephone numbers of subscribers. Write down the first ten names that appear. They will most likely be all businesses. Why do you think businesses choose names like these? You can refer to www.whitepages.com.pg

2. Refer to your current telephone directory.

a. What is the first name in the telephone directory?

b. What is the last name in the telephone directory?

c. How many times does your family name occur in the directory?

3. The World Wide Airport Database provides information about airports. There are 98 airports in Papua New Guinea. The table below shows information about ten of those airports.

a. How many of the names of the airports start with the letter 'A'?

b. How many of the airports are international airports?

c. In what order is the database sorted?

IATA	Name	Location
ABW	Abau Airport	Abau
AZB	Amazon Bay Airport	Amazon Bay
ABP	Atkamba Airport	Atkamba
BOQ	Boku Airport	Boku
BMH	Bomai Airport	Bomai
GKA	Goroka Airport	Goroka
KMA	Kerema Airport	Kerema
MDU	Mendi Airport	Mendi

IATA	Name	Location
POM	Port Moresby/Jackson International Airport	Port Moresby
TIZ	Tari Airport	Tari
WWK	Wewak International Airport	Wewak

Airports in Papua New Guinea

4. The database in the table below is made up of the names of a number of cities and towns in Papua New Guinea. The population figures are mostly taken from the census in the year 2000.

a. Which towns are in the Southern Highlands?

b. How many of the towns have a population less than 10 000?

c. In what order are the towns sorted?

Rank	City/town name	Province	Population
1	Port Moresby	National Capital District	254 000
2	Lae	Morobe	120 000
3	Arawa	Bougainville	36 400
4	Mount Hagen	Western Highlands	27 700
5	Goroak	Eastern Highlands	20 600
6	Alotau	Milne Bay	9 800
7	Tari	Southern Highlands	8 200
8	Kainantu	Eastern Highlands	6 700
9	Ialibu	Southern Highlands	5 500
10	Wau	Morobe	5 000

Cities and towns in Papua New Guinea

5. The First Fleet database contains information about people who were transported to Australia as the first white settlers. The figure below shows part of the records for nine members of the First Fleet. Answer the questions below by referring to the figure.

a. How many settlers had the surname 'Abrahams'?

b. What was the date of John Adams' trial?

c. What is the name of the ship on which females were transported?

d. How many convicts had trials before 1786?

First Name	Last Name	Sex	Position	Ship	Date of Trial
Mary	Abel	Female	Convict	Lady Penryhn	5/3/1785
Robert	Abel	Male	Convict	Alexander	15/9/1784
Eshter	Abrahams	Female	Convict	Lady Penryhn	30/8/1786
Henry	Abrahams	Male	Convict	Alexander	7/3/1785
John	Adams	Male	Convict	Scarborough	26/5/1784
Mary	Adams	Female	Convict	Lady Penryhn	13/12/1786
John	Agnew	Male	Convict	Scarborough	26/5/1784
Thomas	Akers	Male	Convict	Charlotte	14/3/1785
Charles	Allen	Male	Convict	Scarborough	7/7/1784

Part of the First Fleet database

What makes up a database?

A database is made up of a collection of files about somebody or something, referred to as an 'entity'. An entity is a person or an object about which data needs to be recorded.

Each entity that is used in a database has a name. Many databases consist of only one entity. These databases are often called 'flat file databases'. The telephone book contains data about people and organisations called subscribers. Therefore the entity used in the telephone book could be called 'subscriber'.

Each entity is made up of a number of attributes. A book for sale will have attributes including the name of the book and the price.

Each piece of information about an entity is called a record. For example, a subscriber whose surname is 'Agua' has the following data stored as a record in a telephone directory:

Agua W J
PO Box 1111 Pt Moresby
Hunter St, PT MORESBY
321 0000

A record is made up of a number of separate pieces of data. Each of these pieces is called a **field**. Each field is given a name so that it may be recognised. In the telephone book, the record is made up of the fields called 'family name', 'initials', 'PO Box', 'town', 'street', 'main town', 'telephone number' (see the table below).

Field name	Data for each field
Family name	Agua
Initials	W J
PO Box	PO Box 1111
Town	Pt Moresby
Street	Hunter St
Main town	PT MORESBY
Telephone number	321 0000

The record for the subscriber

The field 'family name' has the value 'Agua'; the field 'initials' has the value 'W J', and so on.

Unit 11.5 Activity 1C: Field names

1. Write down the field names in the following database, which stores the names and addresses of people.

Family name	Initials	Address	Main town
Abraham	A L	Buimo Rd	Lae
David	C J	Eagle St	Lae
Dotson	J C	Gordonia St	Port Moresby
Bineng	M	Djaul St	Rabaul
Damaka	P	Walnut St	Madang

Address database

2. The next figure shows a personnel record from part of the Northwind database in Access. Write down the field names used in this database.

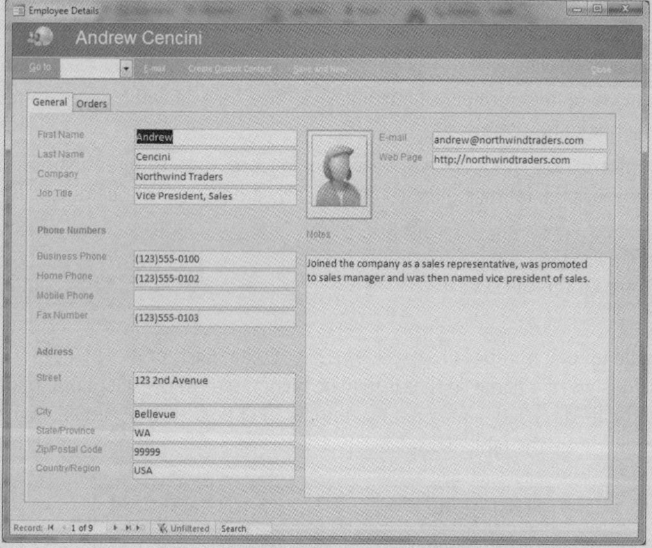

Personnel record in Access

3. The figure below shows one record from a database of runs scored in cricket test matches. Write down the field names used in this database. How is the value in the field called 'Average' worked out?

Player	R T Ponting
Matches	152
Innings	259
Not out	28
Runs	12363
Highest	257
Average	53.52
50's	56
100's	39

Ricky Ponting's record on a database of test cricket aggregate runs

4. For each of the databases in questions 1 to 3, write down the name of the entity about which data is being stored.

What is a report?

An important use of a database is the generation of reports. Reports provide information for the user. This usually involves making a selection from the database and then arranging it in a manner that is easy to understand. A report will normally only show the values from some of the fields in each record. It also often includes the totals of certain fields that will provide summary information for the user.

Example: First Fleet database

On page 301 are the first nine records of a report from the First Fleet database. One selection rule has been applied: POSITION equals CONVICT. For each record selected, the fields 'Given name', 'Last name', 'Date of birth', 'Place of trial', 'Crime' and their values are shown. The report is sorted on the surname. If surnames are the same, then it is sorted on the given name.

Unit 11.5 Activity 1D: Reports

Last name	First name	Value	Purchase Date	Department
Braun	Jacob	475	12-Jan-11	Sports
Brencic	Kate	398	22-Jan-11	Sports
Brencic	Kate	34	23-Jan-11	Book
Brencic	Kate	56	04-Feb-11	Clothing
Byrne	Marianne	88	31-Jan-11	Cookware
Cefai	Desmond	97	05-Jan-11	Book
Cook	Russell	675	12-Feb-11	Sports
Cook	Russell	872	26-Feb-11	Clothing
Denaro	Paula	335	22-Jan-11	Cookware
Denaro	Paula	98	01-Feb-11	Book
Giacomelli	Sam	87	13-Feb-11	Book
Giacomelli	Sam	37	22-Jan-11	Cookware
Hudson	Sandra	44	23-Jan-11	Book
Saunders	William	284	12-Feb-11	Clothing

Customer records from a store

The figure on the previous page is part of a database of customers for a department store. It shows the customers' names, the value of their purchases and the department where the purchases were made.

1. How many of the purchases were made on 22 January 2011? What is their total value?
2. How many purchases were made in the book department? What is their total value?
3. How is the database sorted? Suggest two other ways that it might be sorted and explain why it would be useful to sort in these ways.
4. Generate two different reports with subtotals that might be useful.

Why use a computer for a database?

Computers are used for databases because they:

- Can store large amounts of data.
- Can find and display data quickly.
- Can be updated or changed quickly.
- Present the data in a way that is useful (summaries of data can readily be obtained).
- Make the data available in many locations.
- Allow for data to be transferred easily.
- Allow a large number of people to use a database at the same time.
- Allow data to be available on the Internet.

Common database file formats

This table shows the common database file formats.

File extension	File type	Use
.mdb	Microsoft Access	Microsoft database file format
.txt	tab-separated text	transfer information to other applications
.csv	comma-separated values	transfer information to other applications
.fmp12	FileMaker Pro	FileMaker Pro database file format

Database file formats

Designing and creating a database

In business, designing and creating a database is a complex process and it comes after a lot of analysis.

The following is a typical list of questions that need to be answered:

- What is the entity about which data will be collected?
- What data about the entity needs to be collected?

- Which pieces of data are going to be used for searching and sorting?
- How can each different record in the database be uniquely identified?
- What information will need to be retrieved from the database?

Creating and using a small database involves the same steps.

- Identify the entity that is going to be used in the database. That is, identify the person or thing about which you are going to store data. You also need to know what results you expect to get from your database.
- Define the database by identifying the fields that will make up each record.
- Enter the initial data into the database.
- Check that the data is correct. This could be done by printing out some of the records and checking them against the original documents.
- Work out reports and searches that will be used often.
- Modify the database as required.
- Back up the database regularly by making copies of it and storing them in a safe place.

Creating a database

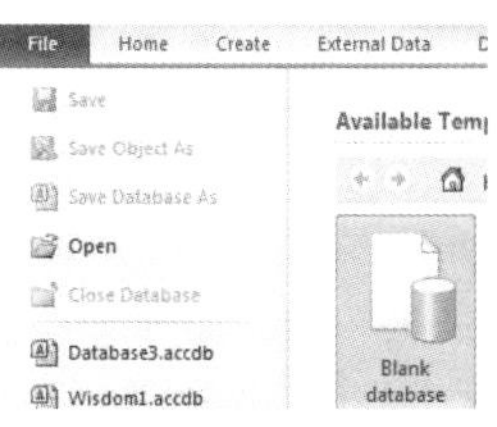

Starting Microsoft Access

To create a new, blank database in Microsoft Access:

- Start Microsoft Access.
- Choose **Blank database** from the available templates.

To create a database to keep track of members of a tennis club or similar group, you may need to include the members' names and addresses as well as their ages (this is needed for under-age competition).

The entity to be used is 'member', with the fields as requested. It is written:

member (id, surname, first name, address, town, telephone, age).

This data will be stored in a table.

The entity will need a primary key, ie a field that has a different value for every row in the table. The primary key enables you to uniquely identify each record.

When creating a table in Access, the first field is the primary key by default.

To create the table, enter the field names and choose the field type. The field types include:

- Text.
- Number.
- Currency.
- Date and time.

Field types in Access

By default, the first field in the table has the field name 'ID' and is the primary key. Clicking on the **Click to Add** button gives you the opportunity to select the field type and also to enter a new field name.

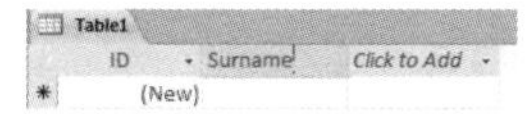

Starting a new table

Entering the field names creates a datasheet that can be used to enter data. The figure below shows the completed table with some data entered.

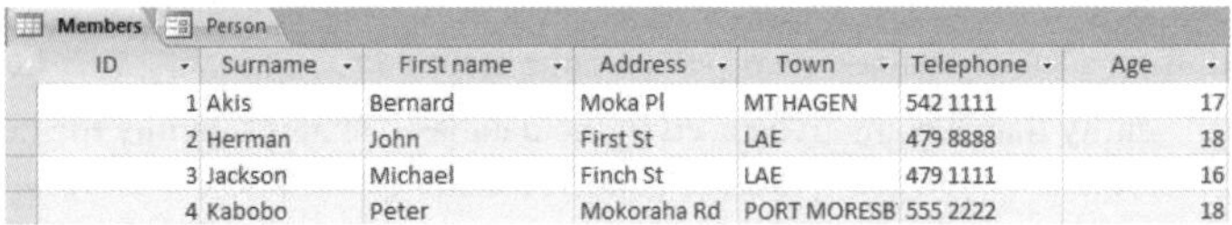

Members | Person

ID	Surname	First name	Address	Town	Telephone	Age
1	Akis	Bernard	Moka Pl	MT HAGEN	542 1111	17
2	Herman	John	First St	LAE	479 8888	18
3	Jackson	Michael	Finch St	LAE	479 1111	16
4	Kabobo	Peter	Mokoraha Rd	PORT MORESB	555 2222	18

A table has been created and data entered

Note that the ID for each person is a number that has been entered automatically.

When you first save the file, you are able to change the table name. In this case, the table name has been changed to 'Members'.

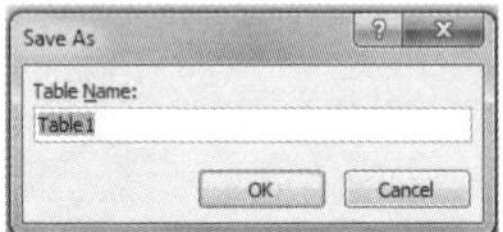

Creating a new table name

Unit 11.5 Activity 1E: Designing a database

Create a database to keep track of members of your tennis club or a similar group. The database will need to include the members' names and addresses as well as their ages (this is needed for under-age competition).

The entity to be used is 'member', with the fields as requested. It is written: member (surname, first name, address, town, telephone, age).

The database is defined using a database management package such as Microsoft Access. Each field will need to be defined using names, making sure they are meaningful. Each field can be defined as text or number. In this case, all the fields except age and telephone are text (the others being whole numbers).

1. Now enter the data. See page 307 for a sample database.
2. Check the data carefully. Look at each record in turn and compare it to the original data. Make any necessary changes.
3. Make sure at least one copy of the database is stored on a disk or memory stick and kept in a safe place. Backups should be carried out whenever the database is altered.

It can be useful to have standard reports and searches saved. Most database management systems allow some of the sorts and searches to be pre-defined. For example, Microsoft Access allows a number of reports to be saved. One useful report might be to produce mailing labels.

If a database is to be of use, its definition will need to be modified. That is, in time new fields will be added and some fields will no longer be of use. More or different information will need to be stored.

Member nu	Title	First name	Surname	Address1	Town	Telephone
3	Mr	Chris	Bandi	Ramu Madang Hwy	LAE	435 5656
2	Ms	Alice	Albert	Vunamami Rd	RABAUL	534 1111
1	Mr	John	Aguil	Senofi St	GOROKA	537 1025
4	Mr	Peter	Wilson	Hoffman St	GOROKA	537 2222
5	Ms	Jennifer	Daniel	Goilanai St	PT MORESBY	641 0000
6	Mr	Joseph	Dandava	Samarai Cres	PT MORESBY	641 0909

A sample database of tennis players

Unit 11.5 Activity 1F: Creating databases

1. A small business requires a database to track its customers and to be able to contact them. You are to create that database and enter test data for 15 customers with their names, addresses, telephone and facsimile numbers. You will need to produce the following reports:

- **a.** Mailing labels for the customer file.
- **b.** An alphabetic list of all customers.
- **c.** A list of customers in postcode order.

You will need to be able to search the database for:

- **a.** An individual customer.
- **b.** All the customers who have an address with a particular postcode.

2. A small business requires a database of employees. Identify the information that would be needed. Identify the reports that would be required. Create a form to collect that information together with anything else of use. Create ten records for testing purposes. Develop the interface needed to:

- **a.** Add records.
- **b.** Modify records.
- **c.** Delete records.

Ensure that there is a method of searching the database.

3. Use a database to track the most popular television programs using your fellow students as the audience.

- **a.** Design a database so that you can track the programs your fellow students watch.
- **b.** Create a form and ask other members of your class to enter the television programs they watch during a week.
- **c.** Enter the data into your database and produce a report that lists the programs in order of popularity.

Online databases

Many databases are now accessible via the World Wide Web.

Programs such as FileMaker Pro and Microsoft Access can be configured so that the data can be accessed using a web browser.

Microsoft Access integrates well with Microsoft SharePoint on the Internet.

Microsoft SQL Server is used in many organisations for database access. Products such as Cold Fusion and Dreamweaver MX can be used to develop the Web front end provided for end users.

Many organisations now provide access to online databases. Within businesses, this is done on **local area networks**. However, the World Wide Web is being widely used to provide many people with access to databases. Databases are searched and the results displayed using the browser.

Telephone directory

The White Pages telephone directory is available on the Web. The PNG White Pages has the URL:

www.whitepages.com.pg

Searches can be made for subscribers based on a number of fields including surname and location.

Searches can be made for residential, business and government addresses.

Unit 11.5 Activity 1G: Using the White Pages

1. Access the White Pages directory on the Web. Look up the telephone number of your home. How many other telephone numbers did it find? Did it show any mobile phone numbers?
2. Repeat the steps in question 1 for two of your friends or relatives.
3. Access the White Pages directory on the Web. Look up restaurants in your area. Find a restaurant near you.
4. Use the White Pages directory to find your school.

Papua New Guinea White Pages

The Australian Parliament website

The Australian Parliament website provides online information. It consists of a number of different but connected files: members, senators, electorates, ministry, Parliament House information and legislation.

The website contains information about members of the House of Representatives. For each member, it includes data about parliamentary service, ministerial appointments, committee service, party positions, qualifications and address, contact telephone and facsimile numbers and email address. The figure below shows an example of an entry on the Parliament website.

The site is updated regularly. The URL for the site is www.aph.gov.au.

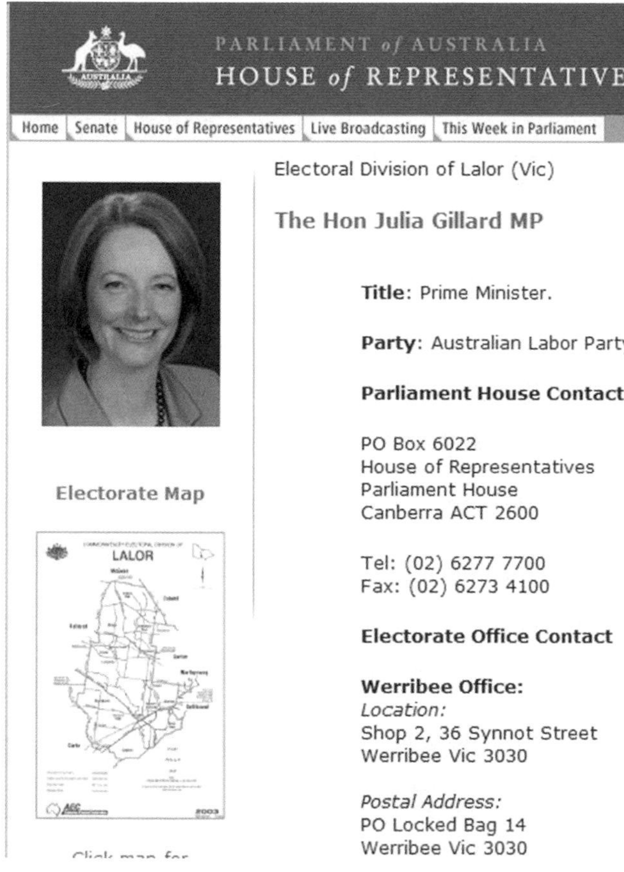

The Parliament website entry for the prime minister of Australia

Privacy and databases

On 21 December 2001, the *Privacy Act* came into law in Australia. It affected many organisations and individuals and is concerned with the collection, storage and access to personal information. Many other countries have also introduced privacy legislation.

The Act has set up ten privacy principles to which organisations must adhere. These principles include:

a. Collection of data.

b. Use and disclosure of data.

c. Data quality and collection.

d. Data security.

e. Privacy policies.

f. Access and correction.

g. Collection of sensitive information.

Most organisations must have a privacy policy that relates to the above principles. The policy should explain how individuals get access to data that is stored about them and what individuals can do to ensure that the data is correct and up to date.

Most countries have set up privacy laws to protect organisations and individuals.

Unit 11.5 Activity 1H: Privacy

1. All schools keep student records on a database. These records include name and address, telephone number, classes in which each student is enrolled, assessments for each class, plus a range of other useful data.
   - **a.** List the types of data that you think your school would keep about you on a database.
   - **b.** Which parts of the data do you think each of the following people or groups of people should be able to see about you: principal, teachers of the classes in which you are enrolled, teachers of classes in which you are not enrolled, your parents, you, other students.

2. With regard to yourself, list three pieces of information that you think
   - **a.** your school
   - **b.** your doctor

   should not disclose to your friends without your permission.

3. Log on to the Telstra website at www.telstra.com. Can you find Telstra's privacy policy? What information do they agree not to disclose?

4. If you have created an account with either Yahoo or Microsoft Hotmail, what do you have to do to change your password? What type of data do they require to ensure that you are a legitimate customer? Do these organisations have a privacy policy? What rights do the privacy policies give you?

5. Define these terms: field, record and file.

6. Why is it important to back up a database?

7. How often should a database be updated? Explain your answer, using an example.

8. What is a key field in a database? How is it used when sorting records?

9. What does the term 'report' mean when considering a database?

10. What is involved in a search of a database?

11. What steps need to be taken to create a database?

12. Explain the difference between data and information.

13. Give four reasons why businesses now use computers rather than paper files to store data.

14. What is test data? Why is it important?

Unit 11.5 Databases
Topic 2: Working with data

Topic 2 provides an introduction to working with data in a database (see ICT Syllabus p. 24).
It covers:
- Managing data.
- Controlling and searching records.

Managing database data

A database is only useful if the data it contains is correct and up to date.

A new telephone book is published every year. As people move house, have new telephone numbers connected or old numbers disconnected, the directory is altered. There is a database that keeps an up-to-date list of all telephone numbers. Making changes to the data is called 'updating the database'.

Databases are updated at various intervals, depending on the nature of the database. The telephone directory for each city or country area is printed each year. The printed directory is always out of date to some extent, as people may have moved house or changed their telephone number by the time the book is printed and distributed.

The stock exchange carries out its trading of shares using computers. Its database is updated online, ie as soon as the transaction takes place. Enquiries to the stock exchange database reflect the latest up-to-date information.

What changes are made to the data in a database?

Three types of changes are made to the data in a database. These are:
- Adding new records.
- Deleting records.
- Altering records.

Each of these types of changes needs to be made regularly and promptly.

The telephone directory might be changed in the following circumstances:
- Adding new records: a new subscriber is added to the network.
- Deleting a record: a subscriber decides not to continue with the service; an organisation closes down and no longer needs a telephone.
- Altering records: a subscriber changes address and/or telephone number.

A school might make changes in the following ways:
- Adding new records: a new student is enrolled in the school.
- Deleting a record: a student has left the school and is not expected to return.
- Altering records: a student changes his or her address.

Deletions are made with a great deal of care. The accuracy of the database depends upon records being deleted when they are no longer of use.

Records must also be altered with care. It is important that the record being altered is the correct one, ie it must be uniquely identified. Large databases such as those kept by Telikom will have many subscribers with the same name and initial.

Unit 11.5 Activity 2A: Updating databases

1. The table on the next page shows the batting averages for some test cricketers.
   - **a.** Under what circumstances would a player be added to the table?
   - **b.** Under what circumstances would a player be deleted from the table?
   - **c.** In which fields would the data never need to be altered?
   - **d.** In which fields would the values be altered?
2. The AFL website includes statistics for each of the teams playing in the AFL. The table below shows six of the records for AFL players at the start of the 2012 season. This is part of the database of all AFL players.
   - **a.** How many games in total has Chris Judd played? If he had played another 12 games in 2012, which field values might need to be changed? Which fields would not need to be updated during the season?
   - **b.** When would a player be deleted from the database?
   - **c.** When would a player be added to the database?
   - **d.** In which fields would the values never need to be changed?
   - **e.** What changes would need to be made at the start of a new season?

Surname	First Name	Club	Games Played	Goals
Swan	Dane	Collingwood	175	133
Judd	Chris	Carlton	222	193
Brown	Jonathan	Brisbane	210	498
Goodes	Adam	Sydney	300	352
Cox	Dean	West Coast	227	120
Cornes	Kane	Port Adelaide	223	81

AFL playing records

(Source: www.afl.com.au)

Unit 11.5 Activity 2B: Database maintenance

1. List four types of changes that would need to be made to the parliament database at the end of each six-month period.
2. What changes would have to be made following an election for the House of Representatives?
3. What changes would have to be made to the database when:
   - **a.** A member of parliament resigns and there is a by-election?
   - **b.** A member of cabinet resigns but remains a member of parliament?

Searching a database

A database needs to be accessed to be of any use. It is possible to select the particular parts of the database that are needed. Each database software package has its own way of finding the required data.

For example, when using the telephone directory, a typical query is to look up a name in the directory and find the telephone number. You will need to know the surname and, probably, the initials and at least some of the address. Finding a telephone number is known as 'searching the database'.

Each database language makes queries in different ways. A typical query made from the telephone book might be:

FIND ALL SUBSCRIBERS WITH SURNAME = 'Agua' AND INITIALS = 'W J'.

A query or search of the database is made up of the following things:

- The field to be used to make the selection: for example, '*Surname*'.
- The value or values that are to be looked for: for example, 'Agua'.
- The operator that is used for the selection: for example, '='.

In Microsoft Access, records are selected by choosing the value for comparison.

Unit 11.5 Activity 2C: Searching a database

The table overleaf shows the batting averages for 12 of the leading run scorers in test cricket.

1. How many players are Australian?
2. Which player has the highest average?
3. Which player has scored the most number of runs?
4. Which player has the highest score?

Player	Country	Matches	Innings	Not Outs	Runs	Highest	Average	Centuries
Ponting, R T	Australia	156	267	28	12557	257	59.04	39
Clarke, M J	Australia	74	123	12	5122	168	53.68	16
Watson, S R	Australia	32	58	2	2135	126	51.22	2
Cook, A N	England	72	125	7	5868	294	49.06	19
Strauss, A J	England	89	157	6	6340	177	49.63	19
Pietersen, K P	England	78	133	7	6361	227	62.64	19
Laxman, V V S	India	130	217	34	8626	281	49.58	17
Tendulkar, S R	India	184	303	32	15183	248*		51
Dhoni, M S	India	64	100	11	3407	148	60.04	5
Smith, G C	South Africa	93	163	10	7642	277	60.37	23
Amla, H M	South Africa	53	94	7	4136	253*	50.32	14
Prince, A G	South Africa	64	101	16	3608	162*	43.79	11

Batting averages for some test cricketers

Sorting a database

Data is usually sorted in some manner. The data may be sorted in ascending or descending order based on any one field (or more) that makes up the records in the database. The field that is used to sort the database is called the key field. Key fields are used to identify records in a database. Usually, each record has a key field that uniquely identifies that record.

Ascending order means going from smallest to largest. Names in the telephone directory are arranged in ascending order.

Descending order means going from largest to smallest. Teams on a sporting ladder are usually arranged in descending order; for example, the NRL ladder or the NBL ladder.

Example: Name and address database

The name and address database below has been sorted in ascending order on the surname.

Title	First name	Surname	Address1	Town	Telephone
Mr	John	Aguil	Senofi St	GOROKA	537 1025
Ms	Alice	Albert	Vunamami Rd	RABAUL	534 1111
Mr	Chris	Bandi	Ramu Madang Hwy	LAE	435 5656
Mr	Joseph	Dandava	Samarai Cres	PT MORESBY	641 0909
Ms	Jennifer	Daniel	Goilanai St	PT MORESBY	641 0000
Mr	Peter	Wilson	Hoffman St	GOROKA	537 2222

Names and addresses sorted on the field 'Surname'

The name and address database below has been sorted in ascending order on the telephone number.

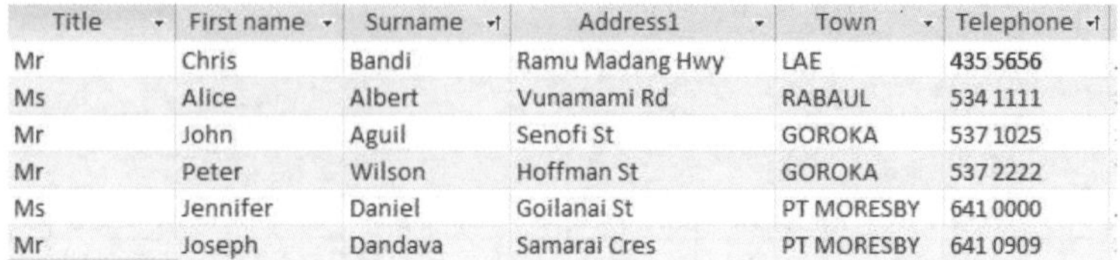

Title	First name	Surname	Address1	Town	Telephone
Mr	Chris	Bandi	Ramu Madang Hwy	LAE	435 5656
Ms	Alice	Albert	Vunamami Rd	RABAUL	534 1111
Mr	John	Aguil	Senofi St	GOROKA	537 1025
Mr	Peter	Wilson	Hoffman St	GOROKA	537 2222
Ms	Jennifer	Daniel	Goilanai St	PT MORESBY	641 0000
Mr	Joseph	Dandava	Samarai Cres	PT MORESBY	641 0909

Names and addresses sorted on the field 'Telephone number'

Unit 11.5 Databases

Topic 3: Working with tables and relationships

Topic 3 explains how to work with tables and relationships (see ICT Syllabus p. 24). It covers:

- Relational databases
- Creating and customising tables.
- Getting external information.
- Managing relationships between tables.

Relational databases

A **relational database** is one that is composed by a collection of tables. The tables are related to each other by key fields.

The first databases were known as flat file databases. In these databases, all the information about an entity was stored in one record in the database. There was only one table. Flat file databases are good for small, simple systems but are inadequate for complex systems. In particular, accessing information from a flat file database can be difficult.

In 1970 E.F. Codd, a researcher at IBM, wrote a paper outlining the theory of relational databases. This theory was adapted in database design and many vendors including IBM and Oracle created relational databases.

His theory had an impact on data analysis and a set of rules, called '**normalisation**', was invented to allow the allocation of data to **tables**. Normalisation is now widely used in the design of databases.

Relational databases are manipulated using the Structured Query Language (SQL). The rules and standards for SQL have developed over time.

Normalisation

The process of normalisation is used to analyse data and to identify the tables that are to be used in a relational database. Normalisation is a set of rules that is applied to the data to eliminate redundant data and to create the tables that will be used in the structure of the database.

Normalisation is a complex process but is necessary for large databases to ensure that the data can be kept accurate and up to date without repeating data in different tables.

The process of normalisation reduces the data to a number of tables. Each table will have a key field that uniquely identifies the entity the table represents.

A data analyst will go through a process of writing down all the fields that make up an entity. This will be the first normal form.

There will almost certainly be repeating groups in the entity. This leads to the definition of a new entity and the removal of the repeating groups. Once the new entity is defined the data is now in the second normal form.

The process is repeated again until new repeating groups appear. The data is then in third normal form. Once the data is in third normal form, the definition of the database can begin.

Each table has a key field, ie a field that is used to access the records in the table directly. Each record will have a unique value in the key field.

In some cases, a foreign key will also be used in an entity. A foreign key is one that is a key field in a different entity but is also used in an entity.

For example, a sales system might include:

Customer(**customer_number**, name)

Orders(**order_number**, order_details, customer_number)

In this case, customer_number is a foreign key in the Orders table but is the key field in the Customer table.

Example: a tennis club

A tennis club is made up of members about whom data needs to be kept. The data includes name, address and contact information, similar to that in a contacts database. The database also needs to include data about the membership type and the membership fee.

If the club has three membership categories (junior, senior, weekday), each with an associated fee, these fields could be added to a flat file similar to the contacts database. But doing this has some significant disadvantages. Every time the annual fee is adjusted, every record in the database will need to be adjusted: all the junior members will need to be selected and the fee changed, and then the same process repeated for the senior and weekday members. Not only is this time-consuming and cumbersome, a lot of data is stored unnecessarily.

Member Number	Surname	First name	Town	Membership type	Membership fee
1	Aguil	John	GOROKA	Senior	195
2	Albert	Alice	RABAUL	Senior	195
3	Bandi	Chris	LAE	Junior	120
4	Wilson	Peter	GOROKA	Weekday	150
5	Daniel	Jennifer	PT MORESBY	Junior	120
6	Dandava	Joseph	PT MORESBY	Senior	195
7	Biti	Mary	MADANG	Weekday	150
8	Klink	Tom	MADANG	Senior	195

Sample data for the tennis club

The figure above shows sample data for the tennis club. Data repeats in the fields *Membership type* and *Membership fee*. These are therefore identified as repeating fields. A new entity called *Membership* is then created, as seen below.

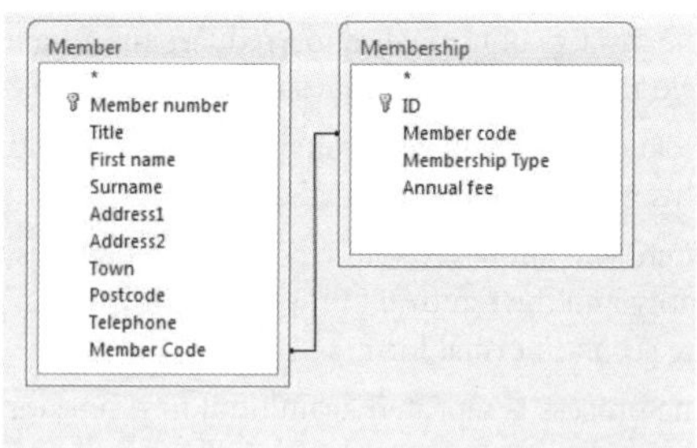

Each member has one membership type

If the club records are organised as two tables, then the membership information can be stored in its own table. When the fee is changed, it needs to be updated in only one place, in the membership table.

The figure on the right shows how this could be designed. There are two entities: Member, which stores data similar to a contacts database, and Membership, which stores membership categories and fees. The tennis club database is based on the Member entity and includes the fields Member number, which is a unique number for each member so that any member can be identified unambiguously, and Member code, which is used to represent the membership type.

Membership is a table with only three rows, as shown in the figure below.

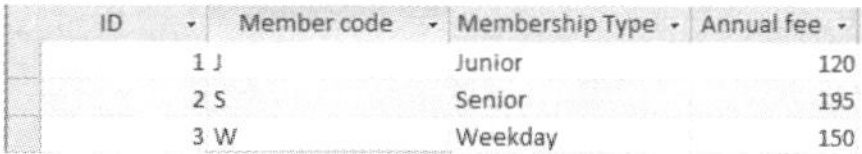

ID	Member code	Membership Type	Annual fee
1	J	Junior	120
2	S	Senior	195
3	W	Weekday	150

Membership table

The two tables are related together by the common field *Member code*. A relationship between the tables has been defined so that this can be used.

Data from the two tables can now be joined together in the one report.

To create the relationship, use the **Relationships** command on the **Relationships** section of the **Table Tools Table** tab.

Using the above example:

- Click the **relationships** command.
- **Add** both the tables.
- Click **Close**.

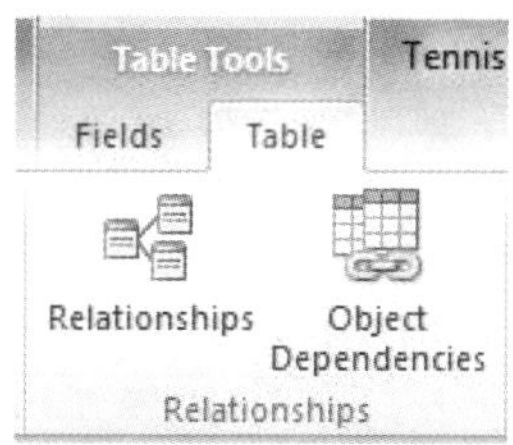

Relationships command on the Table Tools tab

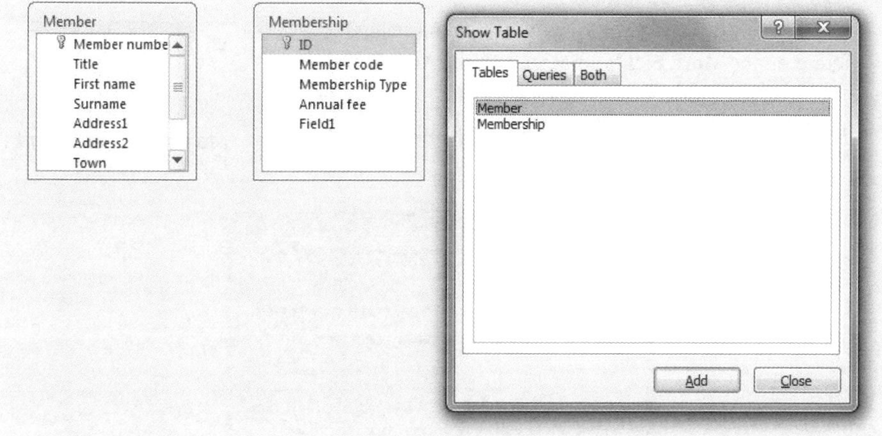

Creating a relationship

- Click on the **Member code** field name in **Member**.
- Drag to the **Member code** field name in **Membership**.
- Click **Create** in the **Edit Relationships** window that appears.

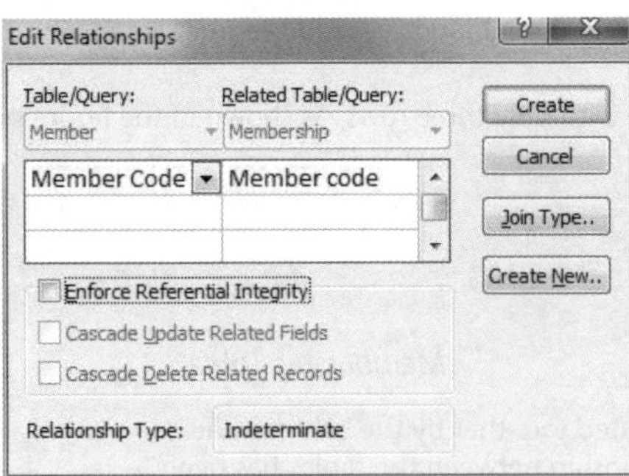

Edit Relationships window

The relationship is now created.

Creating lookup values

The Lookup Wizard allows the use of drop-down lists for data entry. The drop-down list can be used to restrict data to allowable values only and thus make it easier to ensure data integrity.

To create a field with lookup values:

- Choose the field type **Lookup & Relationship** which is found on the **More Fields** command on the **Add & Delete** section of the **Table Tools Fields** tab.
- The **Lookup & Relationship** option opens the Lookup Wizard.

More Fields command

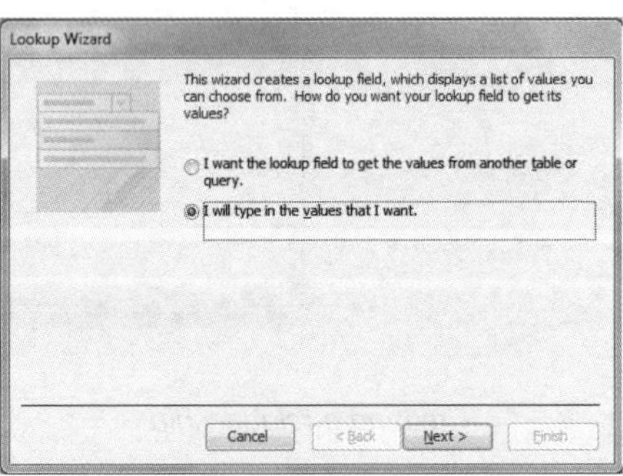

Lookup Wizard

- The values for the lookup table are entered in the columns.

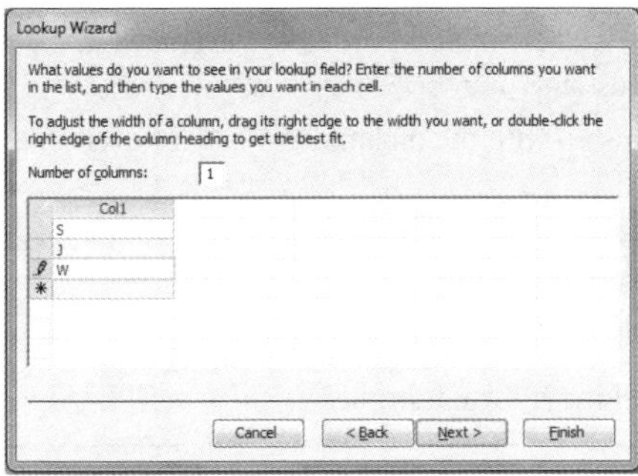

Entering Lookup values

- Once that is done, only the values in the table are allowed in the database for that field.

Unit 11.5 Activity 3A: How do databases identify people?

1. Sheryl Jankovic is a Year 11 student at Mount Hagen High School. She is in 11A. She is a member of the local tennis club, has a mobile phone and works at the local supermarket part-time. She has a statement savings account with her bank. The following table shows other relationships.

Complete the table of the relationships and methods.

	Organisation	**Nature of relationship of organisation to Sheryl**	**Method used to uniquely identify Sheryl**
1	School		
2	Football club		
3	Telephone company		
4	Passenger on a flight with Air Niugini		
5	Bank		
6	Supermarket (part-time)		
7	Video rental store		
8	Online book store		
9	Shareholder in Air Niugini		
10	Government of Papua New Guinea		

2. Listed below are some examples of relationships you could enjoy with a range of institutions, organisations and suppliers of goods and services. Most bodies would require name and address details for identification.

a. Describe your relationship with the organisation, eg school and student, business and customer.

b. What information is likely to be recorded or developed in the system by the organisation, eg customer number?

c. Does your relationship with the organisation change over time, eg. debtor, change in year level at school?

d. How is information communicated between the organisation and you, eg invoice, school report, quarterly statement?

e. How long is the information likely to be recorded and maintained?

f. How 'private' will the information be?

Unit 11.5 Databases

Topic 4: Creating and customising queries

Topic 4 focuses on how to create and customise queries (see ICT Syllabus pp. 24–5).
It covers:

- Creating select queries.
- Controlling queries output.

The ability to make **queries** of a database is an essential part of the database tools. Queries can be used to select records. Queries can be used to combine information from different tables.

Creating select queries

Creating queries quickly: the Simple Query Wizard

The Query Wizard quickly generates simple select queries. The Query Wizard is available on the Queries section of the Create tab.

The Query Wizard on the Create tab

The Query Wizard has the following properties:

- You cannot use it to include selection criteria.
- You cannot specify the sort order.
- You cannot use the Wizard to change the order of the fields from the sequence.
- You can produce a summary query for numeric fields.

To create a query:

- Click the **Query Wizard** icon on the **Create** tab.
- On the **New Query** window, select the **Simple Query Wizard** option.

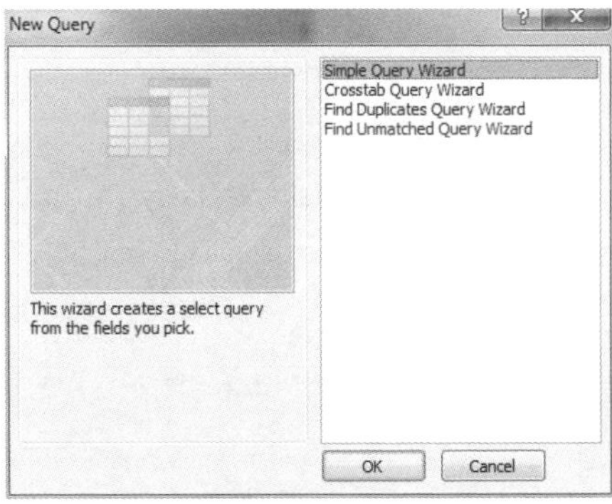

*Starting the **Simple Query Wizard***

- Select the table that is to be queried from the drop-down list.
- Select the fields to be listed from the table.

For example, to select the employee names and their email addresses from the Northwind database:

- Select the table called **Employees**.
- Select the fields, **First Name, Surname, E-mail Address**.
- Click **Finish**.

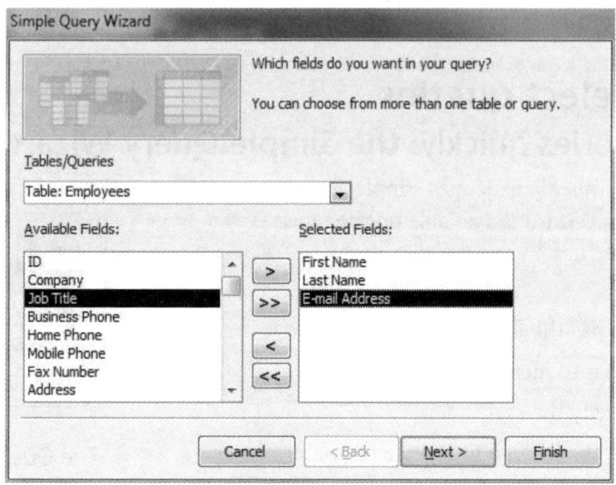

Creating a simple query

The results of the query show in the centre of the screen.

First Name	Last Name	E-mail Address
Nancy	Freehafer	nancy@northwindtraders.com
Andrew	Cencini	andrew@northwindtraders.com
Jan	Kotas	jan@northwindtraders.com
Mariya	Sergienko	mariya@northwindtraders.com
Steven	Thorpe	steven@northwindtraders.com
Michael	Neipper	michael@northwindtraders.com
Robert	Zare	robert@northwindtraders.com
Laura	Giussani	laura@northwindtraders.com
Anne	Hellung-Larsen	anne@northwindtraders.com

Results of a simple query

The Simple Query Wizard has actually generated the data from a SQL query. The figure below shows the query.

```
SELECT Employees.[First Name], Employees.[Last Name], Employees.[E-mail Address]
FROM Employees;
```

SQL query

Controlling queries output

Opening or switching query to design view

When a query is created, it is named and stored in the navigation pane on the left of the screen.

To design a new query:

- Choose **Query Design** on the **Queries** section of the **Create** tab.
- Choose the table that is to be used for the query.

Note that the Northwind database is used for this example.

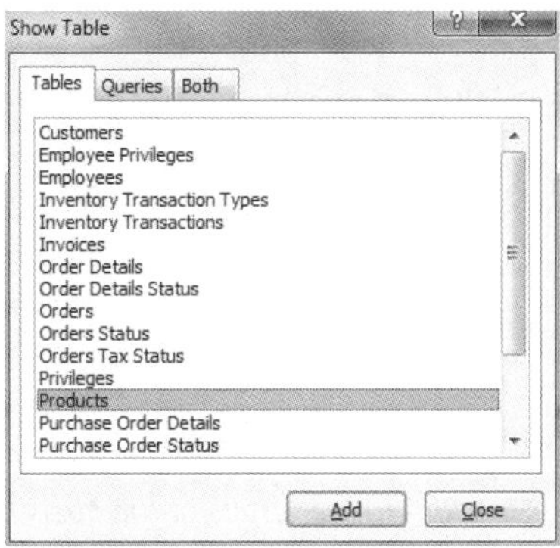

Choose the table for the query

- In this case, the *Products* table is selected.
- Click **Add** and then **Close**.
- The Products table appears in the query window.

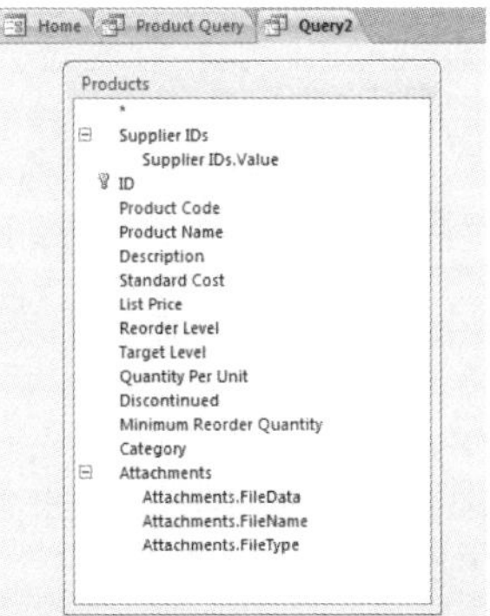

Fields can be selected from the Products table to appear in the query

- The query is now in **Design View**.
- Double-click on the fields to be included in the query, eg *Product Name, List Price*.
- These field names appear at the bottom of the **Design View** Window.

Field:	Product Name	Standard Cost	
Table:	Products	Products	
Sort:			
Show:	☑	☑	☐
Criteria:			
or:			

Fields selected for the query

- Now select **Run** from the Results section of the **Query Tools Design** tab.

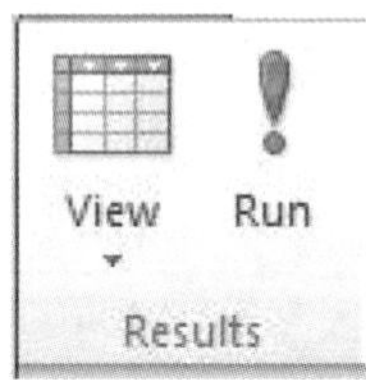

Click Run to see results of the query

- The results appear in the query window.

Product Name	Standard Cost
Northwind Traders Chai	$13.50
Northwind Traders Syrup	$7.50
Northwind Traders Cajun Seasoning	$16.50
Northwind Traders Olive Oil	$16.01
Northwind Traders Boysenberry Spread	$18.75
Northwind Traders Dried Pears	$22.50
Northwind Traders Curry Sauce	$30.00
Northwind Traders Walnuts	$17.44
Northwind Traders Fruit Cocktail	$29.25
Northwind Traders Chocolate Biscuits Mix	$6.90

Results of the query

Adding a field

To modify the query, open the **Design View** window by right-clicking on the query name (Query2) and selecting **Design View**.

To add a field:

- Double-click on the field name eg *Reorder Level*.
- The field is now added in the **Design View** window.
- Click **Run** to see the results.

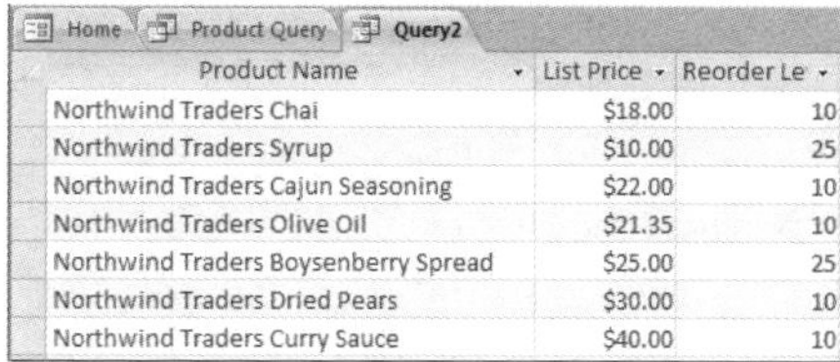

Product Name	List Price	Reorder Le
Northwind Traders Chai	$18.00	10
Northwind Traders Syrup	$10.00	25
Northwind Traders Cajun Seasoning	$22.00	10
Northwind Traders Olive Oil	$21.35	10
Northwind Traders Boysenberry Spread	$25.00	25
Northwind Traders Dried Pears	$30.00	10
Northwind Traders Curry Sauce	$40.00	10

A field is added to the query

Deleting fields

Open the **Design View** window by right-clicking on the query name (*Query2*) and selecting **Design View**.

To delete a field:

- Select the field name in the bottom section of the Design View window, eg *Reorder Level*.
- Click somewhere else in the window.
- The field is now deleted.

Rearranging fields

Open the **Design View** window by right-clicking on the query name (*Query2*) and selecting **Design View**.

To move a field:

- Select the field name in the bottom section of the Design View window, eg *Reorder Level*.
- Right-click on the selected field name and select **Cut**.
- Click in the destination area and choose **Paste**.

Sorting the query output

To sort the query output, choose the **Sort** command from the **Sort & Filter** section of the **Home** tab.

Note that there are two sort options: **Ascending** and **Descending**.

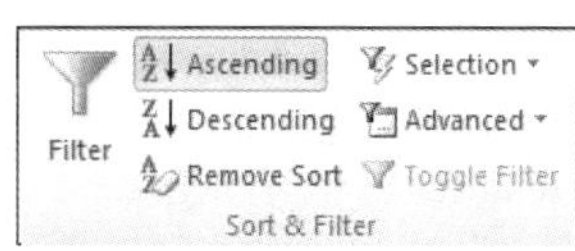

Sorting the query output

For example, to sort the product name in descending order of price:

- Click on the field name **List Price** in the query output.
- Choose **Descending** from the **Sort & Filter** section of the **Home** tab.
- Once the **Descending** button is clicked, the records are sorted.

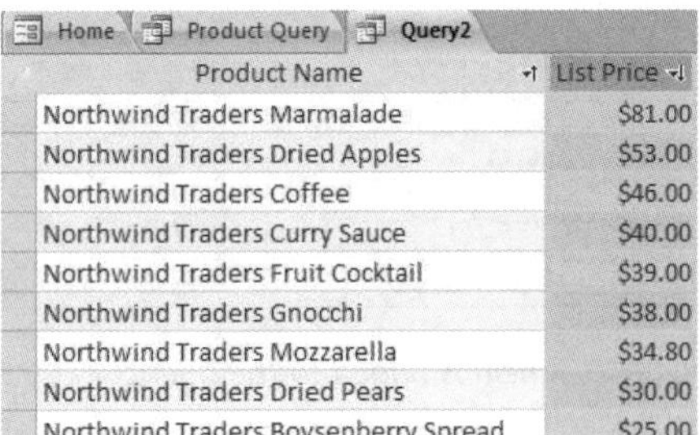

Product Name	List Price
Northwind Traders Marmalade	$81.00
Northwind Traders Dried Apples	$53.00
Northwind Traders Coffee	$46.00
Northwind Traders Curry Sauce	$40.00
Northwind Traders Fruit Cocktail	$39.00
Northwind Traders Gnocchi	$38.00
Northwind Traders Mozzarella	$34.80
Northwind Traders Dried Pears	$30.00
Northwind Traders Boysenberry Spread	$25.00

The sorted output

Filtering the query output with criteria

To filter the data, the **Selection** command on the **Sort & Filter** section of the **Home** tab can be used.

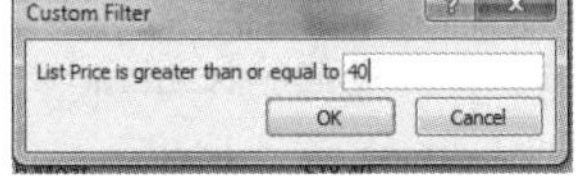

Filtering data

To do this:

- Click on the **Selection** icon.
- Right-click anywhere within the data of the field that is to be used for the filter.
- Select **Number Filters** and then the filter type, eg **Greater than...**
- Enter the value for the filter, eg 40.

The result displays only the records where the List Price is greater than or equal to 40.

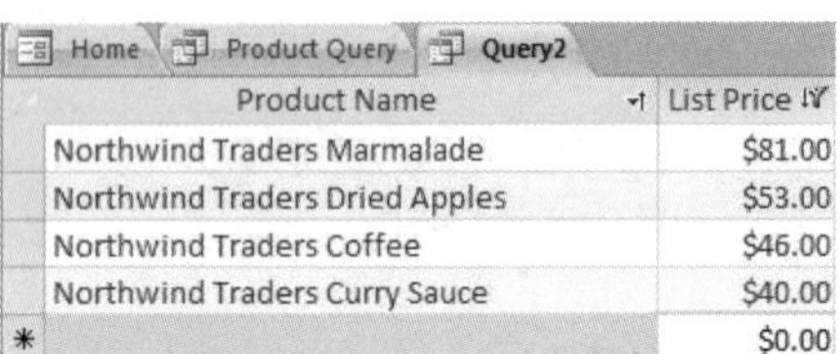

Product Name	List Price
Northwind Traders Marmalade	$81.00
Northwind Traders Dried Apples	$53.00
Northwind Traders Coffee	$46.00
Northwind Traders Curry Sauce	$40.00
*	$0.00

Results of filtering the data

To remove the filter, right-click in the field and choose **Clear filter from List Price**.

Setting multiple criteria

The **Advanced** command on the **Sort & Filter** section of the **Home** tab can be used to set multiple criteria for selection.

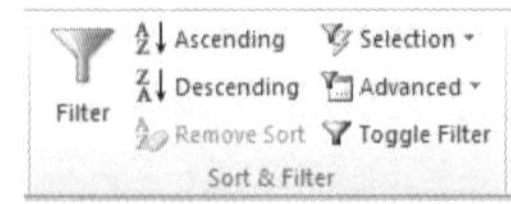

The Advanced command is used for multiple criteria

To do this:

- Choose the **Advanced** command.
- Choose the **Advanced Filter/Sort** option. This opens a filter window with the lower pane that is used to set up multiple criteria.
- Enter the field names in the filter window.
- Enter the criteria.
- Choose the **Advanced** command and then **Apply Filter/Sort**.
- The result of the filter is shown in the window.

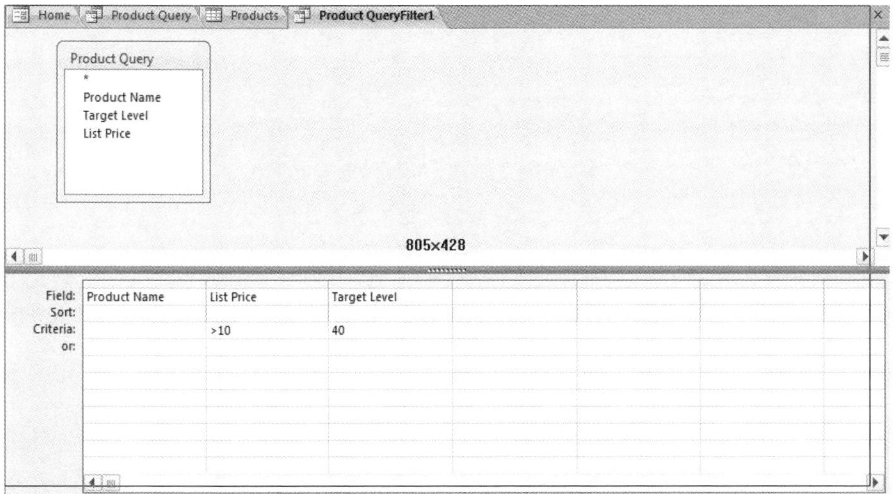

The Filter window with the criteria in the lower pane

The filter query is "*List Price*>10 **and** *Target Level* = 40". The results are shown in the figure below.

Product Name	Target Level	List Price
Northwind Traders Chai	40	$18.00

Results of the filter

The filter can be changed at any time. In the figure below, the filter query is now is "*List Price*>10 **or** *Target Level* = 40".

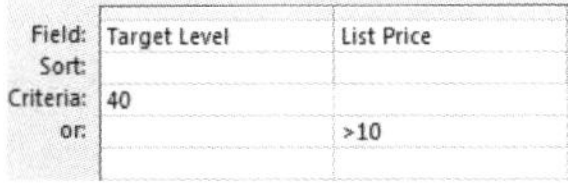

Field:	Target Level	List Price
Sort:		
Criteria:	40	
or:		>10

Changing the filter criteria

Unit 11.5 Databases

Topic 5: Creating and customising forms

Topic 5 focuses on how to create and customise forms (see ICT Syllabus p. 25). It covers:

- Creating forms effectively.
- Customising forms.

Creating forms effectively

Creating a form with AutoForm

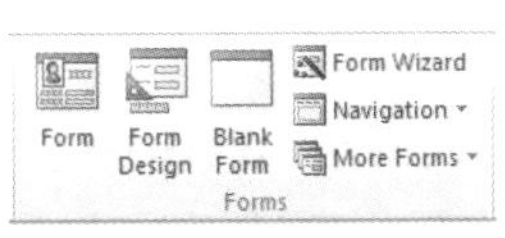

Form command on the Forms menu

The quickest way to generate a form is to use the **Form** command on the **Forms** section of the **Create** tab.

Clicking on the **Forms** command immediately generates a report on the currently selected data.

The form is given:

- A default name.
- Labels for each field.
- All the fields in the table.

For example, using the tennis club members, the form generated is a simple, one-page form.

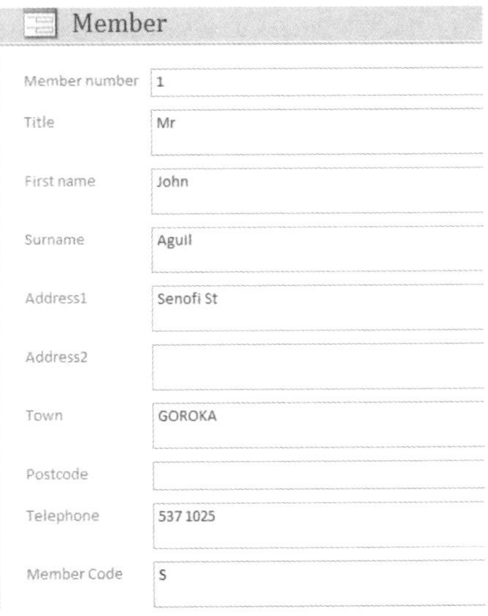

A report generated using the Form command

Saving and renaming a form

A form can be saved by:

- Right-clicking on the form name.
- Choosing **Save**.
- Entering the new form name in the dialog box or accepting the default name.

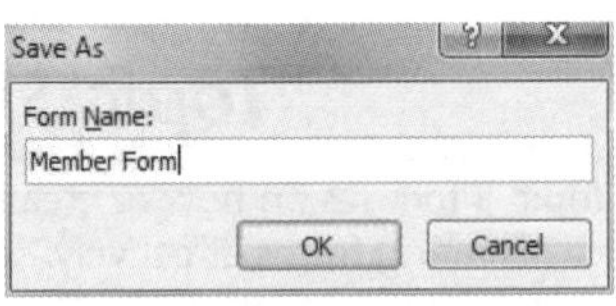

Saving a form

Creating a form using a Form Wizard

The **Form Wizard** on the **Forms** section of the **Create** tab can also be used to generate a form. The **Form Wizard** gives the user more control over the fields that appear in the form and over the look of the form.

The Form Wizard allows the user to select the fields to be used in the form. Fields can be selected from more than one table if a relationship has been established.

To create the form:

- Choose **Form Wizard** from the **Forms** section of the **Create** tab.
- Select the table and the fields required.

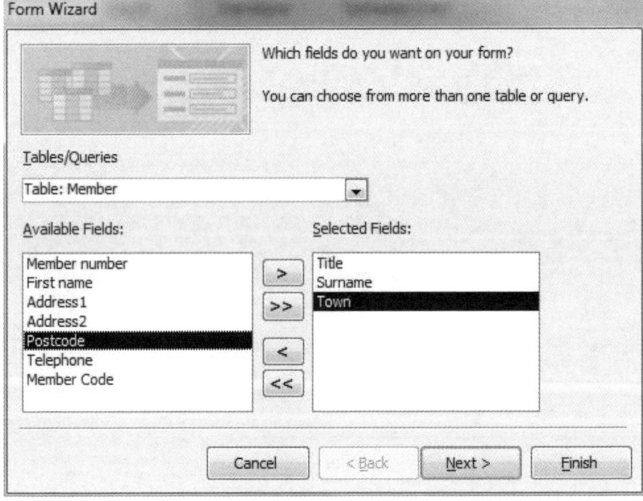

Selecting the fields for a form

- Select the type of layout:
    - Columnar.
    - Tabular.
    - Datasheet.
    - Justified.
- Give the form a name.
- Click **Finish**.

The form is now created and it can be used for data entry and updating or browsing. Note the arrows at the bottom of the form that allow scrolling between records.

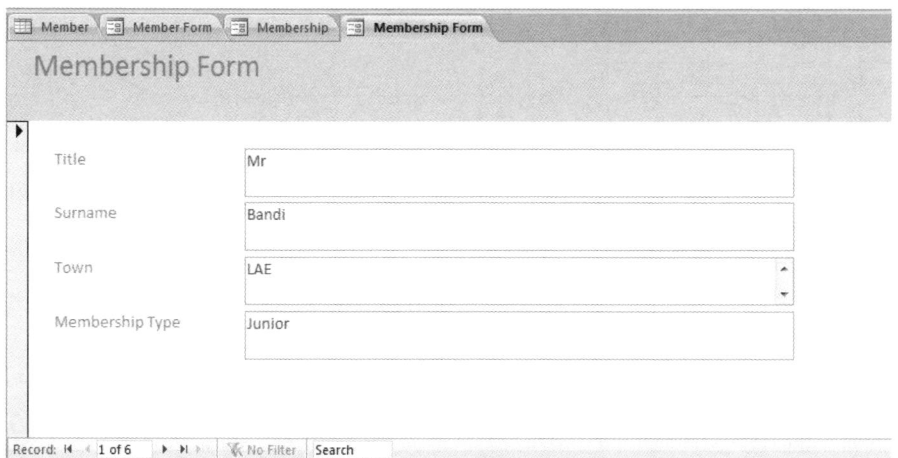

A form created using the Form Wizard

Customising forms

Forms can be customised by the user. This can be done either by creating the form using the **Form Wizard** or by creating it from scratch.

A form created using the **Form Wizard** can be opened and modified using the **Design View**.

Opening Form Design View

The form can be opened by right-clicking on the name of the form and then choosing **Design View** from the drop-down menu.

Form opened in Design View

The user can now see the three parts of the form:

- Form header.
- Detail.
- Form footer.

The header can be modified by changing the title, adding an image and modifying the font, among other things. Similarly, the detail section of the form can be modified: field names can be removed, field sizes adjusted, locations changed and so on.

The user has complete control over the look and feel of the form.

The form in the figure below has been modified in Design View to:

- Include an image from Clip Art.
- Remove some of the field names.
- Modify the layout of the fields.

The modified form

Showing or hiding field list

When modifying a form in the **Design View**, a list of fields can be displayed in a pane on the right the screen.

To display the fields, click on the **Add Existing Fields** command on the **Tools** section of the **Form Design Tools – Design** tab.

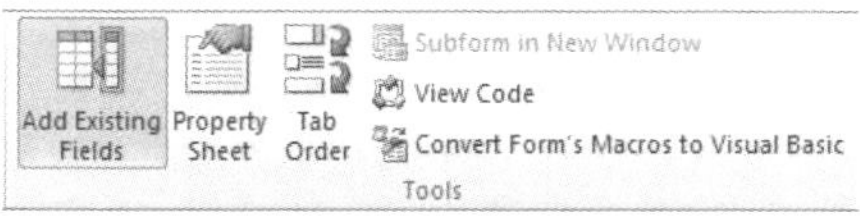

Add Existing Fields command

The field list appears in the right of the screen.

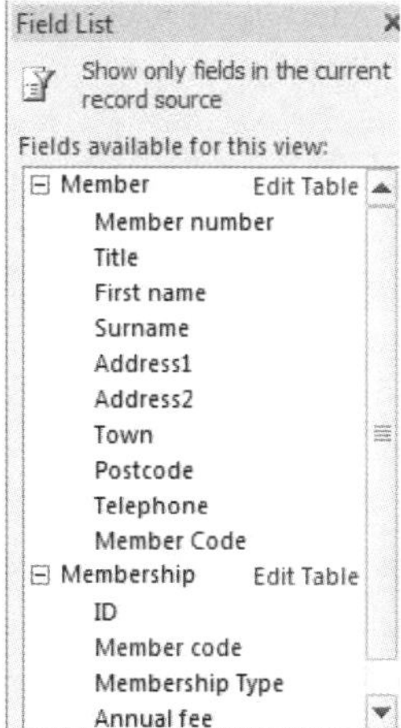

The field list

The field list can be hidden or closed by using the **Add Existing Fields** command again.

Form layout tools

The form layout tools give the designer a range of tools to customise the form and make it easy to use.

Form layout tools

These tools include:

- Text boxes.
- Labels.
- Buttons.
- Hyperlinks.
- Navigation controls.
- Combo boxes.

These tools are available on **Form Layout Tools – Design** tab in the **Design View** and the **Layout View**.

Controls

A control is the part of a form or a report that is used to display and edit data. A text box that displays data in a report is a control. A text box that allows the user to enter data in a form is a control. Other controls include buttons and check boxes.

There are three types of controls:

- Bound controls: the source of data is a field in a table. Bound controls are used in forms to store data that can be text, numbers, dates and other types of values.
- Unbound controls: these are used as labels and have no source of data. They are used for text, pictures and titles.
- Calculated controls: these have the source of data as an expression such as a calculation.

Resizing control

A control can be resized in the Design View by selecting it and then dragging the handles to the required size.

In the figure below, the bound control displaying the field *Membership Type* has been selected and can be resized.

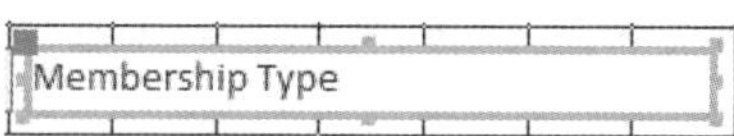

Control is selected for resizing

When the control is selected, it can also be formatted using the commands on the **Form Design Tools Format** tab. In the figure below:

- The control has been resized.
- The font has been changed in style and size.
- A background fill has been added.

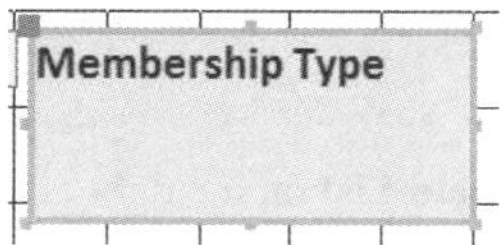

The control is resized and reformatted

Moving both control and label

When a form is created and a field inserted, it is usually done so with a label for the field. These two controls, the field label and the field, are designed so that they can be moved together. To move both controls, ie the label and the field:

- Select one of the controls.
- Click on the outline of the control and drag it to the new position.

Both controls – the label and the field – are moved.

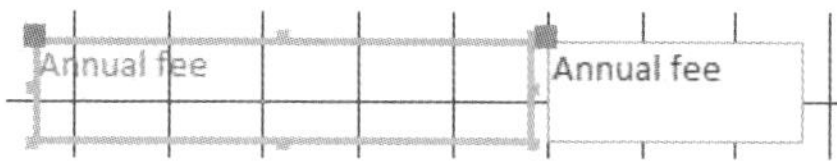

Click and drag on the outline of the Annual fee label control to move both control and label

Moving control and label separately

The two controls can be also be moved separately. This is done by selecting the control to be moved: either the label or the field. Then click on the grey square at the top left of the control and drag. The control will now be moved separately.

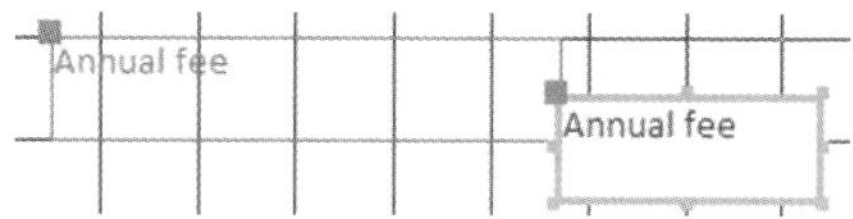

The Annual fee control field has been moved

Deleting a field control

To delete a field control:

- Select the field control in **Design View**.
- Right-click on the mouse and select **Delete**.

Note that this also deletes the label control associated with the field.

To delete the label control:

- Select the label control in **Design View**.
- Right-click on the mouse and select **Delete**.

Note that this deletes only the label control, not the field control.

Adding a field control

To add a field control:

- Select the field name from the **Field List** on the right of the screen.
- Drag the field onto the desired section of the layout.

Note that this also adds the associated label.

If the Field List is not showing, choose the **Add Existing Fields** command on the **Form Design Tools – Design** tab to display it.

Unit 11.5 Databases

Topic 6: Creating useful reports

Topic 6 explains how to create useful reports (see ICT Syllabus p. 25). It covers:

- Creating a report using AutoReport.
- Creating mailing labels.
- Setting page margins.
- Changing page orientation.
- Numbering pages.

A report is the result of a database query or queries that is formatted in a manner that is easy to read. Reports are generally designed to be printed.

Many applications run standard queries that generate reports which are useful for decision-making.

Creating a report using AutoReport

The quickest way to generate a report is to use the **Report** command on the **Reports** section of the **Create** tab.

Report command on the Reports menu

Clicking on the **Report** command immediately generates a report on the currently selected data.

For example, with three columns of product data from the Northwind database – *Product Name, List Price and Target Level* – displayed, clicking on the **Report** command generates the following report.

Note that elements of the form can be modified in either the **Layout View** or the **Design View**. These views are available by right-clicking on the name of the report.

Product Query2

Product Name	List Price	Target Level
Northwind Traders Cajun Seasoning	$22.00	40
Northwind Traders Olive Oil	$21.35	40
Northwind Traders Boysenberry Spread	$25.00	100
Northwind Traders Dried Pears	$30.00	40
Northwind Traders Curry Sauce	$40.00	40
Northwind Traders Walnuts	$23.25	40
Northwind Traders Fruit Cocktail	$39.00	40
Northwind Traders Marmalade	$81.00	40
Northwind Traders Coffee	$46.00	100
Northwind Traders Dried Apples	$53.00	40
Northwind Traders Gnocchi	$38.00	120
Northwind Traders Hot Pepper Sauce	$21.05	40
Northwind Traders Mozzarella	$34.80	40
	$474.45	

Page 1 of 1

Report generated using the Report command

Creating mailing labels

A mailing label report is a multi-column report. There are many different label sizes available to use. The user can either start with a blank page or the **Label Wizard** can be used to create mailing labels.

An advantage of using the Label Wizard is that the dimensions of a large number of commercially produced adhesive labels are included in the design process.

Labels on the Reports section of the Create tab

To create a set of mailing labels:

- Choose the data table to be used.
- Select the **Labels** button on the **Reports** section of the **Create** table.

To generate the labels:

- Open the table to be used and select the data.

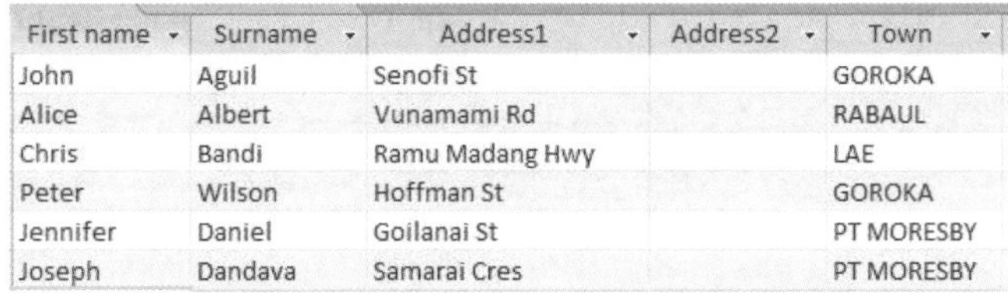

First name	Surname	Address1	Address2	Town
John	Aguil	Senofi St		GOROKA
Alice	Albert	Vunamami Rd		RABAUL
Chris	Bandi	Ramu Madang Hwy		LAE
Peter	Wilson	Hoffman St		GOROKA
Jennifer	Daniel	Goilanai St		PT MORESBY
Joseph	Dandava	Samarai Cres		PT MORESBY

Data to be used in generating mailing labels

- Choose **Labels** from the **Reports** section of the **Create** tab.
- Select the label size to be used from the list.

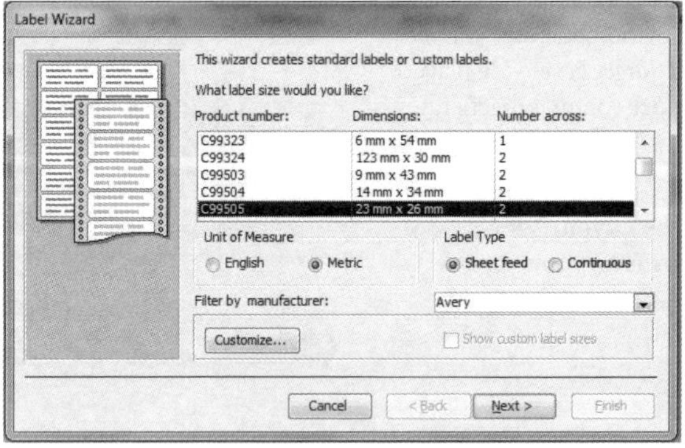

Select the label size to be used

- Select the fields to be used on the mailing labels.

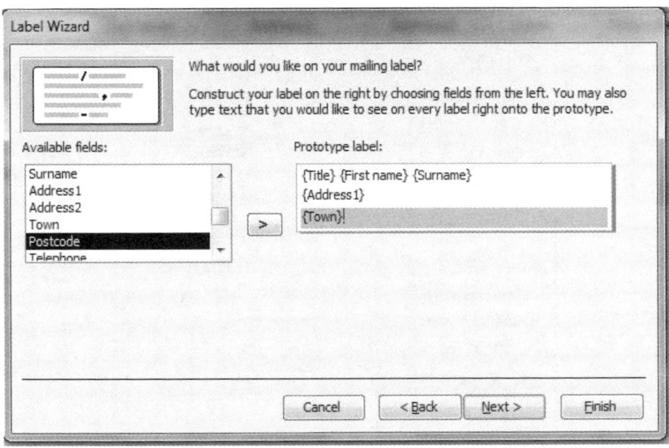

Selecting the fields for the mailing labels

- The mailing labels are now generated.

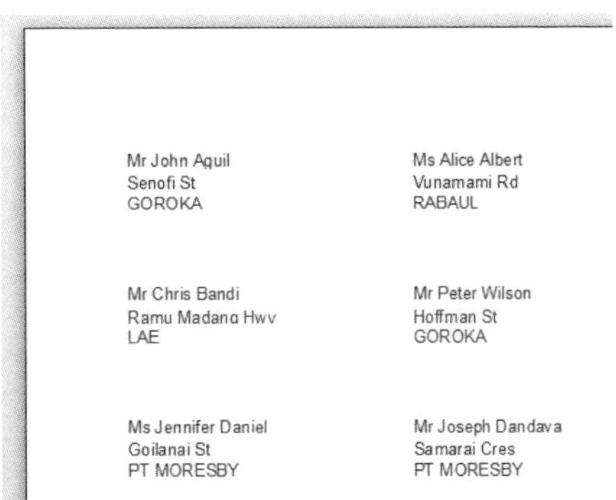

Mailing labels

Setting page margins and changing page orientation

Page margins for a report can be set using the **Page Setup** command on the **Page Layout** section of the **File** tab.

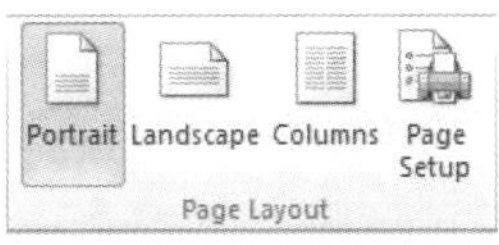

Page Setup command

The **Page Setup** dialog box allows the margins to be set.

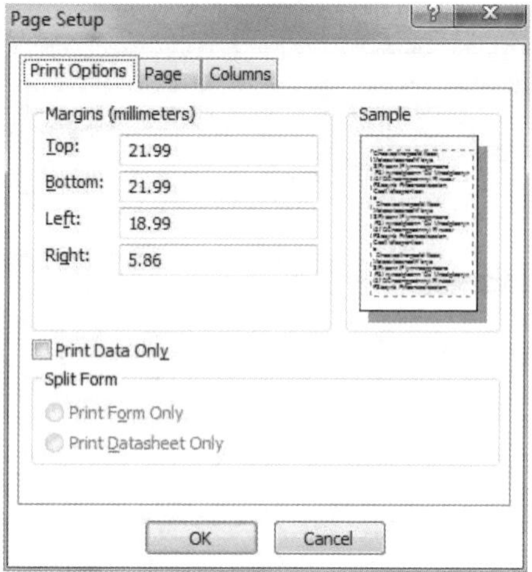

Page Setup dialog box

Margins can also be set using the **Margins** command on the **Page Size** section of the **Print Preview** tab.

The **Portrait** and **Landscape** commands on the **Page Layout** section of the **File** tab allow the orientation to be set.

Margins command

Numbering pages

Pages are automatically numbered when a report is generated using the **Report Wizard**. The page numbers are part of the footer of the report.

The figure below shows the code that is inserted in the report design to generate the page numbers.

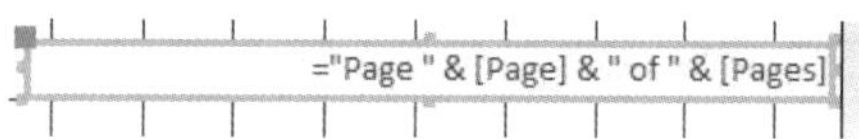

Page numbering in a report

Alternatively, when designing a report there is the **Page Numbers** command on the **Header/ Footer** section of the **Report Design Tools – Design** tab.

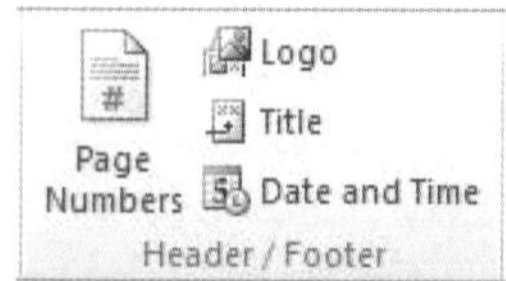

Page Numbers command

External data

Microsoft Access has a number of tools that allow both the import and export of data. This allows Access to work with many different packages. Data can be exported to Excel files, for example. Access can also retrieve data from external databases using the ODBC command.

Data can be imported and exported in from '.txt' and '.csv' files.

Links can also be made to:

- SharePoint.
- HTML files on the Internet.
- Outlook folders.
- External data services.

Some of the links to other applications

Unit 11.5 Activity 6A: Designing and creating an information system

The secretary of the local sporting club has asked you to design and develop an information solution to manage the records of the club. You can choose an actual sporting club that is close to you. The software package should handle the following information set out in the fields below.

1. In the table below, identify the field name and field type for each piece of information. In your answer, show one item of sample data that you would use as sample data for your solution.

Classification	Field type	Field name	Sample data
membership number			
family name			
given name			
title			
number and street			
suburb			
postcode			
telephone number			
type of membership (full, senior, junior, under 18 and midweek)			
date of birth			
date of joining			
date of last payment			

Classification	Field type	Field name	Sample data
method of payment			
amount of payment			
membership status			

2. In the table below are three fields. What validation would be suitable for each field? Provide two items of data which you would use to test each field and the validation you have used.

Field	Validation	Data examples
title		
date of birth		
membership		

3. A data-entry option for the membership could be the 'pop-down' list. How could this assist in data accuracy and ease of data entry?
4. Create some 'dummy' data for ten members so that the system can be tested.
5. Design on paper a layout for the screen for entry of the membership details. Identify each field, the field name and approximate space that would be used for entry of the data. You should also create a screen that shows an alphabetical listing of members. Annotate the design to show the formatting.
6. The treasurer would like a listing of members for the sending of renewal notices. Design on paper a report that would satisfy this need. On the report show the headings and identify how the information is to be arranged.
7. The competition secretary would like a listing of members by their membership category so that she can prepare possible teams for the coming season. Design on paper a report for the secretary.

   Both reports for 6 and 7 are to have name and address of the club, and appropriate information in the header and footer for date of preparation and page number. (Both these items are to be placeholders so that the current date and current page number are inserted).
8. Create an opening menu screen with navigation to the reports.

Unit 11.6 Internet
Topic 1: Web fundamentals

Unit 11.6 deals with the Internet. Topic 1 explores Web fundamentals (see ICT Syllabus pp. 26–7 and Computer Studies Syllabus pp. 25–6). It covers:

- The Internet.
- Browsers.
- Setting up an Internet connection.
- Effective use of browsers.
- Using search engines.

The Internet

The **Internet** is a worldwide network of interconnected computer networks. The networks use the Standard Internet Protocol to connect. This is represented as the TCP/IP protocol.

The Internet consists of millions of computers worldwide: privately owned in homes, in schools, businesses and in government organisations.

The Internet provides a vast range of services including email, interlocked documents available using the hypertext protocol, and communications media including telephone and video using the Voice Over Internet Protocol (VOIP).

The World Wide Web (WWW) or Web is that part of the Internet where webpages are viewed using software called browsers. The browsers use the hypertext protocol (http).

Computers – whether in the home, in schools and universities, in businesses or in governments – communicate with each other. It does not matter where a computer is physically located for it to be able to communicate with another computer.

There is no central organisation, company or government that controls the operation of the Internet. Rather, market forces and industry-based committees determine standards for its operation.

What the Internet means for our society depends on how it is developed and used. The Internet allows the globalisation of information; that is, information is available wherever you are, whenever you need it. For example, weather information from around the world and share prices from stock exchanges in many different cities are instantly accessible.

Development of the Internet

During the 1960s, the United States Defence Advanced Research Projects Agency (ARPA) developed a **wide area network (WAN)** to link institutions, particularly educational institutions conducting research for the US government. The network was known as ARPAnet. Many of the protocol standards of the ARPAnet were further developed to form the basis of standards used today on the Internet.

At the end of 1969, four host computers were linked together and the Internet was under way. During the 1970s, ARPAnet grew into the Internet and protocols were developed to allow computers with different operating systems to connect together. This led to the development of the **Transmission Control Protocol/Internet Protocol (TCP/IP)**, which remains a key feature of the Internet.

Over time, the number of institutions and universities that were connected increased. Electronic mail was the major application that fuelled interest in the Internet in the first instance.

Internet service providers (ISP)

An **Internet service provider (ISP)** is a company that provides access to the Internet. That access is provided by a range of different methods.

Internet service providers have a range of services for users: email accounts, Web browsing, file transfers, etc. Some of them will provide other services including storage on the Internet, hosting of websites and hosting of Web- or cloud-based activities.

ISPs provide services to both corporate customers and home users.

At home, a subscriber pays a monthly access fee to the ISP. The subscriber then receives access to the Internet. The cost of the service depends upon:

- The nature of the connection.
- The speed of the service.
- The amount of data that can be downloaded.

Businesses and organisations also subscribe to services from an ISP. Most organisations will share the service with members of the organisation using its own network.

Types of connection (dial-up, broadband, wireless)

Access to the Internet requires:

- A computer or handheld device such as a smartphone.
- A means of communication: telephone line, cable, wireless.
- A service provider to enable access to the Internet.
- Software on the computer or the handheld device.
- A means of access to the network, ie a modem or a network card.
- Funds to pay the cost of access and charges for time and downloading data.

Dial-up connection

A **modem** is a device that transmits digital data over a telephone line. This makes it possible for the telephone line to be used for access to the Internet and email.

A dial-up modem is connected to a fixed telephone line and to a computer that has had the appropriate software installed.

To access the Internet:

- The software dials a phone number to connect to the ISP through the modem.
- The modem connects and provides Internet access.
- The ISP has a bank of modems that allow the connection to take place.

This mode of access prevents use of the telephone line for voice calls when connected to the Internet.

For many years, this was the standard mode of access to the Internet in homes and some businesses. The disadvantages of this form of access are:

- Speed of access, now relatively slow.
- Shared access to a telephone line.
- Limited bandwidth.

A dial-up modem

Broadband connections

Broadband connections provide a much higher bandwidth than a telephone connection. There are two types of broadband connections available in major cities:

- Cable.
- ADSL.

Cable connection

A cable connection uses a coaxial cable. This cable can also be used to provide other cable services into homes, eg cable television. This requires a cable connection into the house and a cable modem connected to the computer.

Cable provides a much higher connection speed than a dial-up modem.

A cable modem

A cable modem usually allows connections to a number of computers. The cable modem is used to connect to the ISP and then to a computer in a home or a business.

A cable connection requires a coaxial cable to be installed in the location. This requires either a telecommunication company or a pay television company to run the cable in the area.

ADSL (Asymmetric Digital Subscriber Line)

ADSL provides data to the user at a rate of 256 KB per second to 1.5 MB per second and the user can transmit data at up to 256 KB per second.

ADSL is transmitted into the home using the existing telephone network. It allows dual usage of the telephone line for both phone calls and data transmission.

An ADSL modem

As with a cable modem, the ADSL modem can be used to allow a number of devices to connect to the Internet. ADSL modems usually allow both a physical connection, ie via a cable, and a wireless connection.

High-speed ADSL connections are available for both homes and businesses.

Wireless

Wireless Internet access is accomplished using radio waves rather than wires. It is often referred to as a 'hot spot' on a local area network. Wireless access is broadcast from a central hub connected to a computer system and provides connectivity to clients.

Many public organisations provide 'hot spot' access, eg fast-food restaurants and airports.

To access such a network, a computer must have a wireless modem connected to it. Many notebook and netbook computers are configured with an inbuilt wireless card and aerial.

In a home, a desktop computer can be set up to provide connectivity throughout the property. This involves configuring the modem or hub to allow wireless activity. These wireless LANs should be configured to allow only authorised users to have access to the network, usually by entering a user name and password. This prevents neighbors using the Internet bandwidth.

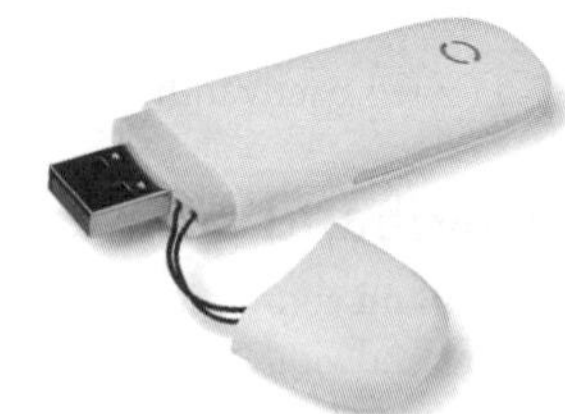

A USB wireless Internet modem

The mobile telephone network can also be used to provide wireless access to the Internet. Many of the telecommunication companies use a 3G or third-generation network. A 3G network uses agreed standards for telecommunications.

The computer must have a wireless network card installed in it or a wireless modem attached.

The telecommunication companies sell plans that include data usage and speed.

There is a range of devices that can use the telecommunications network for Internet access including:

- Notebook computer.
- Netbook computer.
- Internet tablet.
- iPad.
- Smartphone including iPhone and Blackberry.

The Apple iPad can be used to connect to the Internet

Other connection types

Other types of connection to the Internet are available. These include:

- Satellite.
- Microwave.
- ISDN.
- Fibre optic.

Satellite connection requires a satellite dish. Data from the Internet is downloaded via the satellite. This can be useful when taking a significant amount of data to the computer but to upload data another connection is required. It is also useful in areas where cable or ADSL are not available.

A microwave connection requires transmitters between the home or business and the ISP. It requires line-of-sight connection. These are often used between different offices of the one business or between school campuses.

ISDN (Integrated Services Digital Network) is a set of communications standards that allows the digital transmission of services, including the Internet, using the traditional telephone network. ISDN is typically used by organisations.

Fibre optic cable can be used to provide a high-speed Internet service. ISPs have established fibre optic networks in major cities and these can be extended to homes. In Australia, the government is supporting a project to extend fibre optic access to homes.

The World Wide Web (WWW)

In 1992, Tim Berners-Lee at CERN, a Swiss research organisation, released the **World Wide Web**, a system for displaying pages of information containing text, graphics and other illustrations. The web is a hypermedia-based system that supports content types including fonts, graphics, sound and video. Documents are formatted to the specifications of the hypertext transfer protocol (HTTP) to format, store and deliver pages for the web.

Fibre optic cable

The WWW is platform-independent; pages can be viewed on computers with different operating systems.

The early success and dramatic development of the Web is due to its open standards and independence from any particular software or hardware company. The Web is essentially a linking medium where a page is a single page in a sea of pages. Pages can be viewed on devices other than personal computers such as handheld personal assistants, electronic tablets and smartphones.

W3C: World Wide Web Consortium

The W3C was founded in 1994 to promote standards and ongoing development in HTML and other Web technology. For example, the W3C sets guidelines for implementation of 'tags', which if adopted by browser software developers ensure open and flexible Web standards.

According to its website, 'The World Wide Web Consortium (W3C) is an international community that develops open standards to ensure the long-term growth of the Web'. The address of its website is www.w3c.org.

Protocols

Protocols are the rules or standards that allow different computers to interpret messages that are distributed across the network.

Internet, intranet and extranet

Internet technology is used by many organisations throughout the world.

An **intranet** is a privately maintained internal network. It allows only authorised users to access its information. Those users are usually employees of a business or members of an organisation. An intranet usually uses Internet technology and the information is accessed using a browser.

An extranet is usually an extension of an organisation's intranet. An extranet will allow communication between an organisation and people outside the organisation with which it deals. An extranet will be browser-based and may allow limited, authorised access to the organisation's intranet.

Hypertext transfer protocol (HTTP)

The first part of a URL (http://www.) identifies that a site is part of the World Wide Web and its documents are in accord with the **hypertext transfer protocol (HTTP)**.

HTTP defines how messages are formatted and transmitted between different browsers and operating systems. Entering a URL in a browser sends an HTTP command to a web server that then fetches and transmits the requested web page.

A webpage

A **webpage** is a document stored on a web server and available on the World Wide Web. Each webpage has its own unique address.

A webpage can contain a variety of content. Page content can include:

- Text.
- Graphics.
- Links.
- Sounds and videos.

Each page can contain a **hypertext** link or links to another page or other sites. The home page for an individual or organisation is the electronic front cover for the website.

The Web uses a page metaphor. Unlike a printed page, it can be narrow or wide, short or long. For many pages on the Web the text will word-wrap to the size of the window.

HTML

HTML refers to '**hypertext markup language**'. It is a markup or formatting language (rather than programming language) which tells the browser how and where to display text and other content on screen. The instructions about how to display data or links are stored in tags. These tags are not shown on screen when the page is composed. The meaning of each tag is determined by the HTML specifications.

Webpages can be composed using HTML but most people will use an editor that does not necessarily display the tags.

A webfile carries either a (.htm) or (.html) extension to show it has been created in HTML.

Uniform resource locator (URL)

A **uniform (or universal) resource locator (URL)** identifies the address of a page on the web. The Internet address is a unique name that identifies a computer or a user on a network. Addresses are used to send messages between computers.

Understanding the address

The Australian Government has a home page with the address: http://www.australia.gov.au

The first part (http://www.) identifies that a site is part of the World Wide Web and its documents are in accord with the hypertext transfer protocol (HTTP).

Browsers and web servers use HTTP to communicate with each other.

The second part (australia.gov.au) identifies the organisation or body that is hosting the site, followed by the country domain. In this case the country domain is 'au'. All countries, with the exception of the USA, have a country domain. Sites in the United States of America do not include a country domain.

Every computer on the Internet has a unique number. The **domain name system (DNS)** provides a text title for the unique number address. The Internet has a scheme to name companies, institutions and individuals on the Internet.

Domain names

A **domain** name is used to identify the Internet address of a website. Individuals and organisations purchase and register domain names. There is usually a fee to register the domain name and an annual charge to continue using the domain name. Internet service providers often host many different domains. The ISP controls the domain name server (DNS) that directs a URL with a domain name to the actual site.

Some requirements for registering domain names are that:

- The name cannot be already allocated.
- The organisation must be a company or a registered business; this can include individuals who are registered or recognised by appropriate government or industry authorities.
- A business name must be closely derived from the legal name of the organisation.
- Common or generic names or place names are not accepted.

The organisation extension

The organisation extension, which is part of the web address, gives an idea of the primary purpose of a site. The extensions include:

- .com – commercial businesses.
- .edu – educational.
- .net – Internet service providers.
- .org – non-profit and non-government organisations.
- .gov – governments and government departments.
- .info – providing information.

Some examples of the above are:

Air Niugini	www.airniugini.com.pg
University of Papua New Guinea	www.upng.ac.pg
Embassy of Papua New Guinea to the Americas	www.pngembassy.org
Papua New Guinea Law and Justice Department	www.lawandjustice.gov.pg

Country domain

In many countries, the final two letters of the web address identify that country. For example, the address: www.demon.co.uk is an address in the United Kingdom.

Papua New Guinea has the country domain '.pg'. For Australia this is '.au', for New Zealand it is '.nz'. If an address does not have a country domain it is presumed to be the United States.

Microsoft, for example, has servers in the US and Australia. The WWW address for the US is: www.microsoft.com. The address for Australia is: www.microsoft.com.au.

The browser

A browser is a software application that is used to locate and access webpages. Although browsers can have a range of features and creation tools, their primary function is to access a page, download the content to that computer and view the page. Browser software allows users to navigate the World Wide Web.

Pages are accessed using established buttons and links. This software is client-based and platform-independent. This means that the browser software is developed for a range of different computers and operating systems and the same information is accessed on each platform.

Browser software is regularly upgraded and is the focus of much commercial and open-source competition. The most popular browser software is Internet Explorer, a browser that once commanded around 90% of usage.

Browser	Creator	Layout engine	Share (%)
Internet Explorer	Microsoft	Trident	44
Firefox	Mozilla Foundation	Gecko	30
Chrome	Google	Webkit	17
Safari	Apple	Webkit	7
Opera	Opera Software	Presto	2

Browser usage as of May 2011

Browser preferences

Browser preferences and settings customise the manner in which a webpage can be viewed. Basic browser preferences include:

- The font type and font size for pages to be viewed.
- Whether pages are viewed as 'text' only or 'text and graphics'.
- The display colour for visited and unvisited links.
- The URL of the page viewed when the browser is opened.
- The size of the 'cache' for the browser.
- The URL of the favoured 'search' mechanism.

A browser can have a number of windows active at any one time and can access more than one page from more than one site at a time.

Browser cache

Part of a computer hard disk can be used as a storage or 'cache' for the browser. A cache is a temporary storage area that is used to keep a copy of information that has been retrieved. Thus, information from downloaded pages is stored in the cache.

When a URL is accessed the browser refers to the cache to check if the page has previously been downloaded and, if it has, page information can be accessed from the local hard disk rather than downloaded again. For frequently accessed pages it saves time although it may deliver outdated information if the page has been updated on the Web.

Internet Explorer refers to the 'cache' as 'Temporary Internet Files'. It allows the user to set the amount of disk space allocated to storing these files. Choosing **Internet Options** on the **Tools** menu and then selecting the **Settings** option tab provides the opportunity to allocate the disk space.

The option to check for newer versions of the page is used to ensure files stored on a local hard disk do not become out of date.

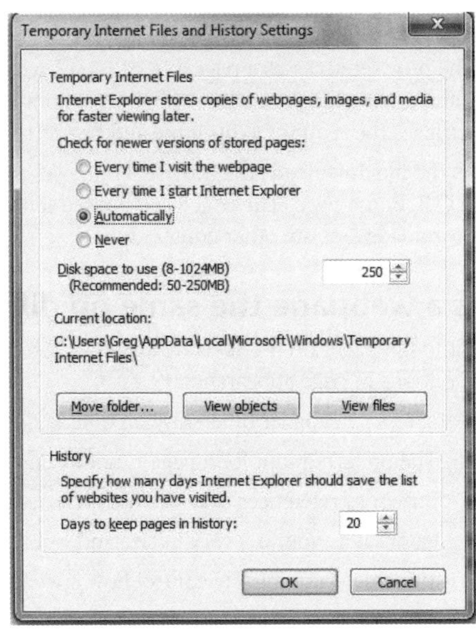

Settings for temporary Internet files

Browser 'plug-ins'

Software created by third-party developers can be used to extend the content types displayed by browsers. The additional software required is installed separately and is called a 'plug-in'. Multimedia technology for the Web, particularly audio and video, is developing rapidly and developers can sell their software product if web developers take up their technology.

Where users are reluctant to install plug-ins for browsers the website developers will restrict their audience.

Plug-in	Creator	Use
Adobe Reader	Adobe	view Portable Document Format (pdf)
Flash	Adobe	view flash movies (.flv)
QuickTime	Apple	sound and audio (.mov)

Three commonly used plug-ins

Are all browsers the same?

The two main browsers, Microsoft Internet Explorer and Firefox, may display pages differently because they:

- Treat some HTML tags differently.
- Offer differing support for plug-ins and other developing technologies.

Web developers often test their pages in commonly used browsers and sometimes in more than one version of the same browser. Webpages should display the minimum browser standards that apply for a particular site. Some sites go to the trouble of preparing different sets of pages for different browsers and different browser versions.

How does a browser compose the page?

The browser accesses a page at a URL on a web server. The server is a computer linked to the Internet which can be accessed by other computers connected to the Internet. The browser retrieves the requested .html file and begins to download the file.

As the file downloads the browser composes the page according to the instructions in the HTML of the page. The page is composed left to right and top to bottom. Graphic images are downloaded, as are other content types.

Is a webpage the same on different computers?

Although pages on the Web are able to be accessed from different computers there can be some variations in page appearance.

Webpages can appear differently on different computers because:

- The preferred font for a page is not installed.
- Browser preferences override the preferred fonts of the webpage designer.
- Computer monitors vary in size and resolution.

It is difficult to completely control how a webpage will be viewed on any computer or monitor. For example, browsers allow an incremental increase or decrease of the font size for all text for a page through a simple toolbar button.

Setting up an Internet connection

Access to the Internet

Access to the Internet is provided through an Internet service provider (ISP). From home, this involves using a personal computer, modem and telephone line. Alternatively, a wireless service can be used at home. An ISP charges for the amount of time you spend accessing the Internet. In some cases, the ISP will also provide for the volume of usage on the Internet.

Hardware

The hardware needed to access the Internet is:

- A computer.
- A modem to connect the computer to a telephone line.
- A telephone line.

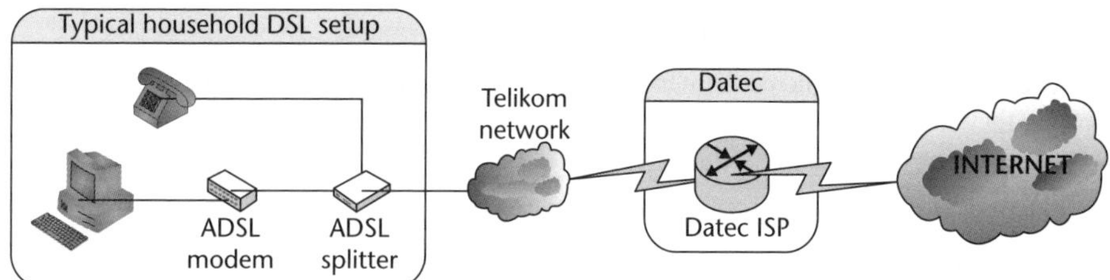

Household set up recommended by Datec (www.datec.com.pg)

The software needed includes:

- Software to drive the modem and allow a connection according to the TCP/IP protocol.
- Browser software, such as Microsoft Internet Explorer or Firefox, to access the World Wide Web.

DIAL UP

Plan	MB	Kina	Excess
Email Tasol	50	K28	40t per MB
Megabyte 50	50	K28	40t per MB
Megabyte 100	100	K48	38t per MB
Megabyte 200	200	K85	36t per MB
Megabyte 400	400	K155	33t per MB
Megabyte 600	600	K185	30t per MB
Megabyte 1000	1000	K290	26t per MB
***Excluding GST**		Dial-Up application form	

Example of a schedule of fees for an ISP (www.daltron.com.pg/Internet-services)

Organisations such as businesses, schools and universities requiring high-speed links can use an Integrated Services Digital Network (ISDN) connection rather than a telephone line. Telecommunications companies are providing different types of high-speed access to the Internet.

Organisations then integrate the Internet services into their own local area network. Individual users will access the World Wide Web through the network and will not need a modem.

The cost of the link to the Internet service provider is part of the cost of the service. From a home in a large city or town, that cost is the cost of a local telephone call that has no time limit. In rural areas, the call may well be a longer-distance call charged according to the length of the call.

Using wireless Internet requires the purchase and installation of a wireless card. A prepaid service allows a certain amount of data. The service is configured on the Internet and requires a user name and password to be set up.

Prepaid wireless access to the Internet

Effective use of browsers

Most people can use a web browser, but there are a number of things that can be useful to understand.

When the browser is open, the address line shows the URL of the page that is being viewed.

The address of a page on the Post-Courier Online

Toolbar

The tools at the right-hand end of the Toolbar are helpful in setting up Internet Explorer how you wish.

Tools on the toolbar

The House icon takes the user to the designated home page.

The Star provides access to the sites that have been set up as Favorites and to the History.

The Gear Wheel gives access to utility functions including Internet Options.

Homepage

The homepage is the web page that people generally access first. The homepage is set using the **Internet Options** window.

Each operating system will have a default homepage (or pages). You can:

- Enter the URL for a new homepage; or
- Use the current page or pages that are open; or
- Use the default pages; or
- Use a blank page.

Note that more than one homepage tab can be created, giving several different tabs as the homepage.

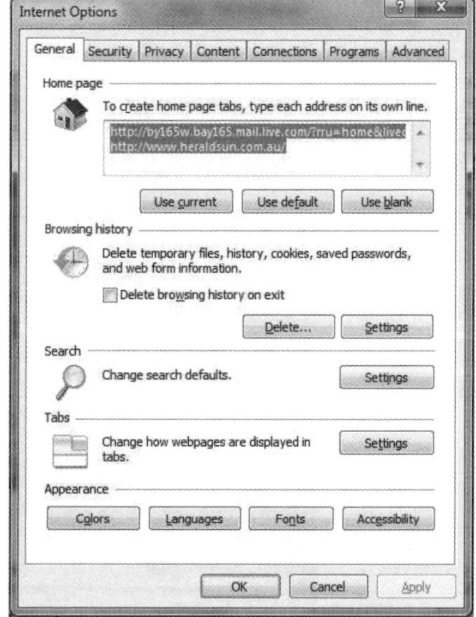

Setting the Homepage

Temporary Internet files

The parameters for the use of temporary Internet files can be adjusted to suit the user's preferences. Temporary Internet files are often used so that not all pages need to be downloaded to a browser. Pages that have not changed are stored as temporary files and can be used when the URL is accessed. This helps speed up access and reduces the amount of data that is downloaded.

Favorites

The Favorites menu allows users to store the addresses of sites that are regularly used and are of interest.

To add a site to the Favorites list:

- Go to the **Star** on the right-hand side of the toolbar.
- Select **Add to Favorites**.
- Click **Add**.

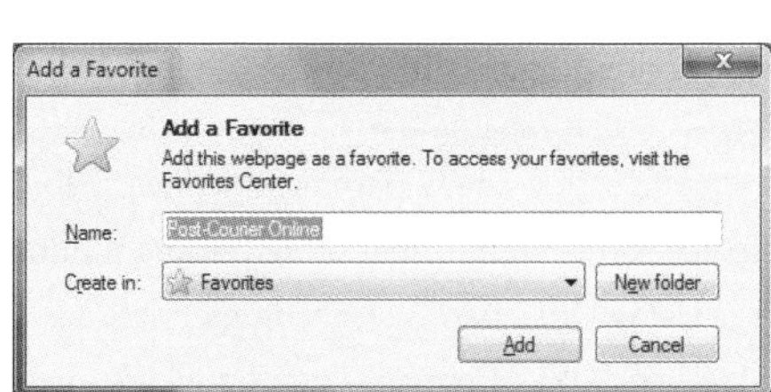

Adding a Favorite

The same menu item can be used to:

- Manage Favorites.
- Import and export Favorites.
- Manage and view the History of viewed sites.

Saving a page for offline viewing

A webpage can be saved to disk for:

- Archiving.
- Viewing offline.
- Viewing the HTML source used to construct the page.

File type	Extension	Features
Webpage	.htm	An HTML page and a new folder automatically created containing non-text content as separate files. Page can be viewed as original
Complete web archive	.mht	A .mht file with all content embedded in one file Suitable to attach to an email
HTML-only text file	.htm	Allows page to be displayed with text only and attributes set by HTML text

Save options for Internet Explorer

Using search engines

Finding information on the Web

The Web does not have a central listing of resources. It is always changing because of its dynamic nature:

- New sites are added.
- New pages are added to sites.
- Sites and pages are deleted.
- Content on existing pages is changed.

There are no reliable statistics about the amount of information on the Web. However, one estimate is that a new page is added every four seconds.

To access useful information requires a number of strategies including:

- Using URLs based on recommendations, such as in a newspaper article or from a librarian.
- Using URLs from sites you know are quality sites that provide quality links.
- Creating **bookmarks** of useful sites from previous searches.

Search engine

A **search engine** is a Web-based service that helps the user find information that is useful. It uses a database that contains an index of pages stored on the Web.

The database stores keywords from websites. The search engine includes the ability to search the database very quickly for words you specify.

There is specialist software, sometimes called 'spiders' or 'web-crawlers', that retrieves information from sites. These extracts are compiled in databases that are accessed when the search engine is engaged. Any search of the Web reflects the database at its last update. Hence, a search might produce results that are out-of-date.

Search engines form their database catalogues by methods such as:

- The title of a page.
- Keywords contained in the text on a page.
- The number of links from other pages to a page, as an indication of popularity.

The most important search engines include:

- Google: www.google.com.
- Yahoo: www.yahoo.com.
- Ask: www.ask.com.
- Altavista: www.altavista.com.

Searching with Google

Google is the most widely used search engine. It offers a range of services other than search including images, maps and videos.

To search for a keyword using Google, go to the Google site at www.google.com. Note that the Google site is localised, ie the location of the computer is used to identify the local Google address.

Now enter the keyword to be searched in the dialog box and press **Enter**. The search results are shown on the centre of the page. However, note the following:

- The first three (or more) sites are advertisements, ie they are sites that meet the search criteria but the organisations have paid Google to have them placed there. These sites have a slightly different background and the letters 'Ad' at the top right-hand side of the window.
- Further advertising also appears in the right-hand side of the page.

Developing a search strategy

Searching for information can be difficult. To be successful you should aim to:

- Minimise the number of possible irrelevant links a search may give.
- Maximise the relevance of those links given.

Searches are based on keywords entered that are matched to data in the search engine database. This requires you to:

- Identify the search topic.
- Identify the key areas.
- Select keywords based on the search topic.
- Select an appropriate search engine.
- Work out the search logic.

Searches can be restricted to sites within a single country.

Unit 11.6 Internet
Topic 2: Web security

Topic 2 deals with Web security (see ICT Syllabus p. 27 and Computer Studies Syllabus p. 26). It covers:

- Spyware.
- Hacking.
- Firewalls.

Spyware

Spyware is software that covertly obtains information about a computer system using the Internet. This is done without the user's permission or knowledge.

Spyware is often hidden in software that is downloaded from the Internet. When it is installed it tracks the activity of the user and sends that information to someone else. Spyware can be used to:

- Collect email addresses.
- Monitor passwords.
- Find out credit card details.
- Use Internet bandwidth.

Spyware is usually installed without the user's knowledge. Users can be tricked into installing spyware. It often masquerades as useful software. It may be distributed using attachments in email messages.

The following will help reduce the risk of spyware on a computer:

- Ensure that anti-virus software is up to date at all times.
- Consider installing and running anti-spyware software.
- Download programs from reputable sources only.
- Open email attachments only from trusted sources.

Hacking

Hacking is the practice of modifying computer hardware and software to do something different from the intended purpose of the hardware or software.

Hacking usually involves unauthorised access to a computer system. Some hackers will access the computer system just for the thrill of it and make no changes. Other hackers will be malicious and may alter the data or steal data for unauthorised use.

There are many tools that hackers use to try and gain access. Some of these tools will capture user names and passwords across a network.

Computer and network security is a complex issue and many organisations engage specialists to reduce the risk of hacking and to ensure data security.

Firewall

A **firewall** is a system that protects a computer system or network from unauthorised access.

On a network, a firewall is made up of:

- Hardware.
- Software.

Large companies such as Cisco and Norton typically provide firewalls for networks in organisations. Every message that enters or leaves the network must pass through the firewall, which blocks those that do not meet the security requirements. Firewall products often include logging and areporting of perceived attacks.

Cisco security devices that are used for a firewall on a corporate network

Personal firewall

Windows includes a personal firewall that is set up to block requests to connect to a computer. This firewall is an application that is accessed via the Control Panel.

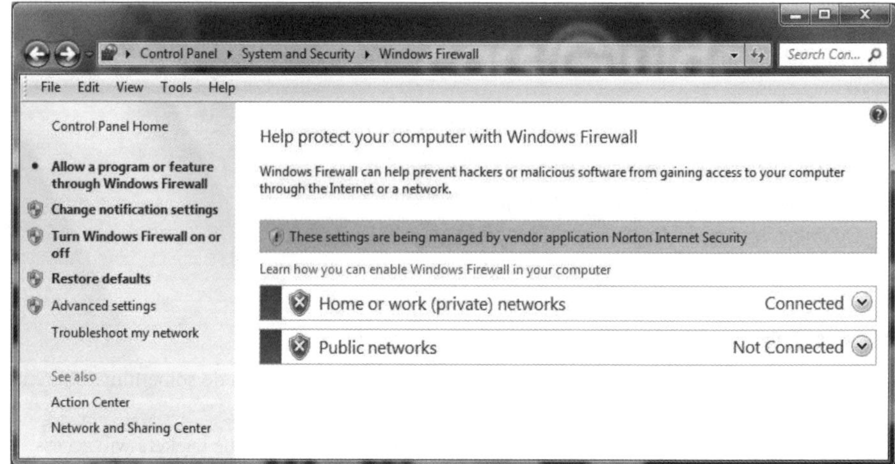

Unit 11.6 Internet

Topic 3: Search techniques

Topic 3 explores the various Internet search techniques (see ICT Syllabus p. 27 and Computer Studies Syllabus p. 26). It covers:

- Simple search techniques (keyword searching).
- Advanced search techniques (Boolean operations, search engines, advanced searching).
- Citing Internet resources.
- Safe use of the Internet.
- Creating bookmark links.

What information is on the Web?

Information on the Web has no classification system. Information is prepared by many different organisations and individuals. Pages are not verified as being accurate or true or useful.

Some sites publish freely to the Web; others require subscription and password access to obtain information at a site.

Regulation of the Internet

The Internet, by its design, is not under the control of governments or other agencies. This could allow access to content that governments do not ordinarily condone.

Information regarded by many as undesirable, such as pornography, is available on the World Wide Web. The government of Papua New Guinea favours self-regulation by Internet service providers as well as uniform national laws to deal with breaches.

Censorship and the Web

No single government or organisation has control over the Web. No one can control the type and quality of the information that is available. There is the possibility that material on the Web could be:

- Contrary to the political views of a particular government.
- Pornographic.
- Used to promote views that are racist.
- Used to promote or incite violence.

Many organisations use software and hardware to restrict access to unacceptable and undesirable sites and content. However, it is impossible to ensure all undesirable links and material can be filtered out.

Simple search techniques (keyword searching)

Information quality

It is unwise to accept information on the Web at face value. Data and information on the Web need to be looked at carefully to determine their quality and use.

Some factors that may assist are:

- The status and reputation of the organisation or individual hosting the site.
- References to the site from other sites.
- References to the site from printed material.
- Your own previous experience with the site.

General search

A search engine can be given specific directions about what to search for. By limiting the search criteria the number of responses will be more manageable. It is easier to conduct another search than to wade through a long list of matches provided by inexact criteria.

General features of search engines include:

- They are not case-sensitive if the search term is in lower case.
- Phrases (or strings) may be searched for if contained in quotation marks.
- Small words (such as 'the', 'and', 'of' and 'on') are ignored.
- Boolean operators can limit or expand a search.
- The absolute number of matches can be limited.
- A 'wildcard' can be used within a search. A wildcard search looks for a sequence of characters. Using Google, the asterisk (*) is used to denote a wildcard search. For example, searching for the string 'crick' gave 7 280 000 results while the string 'crick*' gave 25 700 000 results.

Advanced search techniques

Boolean searches

George Boole was a 19th-century English mathematician whose work became the basis of computer logic. When Boolean algebra is applied to search engines a request needs to be answered with a YES or NO. Further qualifications can be made using AND, OR and NOT.

OR logic

Using the OR logic, *at least one of* the search terms must be present. For example, searching for 'cats OR dogs' will return pages that find:

- Cats.
- Dogs.
- Both cats and dogs.

AND Logic

Using the AND logic, *both* the search terms must be present. For example, searching for 'cats AND dogs' will return pages that find:

- Both cats and dogs.

NOT Logic

Using the NOT logic, *only one* of the search terms must be present. For example, searching for 'cats NOT dogs' will return pages that find:

- Cats, but not dogs.

Citing electronic references in a bibliography

When completing a work in which other materials are referred to, the source of these references should be listed. This allows verification of information and follow-up by others interested in the source material.

The Harvard (author–date) system is an example of a system used for bibliographies.
For references to a webpage and other online material the following elements need to be identified:

- Author's last name.
- Author's first name.
- Title of the document.
- Internet address (URL).

For example, citing an article from the *Post-Courier Online* would be:

> Kana, Konopa, "*PNG's Business Ranking Drops*",
> www.postcourier.com.pg/20111021/frhome.htm, Friday 21 October 2011

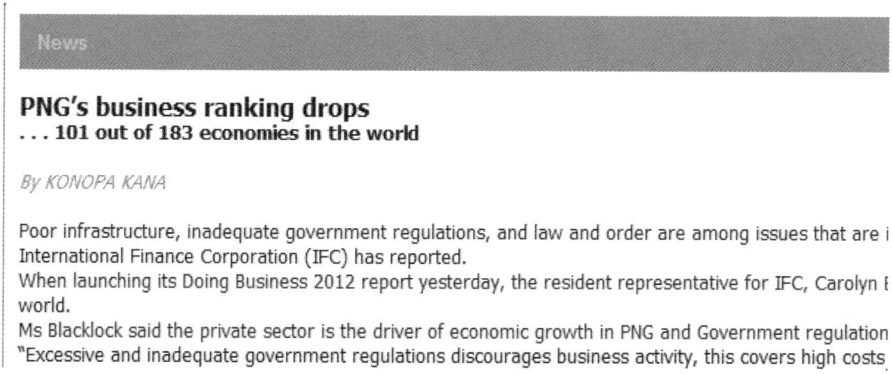

News

PNG's business ranking drops
. . . 101 out of 183 economies in the world

By KONOPA KANA

Poor infrastructure, inadequate government regulations, and law and order are among issues that are i
International Finance Corporation (IFC) has reported.
When launching its Doing Business 2012 report yesterday, the resident representative for IFC, Carolyn I
world.
Ms Blacklock said the private sector is the driver of economic growth in PNG and Government regulation
"Excessive and inadequate government regulations discourages business activity, this covers high costs

Article from the Post-Courier Online

The TeacherVision website has an excellent guide to citing online documents.

> www.teachervision.fen.com/Internet/printable/6396.html

Copyright and the World Wide Web

Information from the Web is subject to copyright law. The Berne Convention and the Universal Copyright Convention protect countries that are signatories to those agreements.

People who copy and use material from the Internet are subject to the laws within their own countries. Material downloaded from the Internet cannot be published unless one of the following conditions is met:

- Permission to use it is given by the owner.
- Use of the material is granted under licence.
- The material is purchased.
- The material is identified as being shareware or royalty-free.

Using the Internet in a safe manner

The Internet enables easy access and sharing of information. People should make sure that they are providing information in safe and secure communication and not endangering their personal safety.

For example:

- Do not give out or reveal to others information such as passwords, home addresses, telephone numbers and login information.
- Do not indulge others by replying to emails and other communications that are offensive.
- Do not make personal contact with someone met via the Internet unless their details and identity can be verified beforehand.
- Do not respond to email from people you do not know.
- Do not open emails and attachments unless the sender is known.

Bookmarks

While browsing websites, the browser:

- Keeps a history of pages visited.
- Allows 'bookmarking' of a URL so that it can be accessed in the future by using the bookmark.
- Allows bookmarks to be arranged in folders decided by the user.
- Allows editing or deleting of bookmarks.

A bookmark is a URL that is stored locally on a computer. In Internet Explorer, bookmarks are known as **Favorites**.

Creating bookmarks

To create a bookmark to a page:

- Go to that page.
- Choose **Add to Favorites...** from the **Favorites** tab on the menu bar.
- Accept or modify the bookmark name.
- Click **Add**.

Many documents on the Internet contain links. To create a bookmark to a link on a page:

- Go to that link.
- Right-click with the mouse on the link.
- Click **Add to Favorites...**

That link is now added as a Favorite or bookmark.

Some sites use image maps to navigate to different parts of the site. An image map is a graphic image that allows users to click on different parts of the image and be taken to a different destination. An image map is intended to be an easy way for a user to navigate to the desired destination.

An image map is created in HTML by inserting tags that refer to particular coordinates of the image. MapEdit is a popular tool for creating image maps.

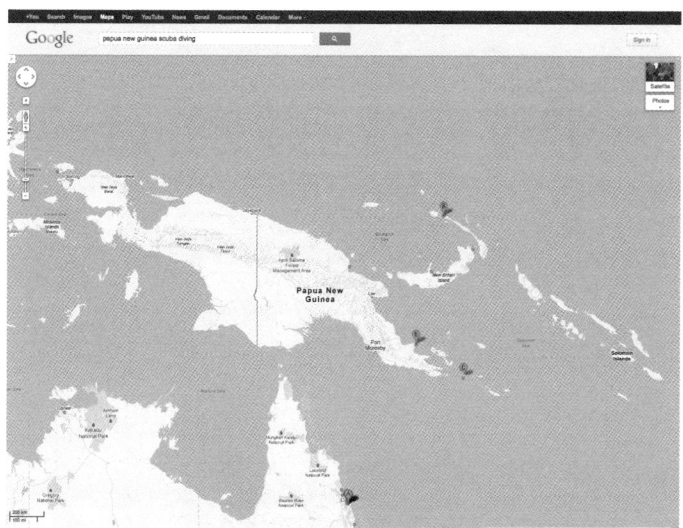

Image map from the Google Maps site

Unit 11.6 Internet

Topic 4: Website evaluation

Topic 4 explores the various factors to consider when evaluating a website (see ICT Syllabus p. 27 and Computer Studies Syllabus p. 26). It covers:

- Download time.
- Navigational ease.
- Attractiveness.
- Content.
- Currency.
- Accuracy.
- Graphics, videos and sounds.

Webpages can be viewed on:

- A single computer, accessing pages from a hard disk or a DVD.
- A local computer on a network, such as an intranet.
- A computer connected to the Internet; pages are accessed from a web server.
- Handheld devices including smartphones and iPads.

Users have a range of connection types and speeds. Some websites offer different versions depending on the type of connection.

Download time

A webpage can be made of:

- The HTML source code of the page.
- Text, images, sound, **animation** and video.
- Hypertext links and hotspots.

Slow response time is one of the factors that frustrate users. Most users have a threshold time after which they will move away from the page. Online retailers such as Amazon need an acceptable response time otherwise customers will not purchase their products.

Download time is the time that elapses between entering a URL and the page being available on the computer. Some research indicates that a download time of more than 8 seconds is unacceptable. It has also been argued that 'fast response times are the most important design criterion for webpages' (Jakob Neilson, 2000).

The download time of a webpage can be affected by:

- The speed of the Internet connection.
- The response time of the web server.
- The amount of content contained on the page; this will be reflected in the number and size of files served to the browser to render the page.
- The type of content on a page: text downloads more quickly than images and video.
- Whether or not the page has been previously accessed: a large part of a page may be stored in the Temporary Internet Files folder on the local computer.

Web designers and engineers spend a significant amount of time and effort attempting to optimise the download speed for sites to ensure an acceptable response for all users.

Navigational ease

Making a site easy to navigate is an important aspect of any website. As websites grow, navigation can become more difficult and complex.

The aspects that are important for successful navigation include:

- A consistent design throughout the site.
- A sense of location for the user, ie the user has an indication of where he or she is on the site.
- Standard navigation tools should be included on every page. These should include a link to the organisation's main page as well as to the main sections of the site.
- A site map can be helpful in navigating a site.
- Providing the shortest possible route to important information; seeking to reduce the number of clicks needed by users.

Part of the site for The Australian *newspaper*

Links on a site

A **hyperlink** or a link on a site is a reference to another page, another part of a page or another site. Clicking on the link takes the user to that other page or site. In some cases, these will open in a new window or a new tab.

Some sites show hyperlinks by representing them in a different colour. On other sites, the cursor will change to a small hand as it moves over the link.

The online encyclopedia *Wikipedia* identifies hyperlinks by the use of text in blue.

It is essential that links be:

- Accurate.
- Up to date.

Part of the Wikipedia *homepage with links*

In some cases, links to other sites can become incorrect very easily.

Some authoring software will check that links are valid.

Attractive pages

The visual design of a website attracts and keeps users on the site.

The design elements on a page are important in making a site attractive to users. To make a site the users enjoy, the following need to be considered:

- The design should be simple and uncluttered – too many elements can make the site difficult to read.
- The site must be written for the Web – the sentences need to be short with links to further information.
- The graphic elements must enhance the user's experience.
- The site should be able to be read by people with sight impairment.

Content: accuracy and currency

The content in a website includes everything that is on the site: text, images, videos, services, etc. Many in the industry have argued that 'content is king'. However, the context in which content is presented and the manner of presentation is also important.

To be useful and authoritative, content needs to be up to date and accurate. Users expect websites to be updated regularly and quickly. Social media such as Twitter and Facebook provide data that is up to date, almost in real time.

Many news organisations operate websites that aim to have up-to-date news items. If the content is inaccurate or incorrect, the site loses credibility and value and hence loses viewers.

The author of content is also important. News sites will generally identify the author of an article or the reporter. However, a lot of breaking news stories come from agencies around the world and it is not always easy to identify the author of the report.

Graphics, video and sounds

Graphic elements need to have a purpose. Images must help to tell a story or support the written text. Graphic images need to be optimised so that the download time is acceptable to users.

Video and sounds can be useful in the right context. Many news sites use video to show important stories. Again, these must be optimised to ensure download time is acceptable. If the video is too slow to download it will break up and be unusable.

Radio stations offer the opportunity to listen live across a website. They also provide podcasts that can be downloaded.

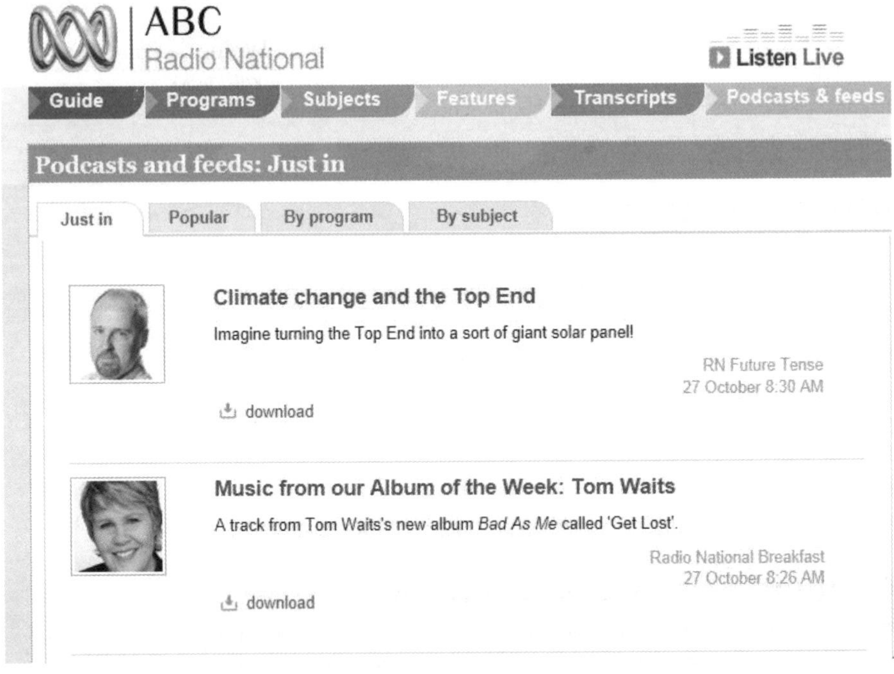

ABC's Radio National site includes live sounds and podcasts

Unit 11.6 Activity 4A: Websites

1. Examine the *Post Courier Online* website: www.postcourier.com.pg/.
   a. When you get to the main news page, how many columns appear?
   b. What is the purpose of each column?
   c. When you go to a particular story, does the content of the columns change? If so, what happens?
2. Examine the *Guardian* website: www.guardian.co.uk/. *The Guardian* is a newspaper published in the UK.
   a. When you get to the main news page, how many columns appear?
   b. What is the purpose of each column?

   - **c.** When you go to a particular story, does the content of the columns change? If so, what happens?
   - **d.** What menus and/or links are provided for the user to navigate through the site?

3. With regard to browsing websites:

   - **a.** What is a Favorite?
   - **b.** Why are they useful?
   - **c.** How do you create a Favorite?
   - **d.** How do you delete a Favorite?
   - **e.** How do you organise Favorites?

Unit 11.6 Internet

Topic 5: Evaluating Internet-based resources

Topic 5 focuses on how to evaluate Internet-based resources (see ICT Syllabus pp. 27–8 and Computer Studies Syllabus pp. 27–8). It covers:

- Author.
- Producer.
- Site.
- Publication.
- Purpose.
- Date of publication.
- Arrangement.
- Intended audience.
- Coverage.
- Writing style or reasoning.
- References.
- Saving pictures or text from a webpage.
- Web browser add-ons.
- Communication protocols.

There is a lot of information on the Internet. Much of it is accurate and informative. Some of it is inaccurate and incorrect. In some cases, incorrect information is deliberately put on the Internet to mislead and deceive people. In other cases, it may be malicious.

Herald Sun
Stories start here.

News | Sport | Entertainment | Business | Money | Travel | Lifestyle

Last Updated: **October 27, 2011**

Vandals seize Robert Doyle's Wikipedia page

Jessica Craven | Herald Sun | October 25, 2011 10:51AM | 50 comments

Melbourne's Lord Mayor's page on Wikipedia *was deliberately altered*

Users need to be able to verify the information that is on a website. The material needs to be checked against another reliable source. ***Wikipedia*** cites a range of sources for much of the information that is available on its site.

References

- Cooke, Lez (2003) (hardback). *British Television Drama: A History*. London: British Film Institute. ISBN 0-85170-884-6.
- Jacobs, Jason (2000) (paperback). *The Intimate Screen: Early British Television Drama*. Oxford: Oxford University Press. ISBN 0-19-874233-9.
- Murray, Andy (2006) (paperback). *Into the Unknown: The Fantastic Life of Nigel Kneale*. London: Headpress. ISBN 1-900486-50-4.
- Pixley, Andrew (2005) (paperback). *The Quatermass Collection—Viewing Notes*. London: BBC Worldwide. BBCDVD1478.

References in Wikipedia *for the Austrian filmmaker Rudolph Cartier*

Site author and producer

In evaluating a website, look at the author of the material. Is the author identified? Is he or she an authority on the topic?

Is the text factual or are there opinions? Are there other viewpoints discussed?

The objectivity of an article is important; is the information biased?

Some websites compile original information; others will collate information from a variety of sources.

Thus, the authenticity and accuracy of the information is important and users need to be able to verify the sources.

Site URL

The URL of the site should be clearly noted. The ending of the URL gives some information about the type of site and its authenticity, eg .edu is an education site, .com is a commercial site.

In general, the location of the site should also be in the URL, eg:

http://www.postcourier.com.pg

This indicates that

- The name of the organisation is the *Post Courier*.
- It is a commercial organisation.
- It is based in Papua New Guinea.

Note that not all sites have a country identification.

Hoax websites may have a strange URL. There is a gallery of hoax websites available on the Internet that shows examples of these hoax sites.

Publications

The purpose of a publication needs to be clearly stated: it may be an information site, it may be reporting research findings or it may be a commercial site inviting transactions.

In all cases, the users need to have a clear understanding of:

- Who or which organisation has published the site.
- The location of the site.
- How to contact the author or publisher of the site.

Most sites will have a note showing when the information was last updated. In some cases, the date of every page published will be shown.

Purpose of a site

The purpose of a site should be clear and easily understood by users. There is a wide diversity in websites with many different purposes and audiences.

Below are some examples of different types of sites:

- The *Papua New Guinea Post Courier Online* site is a news site. Its purpose is to keep readers up to date on current news.
    - http://www.postcourier.com.pg

- *Wikipedia* is an online encyclopaedia. Its purpose is to provide up-to-date, accurate information on a wide range of reference topics.
  - http://www.wikipedia.org/
- Amazon is a sales site. Its purpose is to sell a wide range of items to consumers around the world. It started out selling books but has broadened its range significantly.
  - http://www.amazon.com/
- The purpose of the National Rugby League site is to promote the sport as well as providing information for its supporters.
  - http://www.nrl.com/
- There are many travel sites whose purpose is to sell travel and accommodation throughout the world.
  - http://www.travel.com/
- There are academic research papers available on the Internet. The purpose is to provide access to that research and, in some cases, recover some of the research costs by charging for the papers.
  - http://www.academicresearchpapers.com/

Content arrangement on a site

The design of a website is important to its success. Good design leads to content being arranged in a logical, accessible manner that makes it easy for the user to find information.

Good design includes the use of a page template that has design elements including:

- The logo of the organisation.
- Titles and subtitles.
- A menu and navigation structure that is easy to use and consistent.
- Links that take the user quickly and easily to the required information.
- Navigation links to relevant external sites.

There are many texts available on web style that can be useful when developing a site.

Web Style Guide *by Lynch and Horton*

Intended audience

The intended audience of a site influences the design and the way the content is presented.

A site designed for children might include graphics, animations, sounds and games, with text in small chunks and short words.

Site designed for children and the Dr Seuss books

The site for the Australian Securities Exchange has an audience of investors – both professional and at home – who are seeking information about stock prices and announcements.

Search ASX

Home | Personal Investors | Institutional Investors | Companies | Participants | Information Providers | Product Issuer

- Products
- Prices, Research & Announcements
  - Prices
  - Dividends
  - Announcements
  - Charting
  - Company research
  - Market statistics
  - Industry sectors
- Education & Resources
- Trading Services
- Clearing
- Settlement
- ASX Compliance
- Corporate Governance
- About asx.com.au

Home > Prices, Research & Announcements > Company research > Company information

SITE GROUP INTERNATIONAL LIMITED (SIT)

Vocational education and training, and workforce planning solutions

On this page you will find:

Delayed share price
Company announcements
Price history chart
Exchange Traded Options

LISTED ON ASX

Company details
Closing prices
Dividends
Warrants & Structured Products
ASX CFDs

Delayed share price

Prices are delayed by at least 20 minutes. Retrieving any price indicates your acceptance of the Conditions.

Code	Last	% Chg	Bid	Offer	Open	High	Low	Vol
SIT	0.105	0%	0.100	0.105	0.000	0.000	0.000	0

SITE GROUP INTERNATIONAL LIMITED details

Australian Securities Exchange site for investors

Clearly, there are many different site designs for different audiences. What is important is a clear sense of purpose and a well-defined audience.

Similarly, the information covered will vary. A site such as one for securities will have a great depth of information and be carefully written. A children's site will focus on games and activities.

The writing style will reflect the intended audience.

References

Looking up information online can get quick results. As noted above, the provision of references is important in ensuring the authenticity of the information.

In some cases, there may be links to primary sources. A primary source provides direct evidence of an event – it might be a website recording the scores in a rugby match immediately they happen or it could be an autobiography. Usually these sources are created at the time the event occurs.

A primary source is the most authoritative information available.

The content of the primary source is important. Primary sources can be in digital format.

References in a website need to be properly documented. A reference to a website should contain:

- The complete URL of the article.
- The name of the article.
- The name(s) of the author of the article.
- The date on which the article was written.

The relevance of a reference to the topic under consideration is important, as is the timeliness of the reference.

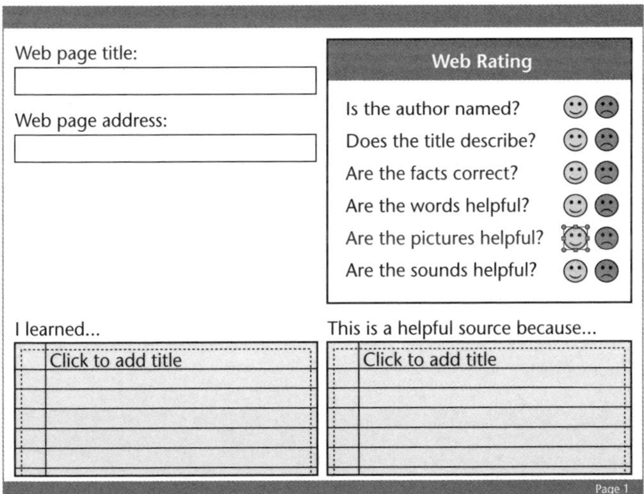

A template developed by Annette Lamb, 2006 (alamb@eduscapes.com) to evaluate a website

Saving pictures or text from a webpage

To save a picture from a website using Internet Explorer 9:

- Place the cursor over the image or picture.
- Right-click on the picture.
- Select **Save picture as...** from the menu.
- This will bring up the **Save Picture** window.
- Note that the name of the file is in the window. This can be changed if desired.
- The file format is also in the window, usually .jpg or .gif.
- The picture is saved in the Pictures folder by default.

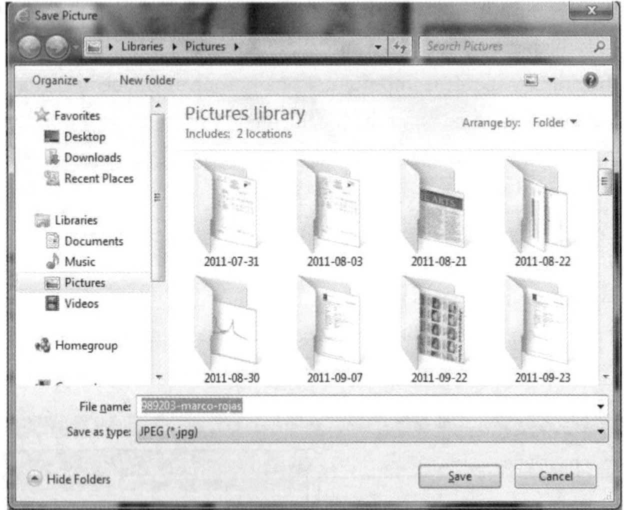

Saving a picture from the Internet

A picture can be printed in a similar manner:

- Place the cursor over the image or picture.
- Right-click on the picture.
- Select **Print picture ...** from the menu.
- Print the picture from the **Print Dialog** box.

To save text from a website:

- Select the text to be saved.
- Right-click.
- Select **Copy** from the menu.
- **Paste** the text into a Word document.

Another option is to send the text to OneNote. To do this:

- Select the text to be saved.
- Right-click.
- Choose **Send to OneNote**.

The text is now saved as a OneNote document. An advantage of this method of saving text is that the origin of the text is also saved.

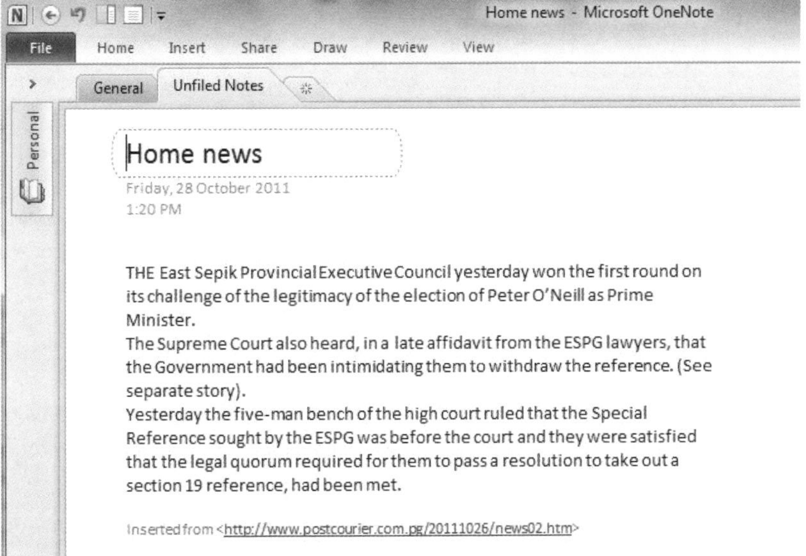

Sending text to OneNote

Web browser add-ons

A web browser add-on is a piece of software that adds extra features to a browser. The add-on is usually written by a third party.

Each web browser has its own unique method of being installed. The user typically follows instructions with the add-on.

One widely used add-on is Adobe Flash Player. This is used to add video and animations to webpages. It is often used in advertisements and games.

Browser add-ons are not always compatible with the browser in use. In particular, a new version of a browser may not be able to use an old version of an add-on. The producers of add-ons work hard to keep up with browser updates to ensure that their add-ons still work.

In some cases, an incompatible browser add-on will cause a browser to shut down.

Users download add-ons as they are needed. Often, a user will be prompted from a website that an add-on is required to carry out a particular activity on the site. The user is then given the opportunity to download and install the add-on.

The Flash add-on can be downloaded and installed

Microsoft Support

Support Home Solution Centers Advanced Search Contact Us Buy Products

Article ID: 968916 - Last Review: August 25, 2011 - Revision: 11.0

The PDFCreator toolbar add-on may not be compatible with Internet Explorer 8

View products that this article applies to.

The third-party products that this article discusses are manufactured by companies that are independent of Microsoft. Microsoft makes no warranty, implied or otherwise, about the performance or reliability of these products.

A warning from Microsoft about an incompatible add-on

Portable Document Format (PDF)

The **PDF** file format was developed by the Adobe software company. This format preserves fonts and layout and can be viewed on the screen looking just as a printed version would appear.

The PDF plug-in is a widely used add-on to browsers.

Many different computer types and different operating systems can be used to view PDF documents.

PDF documents can be viewed:

- Within a web browser using a plug-in.
- Using free reader software from Adobe called Adobe Reader.

PDF documents are used by:

- Software publishers to distribute information and manuals.
- Book publishers to sell online versions of novels and other books.
- Organisations to distribute invitations and brochures.

Downloading a PDF file

A PDF file is often just represented as a link on an HTML page. Clicking on the link will activate the download process.

Once the download has finished the file will be located on the computer hard disk and it can then be opened by double-clicking it. Adobe Acrobat Reader is freely available for download from Adobe's website.

Communication protocols

Transmission Control Protocol/Internet Protocol (TCP/IP)

TCP/IP is the basic communication language of the Internet. These are the rules or protocols that can be used in a network, either private or public. These protocols allow access to the Internet and enable messages to be sent to and from other computers using the same protocols.

File Transfer Protocol (FTP)

File Transfer Protocol (FTP) is the protocol for transferring files from a computer to a host over an Internet-based network. FTP operates on a TCP network. An important use of this protocol is the transfer of updated files from a local computer to a website stored on a web server. FTP users are authenticated on the network using a sign-in or login protocol. Many organisations use the FTP protocol to keep websites up to date.

Unit 11.6 Internet
Topic 6: Electronic mail (email)

Topic 6 explores electronic mail (see ICT Syllabus p. 29 and Computer Studies Syllabus p. 28). It covers:

- Introduction to email.
- Sending email messages.
- Reading email messages.
- Organising email messages.
- The address book.
- Organising contacts and folders.

Introduction to email

Electronic mail, or email, allows people to exchange messages and documents using a computer network. With Internet access, email is a quick and efficient method of communication.

Email has been one of the Internet services that has driven the Internet's dramatic growth. As such, it is one of the core services of the Internet and one that is used worldwide.

People in many organisations routinely exchange email addresses as contact points in much the same way as telephone numbers.

Why do people use email?

People use email because:

- Messages can be created and delivered quickly.
- It is geographically independent: messages may be sent anywhere in the world on the network.
- It is quick and easy to reply to a message.
- It is time-independent: messages can be sent at any time and read at the discretion of the user.
- It is platform-independent.
- Messages can be easily stored and retrieved.

Web email

A number of organisations provide free email for registered users who access their sites. Examples of these include Microsoft's Hotmail, Yahoo! Mail and Google's Gmail.

Using one of these messaging systems, email can be accessed anywhere in the world providing you have access to the Web with a user name and password.

Such accounts allow a certain amount of disk storage for messages. At the time of writing, Gmail allowed a total of 7 GB of disk space for a user.

In the same way as dedicated email packages, users have an Inbox to receive messages, an Outbox to send messages and an Address book in which contacts can be stored.

One of the disadvantages of using such accounts is that the screen usually contains advertising that can be distracting.

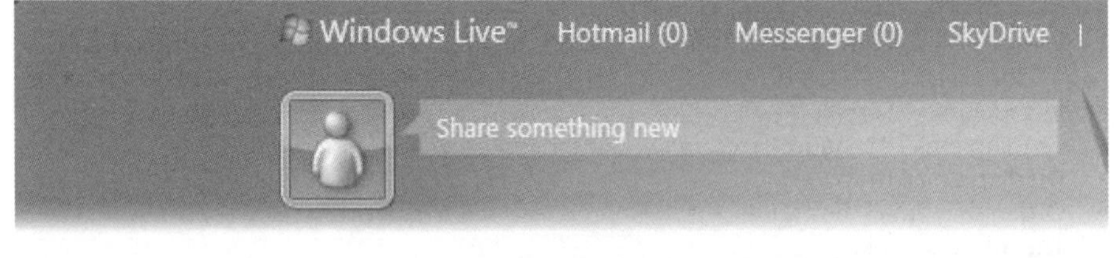

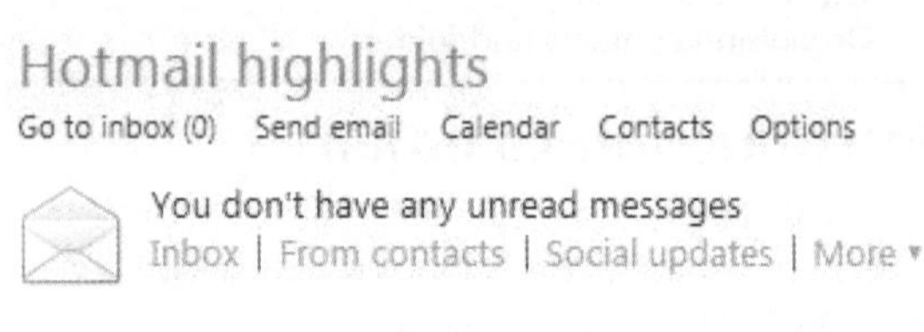

Part of Microsoft's Windows Live web-based email system

Any electronic mail system is made up of:

- People with email addresses.
- A computer network.
- Software.

What is an email address?

An email address is made up of:

- A person's email identity.
- The symbol @.
- The address of the mail server provider.

For example, Jane Pinu may have an email account with Daltron. Her name is identified as Jane. Pinu with a full stop between the first name and family name.

Her email address would be Jane.Pinu@daltron.com.pg.

Many of the public web-based email services have addresses that include numbers to differentiate users, eg JanePinu1998@yahoo.com.

The email address uniquely identifies a person on the Internet.

The Simple Mail Transfer Protocol (SMTP) allows the exchange of mail on the Internet.

What can email do?

Electronic mail systems allow people to:

- Create and send messages.
- Store messages.
- Receive and read messages.
- Reply to messages.
- Attach files to messages.
- Create and maintain address books of contacts.
- Receive notification of the arrival of new mail.
- Check the status of mail that has been sent.
- Forward mail to other people.
- Delete messages that are no longer required.

How does email work?

Email is like having your own electronic post office with a built-in computer filing system. Email requires a mail server on a local computer network. For the home user, Internet access is required.

A mail server is a computer on a network that runs software that manages the mail messages for that network. The server may be dedicated to running mail only or may also have other functions.

For a home user, the mail server is maintained by the Internet service provider. When a message is sent to a user with a unique address, the network software routes that mail to the appropriate mail server. An external message is forwarded across the Internet to the receiver's mail server.

Mail is stored by the provider, although limits may be placed on the amount of mail to be stored or the number of messages.

When a user logs on to a mail system, he or she will receive notification of any new mail that can be read immediately.

After the user gains access with a user name and password, the email software shows lists of messages that have been sent and received. From those lists, individual messages can be displayed for reading.

A message can be saved, printed, deleted or forwarded to someone else.

Email in organisations

Many organisations take responsibility for their own email and related services. The most widely used services are based on Microsoft Exchange Server with the other devices on the network using client software such as Microsoft Outlook.

Microsoft Exchange manages:

- Email.
- Calendars.
- Contacts.

- Tasks.
- Notes.

Microsoft Exchange is a **client/server system**. That is, the messages are received and stored centrally on the Exchange Server and then accessed locally on a client computer running software such as Microsoft Outlook.

In an organisation, a program called Active Directory is used to centrally manage users and their access privileges. It is used to identify and authenticate users on a Microsoft network and it works closely with Exchange Server.

Microsoft Exchange can also be used with:

- Mobile devices such as smartphones.
- The Internet using Web access.
- Integrated telephone services.

Mail folders in Microsoft Outlook client

Microsoft Exchange Server setup

Organisations use products such as Exchange Server to provide:

- High availability of services.
- Full email clients.
- Security and anti-spam features.
- Collaboration tools.
- Email archiving.

Most organisations have acceptable use policies for their members and employees that set out how people are able to use their email accounts appropriately.

Sending email messages

Parts of an email message

An email includes, among other items of information:

- Sender's email address.
- Date and time of message.
- Subject line: a small number of words stating the topic of the message.
- The message.

A message is an unformatted text document that can be copied and pasted into other software applications.

Creating a message in Microsoft Outlook

Composing a message

Short paragraphs of text can be read easily on screen. Most readers of email will scan a message and identify its key elements.

If a reply is required it can be composed immediately and parts of the incoming message can be used if wished.

Long messages can be difficult to read on a computer monitor and the receiver will often print them out.

Sending a message

To send a message the following steps are followed:

- Log on to the mail system.
- Select the receiver or receivers of the message from the address book or enter the email address.
- Enter the topic of the communication.
- Create the message.
- Attach any further documents.
- Include a complimentary close.
- Send the message.

Depending on the package used, the message can be saved in the sender's **Sent Items** mailbox automatically or by choice. It may be possible to request a notification that the mail has been received and read, again depending upon the package and the network.

Reading messages

How is email checked?

Each time the email program is opened the mailbox is checked and a message tells if there is new mail. A message appears when new mail is received if the email application is running.

Mail sent to an email address can be accessed when the receiver of the message logs in.

The user may log in anywhere in the world to email, as long as the Internet service provider has access to the Internet in that part of the world. The computer used must have either:

- Email client software installed; or
- A Web email service.

Receiving a message

Receiving a message involves the following steps:

- Log on to the mail system.
- Receive notification of new mail.
- Read the new mail.
- Save and read any attachments.

Mail messages can be dealt with by reading and then replying, storing them or forwarding them to another user of the system. Mail messages may also be deleted.

Email messages are usually sent to an **Inbox** by default. However, rules can be set up to forward emails from particular people or organisations to particular folders. In Microsoft Outlook, this is done on the **File** tab using the **Rules and Alerts** commands.

Setting up Rules and Alerts in Microsoft Outlook

Email etiquette

The way email is used is important to its usefulness for all people.

Message content

An email message is not necessarily a private document. It might reside on a file server until it is deleted. It is possible to accidentally send sensitive email to the wrong address, such as another employee within an organisation. It is unwise to think that you and the recipient of the message will be the only people who will see it.

Prompt reply

When email is received it should be replied to if there is a request in the message for something to be done. In general, messages should be replied to as soon as possible.

Spam

Spam refers to unwanted and unsolicited emails that are usually sent to a large number of people. These messages promote products or services that may be of no use to the people receiving the messages.

Usually, the true identity of the spammer is not identified. Often, spam messages will purport to come from a reputable organisation. People sending spam messages collect a large number of email addresses from a variety of sources.

The Australian Government has made it illegal for organisations to use spam as a method of promoting products or services. However, there are few legal safeguards from spam originating outside of Australia.

The spam is usually high-volume and automatically generated, often from computers that have been taken over by malware and become part of a botnet where a server controls that computer.

Some ISPs and organisations install software that scans incoming email and can block unwanted spam. Some of the Internet mail services allow users to block email that is unwanted.

Microsoft Outlook attempts to identify spam emails and will forward suspicious messages to the **Junk E-mail** box. By default, Outlook also blocks the download of pictures in messages.

The problem of spam will continue to be a major issue for many years to come.

How to recognise spam

Some of the give-away signs of spam email are:

- The sender is not someone you normally receive email from.
- The subject line of the email may be enticing or vague.
- The email is selling a good or service that you do not normally buy.
- The email may have words with incorrect spelling or used in the wrong context.
- The email may be stating you are entitled to money, perhaps from a lottery or inheritance. These emails invariably require transfer of funds from you to 'initiate' the process.
- The email address may be inconsistent with the organisation the sender purports to represent.

Junk email

Some organisations send email messages to millions of Internet subscribers.

This type of email is usually advertising and is referred to as 'junk email'. It is unsolicited advertising. Most of it is a nuisance to users: it takes time to deal with and it uses up disk space, processing time and network access time.

Direct marketers use bulk email because they can reach a large number of potential customers quickly and cheaply. They are able to distribute their messages without envelopes, stamps and labour to fill the envelopes. Bulk email is thus far cheaper than conventional bulk mailings using the postal system.

Search engines on the Internet enable organisations to create lists of users who have particular interests that can be targeted with promotions.

Some Internet service providers are asked to provide email address lists to marketing organisations.

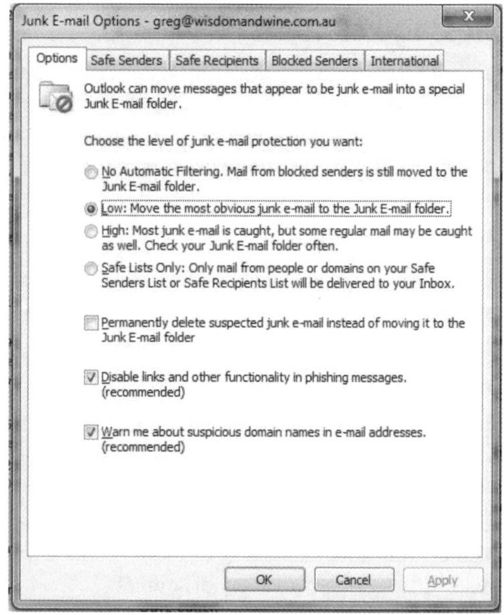

Microsoft Outlook allows user control over junk email

Using email responsibly

The Internet is made up of many thousands of computer networks throughout the world. Messages sent across the network may actually be sent through a number of networks until they reach their destination.

Email lists

People can subscribe to receive information from organisations and individuals via email. Unsolicited email is a potential area for abuse. People are likely to be annoyed if they continually receive email they have not requested.

Phishing

Phishing is the process of sending an email that claims to come from a legitimate organisation. This is usually an attempt to gain private, personal information. That personal information is then used for identity theft. These emails often ask for passwords, bank account numbers or credit card numbers. The email may direct the receiver to a bogus website that is set up to capture such information.

The senders of the email do not actually know the recipients, but they do know that it will reach a percentage, however small, of people who are customers and some of those will treat the email as genuine.

Transfer of viruses via email

An email virus is malicious computer code that is sent as part of an email or as an attachment to an email. The code is often used to destroy particular files on a computer. It can also be self-replicating and can be forwarded on to other email addresses in the receiver's contact book.

At one stage, PDF attachments were being emailed out with viruses embedded.

The best ways to avoid email viruses are to:

- Only open attachments from a trusted and known source.
- Ensure that anti-virus software is installed and up to date and is used to scan incoming emails.

Organising email messages

Deleting an email message

To delete an email message in Outlook:

- Select the message to be deleted.
- Click the **Delete** command on the **Home** tab.

Once the Delete command is clicked, the message is moved to the **Deleted Items** folder. The messages remain in the Deleted Items folder unless they are deleted again.

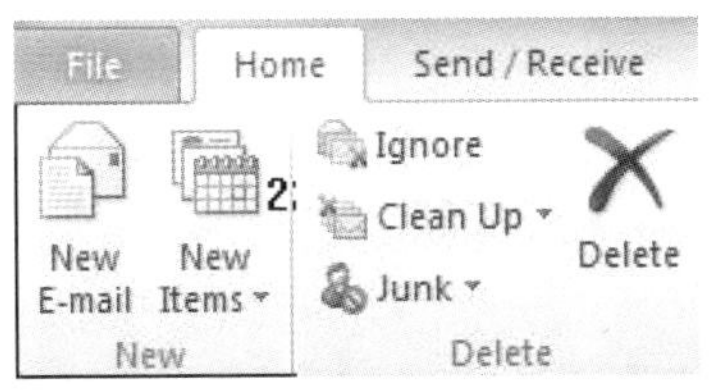

Deleting an email message

To automatically delete these items, go to the **File** tab, choose **Options** and then choose **Advanced**. The **Outlook start and exit** option gives the opportunity to automatically empty the Deleted Items folder when exiting Outlook.

An Exchange Server may be set up to archive all email messages. In some organisations there is a legal requirement to be able to access all email messages over a number of years for e-discovery purposes.

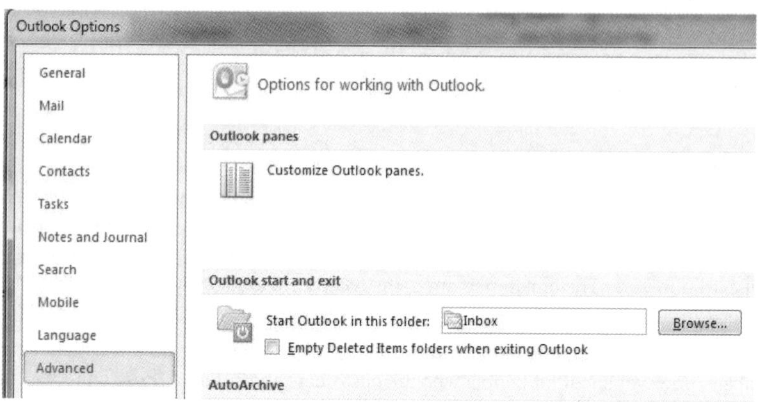

Outlook can automatically delete items from the Deleted Items folders

Saving messages

Mail servers have only limited space for storage of email. Users should save important messages to their own hard disk and delete messages that are no longer needed.

Messages that are saved in local folders can be kept indefinitely.

Messages can also be saved in other folders and then removed from the email system. To do this:

- Select the email message.
- On the **File** tab, choose **Save As...**
- Select the name and folder in which it is to be saved.
- Click **OK**.

Saving an email message

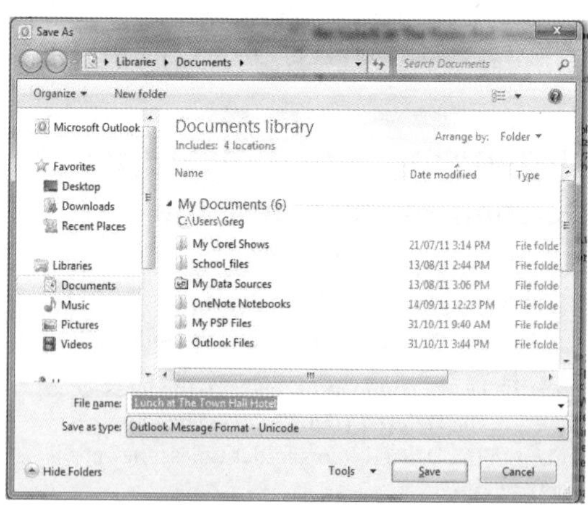

Saving the message

Saving attachments

Attachments should be saved before opening. If you receive an email from a trusted source that has an attachment, you should:

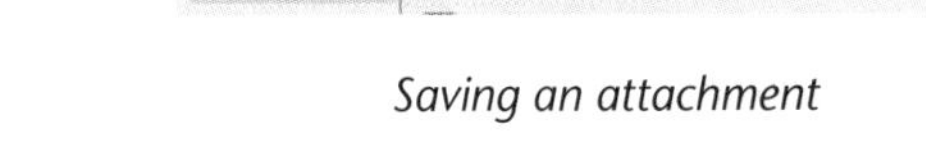

Saving an attachment

- Right-click on the attachment: it is displayed in the message line.
- Choose **Save As...**
- Confirm the file name and save it in the appropriate folder.

The attachment should then be opened using the appropriate application. Do not double-click on an attachment in an email message.

Finding email messages in message folders

To search for an email, use the **Instant Search** box.

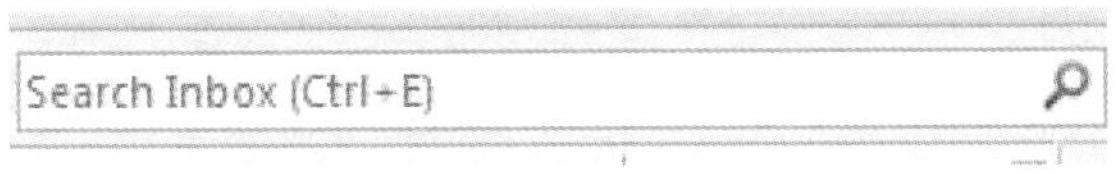

Instant Search box

Click in the box and enter the keywords to be searched. Note that a **Search Tools** tab is now displayed.

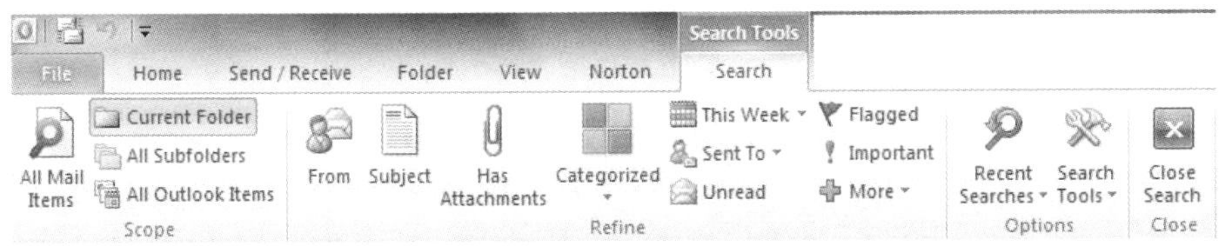

Search tab in Outlook

Note that the search can be narrowed or broadened using the various menu items, eg:

- A particular, selected folder.
- All items.
- From a particular user.
- Sent this week.

The **Search Tools** menu item allows complex searches to be carried out.

Managing email messages with rules

The **Info** menu item on the **File** tab gives the user the option of managing rules and alerts.

Choosing **Manage Rules & Alerts** brings up an **E-mail Rules** window.

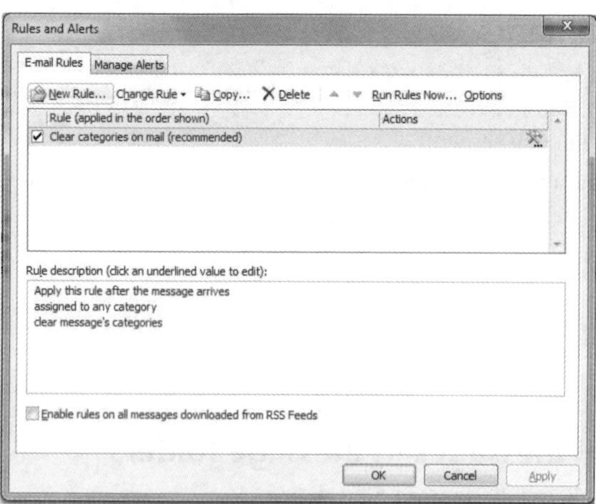

Window for managing rules

In particular, the user is able to automatically move messages from a particular person or organisation to a specified folder. A rule can be established to move messages with a keyword to a particular folder.

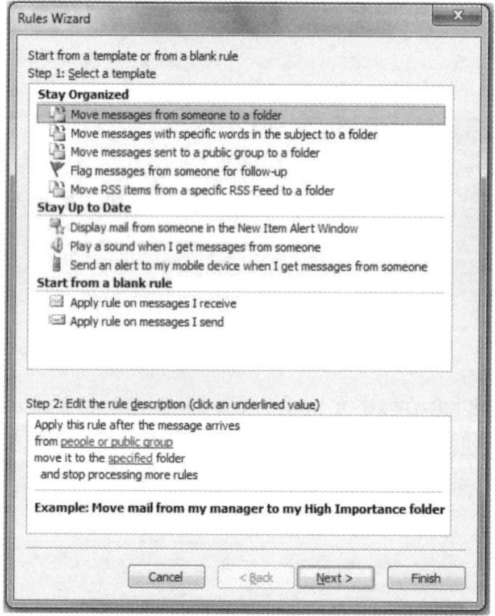

The Rules Wizard allows the creation and modification of rules

Add, delete, or switch folders

Folders can be managed on the **Folder** tab in Outlook.

The Folder tab

To create a new folder:

- Select the **New Folder** menu item.
- In the window that appears, enter the new folder name.
- Choose where you would like the folder to be located. Folders can have sub-folders.
- Click **OK**.

The new folder now appears in the area chosen.

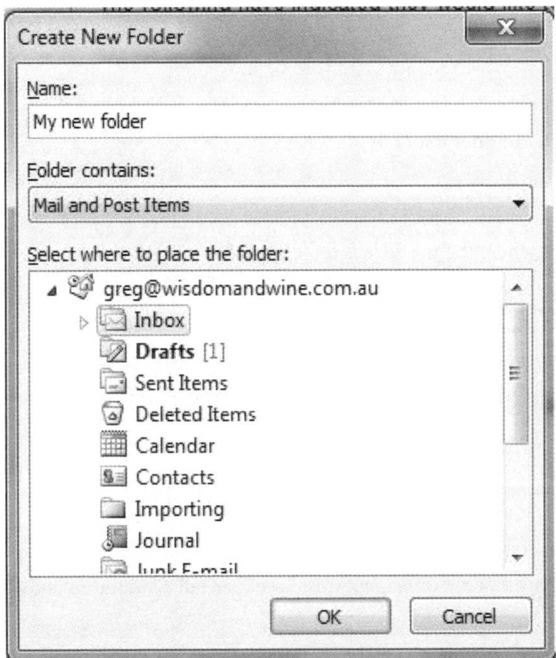

Creating a new folder

The folders appear in the **Navigation Pane** on the left of the screen.

To add a folder to the Favorites:

- Select the folder.
- Choose the **Show in Favorites** menu item on the **Folder** tab.

To remove a folder from the Favorites:

- Right-click on the folder.
- Select the **Remove from Favorites** option.

To delete a folder:

- Right-click on the folder.
- Select the **Delete Folder** option.

To move a folder:

- Right-click on the folder.
- Select the **Move Folder** option.
- Select the location to which the folder is to be moved.

Move or copy a message to another folder

To move a message to another folder:

- Right-click on the message.
- Select the folder to which the message is to be moved; or
- Select the message and drag it to the different folder.

To copy a message to another folder:

- Right-click on the message.
- Select **Copy**.
- Go to the folder where the message is to be copied.
- Press the key combination **Ctrl-V**. The message is copied into the destination folder.

Note that the message also remains in its original folder.

Storing messages on an email server

Each network has rules about the way it is used and what activities are acceptable.

Each electronic mail user is responsible for the maintenance of the mailbox. Users should:

- Check their electronic mail regularly.
- Delete messages that are not wanted.
- Save any messages that are to be kept onto local hard disks rather than on the central mail server.
- Always use language that is acceptable to others; never say anything in a message that would not be said face to face.

When using an email server, messages can be stored on the server simply by leaving them there. Most organisations will have limits about the amount of data that can be stored on an email server such as Exchange. Once that limit is reached, email will no longer be received in a mailbox.

For example, Strathclyde University in the UK provides 100 MB of storage for students and 2 GB for staff.

> To efficiently manage resources, IT Services has placed limits on the amount of mail each person can store in Exchange. As the limit is approached, a warning message will be delivered to the mailbox. If the limit is exceeded for a mailbox, mail will continue to be received, but no more email can be sent. Finally, when the amount of mail reaches an upper threshold, no mail can be sent or received.
>
> The current mailbox limit is 100Mb for students, and 2Gb for staff.

Managing email
(www.strath.ac.uk/exchange/)

It can be useful to store email on a central server, particularly when accessing email on the Web using tools such as Outlook Web Access.

Additional email management

Outlook has a number of additional email management features that can be useful. These include:

- Drafting messages before sending.
- Sending messages to more than one person.
- Sending copies of messages to people.
- Sending blind carbon copies of messages to people (this conceals the recipients of the message).
- Attaching documents including images.
- Forwarding received messages to other people.
- Sending a message to create an appointment.
- Sending an email to OneNote.
- Requesting a message when the email is opened by the recipient.
- Using a voting button when asking a question.

The address book

Email software can store email addresses and other information about people with whom you communicate. Email addresses can be stored in a database and inserted into a new message by selecting from the menu.

In Microsoft Outlook, names and addresses are stored in the **Contacts** part of the application. Contacts are found in the **Navigation Panel** on the left-hand side of the Outlook window.

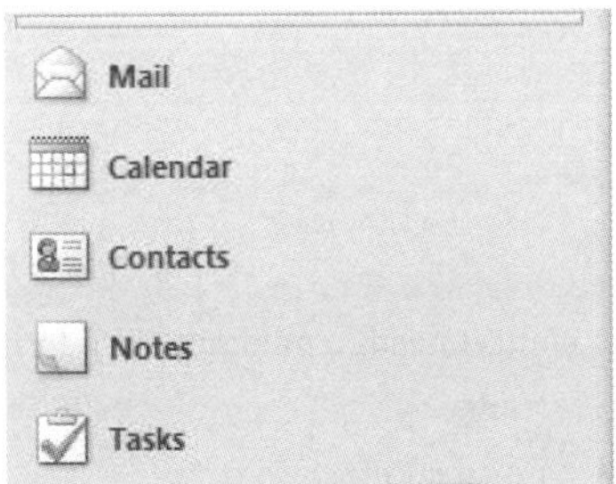

Contacts are accessible in the Navigation Panel in Outlook

Open the address book

To open the address book, click the **Contacts** icon in the **Navigation Panel**.

In a system that uses Exchange and Outlook, there are two different address books:

- One address book is stored centrally on the Exchange Server and is available to all authorised users.
- Another address book is stored locally on the client computer and is available only to the user of that computer.

Add a contact to the address book

To add a Contact to the Address Book in Microsoft Outlook:

- Choose **New Contact** from the **Home** tab.
- Enter the data in the form that is displayed.

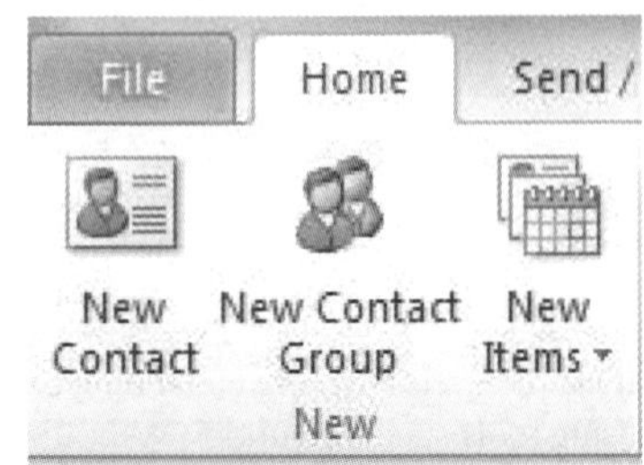

Adding a new contact

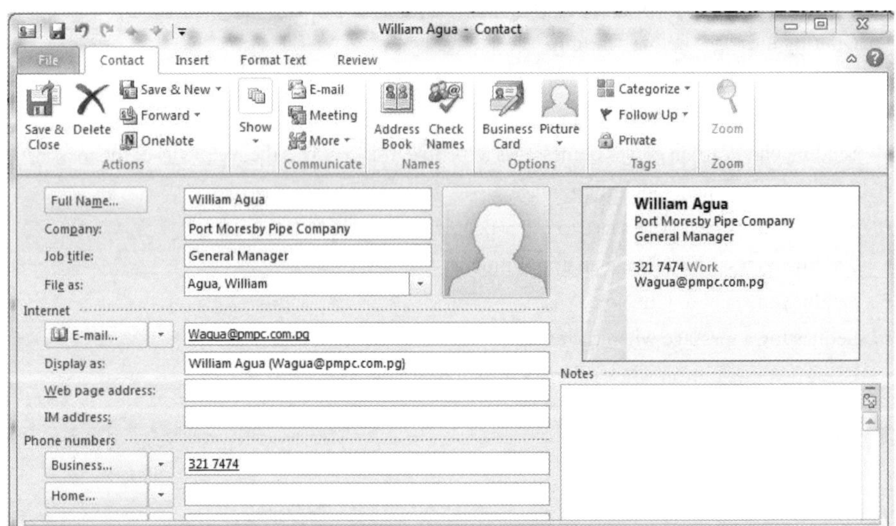

Entering a new Contact in Microsoft Outlook

A contact needs a minimum of information to be useful:

- Name.
- Email address.

Microsoft Outlook can use these Contacts when sending emails.

The **Email** option on the **Communicate** section of the **Home** tab allows the user to send an email to a Contact.

Add names from email messages

To add a name to the Contacts from an email message:

- Open the email message.
- Right-click on the name that appears in the **From** part of the email message.
- Select **Add to Outlook Contacts** from the menu that appears.
- Confirm the information in the **Contact** window.

Business Cards

A Business Card is one way in which a Contact may be viewed.

To view a Business Card for a Contact, select **Business Card** from the **Options** menu items on the **Contact** tab when the Contact is open.

A user can send a Business Card as an attachment in an email. This is done as part of the signature. A signature is information that appears at the end of an email message. Users can create different signatures and choose which one to use depending on the context.

View a Contact as a Business Card

To add a signature to an email:

- Create a new email message.
- Choose **Signature** from the **Include** section of the **Message** tab.
- Enter the signature information.
- Click on the **Business Card** option.
- Select the Contact whose business card you wish to attach.

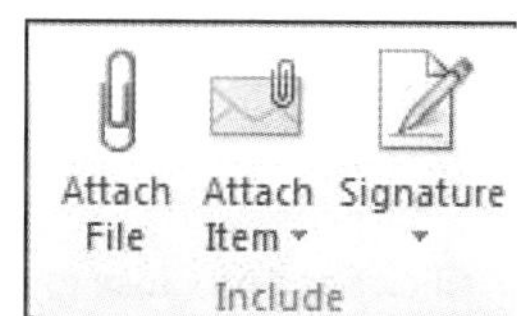

Add a signature to an email

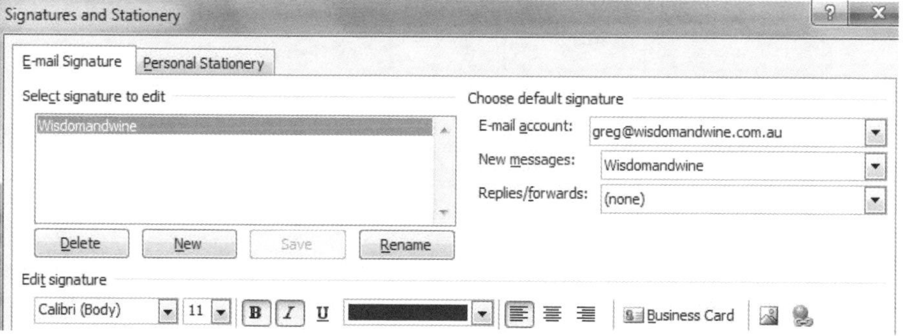

Add a Business Card to a signature

The electronic Business Card is now attached to the email as a '.VCF' file. This Business Card can be downloaded and entered into Outlook.

When receiving an email with a Business Card attached, double-click on the Business Card file and then choose **Save As...** to save the information to the Contacts file.

Double-click on the '.vcf' file to open the Business Card

Change contact information

To change the information in a Contact record:

- Open the Contact and enter the changes.
- Choose **Save & Close** from the **Actions** section of the **Contact** tab.

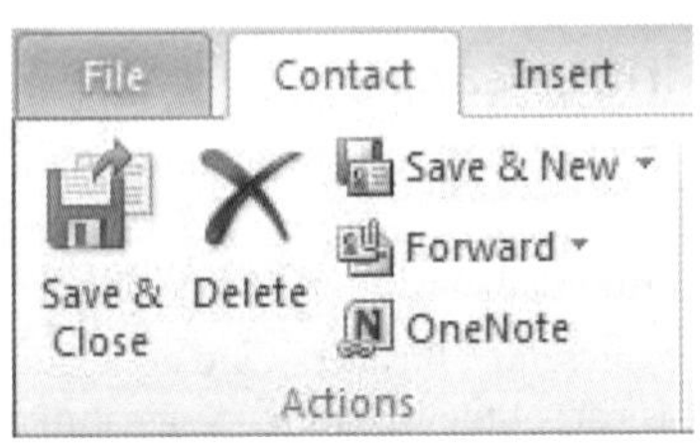

Modifying contact information

Create a group of contacts

It can be useful to create groups of contacts. To create a group:

- Choose **New Contact Group** from the **New** section of the **Home** tab.
- Give the Contact Group a name.
- Now choose **Add Members** from the **Members** section of the tab.
- Members can be selected from Outlook Contacts.
- Click **Save & Close** to save the group.

Create a Contact Group

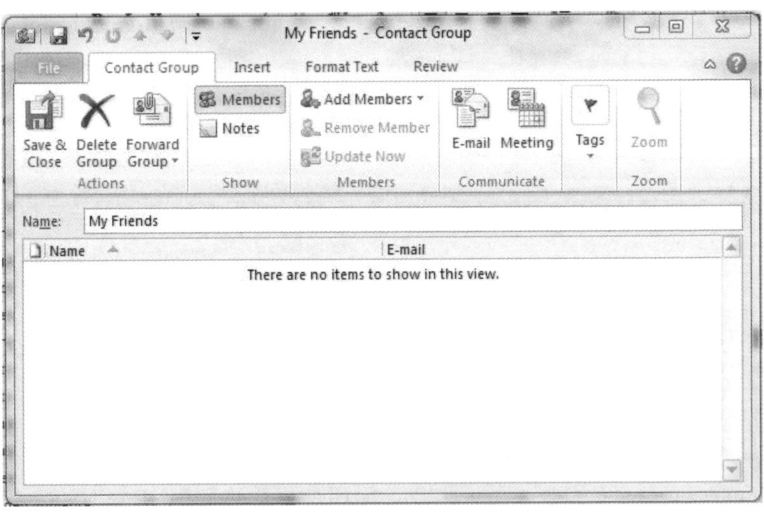

Creating a Contact Group

The group is now listed in the Contacts as a group.

The new group in Contacts

Modifying a group

To add a contact to a group:

- Open the group.
- Choose **Add Members** from the **Members** section of the **Contact Group** tab.
- Add members in the same manner as was done when creating the group.
- Click **Save & Close**.

To remove a member from a group:

- Open the group.
- Select the member of the group to be removed.
- Choose **Remove Member** from the **Members** section of the **Contact Group** tab.
- Click **Save & Close**.

Modifying a group

Digital ID

A **digital ID** or digital certificate is used to prove who you are on the Internet. It is an electronic document that conforms to an international standard.

A digital certificate can be inserted into a Microsoft document via a third party. The digital ID enables you to sign legally enforceable contracts across the Internet.

The digital ID can be connected to an email address and it will allow the sender to both digitally sign a document and encrypt all digital transmissions.

A digital ID is purchased from a third party and an annual fee is payable for the service.

In Microsoft Outlook, a digital ID can be established via the **File** tab. To do this:

- Click **Options**.
- Choose the **Trust Center**.

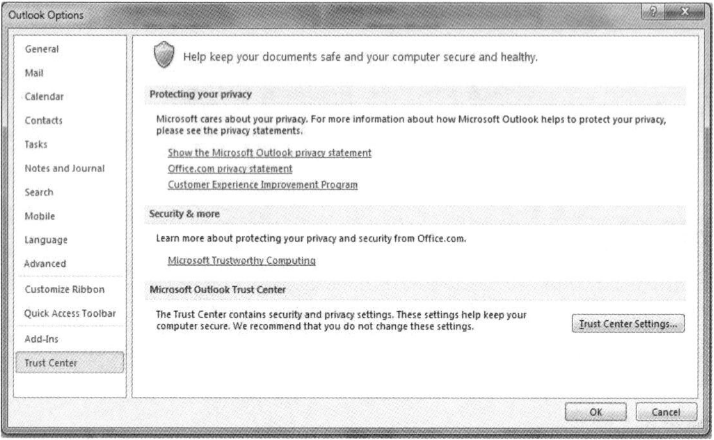

Using Microsoft's Trust Center

- Now choose **Trust Center Settings…**
- Choose **E-mail Security**.
- Select **Get a Digital ID…**

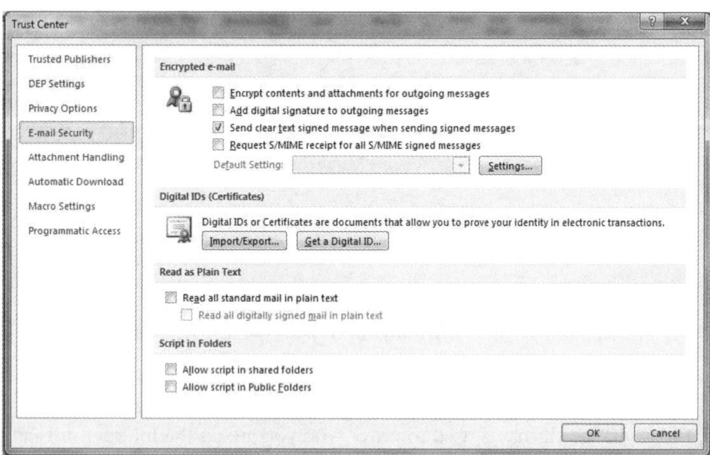

Obtaining a digital ID

This now takes the user to a website that allows the purchase of a digital ID.

Once the digital ID has been purchased, the **E-mail Security** tab can be used to attach the ID to messages.

Recipient's digital ID

A digital ID can be added to a Contact. To do this, you must receive an encrypted email message from that Contact.

When an encrypted message with a digital ID is received, right-click on the name in the **From** box and click **Add to Contacts**. If the Contact already exists, then the Contact Data should be updated.

The digital ID can be checked using the **Certificates** command on the **Show** section of the **Contact** tab when the Contact is displayed.

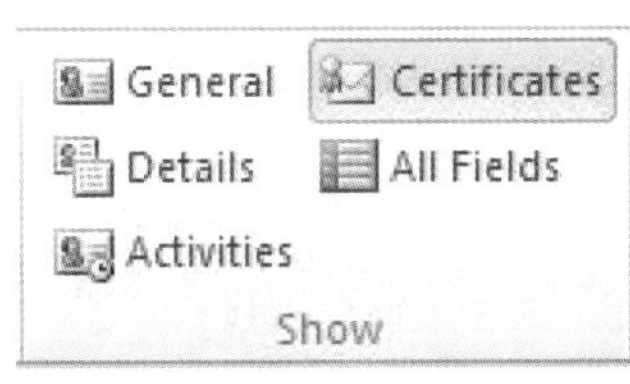

Checking the Certificates for a Contact

Organise names in the address book

Contacts can be organised and viewed in a number of different ways. A Contact can be viewed:

- As a Business Card.
- As a Card.
- By phone number.
- As a list.

This is done on the **Current View** of the **Home** tab.

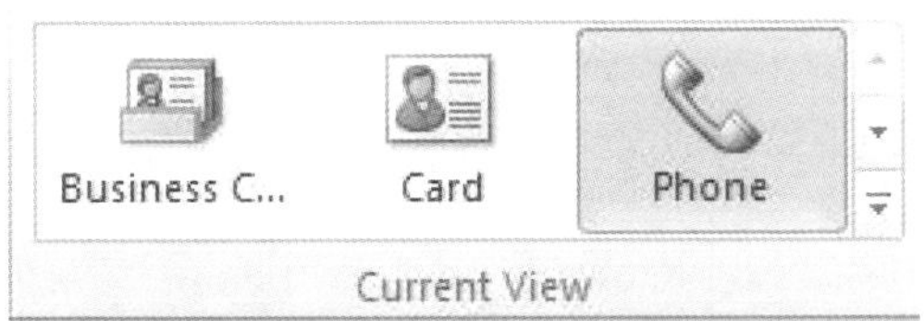

Different views of a Contact

Agua, William	
Full Name:	William Agua
Job Title:	General Manager
Company:	Port Moresby Pipe Company
Business:	321 7474
E-mail:	Wagua@pmpc.com.pg

*A **Card** view of a Contact*

Contacts can be sorted using the **View Settings** command on the **Current View** section of the **View** tab.

The **Sort...** button allows the user to change the selected sort order.

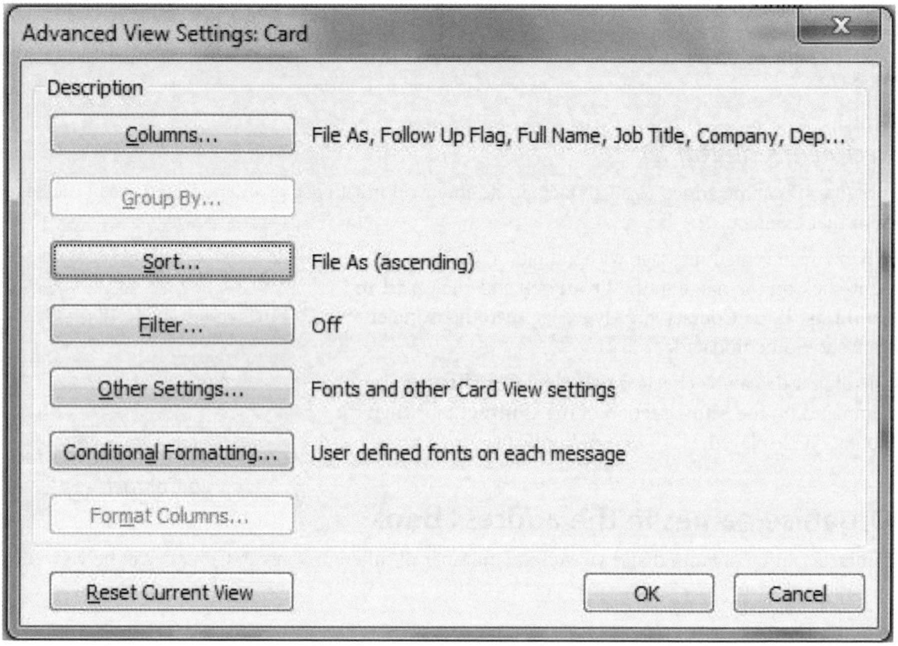

Advanced View Settings: Card
Description
Columns...
File As, Follow Up Flag, Full Name, Job Title, Company, Dep...
Group By...
Sort...
File As (ascending)
Filter...
Off
Other Settings...
Fonts and other Card View settings
Conditional Formatting...
User defined fonts on each message
Format Columns...
Reset Current View
OK
Cancel

Advanced settings for Contacts

Three commands on the **Arrangement** section of the **View** tab allow a quick method of sorting. Those commands are:

- Categories.
- Company.
- Location.

end / Receive
Folder
View
Norton
Categories
Company
Location
Reverse Sort
Add Columns
Expand/Collapse
Arrangement

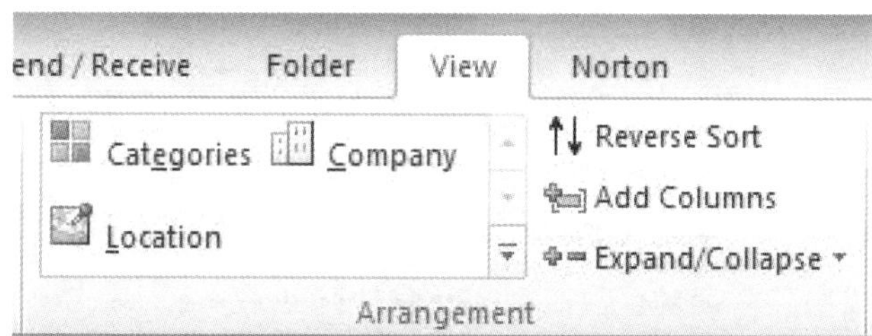

Sort categories

Contacts can be easily searched using the **Search** bar.

Search Contacts (Ctrl+E)

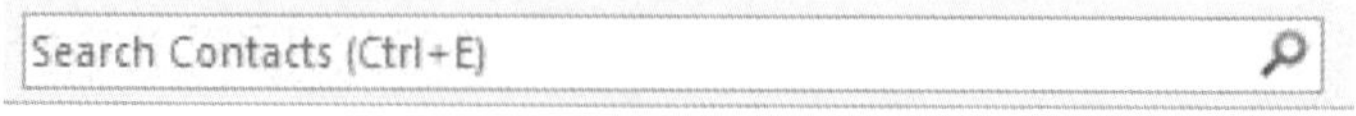

Search bar in Contacts

When the cursor is moved into the search window, a new **Search Tools** tab appears and this can be used for more complex searches.

Search Tools tab

Deleting Contacts from your address book

To delete a Contact:

- Select the Contact.
- Select **Delete** from the **Delete** section of the **Home** tab.

Delete command

Printing address book information

Contacts can be printed in the following manner:

- A single Contact.
- All the Contacts.
- A selection of the Contacts.

To print a single Contact:

- Open the Contact by double-clicking it.
- Go to the **File** tab.
- Select **Print**.
- Check the **Print Preview** on the right-hand side of the screen.
- Click on the **Print** icon.

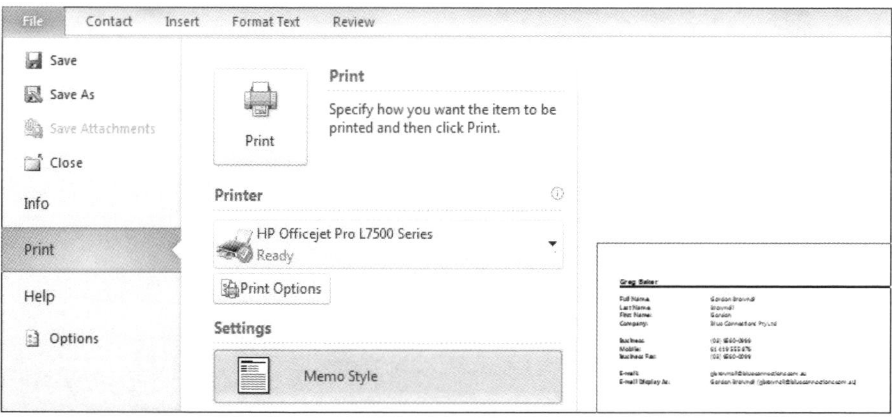

Printing a Contact

To print all the Contacts:

- In the **Contacts** pane, click on **Contacts**.
- Go to the **File** tab.

- Select **Print**.
- Choose the required settings.
- Check the **Print Preview** on the right-hand side of the screen.
- Click on the **Print** icon.

To print a selection of Contacts:

- In the **Contacts** pane, click on **Contacts**.
- Go to the **View** tab and select the **View Settings** command.
- Click on **Filter** in the **Advanced View Settings**.
- Enter the criteria to select the Contacts.

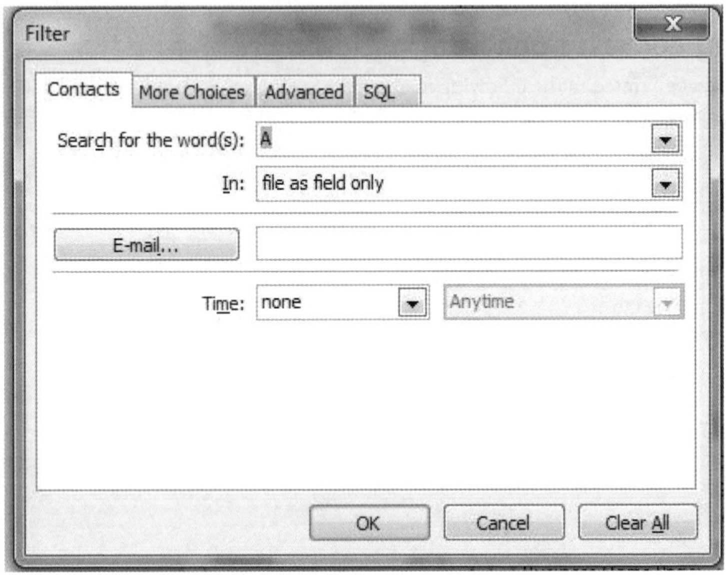

Filtering Contacts

- Go to the **File** tab.
- Select **Print**.
- Choose the required settings.
- Check the **Print Preview** on the right-hand side of the screen.
- Click on the **Print** icon.

Conclusion

Microsoft Outlook is a powerful package that integrates email, contacts, tasks, notes and calendars in a consistent interface.

Unit 11.6 Activity 6A: Email

1. Explain how to carry out the following tasks.
   a. Create an address book.
   b. Add a name, address and email address to the existing address book.
   c. Enter an email address in a new message
   d. Send an email to one recipient and a carbon copy of the email to another recipient.
   e. Delete an existing email.
   f. Create folders in which to store the emails from particular senders and groups.
   g. Sort an email inbox or outbox by date or sender.
   h. Create filters on your email to sort by address.
   i. Add attachments to an email message.
   j. Create a nickname for someone you email on a regular basis.
   k. Forward an email you have received to another person.
   l. Add a signature to your email.
   m. Set the time period where email is automatically checked.
2. Comment upon the following matters of email etiquette.
   a. Email should be concise and to the point.
   b. Email should be checked on a regular basis and replies sent at your earliest convenience.
   c. You should allow a reasonable time from sending your email until you expect a return email.
   d. Do not create an email using upper case letters, as this is the equivalent to shouting.
   e. Do not use email for sending junk mail to others on email lists.

   What other rules of email etiquette can you find?
3. Email has been termed a 'killer application' of the Internet and has been a factor in the massive growth in Internet usage. Many organisations have introduced email without adequate education or training to ensure users fully understand how to use email responsibly.

   Comment on the following statements about the use of email:
   a. Creating and sending email is private if a person has password protection on their computer.
   b. The intended email recipient always receives messages.
   c. People tend to respond in an informal manner with email, such as replying by 'Gidday' rather than 'Dear Sir'.
   d. People will respond to email as a one-to-one communication; it can be regarded as clear, frank, brief, honest and unambiguous.
   e. An email is owned by the sender of the email, rather than the organisation they work for.

f. Emails are not normal communication and therefore cannot form evidence in a court of law.
g. Employers are obliged to tell their staff if email is being monitored and read.
h. Email attachments can be infected with viruses.
i. People sending 'joke' and 'fun' programs to friends can circumvent normal network security in organisations.

4. If you receive an email from someone and you do not have his or her address, how do you add the name and address to your email contacts?
5. Is the following use of email in an organisation acceptable?
   a. An employee uses email in the workplace to notify other employees of a union meeting to be held at lunchtime.
   b. An employee uses email in the workplace to send a message to all other employees to advertise a bicycle he or she wishes to sell.
   c. An employee uses email to criticise the actions of another employee to that employee's superior.
   d. An employee sends an email to a number of colleagues commenting upon company policy regarding employment practices.
   e. An employee uses email to send a private message to a person in another company during work time.
   f. An employee uses email to send a private message to a person in another company after they have finished work.
6. Microsoft Hotmail is an example of an email account accessed through a web browser. The service has a number of levels including a free account and an account with a service charge that offers more features. Web email messages reside on the mail server of the provider.
   a. How do you set up a web-based email account?
   b. Why do people use web-based email accounts?
   c. List the advantages and disadvantages of using web-based email accounts.
   d. How are providers of free email services able to make it a free service?
   e. If you have a web-based email account, find out details about the account and fill in the following table.

	Feature	Details of 'free' service	Details of account with 'service charge'
1	What is the amount of hard disk space allocated for email?		
2	What restrictions are placed on account names?		
3	What happens if you wish to use an account name that is already in use?		
4	How many accounts can one person have?		
5	How often must you use the account for it to remain active?		
6	Does the email provider maintain privacy of the email?		
7	Can the 'free' email service be refused by the provider to any applicant?		
8	If you delete messages using the web browser, is the message deleted from the storage records of the provider?		

Unit 11.7 Desktop Publishing

Topic 1: Working with publications

Unit 11.7 explores all aspects of desktop publishing. Topic 1 provides an overview of working with publications (see ICT Syllabus p. 30 and Computer Studies Syllabus p. 23).
It covers:

- Introduction to desktop publishing.
- Creating a publication from a design template.
- Adding and editing personal information.
- Crafting a publication.
- Managing a publication.

Introduction to desktop publishing

Desktop publishing (DTP) means using a computer system to create a publication for printing. It includes entering text, creating and placing graphics and combining all the elements for a flyer, document, report or magazine.

A document is prepared with a predetermined page size such as A4 or A5. The final stage is printing the document in a complete form. The content becomes fixed when transferred to paper. However, document settings and content can be reworked for a future document.

Desktop publishing software is concerned with the arrangement of text and graphics on a page. A document can be a single-page advertising flyer, a business card, an invitation, a four-page newsletter, a magazine of many pages or a book. Most magazines and newspapers are produced using computers and page layout software.

Desktop publishing software offers the opportunity to design a publication with almost any type of grid for setting out the elements. Looking at magazines, newspapers and books can give ideas about the grid design that is most suitable for your own publication.

Why not use a word processor?

Many word processors offer some of the features of a desktop publishing package. However, it is generally more difficult to work in columns, to manipulate and move graphics and to create master pages in a word processor than it is using a package such as Microsoft Publisher.

If a document consists of text only and does not require graphics, then a word processor is the most appropriate software to produce the document.

Purpose of publishing

The purpose of publishing is to communicate effectively with others. This involves:

- Determining the target audience.
- Creating the content for that audience.
- Delivering the content using the most appropriate medium.

Publishing for screen and paper

Documents produced by a computer are prepared for:

- Printing on paper, called desktop publishing.
- Display on screen, called digital publishing, such as on the Internet.

Apart from developing quality content, digital and desktop publishing require different approaches to document creation and presentation.

Content quality

The quality of the content is the single most important feature of any publishing task. Although computer technology can use many different content types, it cannot enhance poor content.

Creating a publication from a design template

A mock-up of the publication

Before using software to create a publication, it is useful to have a 'mock-up' of the finished publication. A mock-up is a rough, hand-drawn sketch of the page that shows the approximate positions of all of the important elements of the page. For example, if the page size is A4 then some blank sheets of A3 paper could be folded in half to give the required number of pages. Key parts of the publication would be allocated to the appropriate page; for example, the table of contents may be on page one.

Templates

Microsoft Publisher has a number of templates that can be used to create a document. As with other Microsoft Office software, some of the templates are installed with the program and others are available online.

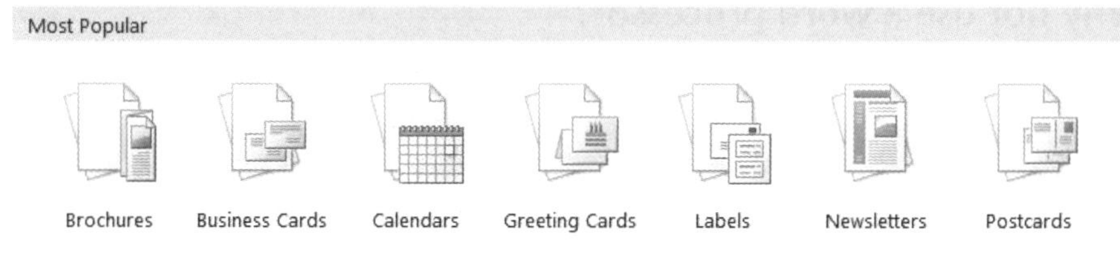

Some of the types of templates available using Microsoft Publisher

Paper sizes

There is a range of standard paper sizes used by printers.

The standard A series of paper sizes is based on the paper size A0 which is 841 mm × 1189 mm. The area of this paper is 1 square metre and the size of each succeeding ratio of length to width is the same. Succeeding sizes are half the previous size. Thus, the series of sizes is:

A0	841 mm × 1189 mm
A1	594 mm × 841 mm
A2	420 mm × 594 mm
A3	297 mm × 420 mm
A4	210 mm × 297 mm
A5	148 mm × 210 mm
A6	105 mm × 148 mm

A4 is the most frequently used size.

There is also a B series size of paper that has a different aspect ratio. The B series is often used for posters and smaller sizes for envelopes.

In North America, there is a local standard called US letter which is 8.5 inches × 11 inches or 216 mm × 279 mm.

One of the standard sizes for business cards is 90 mm × 54 mm. CD inserts and covers are 120 mm × 120 mm.

Master pages

A **master page** is used to create elements that will appear on each page in a document. These items usually include:

- Number of columns and column guides.
- Page numbering.
- Repeating text, eg headers and footers.
- Graphic elements such as lines or a logo.

In a multi-page document, master pages can be used to ensure a consistency of design throughout the document. Most of the elements on a master page can only be changed on the master page.

Master Page command on the Views section of the View tab

Most of the Publisher templates use a blank master page to allow the user complete flexibility in design. The templates include a range of design elements that might be useful to the user.

To make a change to a publication's master page, access the **Master Page** command on the **Views** section of the **View** tab.

Left and right master pages

Master pages can be set up for both the left and right pages of a publication.

The toolbar buttons allow you to:

- Add a new master page.
- Duplicate or modify a master page.
- Add guides to a master page.

Adding and editing personal information

Personal information for a publication can be added using the **File** tab in Microsoft Publisher. Select the **Info** command and then choose **Edit Business Information**.

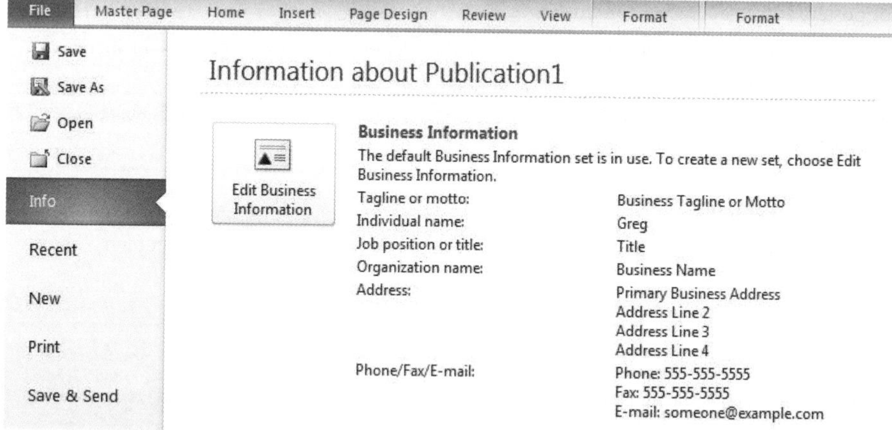

Information about a publication

The information about the business can now be entered and it becomes part of the file.

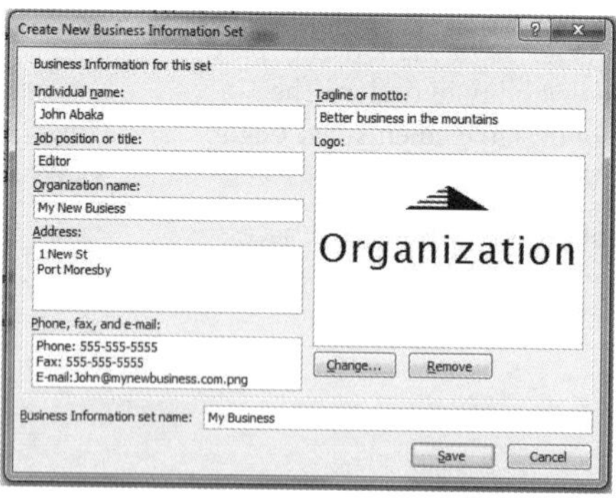

Entering business information

Crafting a publication

The audience

The intended audience influences design decisions. An end-of-year school magazine will be designed and laid out differently from a flyer advertising a rock concert.

Organisations use publications to build images about the organisation, often referred to as its brand. The image needs to be reflected in the type of publication that is built.

Some of the important components of such a brand will be:

- Logo: an image that often combines graphics and text to represent the organisation.
- Font scheme: the colours and types of fonts used can change the image of the organisation.
- Images: the range and types of images used in the publication.

The person using the desktop publishing software can determine the:

- Number of text columns per page.
- Size and style of the body text.
- Size and style of the heading text.
- Amount of white space on a page.
- Position of graphics and photographs.

The design will also allow a variety of other elements to be incorporated, including:

- Sidebars.
- Pull quotes.

Managing a publication

Publication of a magazine

The steps below apply to a class newspaper of one or two A4 sides as well as to a professionally produced publication such as a monthly magazine.

The first steps are to find out:

- Audience: who is going to read the publication?
- Articles: what is going to make them interesting to read?
- Purpose of the publication: why is the publication needed?
- Frequency of the publication: how often will it be produced?
- Time lines: when is it needed?
- Printing: who will print it and what are the specifications?
- Format: what will it look like when printed?

Submission of material

The material received may be:

- Written text.
- Cartoons.
- Images.
- Photographs.

It may be necessary to advertise that submissions are being invited. In some cases a competition could be run with a prize for the best entry.

Style guide

A style guide is a set of standards for the writing and design of a document. The aim of a style guide is to ensure uniformity and consistency within a publication.

Some style guides will focus on the type of language to be used.

Unit 11.7 Activity 1A: Publications and paper size

1. Listed below are examples of paper sizes and common publications produced by many organisations. Fill in the table showing examples of use, paper size and key features.

	Publication	Paper size (mm)	Examples of use	Key features
a	A4 flyer			
b	A3 poster			
c	A4 letter			
d	Envelope			
e	Booklet			
f	Annual report			
g	Magazine			
h	Calendar			
i	Business card			
j	Product catalogue			
k	Leaflet			
l	Newsletter			
m	A5 letter			

2. Create your own calendar for a year. Include a different photograph or illustration for each month.

Unit 11.7 Desktop Publishing
Topic 2: Planning and designing a page

Topic 2 focuses on how to plan and design a page (see ICT Syllabus p. 30 and Computer Studies Syllabus p. 23). It covers:

- Choosing a page layout.
- Navigating a page.
- Adding headers and footers.
- Applying background.

How important is design for a print publication?

Design principles and typography are important in an effective publication. The purpose of any publication is clear communication.

How something is said is just as important as *what* is said. Graphic design is an essential element in an effective magazine, leading the reader through the publication.

A successful publication is one that:

- Is easy to read.
- Has a clear purpose that is reflected in the text and the design.
- Has graphic elements that are relevant.
- Has a logical sequence of direction throughout the document – most people scan a page from top left to bottom right.
- Has page-to-page consistency throughout the document.

Design and layout

The design and layout of a document will determine:

- How easy the document is to read.
- The impact the document makes on the reader.
- How successfully the reader understands the message of the document.

Choosing a page layout

The grid that is chosen for the layout will define the look and feel of the publication. The grid should allow the user to add other design elements and graphics.

What is a grid?

A grid is the system of columns and rows that is used to create the structure of publication. It provides continuity throughout the publication.

It is made up of a series of lines that divide the page. The grid shows how many columns are being used, the width of the margins (both top and bottom) and the space between columns.

The structure that the grid creates is very important in helping to produce an effective publication.

Single-column grid

A single-column grid is the simplest to work with and very useful for one-page newsletters or advertising flyers. It is particularly suitable for those publications that do not have a large amount of text. However, it is very limiting in terms of layout. A large font size is needed and plenty of space will have to be added to help readability. It is difficult to place graphics on the page and still get an effective publication. The figure below shows an example of a single-column grid.

Most books are published using a single-column grid.

A single-column layout for a newsletter

Two-column grid

A two-column grid is used in more newsletters than a single column, but the design can be repetitive and there is often not enough white space. Again, the size of the font is limited. Graphics can be difficult to include as they should either extend across one column or across the full width of the page. The figure below shows an example of a two-column layout.

A two-column layout for a newsletter

An option with a two-column grid is to make the columns off-centre on the page. On the left-hand pages, move the grids to the right and allow space on the left. Similarly, on the right-hand pages, move the grids to the left and allow space on the right.

Three-column grid

Three-column grids offer more flexibility. Headlines can be extended across two or three columns and graphics can be placed more easily. A graphic generally looks better if it extends across complete columns: one, two or three. Vertical graphics placed in a single column can be very effective. However, there can be limitations on the amount of white space available. The figure below shows an example of a page with a three-column grid.

An example of a three-column grid

Other grids

Other grids can include up to seven columns, sometimes leaving a column blank to provide white space, and variable-width columns. Generally, as the number of columns increases so does the flexibility of layout and the complexity of the task.

Navigating a page

Adding headers and footers

Headers and **footers** are set up as part of the master page.

A header is an area at the top of the page that presents information to help the reader determine what the document is and where he or she is in the document. Headers can include text, graphics and clip art. The date and time can also be used in a header, as can page numbering. A footer is an area at the bottom of the page that can serve the same function.

To insert a header:

- Go to the **View** tab, select **Master Page** on the **Views** section of the tab.
- The **Header & Footer** section of the menu now appears.
- Clicking near the top of the page brings up the header in which information can be added.
- Clicking near the bottom of the page brings up the footer in which information can be added.
- It also brings up two new tabs that can be used: **Drawing Tools** and **Text Box Tools**.

Header and Footer menu items

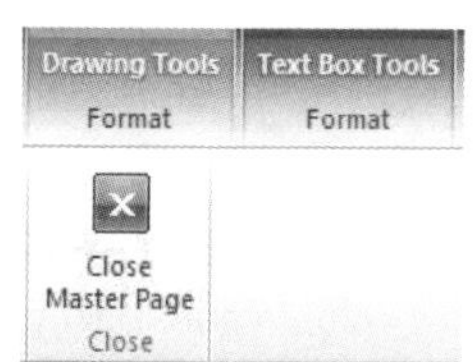

New tabs that can be used in headers and footers

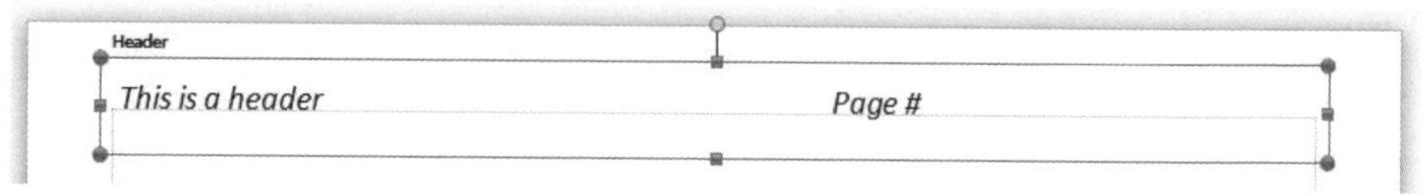

Editing a header

- Once the header or footer is complete, click on the **Close Master Page** button.

Applying a background

A background can be added to a document. The background can be a solid colour, a colour gradient or a picture. Backgrounds can help emphasise text or make photographs stand out. However, backgrounds should be used with care to ensure they do not interfere with the readability of the document.

The **Page Background** section of the **Page Design** tab includes the **Background** command.

Background command on the Page Design tab

To add a background:

- Click on the **Background** command on the **Page Design** tab.
- A range of backgrounds is displayed. Moving the cursor across the backgrounds gives a preview of what the background will look like.
- If the required background is not there, click on **More Backgrounds…**
- A range of backgrounds is displayed and one can be selected.

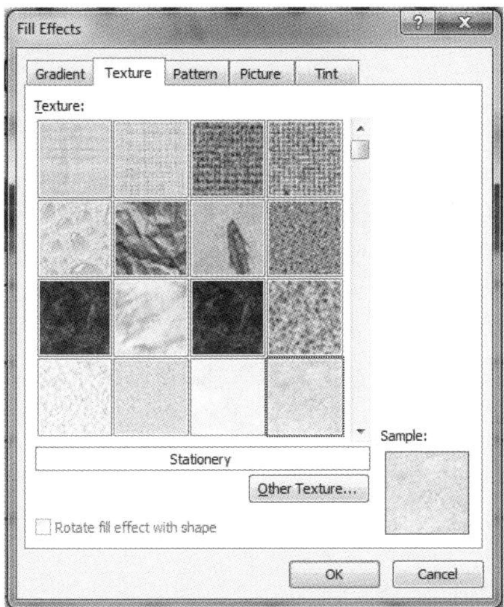

Some of the backgrounds available

Note that an image can be selected here as the background:

- Choose the **Picture** tab.
- Scroll to the image on your computer and select it.

Unit 11.7 Desktop Publishing

Topic 3: Working with text

Topic 3 focuses on how to work with text (see ICT Syllabus p. 31 and Computer Studies Syllabus p. 23). It covers:

- Creating and formatting text boxes.
- Linking text boxes.
- Formatting fonts.
- Formatting text.
- Inserting and formatting WordArt.

Preparing text involves:

- Checking the article for spelling errors and correct use of grammar.
- Checking that the article is appropriate for the publication.
- Checking the length of the article – most publications will have guidelines about the number of words needed.
- Entering the text into a word processor.
- Scanning text using OCR if necessary.

Text should be have limited formatting applied to it before bringing it into a publication. The formatting of the text is best done within the publishing software.

Creating and formatting text boxes

Text boxes are used for stories in documents. A text box is added using the **Draw Text Box** command on the **Objects** section of the **Home** tab.

Text can be pasted into a text box. The text box can be easily resized and moved around the publication.

The number of columns can be set using the **Columns** command in the **Text Box Tools** section of the **Format** tab. The number of columns can be 1, 2 or 3 or another number specified.

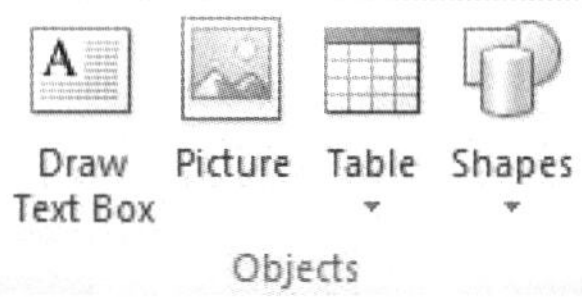

Draw Text Box

Linking text boxes

Text can continue across different pages or different sections of a document. To ensure the continuity of text, text boxes can be linked.

To do this, use the **Create Link** command on the **Linking** section of the **Format** tab (see the figure overleaf).

The **Create Link** command will produce three dots in the first text box. Moving the cursor to the second text box allows the text to flow.

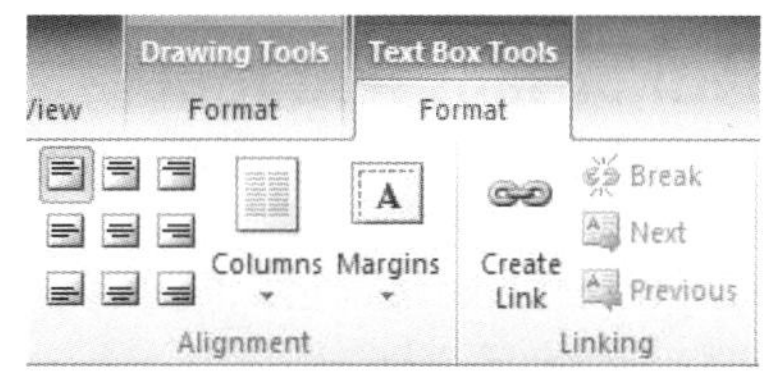

Columns in a text box

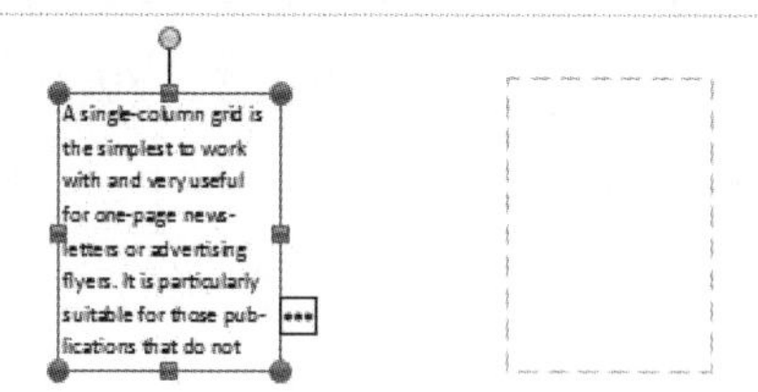

Creating a text box link

Once the link has been created, a triangle points to the linked text box.

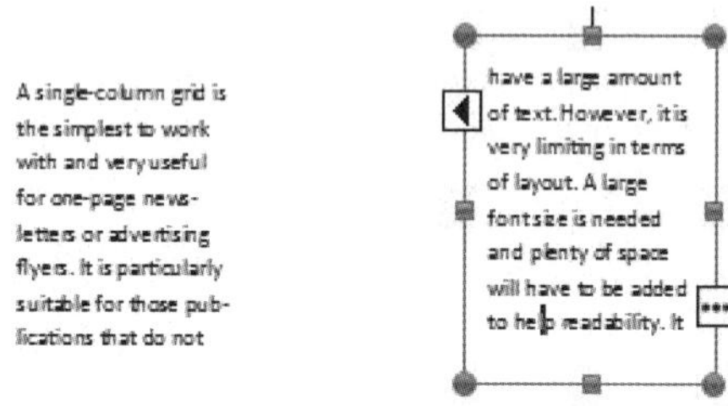

Linked text boxes

Formatting fonts and text

Once in text boxes, text can be formatted by using:

- The **Font** section of the **Home** tab.
- The **Styles** command on the **Home** tab.

Special effects can also be created using the **Effects** section of the **Text Box Tools** menu on the **Format** tab.

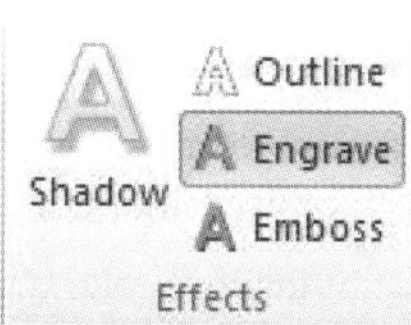

Special text effects

Part of the design process is to choose a typeface to use for the body text that is easy to read and suits the image of the publication. Some typefaces work well as headings but are difficult to read as body text.

Serif or sans serif font

Serif body typefaces have small strokes at the ends of the characters. Books have traditionally been printed using serif texts but sans serif text is often regarded as more modern.

Publisher provides built-in font schemes with each publication. This makes it easy to change the font scheme in a publication.

The font schemes can be found on the **Fonts** menu in the **Schemes** section of the **Page Design** menu.

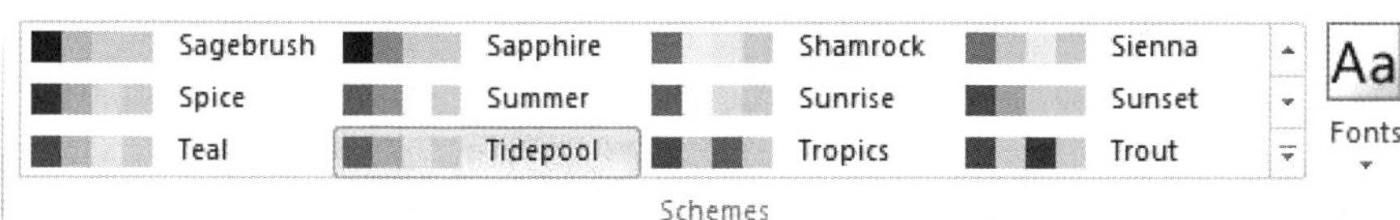

Schemes on the Page Design menu

The Schemes section also provides a range of color schemes that can be used.

Note that font properties can always be changed on the **Home** tab using the **Font** section.

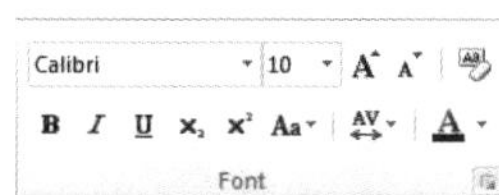

Font section of the Home tab

The **Styles** menu on the **Home** tab can also be used in the same way as it is in Microsoft Word.

The design of any publication should make the articles easy to read. There are a number of techniques to use to help make it readable.

Styles command

Headlines

Headlines attract readers to an article. Well-presented headlines draw more readers to an article. To be effective they need to stand out, so they must be larger in size than the body text, have a 'weight' that provides a contrast to the body text, and be well written to lead the reader into the article. Weight refers to the thickness of type. Using lower case letters rather than all capital letters helps to make the headlines more readable.

Consider the following when choosing a style for a headline:

- Size: make sure the headline is significantly larger than the body text.
- Typeface: a sans serif font can work well with serif body text.
- Style: bold face and italic help with emphasis.
- Colour: a different colour can provide a helpful contrast from the body text.

Subheadings

Subheadings are used to break up text in an article and to provide cues to the reader about the content of the article.

Subheadings use a larger type size than body text and, like headlines, should stand out.

Do not put subheadings near the bottom of a column or a page – allow at least four lines before a column or page break.

Pull quotes

A pull quote is a quotation from the article set in a large font; it is used to draw attention to an important part of the article. These are very useful for enticing readers into an article.

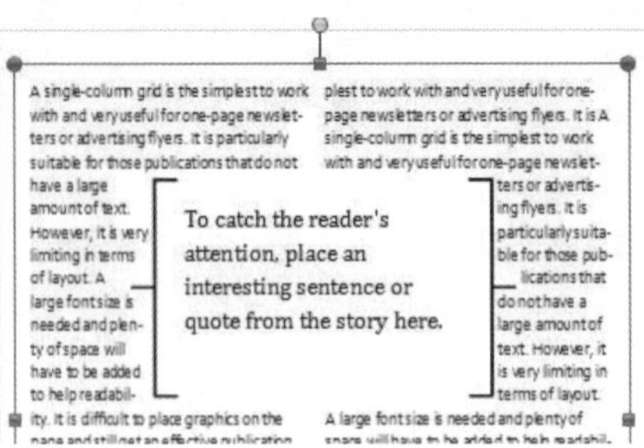

A pull quote

A pull quote can be added in Publisher using the **Page Parts** menu item on the **Building Blocks** section of the **Insert** tab.

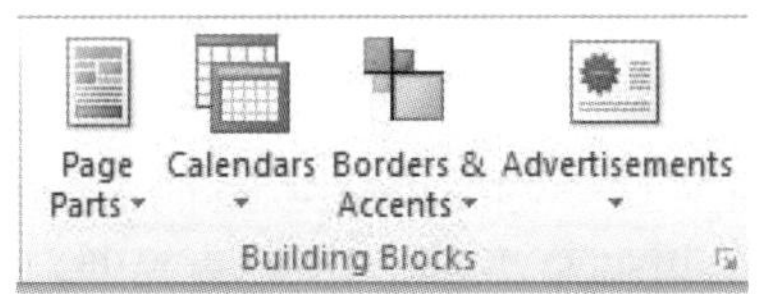

Page Parts allows the addition of a pull quote

Drop caps

A 'drop cap' is a large first letter in an article or paragraph. Its function is to provide a visual cue about the article and to force white space around paragraphs. Drop caps can be easily created in Publisher.

To create a drop cap:

- Choose the first letter in a text box.
- On the **Typography** section of the **Text Box Tools** section of the **Format** tab, select **Drop Cap**.
- The drop cap is created.

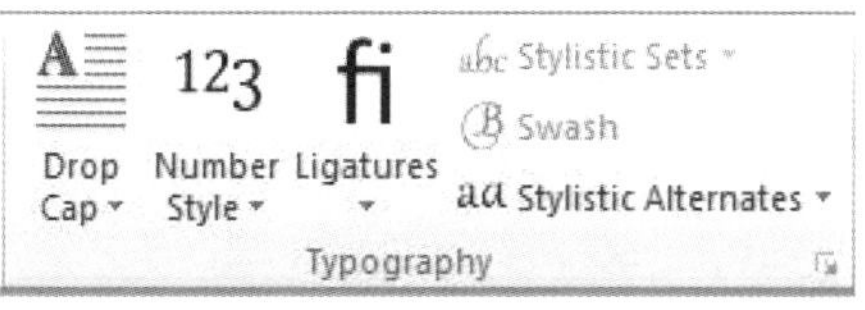

Setting a drop cap

Side bar

A side bar is another effective way of creating interest. A side bar can be added in Publisher using the **Page Parts** menu item on the **Building Blocks** section of the **Insert** tab.

See the side bar in the figure at the bottom of page 426.

Copy fitting

Paying attention to copy fitting can save a lot of time when putting together a newsletter. Copy fitting refers to ensuring that the text that has been prepared will fit into the space that has been allowed for it. Giving the correct parameters to authors also makes it easier for them to prepare the text.

Work out the word count per column inch

To work out the word count in a set piece of text, do the following:

- Create a column with the same width as the columns in the publication.
- Make the column 6 inches in height.
- Prepare a text file that is similar to the type of text in the publication.
- Place this text in the column using the same font size as in the publication.
- Highlight the text in the 6-inch column.
- Count the words that are highlighted.
- Divide the result by 6.

The result is the number of words per column inch. This can be used to advise authors of the number of words to write.

This assumes that the number of column inches for a story is allocated by the designer. For example, you may find that a column inch typically contains 50 words. Hence, a 500-word text article will need 10 column inches.

Inserting and formatting WordArt

WordArt can be used to add a fancy title to a document or publication.

The **WordArt** menu item is found on the **Text** section of the **Insert** tab.

WordArt menu item

To add a WordArt title:

- Select the **WordArt** menu item.
- Choose one of the **WordArt Transform Styles**.
- Click **OK**.

The text appears in the publication.

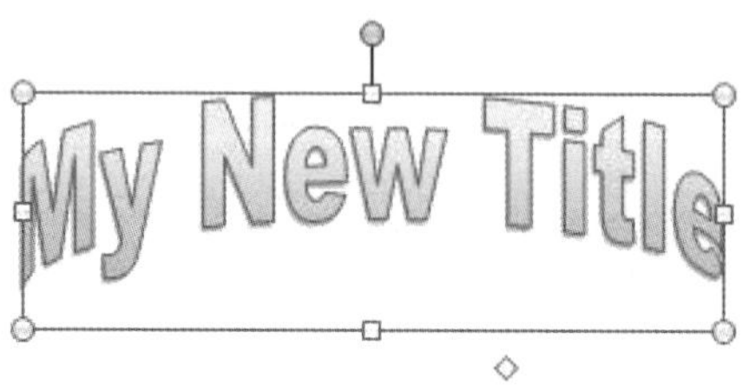

A WordArt title

When the shape is selected, it can be modified:

- The circles on the corners of the rectangles can be dragged to resize the shape.
- The squares in the middle of the lines can be used to stretch the shape either horizontally or vertically.
- The green circle at the top of the shape can be used to rotate the shape.

Also, when the shape is selected, a new tab appears: the **Format** tab with **WordArt Tools**.

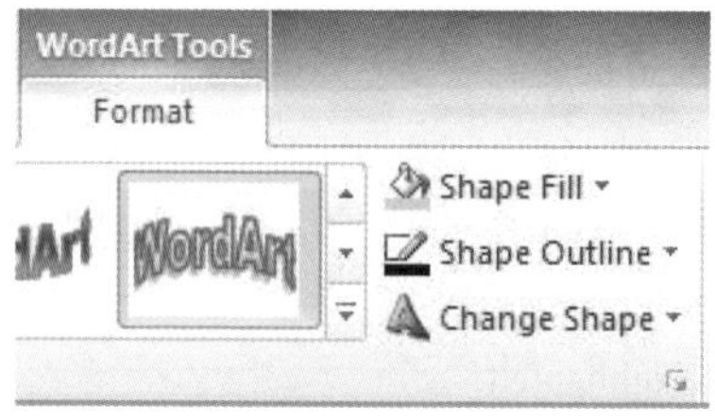

WordArt Tools

Using the menu items here allows the nature and colour of the shape to be easily altered.

Unit 11.7 Desktop Publishing
Topic 4: Drawing and working with graphic objects

Topic 4 explores drawing and working with graphic objects (see ICT Syllabus p. 31 and Computer Studies Syllabus p. 24). It covers:

- Graphic file formats.
- Using the drawing tools.
- Using peripherals to transfer data and pictures.
- Inserting clip art and pictures.
- Working with a design gallery.

Graphic images

Publisher can use a range of different graphic file formats. Each of these has its advantages and disadvantages.

There are two basic types of images: bit-mapped and vector. Bit-mapped images are made up of different-coloured pixels. The larger the number of pixels, the higher the quality of the image. Vector images use mathematical formulae to describe the image.

In general, paint programs create bit-mapped images, eg Microsoft Paint, Adobe Photoshop; while draw programs use vectors, eg Adobe Illustrator, Corel Draw.

There are many different formats for graphics files. Publisher can use many of these. Some of the most frequently used are:

- JPEG (Joint Photographic Experts Group) is a file format that uses a lot of compression. These images are widely used on the Internet. Most digital cameras can use this format.
- TIFF (Tagged Image File Format) is a bit-mapped image format. It is widely used for photographs in the printing industry. TIFF images are quite often very large.
- BMP (Bit Mapped Format) is the format used by Microsoft Windows.

Drawing tools

Publisher has a range of drawing tools that can be used in a publication. These are found on the **Illustrations** section of the **Insert** tab. The **Shapes** command gives a large range of different shapes.

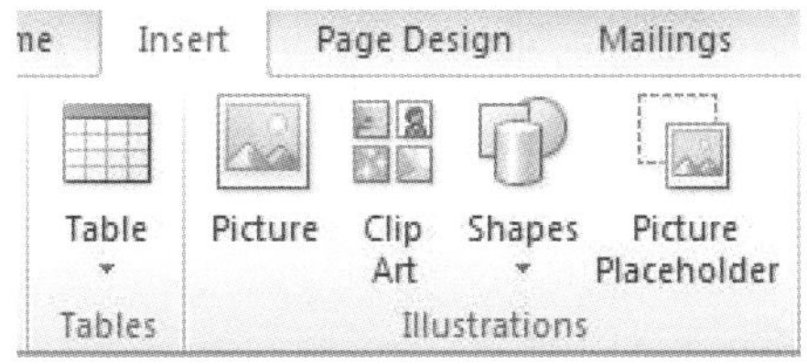

Shapes menu

Once a shape is chosen, a new tab appears: **Drawing Tools Format**. This provides a range of options that can be used with the shape in terms of style, colours, lines, shadows and three-dimensional effects.

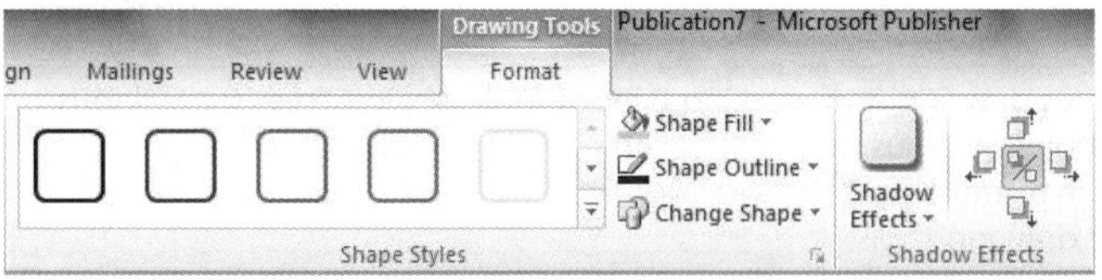

Drawing Tools menu

Once a shape is drawn, it can be modified in the same way as WordArt objects:

- The circles on the corners of the rectangles can be dragged to resize the shape.
- The squares in the middle of the lines can be used to stretch the shape either horizontally or vertically.
- The green circle at the top of the shape can be used to rotate the shape.

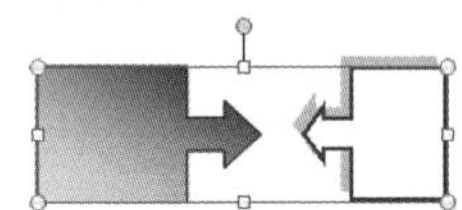

A simple shape that can be modified

Note that objects can be grouped into one object. To do this:

- Use **Shift-Click** to select each object.
- Choose **Group** from the **Arrange** section of the **Format** tab.

Using peripherals to transfer data and pictures

Using a scanner

A scanner is a device that optically scans an image or text. The scanned image is converted into a digital image that can be used in a publication.

Desktop or flat-bed scanners are found in many offices. The image to be scanned is placed on a glass window for scanning.

The scanner is usually connected to a computer via a USB cable. Software on the computer is used to control the scanner.

A flat-bed scanner

To scan a photo, you would typically do the following:

- Place the image in the scanner and start the scanning software.
- Get a preview of the image.
- Select the part of the image that is to be scanned.
- Select the format, resolution and file type.
- Click **Scan**.

The image is now scanned and saved in a folder on the computer. Exactly where it is saved will vary from one computer to another. However, in Windows it would usually be saved in a folder called **My Pictures**. The file name it is given is usually a number.

The image can now be displayed and/or edited. It can be used directly in Publisher if required.

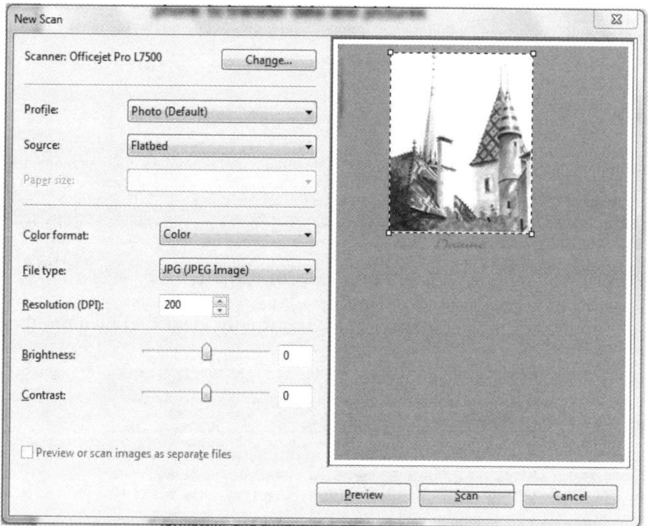

Scanning an image

A flat-bed scanner can also be used to recognise text. The scanner will use Optical Character Recognition (OCR) software to scan a document and save it as a text document.

Scanned image saved in a Pictures folder

Using a digital camera or mobile phone

Photographs from a digital camera or a mobile phone can be downloaded to a computer. The connection between the camera or phone and the computer is usually with a USB cable. The camera or phone acts as an external storage device.

When the device is connected, it is opened in the same manner as a storage device. The images can be copied to the computer for editing.

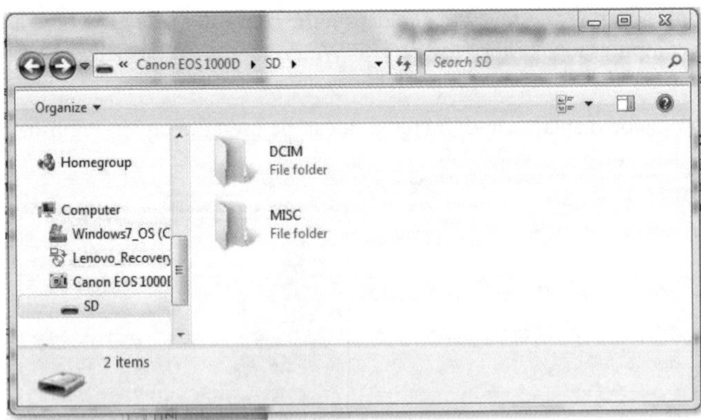

Folders on a digital camera

When the images are copied to a computer, they are usually identified by a number for each file.

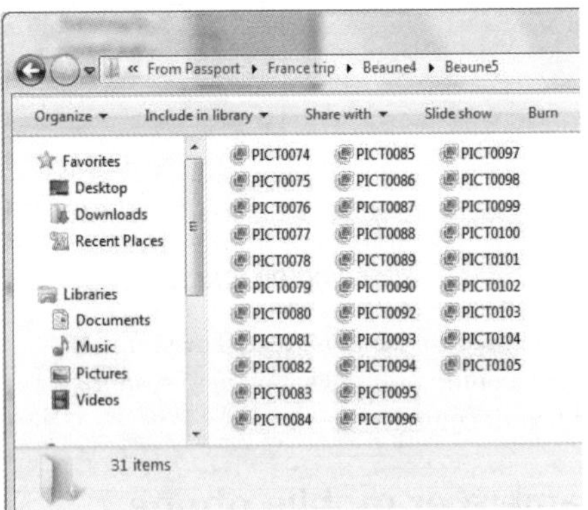

Photographs copied from a digital camera

Some cameras and mobile phones have proprietary software that can be used to manage the images. For example, the Apple iPhone works very well with Apple's iPhoto.

Formatting and enhancing graphic objects

To prepare a graphic involves:

- Choosing an image that is appropriate for the publication.
- Ensuring that the graphic is in a form that can be effectively reproduced.
- Ensuring that the graphic can be resized or cropped so that it is appropriate for the publication.
- Ensuring that the image enhances the publication – every image should tell a story.

Images can be imported into page layout programs, which recognise a range of graphics formats.

The figure below shows a graphic image that could be imported into a page layout program. This image can be resized in proportion.

Image to be imported

The image below contains the same subject matter in a different size. If required, only a part of the image can be retained. This is called 'cropping'. The retained image is different from the imported image. The figure below shows a resized (enlarged) and cropped image. Images can also be distorted for effect. The second figure below shows the image from the figure above after it has been stretched.

A cropped and resized image

A stretched image

Inserting a graphic object

A graphic image is inserted into Publisher using the **Illustrations** section of the **Insert** tab.

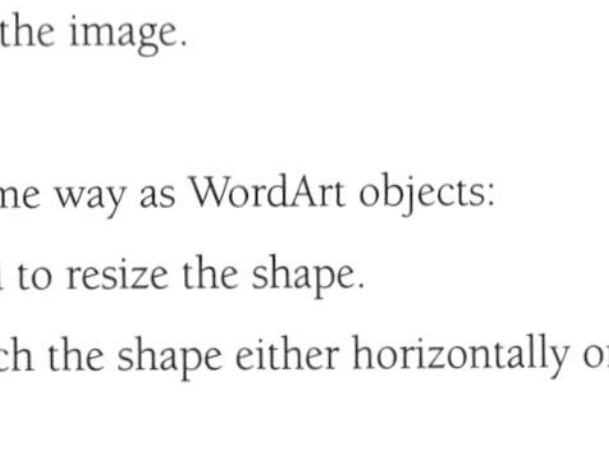

Illustrations on the Insert tab

To insert an image:

- Click **Picture.**
- Locate the image and click **OK**.

Once the image has been inserted, you are able to:

- Resize the image.
- Rotate the image.
- Crop parts of the image, ie remove any unwanted parts of the image.
- Compress the image to reduce the file size.

Once an image has been inserted, it can be modified in the same way as WordArt objects:

- The circles on the corners of the rectangles can be dragged to resize the shape.
- The squares in the middle of the lines can be used to stretch the shape either horizontally or vertically.
- The green circle at the top of the shape can be used to rotate the shape.

To crop the image, use the **Crop** command on the **Crop** section of the **Picture Tools Format** tab.

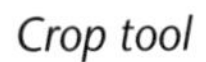

Crop tool

To crop an image:

- Select the image with the **Crop** tool.
- Move the horizontal or vertical line in the middle of the sides to reduce the image size.
- Click on the **Crop** command.

Cropping an image

Once an image is selected, it can be modified.

To modify the image, use the commands on the **Adjust** section of the **Picture Tools Format** tab.

Tools to modify an image

Scrolling over the command will give a preview of the changes that can be made, including altering:

- Brightness.
- Contrast.
- Colour.

Note that the Compress Pictures command will reduce the physical size that the images use in the file.

Inserting clip art

Clip art refers to licence-free graphics. Microsoft supplies a range of clip art with Microsoft Office.

Clip art is inserted into Publisher using the **Illustrations** section of the **Insert** tab.

To insert a clip art image:

- Choose **Clip Art** on the **Illustrations** section of the **Insert** tab.
- Browse or search the clip art in the window on the right of the screen.

Note that clip art images can be modified in the same manner as the other images referred to above.

Clip art can be in a range of formats, eg illustrations, photographs, sound or video.

Choosing a clip art image

Design Gallery

The **Design Gallery** provides a range of ready-made visual elements that can be inserted into a publication. The colour schemes used can also help to give a publication a consistent look and feel.

The Design Gallery is accessed on the **Building Blocks** section of the **Insert** tab. The small arrow at the bottom right of the section needs to be clicked.

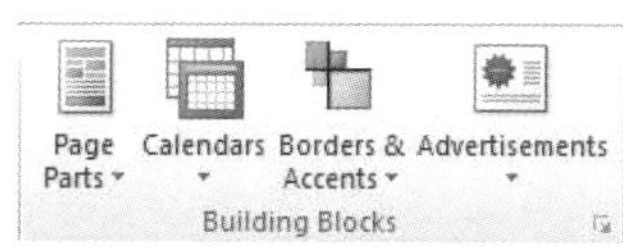

Accessing the Design Gallery

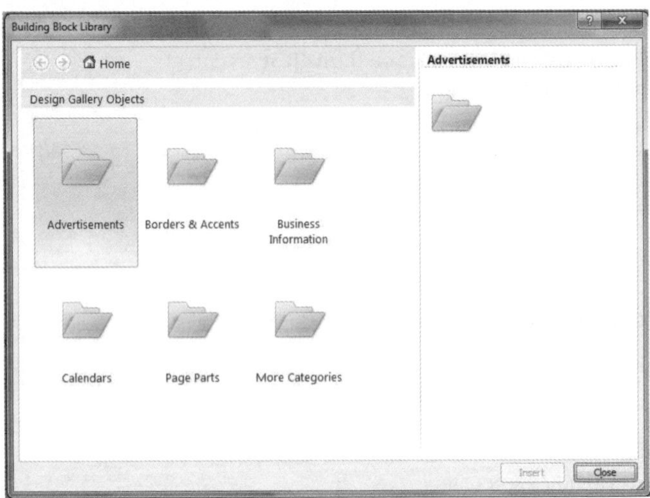

Design Gallery Objects

For example, opening the Calendars folder allows a calendar to be inserted into the document. The calendar is an object that can be moved, resized or rotated in the same manner as other images.

October 2011						
Mon	**Tue**	**Wed**	**Thu**	**Fri**	**Sat**	**Sun**
					1	*2*
3	*4*	*5*	*6*	*7*	*8*	*9*
10	*11*	*12*	*13*	*14*	*15*	*16*
17	*18*	*19*	*20*	*21*	*22*	*23*
24	*25*	*26*	*27*	*28*	*29*	*30*
31						

A calendar inserted from the Design Gallery Objects

Unit 11.7 Desktop Publishing
Topic 5: Working with tables

Topic 5 explores working with tables (see ICT Syllabus p. 31 and Computer Studies Syllabus p. 24). It covers:

- Working with tables.
- Formatting tables.

Working with tables

A table can be inserted into a Publisher document using the **Table** command on the **Tables** section of the **Insert** tab.

As soon as a table is inserted into Publisher, the **Table Tools** tab becomes available. This tab contains two tabs: **Design** and **Layout**.

Once a table is inserted into Publisher, it is treated in the same manner as other graphic objects and can be rotated, moved and resized with ease.

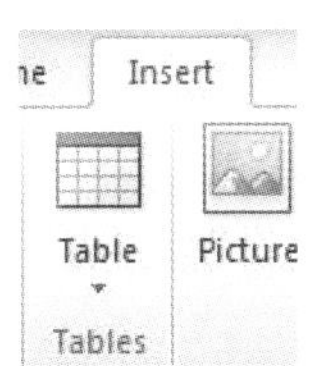

Tables command

Lake	Province	Size (ha)
Murray	Western	64,700
Chambri	ESP	21,600
Wisdom	Madang	8,592
Khanda-Szaga	Western	7,840
Kutubu	SHP	4,924
Dakataua	WNB	4,920
Yonki	EHP	2,120
Aesake Lagoon	Western	2,120
Sirinumu	Central	4,100
Bossett	Western	1,680

A table inserted into Publisher

Formatting tables

The **Table Formats** section of the **Table Tools Design** tab can be used to apply pre-set formats to a table.

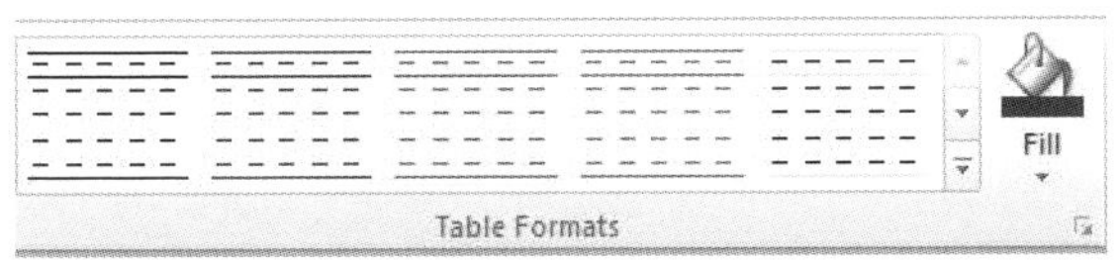

Table formats in Publisher

With the table selected, moving the cursor over the various table formats gives a preview of the various formats.

Clicking on one of the formats applies that format to the table.

- The **Borders** section of the same tab allows you to modify the borders of the table.
- The **Arrange** group allows you to set text wrapping around the table and you can also rotate the table.
- The **Table Tools Layout** tab contains a range of tools that allow you to manage the table.
- The **Rows & Columns** section of the tab makes it easy to add or delete rows and columns.

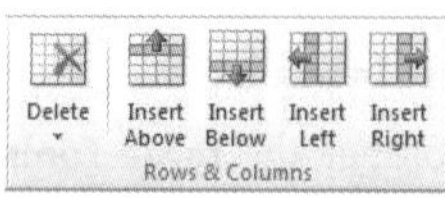

Managing rows and columns

Unit 11.7 Desktop Publishing

Topic 6: Sending and printing a publication

Topic 6 explains how to send and print a publication (see ICT Syllabus p. 31 and Computer Studies Syllabus p. 24). It covers:

- Sending the publication.
- Previewing and printing the publication.

Sending the publication

Publisher provides a range of options for sending a publication. These are available on the **File** menu by selecting **Save & Send**.

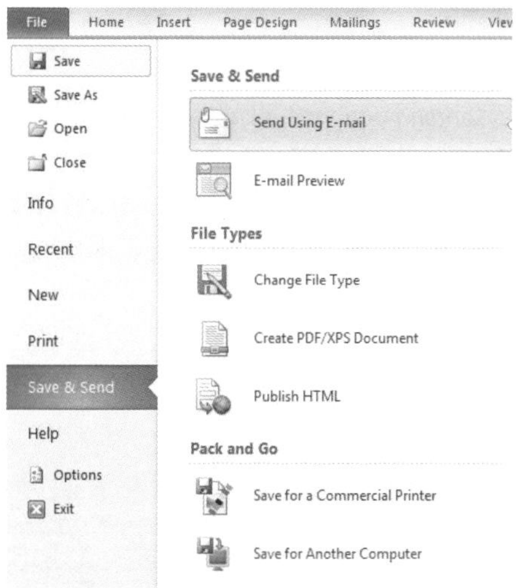

Options to save and send a publication

Note that Publisher provides a range of options for sending a publication:

- Within an email.
- As an attachment with an email.
- As a PDF document.
- As an XPS file that can be viewed online.

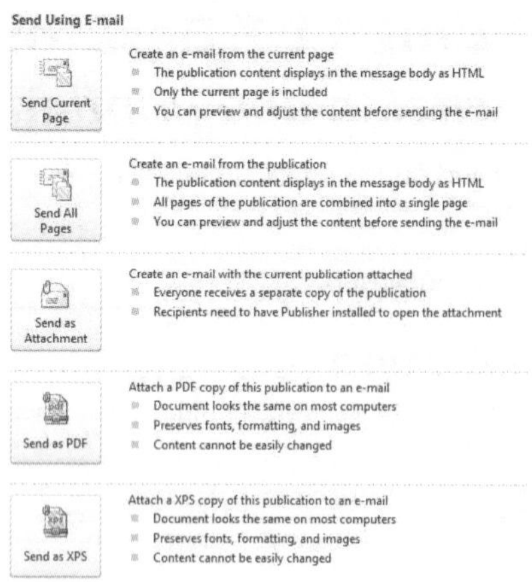

Sending options for Publisher document

Previewing and printing the publication

A document can be printed directly from Publisher. This is done using the **Print** command on the **File** menu.

There is a range of print options that need to be selected. Some of these are used when sending the document to a specialist printer.

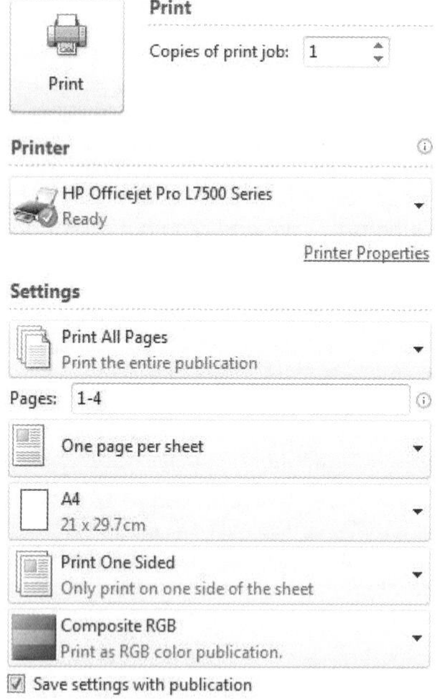

Print options in Publisher

When the **Print** menu item is selected, a preview of the publication shows in the window on the right. Note that there is an option that enables multiple sheets to be displayed and this allows thumbnails to be viewed.

Viewing thumbnails in Print Preview in Publisher

Unit 11.7 Activity 6A: Publishing project

You are involved in a project to create a school newspaper that will have two editions per term: one in the middle of the term and one at the end of term.

Many tasks would need to be arranged, organised and managed to enable deadlines to be met and the newspaper to meet its goals. The project could be organised under the following:

- Specifications
- Investigation
- Drafts
- Producing
- Evaluation or testing

You will need to:

1. Brainstorm the publication
2. Use concept diagrams to determine key areas of content and nature of publication that may include:
   - **a.** Item by Principal
   - **b.** Whole-school news
   - **c.** News about the school and the community
   - **d.** Half page for each year level
   - **e.** Coming events
   - **f.** Sports news
3. You will need to consider the layout and design
   - **a.** Sketch of layout for the basic design
   - **b.** Margins
   - **c.** Columns
   - **d.** Balance of text and images
   - **e.** Template analysis
   - **f.** Template design and selection
   - **g.** Grid selection
   - **h.** Information to be contained in headers and footers
   - **i.** Headings and size of headings
   - **j.** Font selection for headings and body text
   - **k.** Development of styles for text and images
   - **l.** Banners and logos design

4. Production will require:

a. Software and hardware selection

b. Process of file naming, file location, storage and production of product

c. Editorial decisions

d. Subediting

e. Page proofs

f. Final approval

g. Printing

h. Distribution

Answers

Please note that some exercises do not have answers as they are practical in nature.

Unit 11.1 Computer Fundamentals

Topic 1: Information processing cycle

Unit 11.1 Activity 1A: The water cycle (page 4)

Answer on diagram.

Unit 11.1 Activity 1B: Making a cup of hot chocolate (page 4)

1. Source of hot water eg electric kettle, cup, spoon, ingredients (chocolate powder, milk, sugar).

2.
- **i.** Check you have the necessary tools and ingredients.
- **ii.** Bring some water to the boil.
- **iii.** Put some hot chocolate powder in the cup.
- **iv.** Add hot water to the cup.
- **v.** Stir the mixture.
- **vi.** Add milk and sugar to taste.
- **vii.** Stir the mixture.
- **viii.** The mixture should be ready to drink.

Unit 11.1 Activity 1C: Investigation into an airline information system (page 5)

1. Passenger would need to nominate the date, time, origin, destination, seat class, and fare type. This would lead to payment details to process the reservation and book the seat.

2.
- **1.** Airline would have record. Passenger would input name and verify address.
- **2.** Airline could have on file from previous transaction, Passenger could verify.
- **3.** Airline flights have destinations. Passenger would have to inform the airline which flight they want to take.
- **4.** Airline would have frequent flyer number and details. Passenger may need to enter the frequent flyer number to access this information.
- **5.** Status points, as above.
- **6.** Airline may have recorded a profile of the passenger and special requirements. Passenger may need to order a vegetarian meal.
- **7.** Number of items of baggage, unique to a particular flight, entered by airline upon receipt of passenger's bags.
- **8.** Payment details would be unique for a particular flight; could be the same as previous flights or different.
- **9.** Airline may record the gender of a passenger; may be entered by passenger if an online booking is made for a flight.
- **10.** Airline may keep records of flights taken by a passenger. Not entered by the passenger.
- **11.** Airline would record that a passenger has checked in for a flight, if a boarding pass has been issued, and if the passenger has boarded the flight.
- **12.** The seat number on some systems could be selected by the passenger; on others it may be allocated by the airline or selected at random upon boarding by the passenger.

3. Answer from research.

   1. Paper tickets, e-tickets. Some airlines are moving to tickets stored on smartphones.
   2. Paper boarding pass. Can be printed from self-service kiosk as well as check-in desk.
   3. Baggage check for checked in luggage. Printed on receipt of luggage; the check is given to the passenger as a record.
   4. Receipt for payment. Printed as part of the e-ticket, payment verification of credit card or other payment method.
   5. Issue of ticket is confirmation of flight; airlines reserve the right to alter schedules and reschedule passengers if required.

Topic 4: Classification of computers

Unit 11.1 Activity 4A: Notebook computer or netbook computer? (page 16)

1. Netbooks are normally distinguished from a laptop computer by:

   a. Lower cost.
   b. Smaller size and lower weight.
   c. Smaller screen size.
   d. Less hard disk capacity.
   e. Having a modified operating system that is less featured.
   f. A reduction in connection points.
   g. and alternatives for connection methods.
   h. A different configuration is not usually a factor to alter manufacturer's warranty conditions.

2. Preference to own would depend on individual preferences, purpose and use of the computer. For example, a person who does a lot of travelling could favour a netbook computer due to its lighter weight.

Unit 11.1 Activity 4B: Apple iPad (page 17)

1. The iPad is a very personal portable device. Features: access to the world wide web and email; lightweight; location aware; clear screen; simple and intuitive to operate (use of gestures, virtual keyboard); apps can be installed; syncs to other devices through Bluetooth; automatic saving of documents created; inbuilt camera; backup to a normal computer through iTunes; use of flash memory means the device will start immediately.

2. Disadvantages: learning a new operating system; no USB connection; adapting to a virtual keyboard.

3. Airprint is built into the operating system; it allows a document to be printed from the iPad over wireless.

Unit 11.1 Activity 4C: Advantages and disadvantages of e-books (page 17)

1. Lower costs of production (no paper and printing cost). Distribution costs much lower. Overall prices for e-books are lower than printed books. There is no such thing as a print run or unsold copies for an electronic book.

2. E-books require fewer physical resources for production, therefore are better for the environment.

3. An e-book allows electronic linking within the book and to other sources. The book form is extended to a new form.

4. New editions can be created from the digital materials. The new editions can be created at will and as often as required.

5. The text in an e-book can be viewed on a device at different resolutions and is generally not fixed to a particular physical size.
6. E-books are portable, as are printed books; however, e-books are not heavy as printed paper products such as books are. An e-book reader can hold a vast quantity of information in e-book format.
7. That e-book readers have illumination is a significant advantage.
8. E-book formats are varied and this has implications for transferring a book from one device to another. It may be that there will be a number of formats competing in the marketplace.
9. E-books require a reader that has power, battery and/or recharge. Most e-book readers have 'flash' memory and can be switched off and on instantly with a quick 'standby' mode.
10. The smaller screen size is an advantage in some cases, eg public transport, aircraft.
11. E-books will have a 'default' or 'given' font size, however a digital device such as an e-book reader allows the reader to modify through 'zoom in' and 'zoom out' and generate a viewing size that suits.
12. Paper is a very old technology. It is a valuable technology and as it is physical it has advantages over e-books: we can easily get a feel from a physical book of its size and how big it is; by flipping through the pages we get a sense of its linear form. In some cases the physical book is superior to the e-book.

Topic 5: Input devices

Unit 11.1 Activity 5A: Use and care of keyboards (page 20)

1. Keyboard has: keys a–z, with shift key for A–Z, caps lock for continuous A–Z; numeric keys 0–9; modifier keys, eg Alt, command, option, control, windows; a variety of symbols (sometimes separate keys, sometimes the 'shift' of the number keys); special purpose keys F1 to F12 that perform various hardware settings, eg screen display brightness; arrow keys, used to navigate around documents; tab key, for setting text, moving around applications such as spreadsheets and databases. The configuration of a keyboard could be set by the settings on a computer to alter from the default settings, although most users probably do not.
2. Touch-typing means operating the keyboard without looking at the keys. It means a user can concentrate on the content and operation of the software rather than a split task of finding keys to effect the task and then using them.
3. Some are standard across operating systems and software. The functions are similar, the keys are in similar positions on the keyboard, just the names of the keys used are different. For example, a modifier key and the letter 'C' is copy; with letter 'P' it is paste. Some keyboards have a numeric keyboard, adjacent to the normal keyboard, for heavy numeric input.
4. Keyboards can be abused and ill treated by spilling liquids on them or eating while using, which makes it easy for foreign matter to get under the keys. Dirty and dusty operating environments can over time make keyboards unusable.
5. QWERTY refers to the first six letter keys on the top row of alphabetic keys. The keys on a QWERTY keyboard were so arranged on a manual typewriter. When keys were depressed on a keyboard to strike the paper wrapped around the platen (roller) the QWERTY arrangement minimised the instances of the keys hitting each other and jamming.
6. Common keyboard shortcuts are cut, copy and paste, file open, save, save as and print.

Unit 11.1 Activity 5B: Using a scanner (page 24)

1. Advantages: converts paper document into digital document; relatively quick process; as a computer file, can be easily transferred and communicated; document can be saved in a variety of formats.

Disadvantages: variety of formats could require a variety of settings to be explored; quality of scan depends on the quality of the original; quality of text recognition can vary considerably, perhaps extra software required to enable this.

2.
- **a.** Turn on the computer.
- **b.** Check that the scanner is turned on.
- **c.** Check that the glass on the scanner is clean.
- **d.** Open the scanning software on the computer.
- **e.** Adjust the scanner settings.
- **f.** Preview the image to be scanned using the scanning software.
- **g.** Orientate the image on the scanner.
- **h.** Crop the scanned image using image-editing software.
- **i.** Save the scanned image to the hard disk (as a TIFF image).
- **j.** Resize the image if required.
- **k.** Save the image in a final format, eg screen or print.
- **l.** Name the file of the scan.
- **m.** Print the scanned image if required.

Unit 11.1 Activity 5C: Capturing information (page 27)

1. A mouse is a pointing device. It is represented on screen as a cursor, pointer or spinning ball depending on the context: it appears as a cursor when entering data in a document, a pointer when selecting a menu item, and a spinning ball while a process is taking place. A mouse may have buttons that enable more powerful functions such as saving and copying files.

2. Scanning converts the information on a piece of paper into a digital file that can be stored on a computer.

3. Scanning text can, with appropriate computer software, perform OCR (Optical Character Recognition), where the characters on the paper can become editable text. The success of OCR depends on the quality of the text being scanned and the sophistication of the software to perform the OCR.

4. Digital cameras store an image as a digital file in a format that a computer recognises.

5. A digital camera has software to enable a file to be transferred from the camera to the computer; the computer and camera recognise each other and the transfer can be facilitated.

6. A computer keyboard is generally connected to a computer by a USB connection. On a netbook or laptop it is part of the computer. Tablet devices such as iPads have a virtual keyboard.

7. A modem enables a fixed phone line to be used for a network connection. It converts the analog signal of a phone line to a digital signal that is recognised by a computer.

8. A microphone records voice and sound. The recording can be edited in a variety of ways.

9. A CD or DVD with appropriate software can be transferred to a computer. The process where the formats on the CD or DVD are translated into files on a computer is termed 'ripping'.

10. Music software on a computer can sometimes 'import' the file from the portable music player to the computer.

Unit 11.1 Activity 5D: Using a digital camera (page 29)

1. Advantages: digital cameras are compact and portable; images, once captured, can be viewed immediately, retained or discarded; images are stored on memory cards and they can be transferred readily; a variety of image settings can be used on a digital camera; some cameras allow editing of the image. Disadvantages: Images can be easily erased and if this happens they are not able to be retrieved.
2. Refer to a manual for a camera of your choice from the Internet. The instructions will differ according to the features of the camera and its technical specifications.

Unit 11.1 Activity 5E: Connecting devices (page 33)

1. For most of the devices the connection will be a USB connection to the computer. The connector to the peripheral device could be a 'B' connector or 'Mini' connector. Some older devices may have other forms of connection. The software will include a 'driver' so that the operating system can recognise the peripheral device. It will also include some application software that will provide features to make the peripheral device perform the tasks for which it is designed. Sometimes the operating system will also have basic software that may support a device.
    1. Scanner: USB connection; manufacturer-provided software (operating system driver and application software).
    2. Graphics tablet: USB connection; manufacturer-provided software (operating system driver and application software).
    3. Keyboard: USB or wireless connection; operating system driver as the keyboard is part of a computer. Third party keyboards have their own specific drivers.
    4. Light pen: USB connection; manufacturer software.
    5. Printer: USB connection; manufacturer software.
    6. Monitor: USB connection; manufacturer software.
    7. Sound input: 1/8" mini jack; operating system software.
    8. Modem: USB connection; manufacturer software.
    9. Web camera: USB connection; manufacturer software.
    10. Digital video camera: USB connection; manufacturer software.
2. Answers from research.

Topic 7: Storage devices

Unit 11.1 Activity 7A: Binary–decimal conversion (page 44)

1. a. 101101
   b. 1000011
   c. 1101101
   d. 11011101
   e. 1000110111
2. a. 13
   b. 11
   c. 178
   d. 187
   e. 887

Unit 11.1 Activity 7B: Storage (page 54)

1. Compact disk: .cda (CD Audio) file. The .cda file is a shortcut to the audio data. A CD file is 'write once, read many'. Generally all CD players can play CD discs. You need a CD player to read and play the files. CDs are being replaced by digital files. Although a CD holds around 700MB of data, a large music collection would need a many discs.
iBook (example of a computer): When a music file format from a CD is transferred to a computer it becomes a .wav (Windows computer) or .aiff (Apple computer) file. It requires a software player to play the file. There is a wide variety of digital file formats depending on the levels of compression and quality required. Hard drives are fragile.
Portable music player: MP3 is the main format for music. Devices are flash memory and they do not have moving parts. Device is small and easily portable. Relatively limited storage capacity when compared with a hard drive. Low battery requirements. Does not have network connection and requires computer to manage the files and update the listings.
Smart phone: The smart phone is essentially the same as a portable music player for music files saved in MP3 format. Files can be downloaded from the Internet as well as transferred from a computer. Limited storage capacity.
Cloud: Relatively new technology. A variety of options for a user: some are by subscription, while others are free, or free to a certain amount of storage. With a network there is access to the files. The Cloud provider may perhaps change the terms and conditions of the storage. It should be considered whether the Cloud provider will remain in business or withdraw the service.

2. Answers related to capacity should refer to current examples or examples known to the student. Changes in technology mean that the type, capacity and use of various storage devices are changing.

1. ROM: Read only memory. Instructions are permanently written to silicon chip and accessed by computer during 'boot up' to enable the computer to operate.
2. RAM: Random access memory. Capacity is determined by manufacturer; there is usually an option to extend the minimum provided to an upper limit (intensive computer users usually require more than the minimum). Temporary storage location on a computer used to store unsaved documents and parts of application software currently being accessed by the operator.
3. Floppy disk: storage media requiring floppy disk drive, 1.44MB capacity. Only used in very old computers.
4. USB flash memory: becoming a very low cost portable storage option. Small and easy to lose. Can pose security risks given the ease with which the data can be copied.
5. Smart cards: very common for photographic and video cameras Some computers have smart card slots to enable easy transfer; otherwise transfer occurs by cable.
6. Compact disk: 700MB capacity. Cheap and inexpensive storage. Becoming redundant. For large storage needs it is inadequate given the number of disks and storage administration.
7. DVD disk: 4.7GB capacity. Cheap and inexpensive storage, extensively used for video.
8. BluRay disk: a single layer 25GB, dual layer 50GB capacity. A variety of formats. No standard format or standard adoption in computers.
9. Laser disk: not being developed as a technology.

10. Internal hard drive: still the key storage device for a desktop computer. A variety of options and storage sizes; usually size is optioned at time of purchase. Relatively cheap storage. Fragile and needs to be treated with care.
11. External hard drive: steadily falling in cost while capacity is increasing. Durability improving.
12. Raid system: For larger-scale commercial enterprises the raid system allows speed and capacity.
13. Magnetic tape: still used in large organisations although mainly for backup given the cheap cost of the media.
14. 'The Cloud': online storage. Relatively new and developing storage option. Effectively 'outsourcing' storage to external provider. Variety of payment and storage capacity options. Access to network required.

Topic 8: System box

Unit 11.1 Activity 8A: The active desktop (page 63)

Note that the image may vary from the computer you are using. The answers are indicative of what would normally occur, particularly with the icons that do not represent devices.

1. Back: go back to the screen just visited.
2. Forward: alternate to other screen just visited.
3. Up: to the next folder in the hierarchy.
4. Open: the currently selected folder (if any).
5. Options for viewing files: include icons, list and tiles.
6. Minimises currently active window.
7. Currently active window will enlarge to full screen.
8. Closes the currently active window.
9. Shows the current folder/file location according to directory path.
10. Go: will search for text (eg a filename) on the computer.
11. Drives that are currently seen by the computer.

Unit 11.1 Activity 8B: Computer drives (page 64)

Drives would normally be:

A: Floppy disk drive.

B: Second floppy disk drive if present.

C: Hard drive; first hard drive if partition is present.

D–Z: Other disk partition.

E: Device with removable storage, eg USB flash drive

H: Home directory on a network server.

Unit 11.1 Activity 8C: File handling with Windows (page 67)

1. In Windows Explorer, select the USB flash drive, right-click to format.
2. In Windows Explorer, on the hard drive, open the folder in which the document resides, click the file to select, right click and nominate the USB drive to send the file to.
3. In Windows Explorer, right-click to explore the USB drive, select the file, right-click and nominate a drive or location on the hard drive to send it to.

4. In Windows Explorer, locate the file, click on the filename to highlight, type a new filename (the first press on the keyboard will delete the old filename).
5. In Windows Explorer, locate the file, click on the file to highlight, right-click and copy, then click in the appropriate destination, right-click and paste.
6. In Windows Explorer, click in the folder, right click, New > Folder.
7. In Windows Explorer, click on the folder to select, hold down the mouse button and drag to the new location.
8. In Windows Explorer, click on the file to select, right-click and select 'Delete'.
9. In Windows Explorer, click on the file to select, right-click and select 'Create shortcut'.
10. In Windows Explorer, right-click on the file, select 'Properties'; the 'Properties' window will open with details about the file.

Unit 11.1 Activity 8D: Document files (page 69)

Note: a variety of applications can create certain file formats. Filename and application (left to right, top to bottom):

File/Folder	Application(s)
AFC58.zip	WinZip, compressed files in one folder
Book1.xls	Microsoft Excel
conceptmap	Inspiration (determined by icon)
DSC_5018.jpg	JPEG image file, imported from camera, Photoshop
myFirstmov	Movie file, Apple Quicktime among others
Pre.ppt	Microsoft PowerPoint
scene1.avi	Audio and video file, Windows Movie Maker
ResumeDecem	Microsoft Word
schola.rtf	Text file – rich text format, Wordpad, Microsoft Word among others
states.psd	Photoshop format
untitled.psd	Photoshop format
WBN-Jan-O	Adobe Reader, .pdf format
Untitled-1.fla	Adobe Flash (authoring file)
index.htm	Web page; many applications can publish a document as .htm
project Folder	Microsoft Visual Studio is an example of an application that saves files relevant to a 'project' in a folder

Unit 11.1 Activity 8E: Using a computer (page 71)

1. 'Start' menu > Control Panel > 'Date and Time'.
2. 'Start' menu > Control Panel > 'Keyboard'.
3. 'Start' menu > Computer > right-click on disk icon, select 'Format'.
4. 'Start' menu > Control Panel > 'Backup and Restore', select the network disk or external hard drive.

5. 'Start' menu > Control Panel > 'Window Defender'. It is likely that your computer may have third party virus protection installed and its settings should be accessed to see if they are appropriate.
6. Ordinarily if a new printer is being connected the operating system will determine if it has the appropriate drivers. A printer manual will have instructions about where to obtain software if it is not accompanying the printer.
7. 'Start' menu > Control Panel > 'Display'.
8. 'Start' menu > 'Search programs and files': search box will show adjacent to the 'Start menu' icon, enter the name of the file and press return.
9. 'Start' menu > Control Panel > 'Fonts'.
10. 'Start' menu > Control Panel > 'Personalization' > 'Screen Saver'.
11. 'Start' menu > Control Panel > 'Sounds' > 'Sounds'.
12. 'Start' menu > Computer. Brings up the Windows Explorer window, enabling viewing of folders and files.
13. In Windows Explorer, right-click to explore the USB drive, select the file, right-click and nominate a drive or location on the hard drive to send it to.
14. 'Start' menu > Control Panel > Devices and Printers > 'Add a device'.
15. 'Start' menu > 'All Programs', then select the program name from the list.
16. In the Windows Explorer window, click on the '?' icon in the top right of the window.
17. 'Start' menu > Control Panel > 'Programs and Features'. Select the program from a list and then select 'Uninstall'.
18. 'Start' menu > Control Panel > 'Power Options'.
19. In Windows Explorer, find the file, click to select, then right-click and select 'Properties'.
20. In Windows Explorer, locate the file, click on the filename to highlight, type a new filename (the first press on the keyboard will delete the old filename).

Unit 11.1 Activity 8F: Components of information systems (page 72)

Handheld computer: see page 16.
Cloud: this is the symbol of a cloud, where computing services are delivered over the Internet.
Desktop PC: see page 14.
IP phone: see page 39.
Modem: see page 344.
Workstation: see page 14.
Server: a computer that is part of a network to host a service for the network users, eg mail server for email.
Switch: network hardware to connect parts of a network. It receives messages from a connected device and then sends the message to the device it is intended for. (A hub sends messages to all devices on a network.)
Smartphone: a phone (computer) with multi functions, network access, medial player, GPS device.
Hub: connects devices on a network, meaning they can work as a single network.
Scanner: see page 24.
Laser printer: see page 37.
Wireless router: wireless device used by networks to transfer data packets.
ADSL modem: see page 345.
Bus: simple network architecture, all network computers share the one communication cable.
Satellite dish: see page 346.
Radio tower: physical structure to receive and transmit radio waves.
Data: see page 2.

Firewall: hardware or software to monitor and control incoming and outgoing traffic between one network and all other networks.
Compact disk: see page 48.
Satellite: see page 346.
Tape: see page 53.
Raid drive: see page 52.
Router: device used by networks to transfer data packets.

Unit 11.1 Activity 8G: File extensions (page 73)

The names of file extension on a computer can be visible or hidden depending on the computer setup and user preference. It is quite common for them not to be shown. A variety of programs can save files in a variety of formats using 'save as' .exe, Computer Programs on a windows computer have an .exe extension

Extension	Application software	Description of the application
.xls	Microsoft Excel Spreadsheet	can also be .xlsx
.ppt	Microsoft Powerpoint	can also be .pptx
.txt	Notepad	a simple text editor
.pdf	Adobe Portable document format	preserves the characteristics of a print version of a document for viewing on screen
.isf	Inspiration	Concept and mind mapping software
.cws	Claris Works	template file
.rtf	rich text format	Microsoft file format, various Microsoft software
.avi	audio video interleave file	a variety of video software can create, view, save and convert .avi files
mov	audio video file format	mostly associated with 'Quicktime' by Apple
.bmp	Windows bitmap graphics file format	a variety of software can save as a .bmp file
.pub	Microsoft Publisher	desktop publishing
.wmv	Windows media file	can be played by Windows Media Player and other applications
.wav	Waveform Audio File format	Windows file format for storing audio. A variety of applications can create, edit, save and play .wav files
.jpg, also .jpeg	file format for digital photographic images	provides a trade off between level of compression and quality of the image. Variety of applications can save in 'jpg' format.

Unit 11.2 Word Processing

Topic 2: Creating and saving a new document

Unit 11.2 Activity 2A: Writing with a word processor (page 79)

Practical exercise.

Unit 11.2 Activity 2B: Saving a document (page 81)

1. Until a document is saved its contents are saved only in RAM (Random Access Memory). In the event of a power off or computer crash the contents will be lost. Saving a file means the contents will be stored on disk in the nominated location. Some other important stages could include:
   - **a.** File > New: starting point for the creation of a new document.
   - **b.** File > Save as: to save a document as a different file, perhaps to preserve the contents of the original and use it to make modifications.
   - **c.** Running the spelling and grammar check to detect errors.
   - **d.** Reading the document on screen to check for meaning.
   - **e.** Printing the final document (either as hard or soft copy) to send to another party, perhaps for review or as final part of document process.

2. File > Options > Save, click 'Auto Recover' box and set a time period.

Topic 3: Formatting documents

Unit 11.2 Activity 3A: Differences in fonts (page 86)

Practical exercise.

Unit 11.2 Activity 3B: Formatting text (page 87)

Practical exercise.

Unit 11.2 Activity 3C: Text alignment (page 89)

Answer in text on page 89.

Unit 11.2 Activity 3D: Formatting a document (page 96)

1. A header is space at the top of each page that can consist of a line or number of lines. The header space could be blank or the author could include information relevant to the document as a whole, such as document name, date, or page number. In Microsoft Word:
   - **a.** Insert tab > Header or Footer.
   - **b.** Header appears in View > Print Layout; double-click at the top of the page where the header is; a dotted line will show the Header region.
   - **c.** Insert tab > Page Number. A variety of number formats can be selected.
   - **d.** A header for an assignment could contain the name of the assignment, the due date, page number, the person to receive the assignment, name of the author, and class.

2. Insert the date symbol. The date will show the current date according to the computer. The document with appropriate header and footer information could be saved as a template for use later.

3. A word processor inserts page breaks automatically according to the amount of content. A manual page break can modify this automatic process and be inserted as desired.

4. Answer will depend on each individual case. Margins could be 3.54 cm for top, right, bottom, left. Paper size could be A4, perhaps US letter. Font could be Times New Roman, 12 points.
5. Page set-up will enable the US Letter to be selected, as well as a variety of other paper sizes.
6. Margins could be smaller, say 2 cm. The international paper size is A4. Font and font size can be individual preference.

Topic 4: Editing text

Unit 11.2 Activity 4A: Cut, copy and paste (page 101)

1. The left and right margin size will determine when the line wraps to the next line.
2. Depending on the version the extension will be .doc or .docx.
3. Practical exercise.
4. Practical exercise.
5. There are numerous options to select text in Microsoft Word. Often a user will have a preference based on their experience and what they find easiest and are used to. The 'Help' file should be consulted and there will be alternatives listed. The steps listed below are just one way of making the selection:
   a. Place the cursor next to the character and drag the mouse though the character.
   b. Double-click anywhere in the word
   c. Put the cursor to the left of the line, then click when it changes to a right-pointing arrow.
   d. Triple-click anywhere in a paragraph
   e. Place the cursor to the left of any text, then triple-click when it changes to a right-pointing arrow.
6. 'Cut' will remove the selection from its current position, 'Paste' will insert the selection at the new point. 'Copy' will make another copy of the selection and leave the current selection where it is. 'Paste' will insert the duplication of the selection at the new position.
7. Both documents should have the same paragraph in each.

Unit 11.2 Activity 4B: Working with a document (page 102)

Practical exercise.

Topic 5: Finalising and printing a document

Unit 11.2 Activity 5A: Checking spelling (page 106)

Practical exercise.

Unit 11.2 Activity 5B: Printing (page 108)

1. a. Print quality on a draft is lesser quality.
   b. A draft is printed more quickly than the final copy.
2. Name of assignment; identifying information of person submitting the assignment: name of person; name of organisation (eg school); year level; class and/or subject; teacher: person receiving the assignment; date of submission; page numbers.

Topic 6: Working with tables

Unit 11.2 Activity 6A: Creating tables (page 114)

Practical exercise.

Topic 7: Working with graphics

Unit 11.2 Activity 7A: Working with graphics (page 118)

Generally to keep the file size of documents manageable it is best to edit pictures before inserting them in a word processing document. The tools in a word processor are, however, suitable for last-minute alterations to save time.

1. **a.** Select the bottom right corner and drag.
   b. Double-click on the image. Handles appear on the image. Select the 'Crop' button on the toolbar and attach to the selection points on the image to determine the nature of the crop.
   c. Right-click on the image, select 'Format Picture', Choose 'Shadow' from the left pane and apply your preferred settings.
2. Insert > Chart. This will show a default table in Excel. Edit and add appropriate data; this will be reflected in the chart that has been entered in Excel.
3. Practical exercise.

Topic 8: Working with styles and templates

Unit 11.2 Activity 8A: Styles (page 122)

1. Arial.
2. 14 point.
3. Bold and Italic. (Before and after are applied to the paragraph, not the font).
4. Place the cursor in the text you wish to alter, select Styles > Apply Styles > Modify. From the window select the 'Format' button and 'Font'. The various settings that can be applied are shown. The window is shown in the textbook, with the 'Format' button in the bottom left of the window.
5. Place the cursor in a paragraph to which you wish to apply the style. Right-click and then select the style you wish to apply from the drop-down list or select the box with 'AA' to make a selection from the list.
6. Colour is selected as one of the settings in Modify Style > Format > Font.

Unit 11.2 Activity 8B: Templates (page 123)

Practical exercise.

Unit 11.2 Activity 8C: Margins and paper size (page 124)

Practical exercise.

Topic 9: Creating mail merge and labels

Unit 11.2 Activity 9A: Create a mail merge letter (page 129)

Practical exercise.

Unit 11.3 Computers and Society

Topic 1: Impacts on society

Unit 11.3 Activity 1A: Working from home (page 171)

1. **a.** Answer on page 166.
b. Answer on page 167.
c. It may be difficult initially to recreate a space at home that would enable a person to work as well as they may in the workplace. There could be distractions of a different type and the need for adequate lighting, desk area and cooling in hot temperature.

Topic 2: Measures to protect computers and data

Unit 11.3 Activity 2A: Disasters (page 179)

Any of the following could cause an information system to fail.

1. Natural disaster: flood, fire, cyclone, earthquake.
2. Technical failure: power outage, hardware failure of a vital component eg server.
3. Criminal act: terrorism, sabotage, theft, vandalism (physical or over a network), malware.
4. Misadventure: accident in the workplace that damages equipment.

Unit 11.3 Activity 2B: Passwords and their use (page 182)

Examples of systems with password or PIN:
Login to computer.
Login to computer network.
Login to access a bank account through an ATM.
Login to a website.
Login to gain physical entry to a secure facility through a door barrier.
Access to a password-protected document.
In some cases an individual may be able to initiate the alteration of the password, either personally or with the organisation. Doing this over a network usually requires establishment of identification and authorisation communicated to an email address.

Unit 11.3 Activity 2C: Setting a password (page 183)

1. 2: Alistair spelled backwards, all letters.
2. 0: common word, three letters only.
3. 0: place name; would be easy for a hacker to generate an attack from a list of place names.
4. 0: birth date; commonly used by people as a password.
5. 1: common name, five letters only.
6. 9: good password; no association with Alistair; eight characters with a mix of alpha numeric, upper and lower case characters.
7. 1: word in dictionary; has no relation to Alistair; four letters only.
8. 1: association with Alistair; all letters.
9. 0: possibly the most common password is actually 'password'.
10. 0: only two characters, both numeric.
11. 3: only five characters; common word; same month as birthday.
12. 0: same name as dog; only alphabetic characters; easy to guess.
13. 0: Alistair's name and year of birth; easy to guess.
14. 3: common name; hacker could generate.

Unit 11.3 Activity 2D: Forgetting a password (page 184)

It is common today for information systems to use a combination of methods of verification of a person's identity in the event of a forgotten password:

a. The person's email address as their user name.

b. A secondary email account to which an email can be sent when a password is forgotten.

c. Security questions, usually at least two and sometimes more, the answers to be provided to assist in verification of identity, eg name of first school, name of football team supported.

d. A mobile phone number, sometimes used to send a text message.

e. Make phone contact with the organisation, such as a bank. Verification questions may need to be answered. The password may be reset and then communicated, or a temporary password could be sent with an activation time limit.

For the examples given:

1. A combination of the above. Most likely to be done by email where the organisations are overseas.
2. Phone contact with the bank.
3. A systems administrator may have a password at a higher level than the normal user and the normal user's password can be reset. Otherwise, seek technical advice from the manufacturer regarding access.
4. If the password is forgotten it is most likely that the document cannot be opened.
5. Contact the system administrator to reset the password.

Unit 11.3 Activity 2E: Computer virus timeline (page 187)

Virus	Description	Year	Details
Conficker	Time Bomb	2008	Worm – Microsoft servers
Elk Cloner	Boot Sector Virus	1981	Boot sector on floppy disks – Apple
Explore Zip	Virus - zip file attachment	1999	Worm – Microsoft Office documents
I Love You	Email with malware	2000	Worm – Visual Basic script
Klez	Spoof email address	2000	Worm – Internet Explorer, Outlook
Melissa	Spamming email	1999	Microsoft Word and Outlook
MyDoom	Email	2004	Worm – mass mailer
Nimda	Email	2001	Worm – Microsoft Windows
Sassar	Computers without security update	2004	Worm – Microsoft Windows
Storm	File disguised	2007	Worm – email spamming, Microsoft Windows

Unit 11.3 Activity 2F: Hardware failure (page 189)

1. Computer card.
2. For a mission critical operation the system should have been tested on a regular basis. There should have been at least two cards used to monitor the level in the tank in case one failed.
3. Orica would need to install a failsafe system, test the system and provide reports that show monitoring of the levels in real time.

Unit 11.3 Activity 2G: Protecting data in the workplace (page 190)

1. Having only one person who can carry out an important procedure is not adequate, even if they work full-time. People may not be at work for many reasons, eg holidays, illness, personal leave. The procedure for backup should be documented and at least one other employee should be able to carry out the task.
2. The backup period is too long. Accounting software is likely to be used daily, so a daily backup (incremental) is required. A full backup at the end of each week would probably be suitable.
3. A 100Mb disk would possibly be inadequate to back up the software. The cost of storage is low and a hard disk with greater capacity is required.
4. The location of the backup disk is only adequate as long as another backup is kept secure in an offsite location. A backup on site could be destroyed along with the information system meaning there would be no records at all to retrieve.
5. Meeting files for 20 employees in an advertising agency would be a key file for running the agency. Irregular interval backup is not appropriate. There needs to be a regular backup procedure.
6. A backup copy should not be the working copy of files. If a backup needs to be accessed the file should be restored to where the original file is located and worked on there. Otherwise the agency will not know which are the current files. In this case the backup file risks being erased by an earlier file.
7. Computer magazines are useful for background information and useful tips and commentary, butthey are not training manuals. Computer manuals are useful as they explain the key elements of computers and software. In the workplace, however, there will be systems and procedures in place and the employee will need training in what their role is and how the information systems work within the organisation.
8. A simple manual check would be to annotate the delivery and state that it had been entered and by whom to avoid duplication. Adline should ensure that the database is modified so that there are ways to verify if a delivery has been entered twice. Information that may assist to avoid duplication would include: date and time of delivery, who delivered the order, who was the supplier of the delivery, was there an order number for the delivery, who within Adline ordered the goods.
9. A document must be saved before it is sent to a printer. If there is a network issue or the computer crashes then a document may not be saved and it would need to be recreated.
10. It is perhaps prudent to do upgrades and changes to systems outside of normal working hours. However, it is necessary to inform employees of changes and how the changes may causes differences to their computer environment.
11. Jane should power down her computer at the end of the day and not leave it running. Power surges could occur and affect her computer even if it reverts to sleep mode after a period of no activity.

12. The flash drive should be used as a storage device to facilitate the transfer of files from one computer to another, rather than being the only copy. Only a very special circumstance would dictate this method of working. For normal business documents with a relatively low level of security, it would be prudent to use the flash drive as only a storage device.
13. A separate file for each letter would be normal practice. The file could become quite large quickly and unmanageable in the event of referral at a later date. It is likely that the letters may be on a range of topics to a range of clients. Jane should have templates for particular types of letters and then store the letters in an organised manner depending on the protocols of the office, eg. letters could be stored in a folder appropriate for each client, according to date or according to the subject matter of the letter. Files should be named appropriately so that they could be located as required.
14. It may be necessary to print memos from time to time. An electronic copy is essential. It is far easier to find information by searching electronic documents.
15. Gail would need to see if the licensing allows her to install the software on multiple computers and also in multiple locations. It may only be for one computer; it could however allow more than one installation and also at home. The licence may depend on the amount paid for the software.
16. It would be ill-advised for Frank to jeopardise the work computers with software downloaded from the Internet. It would be an improper use of his employer's time. If Frank felt that the software would be useful for the business he would need to talk to Gail and see if they could research the software first and then perhaps find an environment to test the software before installing it.

Unit 11.3 Activity 2H: Network password tasks (page 191)

1. Network administrators would like passwords to be altered on a regular basis to ensure that access to networks as recorded by log files accurately reflects who is accessing the network. It is not uncommon for some employees either through collaboration or expediency to learn of each other's passwords. It is inadvisable for employees to access a network using someone else's user name and password.
2. Depending on the size of the organisation, about every three months.
3. Remembering passwords is not easy. There are a variety of programs that can store passwords, and they themselves should be secured by password. Passwords should not be written down and stored in places that are easily accessible. It is advisable to have a range of passwords and use passwords that are very secure for bank accounts, for example. Often these are used on a regular basis so remembering them is perhaps easier.

Topic 4: Government controls and laws on ICT

Unit 11.3 Activity 4A: Breaches of privacy (page 205)

1. Under privacy legislation it is required that organisations ensure that data is secure. User names and passwords should be a high order priority for an organisation. Once breaches like this occur the organisation needs to have appropriate procedures to rectify the breach, such as notifying those affected by the breach and advising what they need to do in conjunction with the organisation.
2. It is possible that the details could be used, perhaps not for their own service, but if people use the same password for a variety of online access then other information could be retrieved that would enable more information to be gathered. Identify theft

is an increasing area of crime that people need to be aware of and take simple steps to reduce the possibility. For example, disposing correctly of important paper documents with account numbers and account details; being vigilant with emails that purport to be genuine and ask people to log on to websites. Websites produced by criminals are very professional, so do not accept a website on face value.

Topic 5: Ergonomics in ICT

Unit 11.3 Activity 5A: Choosing software (page 209)

There may be more than one solution for each task. There is a variety of free applications and applications pre-loaded on a computer that can also perform the tasks. The suggestions are generic names of software with the commonly used applications in business. In some categories there may be very specialist software designed for a particular task, eg accounting software for budgets.

1. Word processor, eg Word.
2. Spreadsheet, eg Excel.
3. Spreadsheet, accounting software, database solution, eg Excel.
4. Operating system, network utility configuration, browser settings.
5. Browser, eg Internet Explorer.
6. Email, eg Outlook.
7. Image editing or drawing software, eg Photoshop, Illustrator.
8. Image editing, eg Photoshop.
9. CAD, drawing, eg Corel Draw.
10. Calendar, eg Outlook.
11. Music, eg iTunes.
12. Database, eg Access.
13. Archive/decompression utility, eg Winzip.
14. Video player, eg Windows Media Player.
15. PDF viewer, eg Acrobat Reader.
16. Web authoring, eg Dreamweaver.
17. Sound recording, eg Audacity.
18. Presentation, eg Powerpoint.
19. Utility provided by operating system, eg specialist software such as Dragon.
20. Desktop publishing eg Publisher.

Unit 11.3 Activity 5B: Software ownership (page 210)

Example answer:
Name: Microsoft Word.
Maker: Microsoft.
Version: Word 2010 (Version 14).
Media: Disk, pre-installed, download, Office 365 subscription.
Licence: Individual, business. Volume licensing for large organisations.
Price: Varies according to type of licence. You will find a variety of options for some software, particularly Microsoft and other large software publishers.

Unit 11.3 Activity 5C: Upgrading to new software (page 212)

Order 3, 15, 16, 17, 4, 2, 5, 6, 10, 11, 7, 19, 20, 1, 12, 9, 18, 13, 14, 8.
Note: some tasks such as checking (11) and timing (12) can be done at the same time or interchanged. At the end of task 9 the installation would take place.

Unit 11.4 Spreadsheets

Topic 1: What is a spreadsheet?

Unit 11.4 Activity 1A: Reading a spreadsheet (page 216)

1. Column A, Row 1.

2. **a.** 12,345
b. 10,565
c. Total

3. **a.** C3
b. F3
c. F7
d. B1

Unit 11.4 Activity 1B: Moving around a worksheet (page 217)

1. Detailed answer in Help file. The arrow key will move the cursor one cell from the current cell. A modifier key (e.g. Control) and the arrow key will move around a particular table within the worksheet. Arrow key: cell to cell. Control and arrow: first and last column in table, top and bottom row in a table. Control and home: Cell A1. Control and End: active cell bottom right of screen. Control G: Enter cell you wish to go to.

Unit 11.4 Activity 1C: Creating different types of spreadsheets (page 219)

Practical exercise.

Unit 11.4 Activity 1D: Formatting a spreadsheet (page 219)

1. Text in a cell is aligned left.

2. A number in a cell is aligned right.

Unit 11.4 Activity 1E: Entering numbers (page 220)

Practical exercise.

Unit 11.4 Activity 1F: Formatting numbers (page 221)

1. There are twelve different ways to format a number.

2. **a.** Default alignment and format.
b. Generally to two decimal places, eg K50.45. For large numbers, just as whole numbers, with a separator, normally a comma, eg K2,500,000.
c. A date can have a range of formats depending on the user preferences. The default for Excel would be dd/mm/yyyy. It is useful in some cases to show a date such as 25/09/2013 as Tue, 25 September 2013. For day and month numbers that are single digits a leading '0' should prefix the number.

   d. Time can be shown using the 12-hour or 24-hour clock, depending on user preference. If using the 12-hour clock, then am or pm should be placed after the time as appropriate. For example, 07:30 in the 24-hour clock is 7:30 am in the 12-hour clock; 19:30 in the 24-hour clock is 7:30 pm in the 12-hour clock. A colon is used as a separator for the numbers.

3. The percentage format takes the value in a cell, multiplies it by 100 and displays the result with a percent symbol. The number of decimal points can be selected in a dialog box.

Topic 1: Formulae

Unit 11.4 Activity 2A: Working with formulae (page 224)

1. Formula for the total in cell B6 should be Sum=(B1:B5).

2. Enter in cell B8, =Sum(B3:B6), then hold cursor on bottom left of cell C8. When the cursor changes shape to a '+' symbol, drag to cell C8, and the formula will be copied.

Unit 11.4 Activity 2B: Sum activity and average function (page 225)

1. In cell B6, the formula is =SUM(B1:B5).

Unit 11.4 Activity 2C: Buying a house (page 226)

Practical exercise.

Unit 11.4 Activity 2D: Using worksheets for comparison (page 228)

Practical exercise.

Unit 11.4 Activity 2E: Simple calculator (page 230)

Practical exercise.

Unit 11.4 Activity 2F: Spreadsheet terminology (page 231)

1. **a.** Function: part of a program that performs a task. Functions in Excel require 'arguments' according to the syntax of the function. The function will return a value.

   b. Formula: an expression that relates cells to each other, eg '=A1*A2'.

   c. Label: text placed in a cell to describe or name a column, row or part of a spreadsheet, eg Betty's Budget.

   d. Value: usually values are arranged in rows and columns. The values in any particular cell are the results of formulae and therefore rely on the values in other cells. If a value in one cell changes, the value in one or more other cells will alter, eg the total cell in a spreadsheet budget will change if a budget item changes.

   e. Number: value in a spreadsheet, characters 0–9.

   f. Result: value returned in a cell after a function performs its calculation or what a formula displays.

2. A relative reference is the default setting for a spreadsheet. When copying a formula in cells the spreadsheet assumes the relationship between the cells will remain constant as the formula is copied. An absolute reference is entered with a $ sign before the cell and row reference. This means that the reference is always to a particular cell regardless of where the formula is copied.

Unit 11.4 Activity 2G: Class mark analysis (page 231)

1. **a.** MAXIMUM =Maximum(C1:C14)

b. MINIMUM =Minimum(C1:C14)
c. SUM =Sum(C1:C14)
d. COUNT =Count(C1:C14)

2. Bar chart

Unit 11.4 Activity 2H: 'What if' analysis (page 232)

1. A 'what if' analysis allows for modelling of data. A variety of results can be calculated to illustrate how a change in one value can affect the other values. With exchange rates, an importer or exporter could model how a variation in exchange rate could alter cash flow through variations in buying or selling price.
2. As entered in the spreadsheet:
   Initial house value 350000
   Inflation rate 0.03

Year	House Value	Formula in cell
0	350000	=B1 (could also be $B$1)
1	360500	=B5+(B5*$B$3)
2	371315	=B6+(B6*$B$3)

2. a. 907,810
   b. 688,503
   c. 666,110; 805,881; 1,167,184

Unit 11.4 Activity 2I: Planning a holiday (page 233)

Practical exercise.

Unit 11.4 Activity 2J: Comparing house prices (page 234)

Practical exercise.

Topic 4: Charts

Unit 11.4 Activity 4A: Extension exercises (page 240)

Practical exercise.

Topic 5: Using advanced functions

Unit 11.4 Activity 5A: Buying a house (page 256)

1. Formula is the PMT function.
   PMT(rate,nper,pv,fv,type) rate is 0.055/12 (rate of interest/12 - number of months in a year, months being the payment period).
   nper is the 20 years × 12 = 240
   pv is 250,000
   Payment per period = 1,719.72
2. a. 1,615.56
   b. 1,889.02
   c. 1,692.43

Unit 11.4 Activity 5B: Goal seek exercise (page 273)

The value of the property would be 172194.6. Follow the steps shown in the Goal Seek example on page 270.

Topic 7: Protecting and auditing forms and templates

Unit 11.4 Activity 7A: Spreadsheets revision (page 294)

1. **a. i.** 100010
a. ii. 1110001
a. iii. 11010101
a. iv. 1111010110
b. i. 11
b. ii. 33
b. iii. 47
b. iv. 202

2. File > New > Sample Templates. Enter the values in cells, using the start of the current month as the start date of the loan. Values for all cells, except the optional extra payments, will enable Excel to fill in the table. Note the layout and setup of the table.

3. What if table (alternative layout to text). Top image is the chart; bottom image shows formula. Note the use of the ABS function to return the value without a '–' sign.

	A	B	C	D
1	Monthly repayment for Vehicles			
2	Rate of interest (p.a.)		6.00%	
3	Term of loan (Years)		3	
4				
5	Car	A	B	C
6	Loan value	6491	5280	11990
7				
8	Repayment per mth	$197.47	$160.63	$364.76
9				

	A	B	C	D
1	Monthly repayment fo			
2	Rate of interest (p.a.)		0.06	
3	Term of loan (Years)		3	
4				
5	Car	A	B	C
6	Loan value	6491	5280	11990
7				
8	Repayment per mth	=ABS(PMT($C$2/12,$C$3*12,B6))	=ABS(PMT($C$2/12,$C$3*12,C6))	=ABS(PMT($C$2/12,$C$3*12,D6))
9				

4. Practical exercise.
5. Highest mark =Max(C2:C16)
   Lowest mark =Min(C2:C16)
   Total marks =SUM(C2:C16)
   Number of Candidates =COUNT(C2:C16)
   - **a.** Enter the function in cell E2 and drag down:
     =IF(D2<$F$3,$G$2,IF(D2<$F$4,$G$3,IF(D2<$F$5,$G$4,IF(D2<$F$6,$G$5,IF(D2>$F$7,$G$6,"")))))
   - **b.** Enter the function in cell E2 and drag down: =VLOOKUP(D2,$F$3:$G$7,2).
   - **c.** The VLOOKUP is a simpler function. Note that it requires the lookup table values to be in ascending order.
   - **d.** Use the RANDBETWEEN function. Enter the function in cell C2:=RANDBETWEEN(0,50).
   - **e.** Any cell that has a function where the result is determined by other cells. Cells C2:C16, cells G11:G17 and cells F3:F7, G3:G7. The cells referred to in the VLOOKUP may however need to be edited at some stage.
6. **a.** Functions to be used include:
   - **i.** MAX
   - **ii.** MIN
   - **iii.** AVERAGE
   - **iv.** AVERAGE
   - **v.** SUM

   b. VLOOKUP
7. Practical exercise. Explanation of data outlining on page 263, and of PIVOT table on page 265.

Unit 11.5 Databases

Topic 1: Getting started

Unit 11.5 Activity 1A: Databases in the local community (page 298)

1. **a.** The tables could include information about:
   1. Family and friends' contact details.
   2. A person's workplace contact details for fellow employees.
   3. Music listings on a portable music player.
   4. Telephone directory of subscribers to network.
   5. Listing of recipes and ingredients for the family cookbook.

   b. The tables could include information about:
   1. Subjects a student is enrolled in for a particular year.
   2. Family contact details relating to a student.
   3. Sports in which the student competes.
   4. Extra-curricular activities of the student.
   5. The student's end of year results.
2.
   1. Sporting club
   2. Government, (medical, taxation records)
   3. A business that you have purchased goods and services from, eg a local business or internet site

4. Social media, eg Facebook, Twitter
5. Business you have entered a competition with and provided your details.

3. The information is expressed in a generic sense, not the actual fields that may exist in the database.
Name, address, contact details such as phone numbers – used to make contact, post important information, membership renewals.
Category of membership (playing, non-playing, social member) – subscriptions may depend on the playing status and also the age of a member.
Playing record and teams played in – Games played, at which competition level.

Unit 11.5 Activity 1B: Finding information in databases (page 299)

1. Practical exercise.
2. Practical exercise.
3. **a.** 3
   b. 2
   c. Sorted by location.
4. **a.** 2
   b. 5
   c. Population (number).
5. **a.** 2
   b. 26/5/1784
   c. Lady Penryhn.
   d. 7

Unit 11.5 Activity 1C: Field names (page 302)

1. Field names: Surname, Initials, Address. The last field should be titled 'Town' or 'City'.
2. First Name, Last Name, Company, Job Title, Business Phone, Home Phone, Fax Number, Street, City, State/Province, Zip/Postal code, Country/Region, E-mail, Web Page, Notes.
3. Player, Matches, Innings, Not out, runs, Highest, Average, 50's, 100's. The average is calculated by totalling the sum of the runs in the 'runs' field, then dividing by the number of the players (count of the field 'Player').
4. Entity for the three databases is: 'Person', 'Personnel' as in employee of the organisation, 'Player' in the test team(s).

Unit 11.5 Activity 1D: Reports (page 303)

1. 3 purchases, 770 value.
2. 5 purchases, 360 value.
3. Sorted by last name. It could be sorted by department to see what the better-performing departments are, or by purchase date to see when the store is busiest.
4. Report sorted by department with totals for each department; report sorted by date with total for each day.

Unit 11.5 Activity 1E: Designing a database (page 306)

No answer required: database shown on page 316.

Unit 11.5 Activity 1F: Creating databases (page 307)

Practical exercise.

Unit 11.5 Activity 1G: Using the White Pages (page 308)

Practical exercise.

Unit 11.5 Activity 1H: Privacy (page 310)

1. **a.** Date of birth, year enrolled at the school, current year level and class, people to contact as well as parents/guardians, medical information about particular conditions.

b. Principal: access to all records. Teachers of your classes: access to all academic records and contact details, perhaps some private information excluded. Teachers of classes in which you are not enrolled: historical academic records and perhaps contact details if they are connected through sport or other school activities, Parents: have ability to check records but not necessarily access at their leisure. Other students: no access to your records.

2. **a.** School: date of birth, academic results, medical information.

b. Doctor: as above.

3. Privacy.

4. Answer though research.

5. Field: see page 301; record: see page 301; file: table (if only one) or the collection of tables that exist within a single computer file.

6. Although databases save automatically, it is possible to lose information if an action such as 'delete records' is performed accidentally. The only recourse is to find a backup copy to restore the records. An important database should be backed up at least daily. There are automatic scripts in some databases that perform this backup as a matter of course.

7. A database only needs to be updated when a particular event occurs, eg a new student enrols in a school or a student leaves a school at the end of their schooling. The database needs to be updated each year as the student moves up a year level.

8. A key field is the field that holds a value unique to that record in the database. It is usually a number or number and letter combination that does not have any connection to the data in the record, but is used only for its identification. If the key field is a unique number, such as a serial number that increments as a new record is entered, then sorting the database would be by date of creation of the records.

9. A report is arranging the data contained in the database to make it more meaningful. It is generally designed for print but could be also for reading on screen. A simple report could just be an A to Z alphabetical order listing based on a field, e.g. Family Name. A more sophisticated report could group people by a particular location, sorted by A to Z within the category.

10. A search of a database isolates certain records by a query. For example, find all customers who live in Port Moresby. Within that group of records they could be sorted by A to Z.

11. See Topic 1, page 297.

12. Information is data that has had added value to make it meaningful. It is sorted, arranged, manipulated and then examined to enable decisions to be made. A piece of data on its own has no meaning or context and it is difficult to make a decision just on a piece of data. A year's supply of climatic data gives a view of the seasons and how they vary.

13. Electronic files have advantages over paper: storage, access, communication, decision making.

14. Test data is used in a system as it is being developed to see if adequate checks exist to prevent the input of unreliable data. For example, the price of a product in a database requires a number; that number is likely to have a range also, so test data could exist of a 'word', that should be rejected, or a large number that is outside an accepted range of values. Some fields such as 'Family Name' would require a person to check, as there is a great variety of spelling of people's names and there can be some uncommon name spellings.

Topic 2: Working with data

Unit 11.5 Activity 2A: Updating databases (page 312)

1. **a.** If a new player is included in the team, this would occur at the time the player is added.
b. If a player is no longer in the team, this would take place at the end of the season.
c. The 'Average' is a calculation field using the 'Average' function, Highest would use the 'Maximum' function.
d. The following would be altered: Matches, Innnings, Not outs, Runs and Centuries.

2. **a.** 222 games. Games Played would be adjusted, Goals if additional goals kicked. Fields not requiring updating in a season: Surname, First Name and Club.
b. A player would be deleted from this database on leaving the competition.
c. A player would be deleted from this database on entering the competition.
d. Surname and First Name would not need updating. The club may need updating as players change clubs.
e. If a player changed clubs the database would need to be updated.

Unit 11.5 Activity 2B: Database maintenance (page 312)

1. The timetable for sittings and committee hearings needs to be adjusted.

2. An election may mean the electorate information may alter if there has been an electorate redistribution. Members may retire or be defeated and new members represent the electorates. If the government changes hands then the database will need to have the positions and details to reflect this.

3. **a.** The new member's electorate details will replace the old member's details.
b. The resigning member will become a backbencher, but remain representing their electorate; another parliamentarian will become the cabinet minister.

Unit 11.5 Activity 2C: Searching a database (page 313)

1. 3

2. Tendulkar, S R. This is calculated by dividing his runs 15183 by the matches played 184: average 82.51.

3. Tendulkar, S R.

4. Cook, A N.

Topic 3: Working with tables and relationships

Unit 11.5 Activity 3A: How do databases identify people? (page 319)

1. The organisations would have a method to uniquely identify the entity, eg Sheryl. Often a number, it could also consist of alphabetic characters depending on the method used.
1. School to student; student number.
2. Club to player/member; membership number.
3. Business to customer; customer number.
4. Business to customer; frequent flyer number.

5. Business to customer; customer number.
6. Business to employee; employee number.
7. Business to customer; customer number.
8. Business to customer; customer number.
9. Business to shareholder; shareholder number.
10. Government to citizen; tax file number.

2. In the answers use examples known to you. Identify the information that is used to uniquely identify you compared with other information that is used in the communication, eg address. Although in one sense address may be unique, it is not used to identify people, as people's addresses my change over time.

Topic 6: Creating useful reports

Unit 11.5 Activity 6A: Designing and creating an information system (page 341)

1.

Classification	Field type	Field name	Sample data
Membership	Number	MembershipNumber	12345
Family Name	Text	FamilyName	Bandi
Given Name	Text	GivenName	Chris
Title	Text	Title	Mr
Number and Street	Text	NoStreet	4 Rabaul
Suburb	Text	Suburb	Lae
Postcode	Text	Postcode	411
Telephone	Number	Phone	999 9999
Membership	Text	Membership	Junior
Date of Birth	Date	DOB	11/5/1998
Date of Joining	Date	JoiningDate	16/7/2005
Date of Last Payment	Date	Payment	14/7/2012
Method of Payment	Text	MethodPayment	Cash
Amount of Payment	Number	Amount	50
Membership Status	Text	MembershipStatus	Current

2.

Field	Validation	Data examples
title	Value List	Mr, Mrs, Ms, Dr
date of birth	Range - Limit date field to dates after 1900	13/3/1940
membership	Value List	Full, Senior, Junior, Under 18, MidWeek

3. The selection from a list restricts the data to items in the list. An incorrect option could of course be selected during data entry.

4. Dummy data as per example shown. Excel is the best option to create dummy data.

5. The design should have an appropriate heading with the name of the organisation and purpose of the screen. Fields should be shown with appropriate titles. The tab order of the fields should direct the user around the screen. The design should show the fonts, font type and any other formatting details. The design should be such that another person could create the screen from the design.

6. A renewal notice would need to have certain information to identify the member and enable the notice to be mailed out. The listing of members would need to filter and find only those members whose renewals fall within a range of dates. Not all fields in the database need to be displayed in the report. The report should have a title, date, page number, date of report. The report could be sorted and grouped, such as by month or member type, sorted by A–Z by family name, and with totals and sub-totals.

7. The report would be grouped by membership, sorted A–Z within each category by family name, with a total count of the number of members for each category.

8. The opening menu screen should consist of buttons leading to: entry screen for membership details, listing of members, listing of members with outstanding membership subscriptions, listing of members by membership category, among others. The screen needs to identify the name of the organisation and give address details.

Unit 11.6 Internet

Topic 4: Website evaluation

Unit 11.6 Activity 4A: Websites (page 370)

1. **a.** Three columns.
b. Left: site links and navigation; Middle: content; Right: links and special content.
c. The right column disappears, and the layout becomes two columns.

2. **a.** Four columns.
b. Column 1: main stories with byline and links to other pages associated with the story; Column 2: key story with image relating to the story; Column 3: particular stories, often under a side heading (eg Sport, Media, Fashion); Column 4: part navigation links, advertising, newspaper offers, promotion of the *Guardian*.
c. it changes to three-column layout.
d. Navigation bar at the top of the page. Hyperlinks (as blue text) in the content. Columns 3 and 4 are link-intensive.

3. **a.** A favorite is where the URL of a website can be saved by the browser and selected from a list to allow access to the URL without needing to type in the address. (A favorite is called a 'Bookmark' in some browsers).
b. One click access; no need to remember the URL; saves time when accessing the site again.
c. Favorites > Add to Favorite.
d. Favorites > Organise Favorites > select the Favorite > Delete.
e. Favorites > Organise Favorites. They can be placed in a folder. Folders can be created as well as folders and favorites being moved.

Topic 6: Electronic mail (email)

Unit 11.6 Activity 6A: Email (page 407)

1. The answers refer to Microsoft Outlook; there are other ways of carrying out the same tasks.

- **a.** Address book is accessed from 'Contacts'. 'Add New Contact' from the 'Home' tab.
- **b.** Add name and email address to the form shown after 'Add New Contact'.
- **c.** Home > New E-mail > enter the address in the field adjacent to the 'To...' button.
- **d.** File > New E-mail. Click on the 'To...' button, in the window that opens. There are three buttons: To – enter the main recipient, Cc (Carbon copy) – enter another recipient, Bcc (Blind carbon copy) – copy to others whose email addresses will not be displayed to the other recipients.
- **e.** In the Inbox listing, select the email and right-click; select 'Delete'.
- **f.** In the navigation panel, select the folder where another folder is to be created, right-click, select 'New Folder'. Email can be dragged from the inbox to the folder, or a rule can be created so that emails automatically arrive in that folder.
- **g.** In the Inbox listing, select the 'From' tab, right-click and select the sort.
- **h.** Home > Filter E-mail (far right of tabs), select 'More Filters'. Click on 'From' and enter the Sender name.
- **i.** Home > New E-mail, click on 'Attach File' and choose the file to attach.
- **j.** Home > Contacts > Details, enter nickname in 'Nickname' box.
- **k.** With an email open, select 'Forward' and enter the address to send it to.
- **l.** File > New E-mail, select 'Signature'.
- **m.** File > Outlook Options > Advanced > Send and receive, then set a time in the 'Schedule an automatic send/receive every ...' field.

2.

- **a.** Yes. People tend browse email and use it for communication. There is a real issue with overly long emails – will people read them?
- **b.** Email should be checked on a regular basis, particularly in the workplace. However, it can be distracting and prevent people from carrying out their tasks effectively.
- **c.** It is up to each individual to determine how responsive they should be to email. There is a tendency to reply immediately when a considered reply is a better option.
- **d.** Email should be written in normal sentences. It is more difficult to read sentences composed in upper case.
- **e.** There is no useful purpose served by sending junk mail.

3.

- **a.** Email is stored somewhere on a network. Password protection on a computer is an essential security step but it will not keep email private.
- **b.** Some email does not get to the intended recipient; however, the sender should receive a message from their email server that it has not been able to deliver the message.
- **c.** The formality of an email message depends on the relationship between the sender and recipient. For business purposes an email would be formal.
- **d.** Email can be one to one or one to many. It is likely that an email could be 'unclear, misleading, long, dishonest and totally ambiguous'.
- **e.** It is likely that if the email is composed at work the employer may regard it as their property.
- **f.** Email can be introduced in court as evidence.

g. Employers should as a matter of policy inform their employees if their email activity is monitored and read. Although there is no guarantee that this will actually occur, an employee would be wise to assume that this is possible.
h. Email attachments are a common form of distributing viruses.
i. Joke and fun programs should not be directed to people in their workplace. Network security will not distinguish between emails based on contents.

4. Open the email and click on the address adjacent to the 'From:'. From the window select the fourth tab (list tab) and select 'Add to Outlook Contacts'.
5. a. An employer would be entitled not to allow the use of the email to notify employees of a union meeting. It would be better for the employee to seek permission from the employer to see if the practice is acceptable.
   b. Selling a bicycle is a private matter. Some employers may allow this to occur as it may help harmonious relationships within the workplace.
   c. If the matter is work-related it is acceptable to use email. An employee would be advised not to express these opinions in a written form and not in an email. It could for instance be accidentally sent to people it was not intended for and this could create problems for the sender.
   d. If the matter is work-related it is acceptable. It would be advisable for the employee in an email to comment on the policy in a constructive manner, even if expressing concerns.
   e. Although employers generally understand that some use of email would be private, employees would be advised to keep this use reasonable and minimal.
   f. As in 5e, sending a private email outside of normal work time would in most cases be deemed reasonable.
6. a. People use browser-based email accounts such as Hotmail, Gmail and Yahoo mail. The set-up is through a website and requires another email address as verification, recording of security questions, and selection of an email address.
   b. For convenience and access by a variety of devices, such as smartphones. These accounts will also be set up so that people have a private email address.
   c. Advantages include: easy to set up, free for basic service, access though browser and Internet connection, more than adequate storage space. Disadvantages include: spam can be a problem as the services are targeted through spam, advertising, and limited control over customisation of the interface.
   d. Free web email can be provided as the providers can use advertising to subsidise the service, it can direct the user to other paid services of the provider, users may wish to pay to get some additional benefits such as more storage.
   e. Practical exercise.

Unit 11.7 Desktop Publishing

Topic 1: Working with publications

Unit 11.7 Activity 1A: Publications and paper size (page 416)

1. Most desktop publishing software will have templates that enable the sizes of these documents to be selected.

	Paper size (mm)	Examples of use	Key features
a.	210 × 297	Advertising, notice of events	Designed to get attention, content is developed to fit a single page.
b.	297 × 420	Poster	To be a sign, to be prominent and draw attention.
c.	201 × 297	Letter	A form of communication with conventions with formal setting out and composition. Usually to put on the record a particular matter.
d.	110 × 220	Mail letter	A variety of envelope sizes are available.
e.	148 × 210	Easy-to-read format	Can be produced by most desktop publishing software from A4.
f.	210 × 297	Company or social organisation	Document of record produced each year.
g.	210 × 297	Commercial publication	Printed for a specific audience.
h.	Various	Dates and organisation details	Distributed towards end of calendar year.
i.	Various	Persons contact details	Easy to store the information.
j.	Various	Catalogue of product items	Advertising of products.
k.	148 × 210	Advertising of event or business	Short, easy to read, draws attention.
l.	210 × 297	Regular publication by organisation	Communicate with the people who are part of the organisation, eg school.
m.	148 × 210	Short letter, usually thank you	Acknowledgement, invitation, compliment.

2. Choose a template from a desktop publishing program. Create or modify the picture or illustration in a graphics program prior to importing into the desktop publishing program.

Topic 6: Sending and printing a publication

Unit 11.7 Activity 6A: Publishing project (page 442)

Practical exercise.

abacus (7): a counting device for making calculations, consisting of a frame mounted with rods along which beads or bails are moved.

absolute reference (230): an absolute cell reference refers to a cell by its row and column number. In Excel, each row and column number is preceded by a "$" sign.

acceptable use policy (194): policy describing what users are allowed to do with the IT resources of an organisation and what they are not allowed to do. It will often define what sanctions are put in place if there is a breach of the policy.

alignment (88): the arrangement of text relative to its position on a page.

animation (367): the rapid sequencing of still images to create the appearance of motion.

anti-spyware (186): a software program that is used to protect your computer against spyware or malware (see spyware or malware).

anti-virus (185): a software program that is used to protect your computer against viruses (see computer virus)

application software (68): software that has been developed to solve a particular problem for users to perform useful work on specific tasks; for example, word processing, spreadsheets and Adobe Photoshop (see system software).

artificial intelligence (AI) (18): where computers carry out tasks in a manner similar to human beings.

backup (174): the procedure for copying computer data with which somebody is working and storing it in another alternative storage device or area for safe keeping as a security measure. A backup of very important files is crucial in any organisation.

barcode (25): a barcode is made up of a number of vertical lines printed on products with a numeric description of the lines below it. These vertical lines can be read by a machine and translated into numbers. The number that the bar code represents uniquely identifies the item to which it is attached.

binary (41): a numbering system that has only two different values: 0 and 1.

biometric recognition (184): the use of measurable, biological characteristics such as fingerprints or iris patterns to identify a person to an electronic system

biometrics (27): the science that measures and analyses biological data. Computer systems can analyse body characteristics including fingerprints to uniquely identify individuals. The recognition of these characteristics is often used for authentication.

bit (45): the smallest unit of information storable in a computer or peripheral device, expressed as 0 or 1. Eight bits make a byte, the common measure of memory or storage capacity. Short for binary digit.

BODMAS (224): a set of rules that tell you the order in which calculations are to be done.

bookmark (356): a URL or website that is stored locally on a computer

boot process (45): loading an operating system into a computer's main memory

broadband (345): a transmission medium designed for high-speed data transfers over long distances. Cable modem services and DSL are examples of broadband networks.

browser (348): special Internet software that connects users to remote computers, opens and transfers files, displays text and images, and provides an uncomplicated interface to the Internet and Web documents.

browser cache (350): a temporary storage area that is used to keep a copy of information that has been retrieved. Information from downloaded pages is stored in cache.

byte (45): unit of computer information: a group of eight bits of computer information, representing a unit of data such as a number or letter; computer storage unit: a unit of computer memory equal to that needed to store a single character.

cathode ray tube (CRT) (35): desktop-type monitor built in the same way as a television set (see monitor).

cell (215): the basic unit of a spreadsheet or some other table of text, formed by intersection of a row and column. It contains a label, value or formula with attributes such as size, font and colour.

central processing unit (CPU) (57): the main circuit chip in a computer. It performs most of the calculations necessary to run the computer.

client/server system (386): a computer network in which processing is divided between a client program running on a user's machine and a network server program. One server can provide data to, or perform storage-intensive processing tasks in conjunction with, one or more clients.

clip art (435): simple drawings held in digital form on a computer. These items are often supplied in large libraries of files that can easily be incorporated into word processor or presentation graphics documents.

cloud computing (170): the hosting of a service to an organisation or an individual via the Internet.

communication (30): the exchange of information between people by means of speaking, writing or using a common system of signs or behaviour.

compact disk (CD) (48): a storage device that uses laser technology to read data (see DVD).

computer (1): an electronic device that accepts, processes, stores and outputs data at high speeds according to programmed instructions.

computer crime (195): an illegal action in which the perpetrator uses special knowledge of computer technology.

conditional formatting (244): the formatting of a cell that is dependent upon the value in a cell.

copyright (203): exclusive legal right that prohibits copying of intellectual property without the permission of the copyright holder (see copyright law).

copyright law (203): law that prevents people from taking credit for and profiting from other people's work.

cracker (196): somebody who gains unauthorised access to a computer system with the intention of doing damage or committing a crime (slang). See hacker.

data (2): a collection of facts about an entity. The data can be numeric or it can be descriptive.

database (297): a body of information held within a computer system using the facilities of a database management system structure of a database and access to data.

desktop (14, 64): the main screen area that you see after you turn on your computer and log on to the operating system (such as Windows).

desktop publishing (411): application software and hardware system that involves mixing text and graphics to produce high-quality output for commercial printing, using a computer and devices such as digital camera, scanners and printers. Microsoft Publisher, QuarkXPress and PageMaker are examples of desktop-publishing software.

digital ID (401): a digital ID or digital certificate is used to prove who you are on the Internet. It is an electronic document that conforms to an international standard.

digital signature (142): a code that is embedded in a document and is used to ensure that the document is authentic and has not been altered by anyone but the author.

digital video disk (DVD) (49): a storage device that uses laser technology to read data from optical disks; sometimes called a digital versatile disk.

disaster recovery (178): the process of restoring to normal operation following a disruption to services caused by a significant event such as a flood or a severe electrical failure.

disk operating system (DOS) (62): the original operating system produced by Microsoft that has a command-driven user interface (command prompt).

domain (349): a location on the Internet. The domain is the second part of the URL, and is the name of the server where the resource is located. For example: www.nri.org.pg.

domain name system (DNS) (349): Internet-addressing method that assigns names and numbers to people and computers. Because the numeric IP addresses are difficult to remember, the DNS system was developed to automatically convert text-based addresses to numeric IP addresses.

download (17): to copy a file from one computer to another using a modem or network.

e-book reader (17): a device used to read an electronic book (e-book). Books that are published in a digital format need to be read on such a device. An e-book reader has been designed to make it easy to read an e-book and it consists of both hardware and software.

electronic commerce (e-commerce) (168): commerce using electronic media. Usually it is taken to mean commerce using the Internet for sale of goods and services.

electronic mail (383): transmission of electronic massages over the Internet. Also known as e-mail.

encryption (179): a method of converting computer data and messages into something incomprehensible using a key, so that only a holder of the matching key can reconvert them.

ergonomics (207): the study of how a workplace and the equipment used there can best be designed for comfort, efficiency, safety and productivity.

ethics (193): the beliefs we hold about what is right and wrong. There are social norms that exist in a society about what we can and should do, or not do, in our everyday life.

field (data field) (301): an item of data consisting of a number of characters, bytes, words, or codes that are treated together to form, for example, a number, a name or an address. A number of fields may be fixed in length or variable.

file server (14): a computer that other computers access; a computer in a network that stores application programs and data files accessed by other computers.

file transfer protocol (FTP) (381): method whereby you can connect to a remote computer called an FTP site and transfer publicly available files to your own hard disk via the Internet.

firewall (360): software or hardware that can help protect a computer from hackers or malicious software. A firewall helps prevent malicious software (such as worms) from gaining access to a computer through a network or over the Internet, and helps prevent a computer from sending malicious software to other computers.

folders (62, 64): a named area on a disk that is used to store related subfolders and files.

font (84): a set of characters with a specific design. Also known as typeface. A font describes a certain typeface, along with other qualities such as size, spacing, and pitch.

footer (420): a block of text that appears at the bottom of each page in a document.

format (241): to the manner in which the contents of a cell are displayed in terms including font size, type and the number of decimal places for a number.

formula (223): instructions for calculations in a spreadsheet. It is an equation that performs calculation on the data contained within the cells in a spreadsheet worksheet.

function (224): a variable quantity whose value depends upon the varying values of other quantities.

goal seek (270): goal seek analysis is the process where the desired result is known but some of the values of the variables are changed to achieve that result.

graphical user interface (40): a graphical user interface allows people to communicate with a computer by the use of symbols and a pointing device such as a mouse.

hacker (196): a computer user who gains unauthorised access to a computer system or data belonging to somebody else.

hard disk (47): a storage device inside the computer case that stores billions of characters of data on a non-removable disk platter.

hardware (1): the equipment and devices that make up a computer system, as opposed to the programs used on it.

header (420): a block of text that appears at the top of each page in a document.

hub (59): a device used to connect computers on a network. The computers are connected to the hub with cables. The hub sends information received from one computer to all other computers on the network.

hyperlink (368): a connection between an element (such as a word, phrase, image) in a document to somewhere else in the same document, or to a different destination on the Web. Hyperlinks are usually in a different colour to the rest of the document or are underlined; they are activated by a mouse click.

hypertext (348): a system of storing images, text, and other computer files that allows direct links to related text, images, sound and other data.

hypertext mark-up language (HTML) (348): a text mark-up language used to create documents for the Web. HTML defines the structure and layout of a web document by using a variety of tags and attributes.

hypertext transfer protocol (HTTP) (348): the client-server protocol that defines how messages are formatted and transmitted on the World Wide Web.

icon (62): a small picture that represents a file, folder, program or other object or function.

identity theft (196): where a person's sensitive and personal information is accessed and is used by another person in an attempt to make fraudulent transactions.

information (3): the meaningful material derived from computer data by organising it and interpreting it in a specific way.

Information and Communication Technology (ICT) (161): the technologies that are used to manage, store, retrieve and modify information that is kept in a digital format.

information system (2): a computer-based system with the defining characteristic that it provides information to users in one or more organisations. Information systems are thus distinguished from, for example, real-time control systems, message-switching systems, software engineering environments or personal computing systems

input device (1): any device that transfers data, programs or signals into a processor system. Such devices provide the human–computer interface, the keyboard being the most common example.

Internet (343): network that links computer networks all over the world by satellite and telephone, connecting users with service networks such as e-mail and the World Wide Web.

Internet protocol (IP) (38): a protocol that that allows traffic to pass between networks. The most widely used is IP, the Internet protocol.

Internet service provider (ISP) (344): company that connects you through your communications line to its servers or central computer, and then to the Internet via another company's network access points.

Internet telephony (39): Using the Internet to make phone calls, either one to one or for audio conferencing.

intranet (347): a private network, set up by an organisation or company, that resembles the World Wide Web but which is inaccessible to external users.

liquid crystal display (LCD) (35): see *monitor* or *visual display unit*.

local area network (LAN) (308): a network of computers, printers and other devices located within a relatively limited area (for example, a building). A LAN enables any connected device to interact with any other on the network. A LAN uses the infrastructure and standards of the Internet and the Web.

mail merge (125): the process of producing a personalised letter for each person on a mailing list by combining a database of names and addresses with a form letter created in a word-processing program.

mainframe computer (13): a fast powerful computer with a large storage capacity that can accommodate several users simultaneously.

master page (413): a template of a page design that includes the essential elements of a page including margins, text blocks and default formatting styles.

microcomputer (14): a small computer in which the central processing unit is a single silicon chip microprocessor.

microprocessor (57): a silicon wafer with electronic switches etched on the surface to make an integrated circuit. A microprocessor is a type of microchip that has memory and logic circuits built in.

modem (344): a device that sends and receives data over telephone lines to and from computers. Modem stands for modulator/demodulator.

monitor (35): a computer screen, also referred to as visual display unit (VDU), that displays data or files that a user is working on. There are two types: cathode ray tube (CRT) and liquid crystal display (LCD).

motherboard (57): the main circuit board in the computer to which other components of the computer, such as RAM, hard disk drive and processor, are attached. Also called 'system board'.

multifunction device (38): a device containing the functions of scanner, printer, copier and fax in one unit.

multimedia (49): the combined used of digitised information representing text, sound, and still or video images, or the media so used.

network (39): a number of computers linked together to share resources and to facilitate communication.

normalisation (315): a set of rules that is applied to the data to eliminate redundant data and to create the tables that will be used in the structure of the database.

OCR (24): the conversion of scanned text or numbers into characters that can be used by a computer program such as a spreadsheet or a word processor. The material is scanned with a scanner and software converts the images to text. OCR stands for optical character recognition.

online (198): attached to or available through a central computer or computer network.

operating system (60): the computer program that manages all other programs on the computer. The operating system stores files, allows you to use software programs and coordinates the use of computer hardware.

output device (2): any device that converts the electrical signals representing information within a computer into a form that can exist or be sensed outside the computer. Printers and visual displays are the most common type of output device for interfacing to people, but voice is becoming increasingly available.

paragraph (84): a number of sentences grouped together.

password (182): a security measure used to identify a user. It is a series of characters, usually letters, numbers and other characters, that is associated with a user name.

peripheral device (1): any component or piece of equipment that expands a computer's input, storage and output capabilities. Peripheral devices can be inside the computer or connected to it from the outside.

personal identification number (PIN) (182): a code used by an individual to identify that individual.

phishing (187): the act of sending an email to someone falsely claiming to be another person. Someone using phishing replicates the email address of a legitimate sender.

portable document format (PDF) (380): a file format that was developed by the Adobe software company. This format preserves fonts and layout and can be viewed on the screen looking just as a printed version would appear.

program (60): a list of instructions in a programming language that tells a computer to perform a task.

query (321): a question or request for specific data contained in a database. Used to analyse data.

radio-frequency identification tag (RFID) (32): RFID transmits the details about an object wirelessly. An RFID tag is scanned by a reader and the details are transmitted to a computer. An RFID tag consists of a microchip that is attached to a radio antenna.

random-access memory (RAM) (46): the main internal storage area the computer uses to run programs and store data. Information stored in RAM is temporary, designed to clear when the computer is turned off.

read-only memory (ROM) (45): built-in computer memory that can be read by a computer but cannot be modified. Unlike random access memory (RAM), the information stored in ROM is not cleared when the computer is turned off.

relational database model (315): a data model that views information in a database as a collection of distinctly named tables. Each table has a specified set of named columns, each column name (also called an attribute) being distinct within a particular table, but not necessarily between tables.

relative reference (228): a relative reference refers to a cell by its position compared to the active cell.

router (72): an electronic device that directs communicating messages when networks are connected together.

satellite (or air) connection (346): connection services that use satellites and the air to download or send data to users at a rate seven times faster than dial-up connections.

scanner (24): device that identifies images or text on a page and automatically converts them to electronic signals that can be stored in a computer to copy or reproduce.

search engine (356): a computer program (such as Google or Yahoo) that searches for specific words and returns a list of documents in which they were found.

sensor (31): a device, often a microprocessor, which measures a physical quantity. The measurement is read by an observer or another piece of equipment such as a computer. Sensors are used to measure temperature and light, amongst other things.

server (14): a powerful computer that manages shared devices, such as laser printers. It runs server software for applications such as e-mail and web browsing.

software (2): computer program consisting of step-by-step instructions, directing the computer on each task it will perform.

spam (389): electronic junk mail; an unsolicited, often commercial, message transmitted through the Internet as a mass mailing to a large number of recipients.

spreadsheet (215): an application software or program that is used to manipulate numeric data and create workbook files. Popular spreadsheet programs are Microsoft Excel, Corel Quattro Pro and Lotus 1-2-3.

spyware (malware) (359): conventionally defined as software that enables an outsider to obtain information from a computer without the user's knowledge and consent. The term is sometimes used to describe brazen advertising programs that slow computer performance and disrupt browser settings.

storage device (45): device that can be used to store data (for example, flash drive, CDRW).

style (119): a collection of formatting characteristics used to provide consistency within a document.

supercomputer (13): fastest calculating device ever invented, processing billions of program instruction per second.

switch (178): a device used to connect computers on a network. The computers are connected to the switch with cables. A switch is similar to a hub, except that it sends the information received from one computer to the specific computers that are supposed to receive it.

system box or unit (57): part of the microcomputer that contains the CPU that houses most of the electronic components that make up a computer system.

system software (60): software that helps the computer perform essential operating tasks; for example, Windows XP Professional, Windows Vista.

table (in database) (315): The list of records that make up the basic structure of a database. Their columns display field data and their rows display records.

tabs (91): a position in a line of text that allows that text to be aligned in a consistent manner.

telecommuting (166): working from home using a computer and telecommunications equipment to link to the employee's place of employment.

template (122): a sample form or presentation that can be used as a pattern to help guide you in designing your own layout.

terminal (39): an input and output device connecting to a mainframe or type of computer called a host computer or server.

text (83): letters, words, sentences and paragraphs.

toolbar (60): bar located typically below the menu bar containing icons or graphical representations for commonly used functions.

transmission control protocol/Internet protocol (TCP/IP) (343, 381): the standard protocol for the Internet. The essential features of this protocol involve identifying, sending and receiving devices reformatting information for transmission across the Internet.

Trojan horse (186): a malicious software program that hides inside other programs. It enters a computer hidden inside a legitimate program, such as a screen saver. It then puts code into the operating system, which enables a hacker to access the infected computer. Trojan horses do not usually spread by themselves; they are spread by viruses, worms or downloaded software.

uniform resource locator (URL) (348): an address that uniquely identifies a location on the Internet. A URL is usually preceded by http://, as in http://www.microsoft.com.

universal serial bus (USB) (59): a narrow, rectangular connector used to attach a device, such as a keyboard or a mouse, to a computer.

upload (29): a process of transferring information from the user's computer to a remote computer.

video (65): moving images displayed on a monitor.

videoconferencing (38): use of television video and sound technology as well as computer networks (including the Internet). Also called teleconferencing.

virus (185): software designed to deliberately harm your computer; for example, worms and Trojan horses are malicious software.

webpage (348): a computer file, encoded in HyperText Markup Language (HTML) and containing text, graphics files and sound files, which is accessible through the World Wide Web. Browsers interpret HTML documents to display webpages.

website (150): group of related webpages.

what if analysis (232): the process of changing cell values to see how those changes impact the final result.

wide area network (WAN) (343): a network that connects geographically separated locations by using telecommunications services.

wireless (345): the transmission of information without a physical connection between the sender and the receiver. Uses radio frequencies, hardware, software and various technologies to transmit information.

word processing (75): the act of creating a word document on a computer using a program (for example, MS Word or ClarisWorks).

word processor (75): an application package designed to work with text and produce documents.

workbook (215): a file containing one or more related worksheets or spreadsheets

worksheet (215): a rectangular grid of rows and columns used in a program like Excel. Also known as spreadsheet or sheet.

workstation (14): computer that is part of the computer network.

World Wide Web (WWW) (347): the interconnected system of Internet servers that support documents in multimedia form and include sounds, photos and video as well as text.

worm (186): a self-replicating program, similar to a virus. A worm can make it possible for a malicious user to take over your computer or can send out enough copies of itself to cause your computer or a web or network server to stop responding.